Dedicated to the City
and the People

*Since Pittsburgh has always been my chief
interest, anything which has been part of it may
be considered worthy of being chronicled.*

—*James D. Van Trump*

Life and Architecture
in Pittsburgh

James D. Van Trump

Pittsburgh History & Landmarks Foundation

Published by
Pittsburgh History & Landmarks Foundation
450 The Landmarks Building,   One Station Square,   Pittsburgh, Pa., 15219
Edited by
Walter C. Kidney and Louise King Ferguson

Illustration Sources

The numbers given below refer to pages of this book on which illustrations from each source are found:

Allegheny County Airport: 80

Art Work of Pittsburgh (1893 edition): 184

Art Work of Pittsburgh (1899 edition): xi

Peter Berndtson Collection, Carnegie-Mellon University Libraries: 68, by permission of Indira Berndtson and Anna Coor.

Cardell Studio: ii

Carnegie Library of Pittsburgh: cover, 7, 14, 38, 60, 74, 103, 106, 133, 188, 204, 205, 208, 218, 223, 227, 230, 234, 240, 246, 247, 262, 268, 272, 275, 280, 303 (both), 316, 318, 322, 340, 344, 347

Mike Crawmer, University of Pittsburgh: 256

Curtis Theatre Collection, University of Pittsburgh: 334

Sigo Falk: 153, 155, 157

Vernon Gay: 50, from *Discovering Pittsburgh's Sculpture,* photographs by Vernon Gay and text by Marilyn Evert

Gulf Oil Corporation: 76

Clyde Hare: xx, 308

Heinz Hall for the Performing Arts: 85

The Historical Society of Western Pennsylvania: 55

Dennis Marsico: 64

Museum of Art, Carnegie Institute, Pittsburgh (Museum purchase, 1942): 336

Randy Nelson, Invision: 20, 24, 28, 46, 78, 91, 110, 121, 124, 130, 147, 160, 166, 170, 198, 266, 282, 286

Pittsburgh & Lake Erie Railroad: 237

Pittsburgh History & Landmarks Foundation: xv, 4, 30, 36, 40, 49, 51, 72, 82, 87, 115, 175, 181, 191, 203, 210, 249, 259, 312

Bill Redic, Carnegie-Mellon University: 137, 140

Charles Morse Stotz, *The Early Architecture of Western Pennsylvania* (1936), reissued as *The Architectural Heritage of Early Western Pennsylvania* (1966); courtesy of the University of Pittsburgh Press: 251

James D. Van Trump: x, xii, 94-95

Grateful acknowledgment is made to *Carnegie Magazine,* Chatham Associates, Inc., Metropolitan Pittsburgh Public Broadcasting, Inc. (licensee of WQED-FM), and the Tribune-Review Publishing Company for permission to reprint essays by James D. Van Trump in *Life and Architecture in Pittsburgh.* The three lines of poetry on page 228 are from "The Dry Salvages" in FOUR QUARTETS, copyright 1943 by T. S. Eliot; renewed 1971 by Esme Valerie Eliot. Reprinted by permission of Harcourt Brace Jovanovich, Inc.

Contributors

Vicki Acklin
Mr. & Mrs. Charles Covert
  Arensberg
Mr. & Mrs. Fred W. Bader
Mr. & Mrs. James Bibro
Gay M. Blair
Mrs. Kenneth S. Boesel
Mr. & Mrs. J. Judson Brooks
Carl Wood Brown
Mrs. Grace J. Burrell
Burt Hill Kosar Rittelmann
  Associates
Celli-Flynn and Associates
Mrs. George L. Craig, Jr.
Mr. & Mrs. John P. Davis, Jr.
Deeter Ritchey Sippel
Mr. & Mrs. James O'Hara
  Denny, III
The Design Alliance, Architects
Mary Lu Donnelly
Mr. & Mrs. Richard Dilworth
  Edwards
Leonore R. Elkus
Mr. & Mrs. Sanford B. Ferguson
Mr. & Mrs. James A. Fisher
Mrs. William A. Galbraith
Mr. & Mrs. David L. Genter
Mr. & Mrs. Richard E. Givens
William T. Hillman
Mr. & Mrs. Henry P. Hoffstot, Jr.
Alfred M. Hunt
Mr. & Mrs. Harry T.
  Hutchinson, Jr.
Interspace Incorporated
William J. and Mildred M.
  Johnston
Mr. & Mrs. B. F. Jones, 3rd
Genevieve Jones
Elizabeth Kimberly
Joel H. Kranich, Associates

Landmarks Design Associates
Edward J. Lewis
Arthur Lubetz Associates
MacLachlan, Cornelius &
  Filoni, Architects
Shirley A. McMaster
Merrick Art Gallery
Mr. & Mrs. Robert S. Merrick
Theodore C. Merrick
Ruth Crawford Mitchell
Mr. & Mrs. Edward A.
  Montgomery, Jr.
Neville Lewis Associates, Inc.
William R. Oliver
James S. Pedone Associates
The Pittsburgh Foundation
Alfred D. Reid, Jr.
Mrs. Sidney Ruffin
Richard M. Scaife
Bill and Helen Schlenke
Christina Schmidlapp
G. Whitney Snyder
Mr. & Mrs. Furman South, III
Mrs. Rose S. Tarasi
Mr. & Mrs. LeRoy Thompson
Mimi Jones Timmons
Professor Franklin K. Toker
UDA Architects
  David Lewis
  Raymond L. Gindroz
  James P. Goldman
  Donald K. Carter
Valentour English and Associates
Congressman Doug Walgren
Mrs. James M. Walton
Brenda Oliver Whitehair
Gilmore C. Williams
Williams-Trebilcock-Whitehead
Mr. & Mrs. Arthur P. Ziegler, Sr.
Arthur P. Ziegler, Jr.

The printing of this second edition was made possible in part by the Revolving Fund for Education which was established in 1984 through a generous grant from the Claude Worthington Benedum Foundation.

Contents

James D. Van Trump (left) at age eight, with his mother and his brother Sherrard.

The Author

James Denholm Van Trump was born on July 20, 1908, on Thomas Boulevard in the Point Breeze section of Pittsburgh's East End. His father was James Coleman Van Trump, who had recently moved to Pittsburgh from Wilmington, Delaware, and was a salesman. His mother, Jeanne Denholm Van Trump, was of an old Scotch-Irish Westmoreland County family.

The family moved several times in Jamie's youth; in 1914 to the Denholm apartment building, at Lincoln and Frankstown Avenues in the East End; in 1916 to South 56th Street in West Philadelphia; back to Pittsburgh in 1921; to Oakmont for 1921-22; then, in 1922, to Thomas Boulevard again, where Jamie lived for the next 44 years. All this time, there were summer trips to Ocean City, New Jersey, and later journeys to other cities in North America and Europe.

Jamie attended public schools, then entered Carnegie Tech (now Carnegie-Mellon University) in 1926, studying painting, decoration, and singing. In 1927, he transferred to the University of Pittsburgh, with a dual major in fine arts and English literature. He received

Thomas Boulevard at the end of the nineteenth century.

At the time of graduation from Pitt in 1931.

his M.A. in 1932, at the very worst time of the Depression. The next 24 years were a period of intermittent job activity against a background of intensive study of Pittsburgh history and architecture, mostly in the Pennsylvania and Fine Arts rooms at the Carnegie Library in Oakland. In 1934-36 Jamie was architectural historian for a WPA museum-extension project whose purpose was to draw plates for a "History of the House," never published. He worked as a bookstore clerk. In 1942-45 he was a clerk with the War Production Board. He wrote short stories, only one of which ("When Yesterday Returns," *Woman's Home Companion,* September, 1947) was ever published.

The Jamie who has become familiar to thousands of Pittsburghers emerged suddenly in 1956, when *The Charette,* journal of the Pittsburgh Architectural Club, published "Pittsburgh's Church of the Ascension" (included in this collection). From then on, Jamie's pent-up knowledge flowed massively and inexhaustibly. The sheer quantity of his writing — in *The Charette, Carnegie Magazine, Western Pennsylvania Historical Magazine, The Pittsburgher,* less frequently in other publications, and in script form for WQED-FM — is obvious from a mere glance at the bibliography at the end of this book. And this is to say nothing of the private journals he has kept year after year.

In 1961, he joined the staff of *The Charette,* first as assistant editor, then as full editor. By that time, he had become active in other ways as well: assistant bibliographer at the Hunt Botanical Library from 1958 to 1962; advisor to the Historic American Buildings Survey between 1957 and 1960; and a steady contributor to *Carnegie Magazine* from 1956 on.

In 1957, Jamie met a young student of English literature, Arthur Ziegler, who became an increasingly close associate in the next few years. First Arthur, who was teaching at Carnegie Tech, joined the staff of *The Charette;* then, in 1964, the two broke away from the current management of the magazine to form Van Trump, Ziegler & Shane, with Charles Shane and Albert Kiefer as partners. The new firm offered advertising and public-relations services, historic-preservation consultation, and publishing, and soon became itself the publisher of *The Charette.* It remained so until 1971, when the magazine was sold to a Philadelphia company that entirely changed its content. Van Trump, Ziegler & Shane was dissolved in 1973, and Landmarks Planning, Inc. was formed to continue the preservation consulting practice. Jamie retired from this nine years later.

Meanwhile, in 1964, another organization was formed. Jamie and Arthur recount that, one winter afternoon in the late 1950s, they were in Liverpool Street in Pittsburgh's Manchester district, looking at a handsome but decayed row of Victorian houses. This was still the time when conventional urban renewal was triumphant: the City went into a neighborhood, destroyed almost everything, and rebuilt. The new neighborhood had no past, and therefore very little character, and much that was beautiful or still useful was gone. Manchester itself was populated in part by refugees from the near-total destruction of the Lower Hill in the 1950s, in preparation for a showy cultural acropolis that materialized only in fragments. Jamie and Arthur determined, then and there on that sad street, that something effective should be done about saving historic architecture. They organized the Pittsburgh History & Landmarks Foundation, found sponsors, and set to work. Jamie was the scholar, Arthur the businessman; both were important to an organization with the authoritative character needed to succeed in saving buildings and, indeed, whole neighborhoods.

Jamie, until then, was a shy, retiring person, but this new work forced him into the open. He spoke, met people, gave information and advice, and became a personality. Between 1975 and early 1983, he had a regular program on WQED-FM, and in 1975 he even ventured into television: his brief weekly news feature with Al Julius on KDKA-TV lasted until 1978. In 1979 he began a television program on WTAE. Always interested in the theatre, he appeared as Mark Twain in *The Iron Clad Agreement* in 1976. Deprived of a regular writing outlet in *The Charette* in 1971, he found another in *The Pittsburgher* between March, 1978 and January, 1981; when that city magazine ceased publication, he went on to write for *Focus*, a supplement of the Greensburg *Tribune-Review*. Since 1981, Jamie has served at the Hunt Institute for Botanical Documentation as the honorary curator of a collection of "old Pittsburgh formal gardens."

On Election Day, 1978, Jamie was crossing Forbes Avenue on his way to the Carnegie Library in Oakland when a speeding car struck him. In recent years he had had two other hospital experiences and had recovered from them, but this time he was in danger of his life; the next few months found him recovering, but slowly and never fully. He now uses a wheelchair. In 1979 the presentation of the Jefferson Award from the American Institute for Public Service stressed Jamie's determination to get well again; on this occasion, he also was named an Outstanding Citizen by the *Pittsburgh Post-Gazette*. Early in 1978 he had moved to the Fairfax, in Oakland, from the nearby

Cathedral Mansions, where he had been since 1966. In 1979, he finally returned to the Fairfax — with what feelings *"Die Heimkehr aus dem Fremde,"* included in this book, tells — and went on with his work.

In the last decade, his personality has emerged increasingly as he has become a public figure. His first *Charette* article was basically the work of a scholar, primarily presenting facts though already with a slight injection of himself and his own attitudes into the text. As he continued to write in the next few years, he retained scholarly objectivity about facts but eschewed the sort of scholarly caution that has given the world so much worthy but dull prose. Jamie writes floridly, impressionistically. Expressing his feelings is a natural characteristic, and addressing the public has allowed him to express his enthusiasm, his nostalgia, his upper-middle-class youth, his Anglo-Catholicism of more recent years. In this way, such a large audience is all to the good; yet Jamie wonders, too, if he really likes being such a public figure: whether the quiet communication with his journals was not, at least, a little less harrowing to his retiring nature.

Walter C. Kidney

Viewing a public clock near Market Square after a street accident, late 1960s.

Introduction

*Nostalgia is perennial, and for those of us who are aging, its
bitter-sweet presence is often experienced, often felt, with various
degrees of poignancy as more years accrue to our calendars. A chance
word, a fugitive view, a rose, a smile, a certain touch, on a fine morning or a dull afternoon, arouses some sleeping memory, and we are
off down the misty corridors of our minds in pursuit of the long-past
complete experience, of which the small signal light in the present
day illumined some minute facet. The process by which we travel from
the moment of recognition to the event now embedded in the far
reaches of our minds resembles one of those camera feats by which
in a few seconds we are given the visual record of a passage through
many years . . .* [1]

These lines are pure Van Trump: recollections of the past as
interpreted by time and emotions, and seasoned by tranquillity. Only
Marcel Proust could remember as infallibly those passing moments
of experience; only Henry James could restate them as subtly.

But Jamie Van Trump, as he has been known to his beloved
city for three-quarters of a century, is a unique writer, for he alone
can pass our architecture and our history through a fine sieve, refining and restating them as his sensitivity plays over them. Whether
the subject is dining *al fresco* on a club roof terrace looking out at
the buildings of Oakland or recalling waiting for a train, as a child,
on a golden summer afternoon at a suburban Philadelphia station,
Jamie captures and conveys the emotional effect that someone — often
himself — felt as his life touched and was touched by that architecture, that day, that experience. "Life, London, this moment of June,"
as Mrs. Dalloway happily remarked.

Odd that in his writings Jamie is so nostalgic. His attitude
toward life has been one of unfettered optimism and looking forward.
As the two of us worked together at the Pittsburgh History & Landmarks Foundation and in several business enterprises, he was the
inspiring leader, always prepared to venture into new projects, excited with fresh plans, never deterred by the unknown.

I first met Jamie in 1957 at a Lenten dinner at a little Anglican
church, on McKee Place in Oakland, called St. Mary's. We both loved
literature, particularly that of the late nineteenth century, books and
printing, and architecture. Our lives became intertwined as Jamie

guided my learning. We toured about Western Pennsylvania — still his favourite pastime — in search of pieces of history that he wanted to remember and to revive in conversation and in prose.

Jamie had been researching daily the history and buildings of this area for over twenty years, but he was only then beginning to write, and I became editor to my mentor. An outpouring of history and architectural criticism soon resulted, increasing when we both worked for *The Charette,* which became a showcase for his great knowledge and voluptuous prose.

The Pittsburgh History & Landmarks Foundation was established in 1964 when the two of us discovered and wanted to save Liverpool Street in Manchester, and sought and found the help of Barbara Hoffstot, Helen Clay Frick, Charles Arensberg, and Calvin Hamilton, followed by the magnificent support of Richard M. Scaife. The Foundation supported Jamie's work and gave it an official basis. At the same time the Foundation depended on him for almost all of its knowledge, which was augmented by a survey of the buildings of Allegheny County that the two of us carried out in 1966-67; our findings were published in *Landmark Architecture of Allegheny County, Pennsylvania.*

Jamie has never been an organized writer or scholar. He has neither great scholarly goals nor any desire to write full-length books. Only once has he tried his hand at one, which deals with his favourite architectural "lion," the Allegheny County Court House and Jail. He invested five years in this effort, producing such a voluminous manuscript that it would occupy two volumes. Funds sufficient to publish it must still be found.

Jamie's on-to-tomorrow spirit infected us all. Landmarks grew because of that; as it did, more of his knowledge became available in our publications. He became a tour leader too, treating hundreds of people to lively information on walking tours around the county on summer Sunday afternoons and on bus tours to distant places. Everyone glowed in the romance that he bestowed on the sites and buildings. And, much to his annoyance, he became a living repository of information, used as a resource by countless scholars, students, and researchers who sought him by letter and by telephone.

Once shy and retiring, Jamie burst forth as a public figure known to hundreds of thousands when, with Al Julius, he began to do short features on the Friday 6:00 PM KDKA-TV News. Widely popular, he signed autographs, fled from adoring teen-agers, and made appearances at public banquets and festivals. He was even asked for advertising endorsements.

On his way to the Library one day several years ago, Jamie was struck by a car and badly hurt. He has since been confined to a wheelchair, although this has in no way deterred his spirit. He is out every day, researching, writing, observing the passing scene.

Jamie is the master of the moment; he takes one that has passed into history, holds it up for us to see, turns it to catch the poetic light, feels it for us through his romantic prose, and gives it a kind of immortality. Buildings, the objects he most cherishes, are never treated in academic detachment; they are described in their human context and venerated through poetry in prose.

His writings take the form of personal essays. During most of his life, he has kept a journal in which he has recorded thoughts, ideas, events, but most often in which he has described an experience of the day. For years he had dinner at the Press Club, atop an older downtown skyscraper, where he could look up the Allegheny River and toward the hills to the north. Night after night he described in his journal what he saw: the same scene repeated but each time different because of the sun, or clouds, or cold, or a change in his own feelings, or — most often — because "a chance word, a fugitive view aroused some sleeping memory."

Moment to moment, building to building, event to event, Jamie moves and Jamie remembers. His work is an integration of a random journal among those misty corridors of our communal mind and an exacting knowledge of what was built and what happened in relation to those buildings. It is the expression of a unique sensibility as it plays over all of its becoming, and the emotional effect knowledge and experience have had. He is not lost in a romantic past; he is captivated by its existence, and by its recurrence in many forms in the present. "All things change, yet all things stay the same," he often reminds us.

Many cities have their historians. I know of none which has an interpreter of the experiences of the past that have affected people, accretion by accretion, who offers them up in such a sumptuous style, beautiful as an art in itself. Jamie reminds us that our buildings reflect lives; they express and symbolize those people who were involved in creating and in using them — and he renders for us with endearment the things that we may have put away, or not even noticed, like those yellow daisies on the golden afternoon at the forgotten train station.

Arthur P. Ziegler, Jr.

---

¹This is an excerpt from a radio broadcast titled "*Crime Without Passion:* a Nostalgic Essay on Re-seeing the Movies of One's Youth," which was broadcast by WQED-FM in 1978.

On the South Side slopes.

Uphill and Downdale in Pittsburgh
A Night Journey at the New Year

New Year's Day has always been a time for new beginnings;
the unknown year seems to stretch ahead wonderfully like a *tabula
rasa* on which we can write as we will with whatever comes to hand.
The days stretching ahead commend themselves to us as fields for
exploration, voyages of discovery — not necessarily to far places, to
perilous seas or fairylands forlorn, but to the familiar streets and hills
of the home landscape, which seem to me, at least, as the years fly
away, to be more infinitely marvelous, more fascinating. Here, I say
to myself, looking along the serrated line of the South Side hills or
the far escarpments up the Allegheny or even the brief tree-hung
streets of Schenley Farms, here is enough to excite forever the
curiosity of the mind or to spur the farthest searches of the heart.
However much time is granted me, how can I ever learn enough, see
sufficient, *know*, know, the secret glory of these hills? How can I
speak, or even in their celebration, sing? Out of my long love, how
can I cease to praise?

So on New Year's Day this year of 1978, these thoughts, feelings, these perennial speculations occupied my mind again in
delighted anticipation, as I spent the whole afternoon at the Old Post
Office Museum [on the North Side], labeling lantern slides — the
bright mementoes of past excursions made during the year just turned
back into history. Beyond the windows of my office, the skeleton trees
of West Park dripped mournfully, but in the land of my slides it was
Spring and Summer.

Pleasant as it was, this preoccupation was essentially concerned
with looking backward; I was, at the moment, intent on looking
forward into the new year. I was aware, at the same time, that I was
to have a renewal of my long acquaintance with the Pittsburgh hills,
a recapitulation of past experience, a re-seeing and, at the same time,
in the new view, a totally different insight into the familiar landscape. I was waiting for my initial New Year's adventure, out into
the hills at dusk.

At lunch my partner at the Pittsburgh History & Landmarks
Foundation had told me that he had been looking for some old
properties, rather out of the usual fields of our activity, that would

lend themselves to our restorational ministrations as good investments in the urban scene and, as such, would yield returns for both the community and our own reputation.

Since we both had some free time on our way to dinner, what better time for him to take me to see the properties — which were both on the South Side, on those hillsides facing the Monongahela River which from a distance look so Romantically complex, so picturesque, but in actual fact are so difficult of access, so intractable to human settlement; and yet, in the late nineteenth century, they were so triumphantly settled, not by mountain goats but by European immigrants who did not seem in the least to mind the steepness of the terrain. They accepted that land and its stiff gradients, not as something picturesque or Romantic, but simply as one of the facts of life, one of the conditions of existence in their new environment.

To us, these assorted houses are transcendently pictorial, abundantly stimulating as visual artifacts of a vanished day, but even to the descendants of their builders they are still simply part of the fabric of existence. True, the inhabitants of these eyries no longer have to walk great distances to reach the busy valley below; they, even as we (who come to look and admire), have motorcars which transport them easily. Ah, nowadays, in beholding the hillside houses with their attendant automobiles, one must consider that the internal combustion engine has been the great leveler in America during the twentieth century.

So it was in my partner's trusty red Rabbit that, shortly after five o'clock in the glooming rainy dusk of New Year's Day, we went off to the South Side to see our prospective purchases. By the most modern of freeways and bridges we journeyed to Smithfield Street, where the Victorian traceries of the Smithfield Street Bridge conducted us to Carson Street, past the great railway walls of marvelously variegated Victorian masonry to the sombre viaduct leading to Arlington Avenue. There was a faint mist in the cold air, an evanescent veil that lent a certain mystery to these familiar vistas. Water splashed under the wheels of the Rabbit, lights gleamed wetly through the fine rain. It was a good night for a Victorian adventure.

As we ascended Arlington Avenue, the dense, dark mass of the city, festooned with innumerable points of light, began to appear below. The avenue twisted upward like a midnight vine. At intervals in the ascent, streets branched off riverward, like gaping mouths leading to unimaginable depths on those perilous slopes. Everywhere was darkness suffused with mist, lit fitfully by patches of illumination from street lights on dimly-seen windows.

We paused at one of those yawning openings. I looked up at a lighted street sign — Hartford Street, it said. The Rabbit swooped downward into darkness; the lights of the city swung upward. Far below was the river; then the car rose again as the city view was obscured by a clump of small houses that seemingly hung by their heels on the edge of the gulf. Clinging close to them were two fairly large Victorian mansarded houses, now deserted and boarded up. In the half-light we considered them and their possibilities — we allowed that the view from the back would probably be magnificent, and that with special treatment the parking problem could be overcome.

Then we moved on to look at the dead end of the street, which, down a roller-coaster gradient, was not far distant. At this sharp angle we could see far up the tenebrous, light-spotted Monongahela valley. Straight ahead, on the next hill, was the sharp, almost needle-like, bulk of the spire of St. Michael's Church; its lighted clock face glowed distantly like a lost moon. At the dead end there was no room to turn around, and we had to back up to the Avenue again.

I sighed with exhilaration and some relief as we descended Arlington Avenue to the McArdle Roadway and then, via Josephine Street, far out into the South Side. At one point, the dark, castle-like mass of the old Duquesne Brewery, with its great lighted clock, loomed remotely. At Twenty-third Street we passed under the railroad and on to Barry Street, where we began what gradually seemed to be an almost Alpine ascent.

Facing out toward the city, the tall houses seemed to climb skyward. At a sharp turn, the street mounted directly up the face of the hill; the grade was so steep that the sidewalk on one side became flights of concrete stairs. At Mission Street we turned off onto a road that had an upper and lower section, the two divided by concrete walls topped by iron fencing. The highly variegated houses on either side faced each other at different levels — an unusual arrangement even for Pittsburgh. Gradually, we seemed to become enmeshed in a web of sharply-angled streets whose names I cannot remember. We examined more houses in the lurking tenebrosity, the damp light. At one end of Mission Street there loomed, like a sign post in a dream, the massy, Baroque tower of St. Josaphat's Church.

Once back again on the flats of Josephine Street, I considered that my small New Year excursion had been a good augur for the coming months. How inexhaustible is the local landscape, how mysterious, how wonderful! From my long love, how can I cease to praise! The streets rise and the streets descend. Who knows where they lead?

Radio script for WQED-FM, 1978.

3

A scene on the Lower Hill, 1930s.

The Hill

A web of years, the Hill,
   A tree not beyond hope,
     Shame's own castle, forum of forgotten footsteps,
Bright blood of the heart
     Moving among the cobble stones
       And the ruined attics,
Deep past the black mask or the white
     Which fences the universal flesh,
       Flowing, flowing like the spring
On the old farm near Fifth Avenue,
     In the arms and lips that move in the streets
... The streets with fancy names
     (and sub-standard housing) ...
And the feet speaking on sidewalks,
     The sidewalks of herring-bone bricks
     Humped with old frosts and dog turds.
Disemboweled cans
   (Campbell's Tomato Soup)
     Gape from the sparkle of old whiskey bottles ...

     This is the Hill,
And the Hill is the City,
   As the City is many hills,
     But this hill, the mucked altar
   And the broken place,
Speak of old streets and passages carpeted in Brussels,
   And the new places that will be ...

High, looking down on the skyscrapers, it speaks
   To the silver glitter of rivers ...
The accents of Carthage, Nubia, and Congo
   Formulate the tribal dances
     Coiling in the streets.
The bronze bucks in stove-pipe pants and Renaissance hats,
   Teeth flashing like swords in the Chicken Shack,
     Mingle under the Byzantine spire

Of the Russian Church.
In a rocketing street of half gables,
    Where ragged shorts hang out to dry,
                                    A sign shouts —
"Triumph the Church and the Kingdom
    Of God in Christ!"
        Here dragon and basilisk hide in gutters
    And the Lamb scratches its back on the Lion.
Among crawling fences and dirty words,
    Cats depart on important embassies,
        Like princes of the night.
On cavern stairs, convoluted like shells,
    Lovers announce the feasts of the heart
        And the cauliflower ear salutes the pomegranate . . .
        A half-eaten pizza rots under Trinity's window . . .

The Hill now is — and was,
And at the old Penn Incline,
    The towers of the Resort, where they drank beer,
    Fell long ago into their own cellars,
A funeral of arches, but
There was a young man once
    With a golden eye, and an elk's tooth
        On his watch-chain, standing
With his girl beside him, on the Incline
    Rising above the city like a god —
                    He said,
Holding the world by the hand,
    His fingers folding seven furnaces,
        St. Philomena's tower and Troy Hill —
"I'll leap the Allegheny's ditch for love,
    For the stretch of my legs, for the
        Eye in my heart . . ."
In Arcena Street there is an ailanthus
    Where the Incline was.

            Now no more the light
Of the Riots in '77, or the furnaces'
    Gleam on the cliff houses.
                Now more the light
Of the old century's sun or even
    The time before which had no measure,
        Neither that gleaming nor the sight

6

Of the vanished eyes laughing,
    For life, in the summer house on Cliff Street —
        survive.
           Who remembers the burning station
Below, or how the woman's hand moved,
    What the preacher said in the Eighth Church,
        Where the horse turned on Centre Avenue?
All lie consumed in the funnel of the past.
        Now dogs sleep on the steps
         And children play,
Children in the sun, fighting Priam's war
    Between a gutted mattress and an apple core.

       In an old house — somebody's "mansion"
Far back in the Hill —
    A farm house once — holiness comes with witches.
Where then the roses in the carpet
    Spoke of six percent and even
The Sunday roast beef was Presbyterian,

Now a marijuana dream spawns in the attic,
And Cerberus, a knife between his legs,
   Roars down the splintered stair,
     Chasing Hesperidean apples.

     In winter, transgressed by shadows,
The breath of the old, vapours a remembered season,
   Fainting toward dead burdock leaves,
Where modillions fall from Second Empire
  cornices,
     The pride of a meat-packer in 1870
     In DeVilliers Street.
And Juliet among the neon flowers
       (Jack's Bar and Grill)
Walks toward a meeting under broken sticks
      Where Romeo bleeds the flow of legend
       Into the rose of Time.
While eastward Verona falters like a dream
And in a molten hour near dawn,
Blossoms its jittered fragments on their heads,
     A curse of stars.

And all the towers that once were
     And all the towers that will be,
Or the wide vision blooming
     Where the young cherish the planets,
       Will be the Hill.
Dream in our dreams new light —
     The steel turret and the linden tree
The earth's lip flowering
     And the old spring falling down, down,
       To the river,
Past the new house on the old rock,
     Holding its heart in its hand.
And here whatever may come,
     The tall towers,
Whatever built, the new leaves
     Singing from the young hands
       At the stairway's head,
         Will come like Spring rain,
The courage of gifts
       Like water flowing.

The Charette, April, 1962.

8

Urbane, Cultivated,
and Formerly "Gracious"

Pittsburghers have always been interested in the visitor's-eye view of their city, and whether the imported observations be well- or ill-natured, the native feels pleased that his habitat has been noticed. Having dwelt under the ponderous shadow of heavy industry, the Pittsburgher has become so conditioned to dolorous descriptions and dark blanket indictments — clouds of smoke and dirt (if not of fire and brimstone) — that he feels his city is not beautiful or amenable even if it is ugly and powerful. While he puffs out his chest with pride, he lowers his eyes in deprecation. The native's own view is often largely negative, even if the Smoky City has long since been cleaned up. The smoke and dirt have become so deeply ingrained in his spirit that, almost subconsciously, he feels his native place is inferior.

He has come to expect the denigratory comment, the sardonic observation, even the supercilious sneer. All the while that he accepts, or even invites, disparagement of his home landscape, he yet hopes for words of appreciation and praise. However, he is often suspicious of the laudatory opinion when, as is often the case, it is offered by a visitor perceptive enough to glimpse the local splendour, the very real beauty of the place. Perhaps, the native says to himself, this is a put-on, but perhaps, *perhaps*, it's true.

I was thinking of all this the other day when my old friend Charley Arensberg[1] sent me a small paperbound booklet. Its cover said simply *Pittsburgh* in classical lettering inside a cartouche that displayed a sketch of the Masonic Temple on Fifth Avenue in Oakland. The presence of the Temple of the Masons was explained on the title page, which bore the legend "113th Annual Meeting Supreme Council 33° A.A.S.R. of Freemasonry N.M.J. — U.S.A. — Pittsburgh, Pennsylvania, September 12-17th, 1925."

The next page bears a further title, *The Pittsburgh Owl*, beneath a sketch of a typical Pittsburgh street with an owl hovering on a tree branch. The next twenty-two pages consist of a printed text interspersed with some delightful sketches of the local landscape, both urban and suburban.

An explanatory note informed me that *The Pittsburgh Owl* had been written by Frances Lester Warner, a New England woman born in 1888 who lived in Pittsburgh from 1922 until 1926. Her husband Mayo D. Hersey was a member of the research staff at the United States Bureau of Mines on Forbes Avenue. All this was made known to me through *Who's Who in America,* where she was abundantly represented from 1930 to 1953.

As I rapidly read through the pamphlet, the fine quality of her prose and the cultivated sharpness of her perceptions seemed at least partially accountable to the fact that she was a graduate of Mt. Holyoke, had taught at Wellesley, had been an assistant to the editor of *The Atlantic Monthly,* and headed the English Department of the New England Conservatory of Music from 1946 to 1949. The Carnegie Library had her book *Groups and Couples,* published in 1923 by Houghton Mifflin, from which the essay *The Pittsburgh Owl* was excerpted. Although the library did not have my pamphlet, it did have another, *Steel and Holly: Christmas in Pittsburgh,* published by Houghton Mifflin in 1925. Like my own pamphlet, this small booklet is as charmingly printed and illustrated as its literary content is choice.

The general tone of the author's prose is undoubtedly urbane, cultivated, and what used to be called gracious, although not unmixed with a touch of feminine archness which lends a certain piquancy to her work in these days of women's lib. Perhaps she tries a little too hard to be brightly humorous and whimsical. As such, she is closely akin to a much better-known American writer of the early twentieth century, Christopher Morley, who was almost Frances Warner's exact contemporary. I was so struck by the resemblance that I took down from my bookshelves Morley's *The Haunted Bookshop,* published in 1919, and discovered the tone, outlook, and style of both writers were surprisingly similar. I recall that in my own youth Morley's work was considered to be quaintly middle-class and coyly urbane to a generation that relished Hemingway.

Morley and Warner were a little old-fashioned then, and they are rather more than that now. But a revival of interest in their work is possible. I now find their literary metier, if not robust and realistic, at least charming and evocative of the graces and amenities of the old upper middle-class intelligentsia. This kind of thing is "period" if you please, but it does have some enduring qualities.

Aside from that, I am concerned here chiefly with the Warner pamphlet as an interesting and valid view of Pittsburgh as it was in the mid-1920s. I was struck with her perceptions and opinions, which agree with some of my own observations as a native Pittsburgher. And such agreement always recommends any writer to his reader. Finally, I thought my study to record what other writers had said about Pittsburgh should include these forgotten opinions.

I confess that I am baffled by her use of the owl as a device in introducing her discourse on Pittsburgh. Also, it seems a little fantastic as an introduction to what is in reality an old-fashioned "familiar essay" — a literary form that does not have much currency nowadays. In any case, we shall just have to allow for the writer's idiosyncrasy and get on to the Pittsburgh views.

"I wish," she informs us, "that Pittsburgh had been named Fort Pitt after the historical stronghold there. Fort Pitt exactly suits it, with its stockade of smoke stacks, its 'Block House,' and the barricading ramparts of its hills. And as a second choice, I should name it Saint Pittsberg [sic] for the sake of mixing up the nationalities and creeds." Although these descriptions come within a hairsbreadth of being a little "quaint," she did express, saliently and briefly, certain undeniable aspects of Pittsburgh — its turbulent topography, its military past, and its still-militant present (c. 1925) along with its more-than-generous ethnic mixture.

The decade of the 'Twenties was — with its prosperity — still eminently part of the local era of the "Great Smoke." It does rejoice *this* ancient heart to see how aesthetically, at least, she valued "Old Smokey" — "its wonderful smoke screen all around it — some from coke, some from dust from ore, much of it not smoke at all in the strict sense, but drifting along the rivers and lingering in the valleys where the wind can not scoop it up over the hills.

"Knowing what hard work all this means for somebody to keep it going, one feels guilty in perceiving any beauty there. But the fact remains that the floating shadows and the indistinctness of outlines and the deep wide spaces in which the smoke drifts and curls, all combine to form a marvelous screen for the play of lights and colors. There are Japanese effects in delicate monotones on winter afternoons; airy Claude Monet color effects at dawn; Whistler bridges and blue twilights; and Turner fires at pouring time after dark."

Ah, how well she does express the beauties of the old dark, polluted, smoke-clouded days "of yore"! And what old Pittsburgher does not remember those spectacular nights when, at "pouring time" in the steel mills, half the sky was suffused with a throbbing curtain of light! What memories and visions of the past she does call up! I have always said that when Pittsburgh un-smoked itself, half of its visual mystery and drama departed. But, to a degree Warner returns it to us.

Again, I have often said of Pittsburgh, as one might of a man, that it is "handsome-ugly." Hear Warner on the same theme: "Nobody, I think, would claim that Pittsburgh is a dainty spot; but nobody can deny that it has (as tactful persons say of a homely friend) an interesting expression. Every part of Pittsburgh has an expression of its own."

I have often said that Pittsburgh is intensely masculine in tone, that it is a purely male city. Warner concurs: "Pittsburgh is above all the most masculine place in the world. It is more masculine than a mining-camp or a logging-settlement or a whaling-ship, because in those one finds only men's rough-hewn, knockabout, haphazard makeshifts, deliberately rude, whereas in Pittsburgh one sees their finished products, the product wrought out by the masterful metal-conquering type of man."

Not a little of the charm of the pamphlet lies in the black-and-white line drawings of the now half-forgotten Pittsburgh artist Christ Walter (1872-1938), who was one of the first local artists to exhibit in the late, lamented Carnegie Internationals.[2] These miniature sketches have an uncanny precision that conveys hauntingly the Pittsburgh atmosphere of the 1920s.

I wish that I could reprint the entire pamphlet, but these small excerpts do convey something of its flavour. As one of its most remarkable "preserved" qualities, Pittsburgh still has a curious openness and freedom in its way, reminiscent of the frontier. As Warner says in a remark that she attributes to her husband: "Pittsburgh . . . makes a dash where Boston would put a semi-colon or a period."

[1]Chairman of the Board of the Pittsburgh History & Landmarks Foundation.

[2]Between 1970 and 1982 the International Exhibitions that had been an intermittent tradition since 1896 were discontinued, though there were several large one- or two-man shows.

"Jamie's Journal," *The Pittsburgher,* April, 1978.

An Antiphon of Stones
Some Random Native Notes in Reply to a Visiting Architectural Critic in Pittsburgh

. . . To call the stones themselves to their ideal places . . .
—*George Santayana*

From a view to a paragraph, from a month's visit to a book, American cities have lent themselves to visiting writers. They have been looked at hurriedly and "capsuled," or slowly savoured and generously "served up." Damnations and faint praise, eulogies and denunciations have attended their histories and their landscapes. At places of special note, mountains of words have accumulated in the wake of visiting pens and typewriters.

A city may mean many things to many people. For statisticians of population or the market place, the urban area may resolve itself into a mounting trellis of figures, a skeleton waiting, as it were, for flesh. For dealers in aesthetic impressions or purveyors of groceries, the streets may convey disparate messages of vistas on the one hand, or dinner tables on the other. The writer of fiction, especially the novelist, may find in the metropolis a world which he can remake into any image he desires. The collected streets, buildings, and houses provide the journalist with a never-failing source of copy.

Pittsburgh has provided material for all comers, and a multitude of visitors have recorded their opinions with varying degrees of accuracy or bias. Most of these *impressions de voyage* now lie forgotten in old travel journals or dusty letter-files. Even so the pronouncements of Mrs. Anne Royall or Charles Dickens[1] may be quoted on occasion, but the once-trenchant observations have now chiefly an historical value. However, the *latest* visiting opinion, from whatever source, may cause the local citizens to sit up and take notice.

Anything said about Pittsburgh architecture will be sure to cause stirrings of interest and impulses of assent or disagreement in our particular corner. Pittsburghers have not forgotten Frank Lloyd Wright's dictum that the Steel City should be abandoned, but his condemnation was so outrageous as to become ridiculous; such displays of calculated intransigence may very well excite laughter rather than anger. H. H. Richardson, on the other hand, found Pittsburgh particularly sympathetic, and as its most famous architectural interpreter he left one of the chief monuments of his genius here.[2]

13

The Allegheny County Jail with the Court House beyond, c. 1890.

It may be both salutary and instructive for the native voice to answer, on occasion, the visiting opinion. The local utterance has, of course, the distinct advantage of familiarity with the terrain, but the visitor will have a certain freshness of approach to the observed phenomena. The indigenous commentator may also, in responding, have the opportunity to check the validity of his pronouncements against those of the larger world. The combination of the two opinions, speaking and answering, may thus present at least a partial mirror of the metropolis (there can never be any complete reflection).

Possibly this situation of statement and answer may be compared to those antiphonal religious services in which vocal statements made by a choir on one side of the chancel are answered by a group of singers on the opposite side.

However, our "service" must start with the visiting voice, in this case that of Mr. Joseph Watterson, the Editor of the *A.I.A. Journal,* who in his March, 1963, issue devoted a page to his impressions of Pittsburgh architecture. We have been moved to answer, and our antiphon, delivered from the "home" side of the chancel, will present the local view of the "stones" of Pittsburgh — its streets, parks, and buildings.

14

Our opposite Editor admirably begins with modest notes and self-effacing words. The reader is requested not to take these paragraphs as considered dicta since they are the surface observations of what might be called a "qualified observer"; these are taxicab vignettes and hotel-window vistas that make no pretension to "expertise." As we attend we applaud the visitor's modesty and perspicuity, but we pause, we nod approval or disagree, and the answering words form.

But how to answer and why? The merit of the visiting voice·is that of its freedom; it is not *engagé,* it need not come home to dinner every night, nor need it dutifully traverse, day by day, the same streets. But the local spokesman comes from a familiar circle of commitments, duties, and responsibilities. He must ultimately realize that he is held by something both as demanding and sustaining as "the wife and kids." The place, the city, may demand a great deal, but it will also give him something back.

The native citizen must speak out of concern, out of duty, but above all, with love. He will also speak with a little hate, with asperity or impatience, because even the noblest emotions are never entirely "pure." Love is, however, necessary. The word may mean everything or nothing, and in a materialistic culture it is often cheapened; but even in an uncertain context, we still dare to speak the great word. It should be spoken with a proper diffidence, delivered, as they used to say on the stage, a little "aside," perhaps "thrown away." Only thus can it take root and blossom in the changing streets of the city.

And there it must blossom, if anything called a city is to survive. The citizen must love, become part of, his city; if he does not, all the money poured into the new schemes and the bright multitudinous plans of the planners will avail nothing.

We have tried to explain why we are standing in the chancel ready to reply. We speak here of our native place; we have been with this city all our life, in sickness and in health, in joy and in sorrow. We have endured much together, and we thus presume to speak.

For courtesy we may take up the theme where our opposite Editor begins — his praise of the rivers and the hills of Pittsburgh. In the nineteenth and early twentieth centuries, commentators not infrequently began with the local soot and the smoke (*"la ville la plus hideuse du monde"* or "hell with the lid off"). We now can be sure that smoke control is an unqualified success, and we are pleased with these civil references to our waters and our verdant topography. However, we must confess, a little ruefully, that much of the drama and the bustle of the city departed with the smoke and the attendant

15

phenomena. The veiled vistas and infernal perspectives of the old dispensation were not without a kind of sulphurous merit.

On the side of amenity, rather than commerce, Pittsburgh, like most other American riverside cities, did *not* take its place. As our visitor says, not too much is made of the local rivers, and they may be considered only in terms of getting across them with as much dispatch as possible. The native voice replies that at certain times and in certain places they do emerge rather gloriously into view, but one must know where and how to look. Alas, it is too true that the riverbanks were preempted in the last century by the railroads, and now it is the turn of the highways. It is doubtful if the cityscape is any better served by the new method of travel than by the old.

If we lament here the absence of well-planned quays seen in foreign cities, it must be remembered that the great sloping commercial wharves of the Triangle, which have but recently disappeared beneath the new highway systems, had a certain spaciousness and a loosely-defined and cobble-stoned grandeur. Much of their effectiveness as open urban spaces was due to a certain density of use, and they disappeared because diminishing commercial traffic no longer warranted their continuance.

Bridges are another "specialty of the house," but Pittsburgh is not so much surrounded (according to Mr. Watterson) as interwoven with them. Tunnels also have a pervasive influence on the local landscape, for without them life in certain sections of the city would be of an almost Alpine difficulty. Our hills and valleys have, of course, imposed extreme difficulties of communication and articulation upon the urban entity. Anne Royall, in her song of hate to Pittsburgh, called it a "vagabond village," but the place might more properly be called a collection of wandering towns which have taken squatter's rights and lodged themselves helter-skelter among the sheltering ridges. Many peoples and races from all the countries and the continents have brought their songs, their towers, and their gods to enrich the native valleys. The metropolitan area is thus a kind of honeycomb of diversities, a roughly-woven cloth of many threads, which is as constantly changing as it is endlessly fascinating.

Our opposite voice takes up the chant again to notice the great brooding ridge of Mount Washington which looms above the Monongahela River (*not* the Allegheny!). Our visitor should have seen it seventy years ago when, bald, bleak, and eroded, it rose starkly from the all-pervading smoke. He comments on the ragged houses fringing its top, and he asks, not without reason, why there is not something grander there. Native voices, even in the last century, were not wanting to lament Pittsburgh's inattention to its hills, and the complaint is still valid.

To the native eye there is a certain homely charm in this great hill with its low cornice of buildings — the usual late-nineteenth-century miscellany of mansard and jigsaw curiosities, dotted with aridities of yellow brick. The whole broad scene presents another of those faintly raffish, haphazard effects in which Pittsburgh abounds. It is as if one of the wandering villages had crept up the other side of the ridge, and with one eye closed, hair all anyway, and cap pulled down, was peering over the edge with a kind of friendly slyness down at the Golden Triangle.

We do not scruple to amplify the strictures of the visiting voice against the iniquitous handling of the historic Point area, where the rivers meet. If that ill-used piece of land now seems to be little more than an insignificant pendant to the enormous coils of the over-riding expressways, if that park is only a fake pearl, or perhaps a pea, attached to a monster necklace of highways, we have at least escaped the use of the site as another vessel of embalmed history — a full-scale "restoration" of Fort Pitt.[3]

This area is haunted for the native by the ghosts of vanished buildings — the Wabash Station with its Beaux-Arts swags and aedicules, crumbling Greek Revival houses on vanished Fancourt Street and Penn Avenue, old loft buildings, railway viaducts that marched stolidly across the area much less oppressively than the freeways do now. All is definitely not "improvement" here.

The Gateway area on the "town" side of the freeways, for all its office towers, seems to be essentially suburban in tone. The placing of the buildings among the ornamented open spaces has been handsomely accomplished, but there is a little too much openness. From the Liberty Avenue entrance of the quarter, one has a sense of tremendous sweep and verve that is entirely pleasing, but even at noonday there seems to be a kind of busy emptiness about these spaces. After five o'clock, when the office workers, like homing pigeons, head for the distant suburban hills, the gardens become really vacant. We, in the past, have dined al fresco on summer Sunday evenings at the Hilton, and the great spaces stretching away from the terrace were often quite devoid of life. Those green pleasances stretching out, all uninhabited, seemed totally ours. How grand and how sad!

The new furniture of the Gateway quarter, we have taken (with some reservations, and after a proper season) to our thorny bosom. That great looking glass Gateway Four is, like all mirrors, at once

17

ominous and fascinating, but we are not altogether sure that reflection is one of the major functions of architecture. The new IBM Building[4] which our opposite Editor extols as "the only fine and daring piece of new architecture . . . in the downtown area" produces in us a rather uncertain impression. There is no doubt that it is a really engaging "stunt," like one of those old vaudeville "turns" in which a whole pyramid of acrobats is supported on the shoulders of one man. To return to the furniture metaphor, however, we might conceive of the building as a great ornamental lantern that might be any size you please, with its present dimensions merely fortuitous. Is this the Pharos of the future? — Lighten our darkness, we beseech thee, O IBM, and by thy great mercy defend us from all perils and dangers of the night!

Here in Gateway Center, that enormous outdoor room, with its rather disconcerting changes of scale, we may observe many of the architectural shapes and textures fashionable in the last fifteen years (there are still notable lacunae, but give the planners time!). This area, which our visitor praises, is still in process of becoming, and we shall reserve any final judgment on it, but we still assert, *forte,* that the most effective piece of site planning in Pittsburgh is Mellon Square, which our opposite number describes as "a Japanese pebble garden at the bottom of a well."

We feel that this elegant out-door living room has been very well tied in to the surrounding old downtown neighbourhood. Despite the tall walls that surround the square, the scale here is "geared" to the people who use it, and it is *used,* which is not the least test of the fitness of any urban space. We are no specialist in the bottoms of wells, but we doubt that any such subterranean area is so felicitously arranged or so well populated.

Toward the end of the antiphonal service, the visitor bows at the appearance of the mystical symbol SOM (represented in downtown Pittsburgh by the YWCA Building[5]), and, genuflecting deeply at the name of Richardson, he launches into a chant in praise of the Allegheny County Jail. We have genuflected to the Jail so often (and we may remember here that Richardson adopted the plan of the church of St. Simeon Stylites in Syria for his building) that our knees are a little stiff, but we yield to no man in our praise of that magnificent heap of granite. We are glad that the chorus of approbation is not only national but international, and we can add nothing but our native note to their voices. The Jail is, after all, the *purest* Pittsburgh.

In a far-from-inspired passage, the visitor asserts that (with the exception of the building noted above) the rest of our downtown architecture is either "cheap and mediocre" or "old and crummy." We assert in response that this is something less than just, and it implies, on the part of the observer, an impression based on meagre examination. There are in the downtown area alone some quite good things of the late nineteenth and early twentieth centuries — structures like the cabstand of the Union Station and the Frick, Oliver, and Union Trust Buildings — which will compare favourably with anything of the same date in America.

But it is finally the area beyond the "good" things — that of the minor, anonymous street architecture, the undistinguished houses and casual shop fronts of a hundred years of Pittsburgh life — which most engage the heart of the native. Our praise must go to the humble multitude of structures, whether of brick, wood, stone, or iron, that have served the past days of the city. As these constitute the most notable evidences of urban life, we here offer a prayer for the faithful departed, and departing, and with it we express the hope that our new housing, if it is not made in heaven, will at least be conceived in love and deployed with intelligence.

As the last antiphon is ended, we salute the visiting voice in the darkened chancel and we go out again into the streets of our city.

---

[1]Respectively, from *Pennsylvania; or Travels Continued in the United States* (1829) and *American Notes for General Circulation* (1842).

[2]The Allegheny County Courthouse and Jail.

[3]In 1983, it must be said that Point State Park has become a much-used amenity.—JVT

[4]Now the United Steelworkers of America Building.

[5]The New York architectural firm of Skidmore, Owings & Merrill, famous especially for its business and institutional designs.

The Charette, July, 1963. This was a response to "Observations on Pittsburgh" by Joseph Watterson, published in "Editor's Page" *AIA Journal,* March, 1963.

A toy castle owned by James D. Van Trump.

Of Castles
A Medley of Dream Towers in Miniature

I cannot remember when castles have not excited my imagination, or when they have not been part of the general climate of my mind. I thought of this the other day when I was dusting and rearranging part of my collection of miniature buildings at the Old Post Office Museum. Among these are several castles, ranging all the way from rooks used in chess sets to fairly large three-dimensional models of medieval castellated structures, complete with miniature men-at-arms.

When I was a child, I used to collect pictures of castles — post cards or photographs and engravings from books. Since I had never visited the castle lands of Europe, they became a spur to my imagination, a point of departure for fantasy and dream, harbours of romance and refuges from the life of everyday.

The castle-lover is always a Romantic by pre-disposition — mere forts or works of defense may be left to the practical or Classical mind, but castles are for poets and those who dream. A castle is part fort and part house, but for its true devotees, howsoever solid it may in actuality be, it is compounded of fantasy and the faraway.

It could have been that, in my own far past, I was introduced to castles by way of fairy tales, which were once part of every child's up-bringing, or at least that of the children of families that read books. In the crowded *mise-en-scène* of the Brothers Grimm, or Hans Christian Andersen, or the multitudinous tales collected by Andrew Lang in the books identified by colour — *The Red Fairy Book,* etc. — there were many castles inhabited by beautiful princesses or evil sorcerers. In our present televisioned day perhaps the fairy-tale land for children may be far to seek, and the present-day young are fed on much more realistic fare. How can a fairy-tale castle, even complete with an enchanted princess, possibly compare with a real modern space ship?

Grounded serenely in Fairyland, my childhood castles loomed remotely in a word and picture. However, at Christmastime in 1916, I received my first miniature building, a toy castle made of wood and *papier-mâché,* a marvelous production of late nineteenth-century German craftsmanship. I can see it now, gleaming and glowing under the Christmas tree lights. I had long wanted a castle of my very own, and there it was. It sat wonderfully on a painted *papier-mâché* hill

21

which included a partial moat crossed by a draw-bridge; it had two courtyards on different levels, which were surrounded by a variety of wooden towers and walls that could be removed and stored in a compartment inside the hill when the castle went with me to the seaside. There it sometimes served as a model for sand castles.

In these far days, how many castles made of sand did I construct, and their speedy vanishment taught me early lessons in the brevity of all human pleasures. Were they never so grand, they would melt away with the next tide, but always there was the wooden fort, which went back to town with me in the autumn. Whether the castles were of sand or wood, I led an elaborate dream life among them. I would concoct about these magic miniatures whole fairy tales filled with kings and queens, beautiful princesses and enchanted princes, ogres and knights, which all *lived*, at the time, a full life of their own. Alas, in due course, the wooden architecture of my castle vanished in my early youth, when I put away childish things. But I have never put it quite away. Even today I often think about it and wish that I had it back.

In the next year, 1917, my mother was given by the local tailor shop a moulded-paper wall calendar in the form of an infinitely complicated German castle, all blue and silver and sprinkled with glitter snow. It was not three-dimensional like my toy castle, but its partly-sculptural quality, its strange metallic colours and its brilliant snowy crags and steep roofs, made it seem like the Ice King's stronghold, where a pale princess, held under enchantment, awaited rescue by a handsome huntsman.

This calendar castle adorned the kitchen, holding in its cardboard Gothic pocket grocery lists and skeins of salvaged string — which crumpled string, striped like peppermint, added a note of gaiety to the icy fantasy. When I was not at school, I would stop in the kitchen to visit the castle and our Irish cook, who, when she was making a cake, would let me lick the spoon and knife with which she had been spreading boiled icing. To sit beneath the shining turrets of the castle eating the crystalline icing from a spoon seemed to me to be entirely cozy and comfortable — having the icing without the ice. It occurred to me, much later, that this is not an uncommon Romantic attitude.

Outside the kitchen window stretched one of those long plains once so common in West Philadelphia, acres that had in the past been pasture and farmland but which, now dim and weedy, waited the ministrations of the house "developer." At a little distance, "bowered," as the fairy tales said, in great ancient trees, was a stone

22

country house, "Whitby Hall," from which long ago, before the Revolution, the High Sheriff of Philadelphia had ridden to hounds.[1] Perhaps that dim ghostly presence was, to the dreamer in the kitchen, the handsome huntsman, high and golden, splendid on a white horse. Was that distant sound on the March wind the baying of hounds? Perhaps ... In the land of fey, anything is possible ...

In this ambiguous field, which sullenly waited for the builder's grid, I made my only foray into actually trying to build a castle of my own. Shortly after America's entry into the First World War, when all the martial virtues were much in the air, I, the dreamer with the book, assisted a group of my male schoolmates, all about my age, to construct a fort on a slight rise about a half-mile from my home. It was their idea, born of a childish notion of constructing a defense work against the Huns, which in the early summer of 1917 meant the Germans. It was not exactly my idea of what a castle should be, but since I was always talking about medieval defense works, the other boys thought that I should be architect and engineer. Just out of school, we worked mightily on our fort — we dug and hoisted stones, and scoured the neighbourhood for old packing cases which provided wood for palisades. We hollowed out trenches and leveled platforms; we even made a tunnel of sorts between an upper and a lower court-yard. It was a crude and very small affair, but I, as designer, when it was finished, felt pleased as I surveyed it from my rudimentary battlements.

Unfortunately, my small companions of the venture felt that, now the fort was finished, we should challenge another group of boys ("gang" would now be too strong a word) to storm our ramparts. Once the place was constructed they felt that we should find a use for it. In other words, function should follow form. I spoke very strongly against this new development, much to my companions' chagrin.

Providentially, my parents, just before school reopened again, took me to Pittsburgh to spend several months with my grandfather, and when we returned we moved to another neighbourhood. My only real castle had, as well, vanished beneath rows of developer's houses.

So began my interest in castles and the inception of my collection of miniature chateaux. Ten years ago I found, at Marshall Field's toy department in Chicago, another version of my small wooden castle of 1916. Presently it sits proudly in my office at the Old Post Office Museum. It is now, as were all my vanished castles, an abode of romance, a hill of dreams.

[1] In 1923, the shell of the house was moved to Haverford, Pa., and most of the fine woodwork is now in the Detroit Institute of Arts. The "long plains" were filled with jerry-built row houses.—JVT

Radio script for WQED-FM, circa 1977.

The Heidelberg apartment house.

Castles on the Allegheny
An Architect's Fantastic Demesne near Pittsburgh

It is no paradox, perhaps, that our "age of conformity" should so admire manifestations of the unusual, the "original," the fantastic. The monumental facade suggests the private corner, the secluded room. Architecture is no stranger to these contrarieties, and embraces both with an impartial indifference. The architectural publicist, whether indifferent or not, still celebrates the forum gesture, the public facade, but he must also be aware of his reader's abounding interest in lateral passageways. So the wayward chimneys, the mysterious towers, once the adornments of the ancient ballad, have become the stock in trade of our art magazines.

Surrealism, with its Freudian overtones, has nurtured the modern cult of the architecture of Antonio Gaudi, which is the largest public symbol of the fantastic impulse. Here the personal creative explosion is everything, and organized caprice and plastic extravagance have achieved a kind of canonization. Since the interest in the bizarre is undoubtedly extensive, the world is searched for similar exotic phenomena. We herewith present our own small "find," our particular, strange flower in the general fantastic garden.

"Il faut cultiver nôtre jardin," and the architect may be as assiduous as any other to comply with Candide's adjuration. His garden, if he can afford it or if he knows how to build with his own hands, may blossom in brick and stone. If, further, he has a bent for fantasy, he may indulge a propensity for dream castles, but the castles are there for everyone to see. A garden of solidified dreams may or may not be an edifying or a pleasing spectacle, but its strangeness will command our interest surely.

Again, the public works of an architect must wait upon the wishes of his clients, but in his private constructions he may do as he pleases. The case of the Pittsburgh architect Fred C. Sauer, who died in 1942, is a case in point, and it is highly interesting that this conservative, successful, but uninspired German-American architect should have enlivened his later years with the production of a colony of fantastic buildings.[1] The locale of this hibernal activity was his hillside estate in the middle-class, turn-of-the century suburb of Aspinwall, on the Allegheny River near Pittsburgh.

25

He was essentially a "minor league" architect — sound, well-trained, practical, and business-like. As a good business man, he dealt in real estate and building products as well as design. His acres of suburban villas are today, even when they can be identified, unmemorable, and his schools, churches, and shops excite no interest even among antiquaries. Representative and typical of his time and place, he built soundly but without imagination; he knew exactly what his American public wanted and he gave it to them. He was (and is) the backbone, if not the heart and soul, of his profession.

A census of immigrant architects working in nineteenth-century America would be interesting; there must have been a great company of them, and Sauer was of their number. He was born in Heidelberg in 1860, and was very thoroughly educated in his chosen profession at the architectural schools of Stuttgart. Part of his schooling, as he himself said later, consisted in his working as a stonemason, bricklayer, and carpenter — good training for the future castle builder. He graduated at the age of nineteen and came immediately to Pittsburgh, where he worked for a time with E. M. Butz, whose office designed the Western Penitentiary buildings at Wood's Run. In 1884 he went into business for himself, and from that time on, plans for a steady stream of buildings issued from his office, testifying to a large and varied practice.

Such extensive building operations as Ben Venue and Boulevard Place in Pittsburgh led to similar activities on the alluvial plain of Aspinwall; he bought his hillside tract of land on Center Avenue and moved there in 1898. In 1904, he organized the Aspinwall-Delafield Land Company and, according to his own account, was for some time its president. There is little doubt that he was active in its promotion. One of his late large architectural commissions was the designing of several structures at the Allegheny County Work House near Aspinwall.

This prosperous, active, architectural-business career was reflected in his Center Avenue home tract, which we may, for courtesy at least, call an estate. It was in its beginnings probably little different from many of its kind. The original, rather staid "1900" centre-hall house of cream-coloured brick still sits in a fold of the hillside, largely untouched by the enchanter's wand, but above and below it, clinging to the hillsides, erupt cascades of turrets, chimneys, terraces, and stairways. It is interesting that this web of dreams seems to emanate from the mansion's fixed and apparently static centre, but it is immaterial to the unfolding of the ballad.

Here in this staid brick house, where the business letter ends and the song begins, it is abundantly evident that the aging architect had begun to dream. One might say that this blossoming phenomenon was a result of that dichotomy in the German character, consisting of the dreamer and the efficient man, which has produced such wonders for the world, and such woe. Certainly on his practical side he was frugal and hardheaded enough; his dreams were also investments on which he expected a return in dollars and cents. Even the chicken house and the garage on the estate were turned into rentable properties.

But this is not to invalidate the dream, nor discount the ballad. As one enters the demesne from Center Avenue past a rather Gaudi-esque mail box, it is a little difficult to discover the "melodic line" of the composition. To the left on the descending side are two houses and on the right the mansion, which is overlooked by the stepped gables and the horrendous pent roof of the stable. This latter structure is reached by a road which loops widely past the apartment house, known as "Heidelberg," and a towered cottage. Downhill near the apartment is a semi-circular lawn garden, upheld by a fantastically-textured retaining wall, past which another branch of the road leads back to Center Avenue. On the town edge of the property were two more houses and a duck pond, which have disappeared beneath a modern expressway.

The "line" here appears to be the road, which is like a branching tree trunk from which the constructions, like foliage and fruit, depend. As against the constructed volumes, the procession of spaces between them seems medieval and accidental, but they are nonetheless effective. The subtle interlocking of varied planes, the abrupt declensions and ascensions of the road, the sharp juxtaposition of angular forms and unconventional textures, the rocketing vistas and beanstalk perspectives make this suburban hillside an exciting visual experience, a ballad of opposing and yet related forms and spaces which is in the strongest contrast to the prose of the streets below.

The largest structure in the complex is the Heidelberg apartments — Sauer's erstwhile chicken house — whose three bold stories jut out at one side of the lawn garden. Remodeled in its present form about 1928-30, it recalls the work of the boulder-and-timber school of architects earlier in the century, but the silhouette is gentler here, the texture more smooth. The fenestration is varied, and the walls are veneered with jagged stone slabs quarried on the property. The stone veneer, probably over concrete block, is the chief surfacing of walls throughout the complex; it is varied only by patches of brick

Benjamin Franklin and the eagle.

and fragments of ornamental stone and terra cotta. There are no stairs within the apartment house; each floor is approached from the road which winds upward around the structure. From the eastern wall, Benjamin Franklin in bas-relief peers down benignly at a militant terra-cotta eagle.

Past Franklin and a superb evergreen tree with glossy leaves, the visitor mounts a multi-directional staircase to the upper level of the road, where he finds himself before the mysterious door of the towered cottage, which according to the architect's son was built about 1940. The battlemented tower is cozily companioned by a wide

Edwardian window of plate glass. From the roof of this little house, one may look through clerestory windows into its high living room or across the battlements of the tower into a maze of descending roofs and chimneys that melt into the town and river in the distance.

The clerestory — a very modern touch — is a reminder that the old man liked to experiment with new forms of construction, forays in which he was not always successful. He was interested in concrete, and about the time of the First World War he built, on Delafield Road in Aspinwall, two tall, box-like cement houses of a portentous ugliness and uncertain stability. One of them collapsed a few years ago, but the other still remains.

But the old architect did not collapse nor did he "retire." He continued building and planning new constructions until the day of his death. There was in those last days an intimate connection between the man and his work, for he had the advantage of being able to shape his creations with his own hands. It might be well if more modern designers possessed the same ability. Above all, Sauer seemed to sense that for the maker, the artist, there is no retirement. The architect, like the poet or painter, should die with his boots on.

The fantastic colony on the metamorphosed estate remains Sauer's monument, his claim to memory. Granted it is a fashionable "fantastic" document, what are we to make of it? There is something a little pedestrian, awkward, and fumbling about these buildings; Sauer's imagination had its limits, and his visions lack any ultimate distinction. There is something here of the old-time amusement park, more than a seasoning of the frantic romanticism of the 1920 real-estate sub-division, a touch of the cinema landscape of Rudolph Valentino, perhaps a memory of the elves' village under the Christmas tree. In the end, the hillside was Sauer's own private Disneyland with profits at six percent. But having said that, there is a charm and an interest about the place that is irreducible. It is a minor but still valid document of humanity's primal love of fantasy and legend. "Once upon a time . . ."

And so we are left with the notes, the words of the ballad on the hill. This is a winter song sung by an old man, but there is something about it forever youthful, forever true. However bumble-fisted and awkward it may be, it is still a real poetic statement. Prose is not enough and the legend never dies. A man must sing as he is able.

---

[1]Fred C. Sauer received some of his training in architecture in Germany. Could this have predisposed him to castles?—JVT

The Charette, March, 1963.

The First Presbyterian Church.

30

Mirror in the West
The Work of Some Philadelphia Architects in Pittsburgh

When one considers the magnitude and grandeur of the Philadelphia architectural image, it seems rather surprising that it was not more largely reflected at the western end of the state, especially in Pittsburgh. That it was not is undoubtedly due in part to the topography and the general tone of the newer city, which has not lacked, be it said, for emanations of architectural light, manifestations of talent, even a flash of genius or two in the western glass — but they have all come from other quarters. Mostly the transmission of images from Philadelphia has been minor, intermittent, and muted. It is as if the great mountain ridges curving across the centre of the state had some mysterious power to obstruct the flow of architectural commissions to the west. Those that did come through, however — the pictures in the western mirror — constitute an interesting phenomenon not unworthy of record.

Pittsburgh did not really cease to be a frontier outpost until the end of the eighteenth century; during the intervening years since its foundation, its construction had ceased to be logs and became brick and stone. Important public buildings like that of the Western University of Pennsylvania (1830)[1] and the Court House (completed c. 1800) reflected the Classical manner of the Eastern Seaboard; but pleasant as this provincial Georgian must have been (the original buildings are long since gone), it certainly lacked the authority of the Philadelphia image.

However, the growing city, enlarging year by year and spreading out beyond the Point into the hills, needed new buildings for special uses. For very specialized building types, either of necessity or amenity, application would have to be made to a more established community where architectural services of the necessary sort were readily available. Philadelphia was the obvious answer in this case. A large prison and a theatre were needed, and thus it came about that the first considerable architectural reflections from the metropolis in the East were penitential and dramatic, an unusual combination.

The prison was the more necessary of the two, as Harry Elmer Barnes, who has documented the history of the building, states: "In March, 1818, an act was passed by the General Assembly of Penn-

31

sylvania appropriating money for the erection of a state penitentiary in Allegheny County, which was to be constructed according to a plan submitted to the legislature by the inspectors of the Philadelphia prison." This building was designed in 1820 by the Philadelphia architect William Strickland (1788-1854), and its plan showed the influence of a prison at Ghent and also of Jeremy Bentham's Panopticon.[2] The Pittsburgh structure, opened in 1826, provided one hundred and ninety cells, and it also operated on the principle of solitary confinement without labour.

From the first the institution was a failure functionally because of the subsequent adoption by the authorities of the practice of solitary confinement with hard labour. Strickland's cells could not be adapted to the new method, with the result that the interior of his prison was demolished and rebuilt in 1833 after the plans of John Haviland (1792-1852). After the construction of a new building at Riverside on the Ohio, the old prison was demolished in 1887, its site now forming part of the West Park in Pittsburgh's North Side. For many years, though, its castellated stone facade provided for Western Pennsylvanians the proper Romantic vision of a prison.

Across the Allegheny River in Pittsburgh the Pittsburgh Theatre (affectionately known to the natives as Old Drury) provided an image of what the proper playhouse should be. According to an advertisement that appeared in the *Pittsburgh Gazette* of July 30, 1833, "The building has been substantially erected . . . after a plan drawn by John Haviland, Esq., of Philadelphia whose justly acquired fame as an architect will be increased by the style and beauty of the Present Edifice."

This building, now demolished, was located on Fifth Avenue between Smithfield and Wood; it was two stories high (with a third false story added to the main facade). The auditorium, which held about one thousand two hundred people, had a gallery and a double tier of boxes. The seats were covered with crimson and edged with velvet and brass nails; there were eighteen chandeliers. The theatre was never very successful, however, and it finally closed in 1870.

In the field of church construction there were numerous reflections from the Eastern city, nor is this too surprising, since building committees might well look beyond the near streets for grander architectural images. The earliest churchly reflection from across the mountains consists of those additions made to the First Presbyterian Church of 1802 by Benjamin Henry Latrobe in 1816. Although Latrobe was much identified with Philadelphia, he cannot properly be called a Philadelphian. . . .[3]

Not of equal merit, stylistically, but designed by the Philadelphia architect David Gendell, was Pittsburgh's First Baptist Church (1867-76) formerly at Fourth and Ross Streets; the organization has since moved on to grander quarters designed by Bertram Goodhue.[4] Demolished in 1909, the Ross Street Church was in its day perhaps the city's most elaborate example of the pre-Richardsonian Romanesque Rundbogenstil, a manner very common throughout America in the mid-nineteenth century. Characteristically, it had a large wheel window in the main facade, which was flanked by two squat towers; the spire at the rear was never constructed. The architect exhibited the drawings for this church at the Forty-fifth Annual Exhibition of the Pennsylvania Academy of Fine Arts in 1868.

Equally uninspired, but pleasant in a picture post-card way, was the second Shadyside Presbyterian Church, formerly at Amberson Avenue and Westminster Place. It was designed by James H. Windrim (1840-1916) and constructed in 1874-75. Windrim was not unknown in Pittsburgh, since he had been supervising architect for the second Union Station, of which we shall speak presently. The sharp needle-like spire of his Decorated Gothic church quite dominated its suburban neighbourhood, but it did not do so very long, because a serious fault in the foundation made necessary the demolition of the entire structure to make way for the present building (1888-92), designed by Shepley, Rutan & Coolidge. . . .[5]

It may seem strange that the very vigorous and masculine Frank Furness never received more commissions in Pittsburgh, but the advent of H.H. Richardson and the Allegheny Court House and Jail so definitely set the city in the Richardsonian course that no other contender had a chance. Only a single small building — that of the Farmers Deposit National Bank, formerly at 220 Fourth Avenue, can be attributed to [Furness'] office on the authority of Maximilian Nirdlinger, who worked in the Furness & Evans' atelier in the late 'Nineties. The records of the Farmers Bank were destroyed in the 1936 flood, and documentation is at present lacking. The structure is, however, definitely Furnessian in both the broad handling of the forms and the rugged detailing.

According to Pittsburgh city directories the Bank was located in this building from 1896 to 1902, so that it must have been designed sometime in the early 'Nineties; possibly comparison with other work of the firm from this period may yield a clue as to its date. Certainly the little structure, which was demolished some years ago, needs further study before anything definite as to its date and authorship can be said.

The writer remembers it as a kind of architectural shock among its bland contemporaries. From the low, cavernous segmental arch of the entrance, the vigorously-defined planes of stone seem to explode upward into the jagged voussoirs of the second-story window. The wrought-iron window grills are almost brutally designed, and their spiked Charles Addams rosettes seem like instruments of torture for unwary birds. In a city where muscular architecture is not exactly uncommon, this is a highly interesting as well as an enigmatic building.

In the wake of Richardson, a group of New Englanders held the field in Pittsburgh — notably the firms of Longfellow, Alden & Harlow (after 1896, Alden & Harlow), Rutan & Russell, and the Boston firm of Peabody & Stearns.

This may explain why so talented a residential architect as the Philadelphian Wilson Eyre (1858-1949) is so little represented in the western city, although he is said to have designed a country house in suburban Sewickley. He also exhibited a sketch for a house and stable at Allegheny City in the Sixty-first Annual Exhibition of the Pennsylvania Academy of Fine Arts in 1891. He did compete for Pittsburgh's Church of the Ascension in 1896, but although his design was looked upon with favour, he lost out to William Halsey Wood. Near the end of his long career, he, then in partnership with John G. McIlvaine (1880-1939), designed the remodeling of the interior (1937-38) of the Shadyside Presbyterian Church. Eyre and McIlvaine's extremely suave and elegant auditorium is a pleasing late-Eclectic exercise in the Romanesque manner.

Before Ralph Cram and Bertram Goodhue executed some of the big Pittsburgh church commissions of the twentieth century, Theophilus Parsons Chandler (1845-1928), a New Englander by birth but a Philadelphian by choice, designed the First and Third Presbyterian churches in Pittsburgh. The latter (the Third Church's third building) [was] constructed [in] 1896-1902 . . . . We will speak here only of the former (the First Church's fourth structure), which was erected 1903-05 and which is located on Sixth Avenue in downtown Pittsburgh.

Both the First and the Third Church display the lush, richly-textured Gothic manner of Chandler at its most lavish, but the former is probably the most interesting structurally. The First Church, with its twin towers, is a prime example of Chandler's facility in manipulating creatively his "Curvilinear" English Gothic forms and ornament to meet the demands of an affluent Protestant clientele. Spatially the interior is extremely effective; a great carved-oak shell in the chancel arch opens to permit the nave and church-school areas to be made into one large room, while either may be a sufficient unit in itself. The view through the whole length of the building when the chancel doors are open is very impressive and displays the architect's imaginative use of Gothic form in meeting the specific problems of his own time. Similarly, the sinuous curvilinear ornament of the exterior seems nearly allied to the Art Nouveau. . . .[6]

Louis Kahn has also appeared at Greensburg — thirty five miles to the east of Pittsburgh — in a characteristic structure, the Greensburg Tribune-Review Building of 1959-60, but it is still too early to say if his influence will be as potent in the west as it is in Philadelphia. Other reflections appear in our glass, but we do not have space to record them — we have merely tried here to summon up some of the more important images known to us. What the glass will contain in the future we cannot say, but we venture a guess that it will not be heavily populated. Each city uses, of course, its own local talent, but when Pittsburgh does go elsewhere for architectural design, it does not seem to go often to Philadelphia.[7]

[1]The institution is now the University of Pittsburgh.

[2]Jeremy Bentham was a British jurist and philosopher who was interested in penology.—JVT

[3]A mention of St. Peter's Episcopal Church follows. This is more fully described in the third part of "The Gothic Revival in Pittsburgh."

[4]David Gendell had a respectable practice in mid-nineteenth-century Philadelphia, but not much is known about him. —JVT

[5]A discussion of railroad stations by Philadelphia architects follows, including the second Union Station and two from the office of Frank Furness. For complete descriptions, see "Pittsburgh Railroad Stations Past and Present."

[6]Discussions of Charles Z. Klauder's work at the University of Pittsburgh follow. These appear in completer form in the fourth part of "The Gothic Revival in Pittsburgh."

[7]Still true: New York mostly, these days.

The Charette, January, 1964.

The interior of the North Side Market House, with the top of an Art Deco fountain.

The North Side Market House

The Allegheny or North Side Market House[1] belongs — or should one say belonged? — to a type of building which both in style and function was once fairly common in this country. The institution of the market place is one of the oldest known to man, and the *covered* shopping space has also a venerable if more recent ancestry. In the nineteenth century, new methods of construction, notably the extensive use of iron, and later steel, had made possible daring innovations in the roofing of these spaces so that they became larger and loftier. This aspiring new splendour of interior arrangement, if not exactly necessary to the sale of vegetables, certainly conferred honour upon an ancient calling while more impersonally it celebrated the triumph of modern technology.

The history of the marketing of food in a city like Pittsburgh would undoubtedly prove interesting if it were ever written, but we can touch on it briefly here only insofar as it concerns the building in question and other contemporary local examples of the same type. The focus of marketing activity in nineteenth-century Pittsburgh had been the area in the Triangle known as the Diamond, and there, in 1854-55, had been erected a market hall that was related stylistically to the later North Side structure built in 1863.

Among the stylistic revivals of the early nineteenth century, the Romanesque had a not unprominent place, and often it would seem to have been more widely used, in all its provincial variations, than the Gothic — at least in the "medieval" section of the revivalist architectural camp. In America, allied with the enormously popular Italian Villa style, this rugged Romanesque manner (what the Germans called the Rundbogenstil) was simplified into an all-purpose, easygoing vernacular that featured round arches and Romanesquoid detailing.

Towers were also, in the more elaborate examples, very much part of the picture, and a really high-style version of the manner like James Renwick's Smithsonian Institution in Washington shows it at its Romantic best. However, the American Romanesque vernacular could be — and was — used for almost any kind of building from a blacksmith's shop to a railroad station. After the log cabin, it may

37

have been the most popular of all American styles until the Georgian revival of the end of the nineteenth century.

These buildings were often constructed of brick (which permitted the solidity of stone construction without its expense), and the Diamond Market of 1854 in Pittsburgh and the Allegheny Market of 1863 made use of this material. Both structures had been erected on land set aside for public use in the late eighteenth century when the respective towns had been laid out. There were differences; the Pittsburgh building was rectangular in plan while that of Allegheny was roughly square, but both were no different in style from that of assorted school houses, city halls, factories, and fire-engine houses that were being built the length and breadth of America.

The Allegheny Market was definitely the more handsome and spectacular of the two, since it was planned on the rather ample scale of the grand Renaissance manner; at each corner of the square plan were simulated pavilions that were connected with each other by curtain walls and tied into a central domed structure by low-pitched roofs supported by columns and trusses.

That this was essentially a one-story building was expressed in the detailing of the outer walls, and that same detailing — the tall round-arched windows, the brick corbelling under the eaves, and the curious rounded-top buttresses — gave the outer envelope of the building an interest that it otherwise might not have had. In this case "style" was merely something that was lightly wrapped around the great central space, with its clerestories and lantern. The interior

Ohio and Federal Streets, early 1900s, with the Market House.

38

of the great enclosure carried in its ample proportions the chief message of the building.

All was by no means "Romanesque," however; the curving gables of the corner pavilions imparted an almost Baroque feeling of movement to the rooflines. These undulations were no doubt reflections of the Second Empire style of Napoleon III's Paris, although they may be actual echoes (however they may have been carried to this place) of the Baroque of the seventeenth century. At any rate, this curling roof gives an exotic, almost confectionery, effect to a utilitarian building, an effect which was further enhanced by the small ventilating turrets, which looked vaguely Chinese. Although these elements all gave piquancy to the over-all design, it was the solid, rugged, round-arched Romanesque vernacular that gave the building its particular character.

Some charming minor notes may be noticed. Over the arches of the main doors were carved representations of the fruits of the earth, all done in the heavy, slightly abstracted manner of the American mid-nineteenth century. These decorative sculptures should be preserved, because they have a fresh, provincial vigour all their own. If today we are to be allowed to retain few large-scale examples of our municipal past, perhaps we may be able to collect a few fragments such as this into a repository of some kind where they could be kept as mementoes. A mortuary museum of such municipal pleasantries would perhaps constitute an ironic riposte to many an urban statement of today.[2]

It was preponderantly the interior, however, that constituted the main interest of the building. This great square hall, with its slim pillars and its large uncluttered space, ornamented above with the delicate tracery of the roof trusses, was like a grand church dedicated to commerce. These huge enclosures of wood, glass, and iron were the real *chefs d'oeuvre* of nineteenth-century construction as well as its valid architectural poetry. Under these new technological "vaults" the buying and selling of food took on almost a dimension of grandeur, and it is one of the tragedies of our own day that we can find no use for these handsome structures.

[1]Demolished in 1966.

[2]This idea was later realized in the garden court of the Old Post Office Museum.

The Charette, March-April, 1967.

J. W. KERR Architect.　　　Otto Krebs lith. Pittsburgh.　　　JAMES STEEN, del.

MUNICIPAL HALL
(NEW CITY HALL)
PITTSBURGH, PA.

The City Hall, from a lithograph by Otto Krebs.

The Old City Hall of Pittsburgh
A Glimpse of Our Victorian Past

Recently, when I was doing some research on the Court House of Philadelphia County, which is contained in the great City Hall of Philadelphia, I was reminded that Pittsburgh once had a High Victorian City Hall of the same vintage, begun in 1868 and dedicated in 1872. This domed structure, in the French manner of the Second Empire, was Pittsburgh's first really elegant municipal building, and sure evidence that the city must be considered in the forefront of important American municipalities. Our fine new French City Hall was the visible sign of our achieved position.

Pittsburgh became a borough in 1793, but even after the incorporation, there was no fixed meeting place for the borough council. Sometimes they met in the new Court House (finished c. 1800) in Market Square, or in taverns — chiefly the latter. Undoubtedly this sometimes encouraged conviviality in the conduct of public affairs.

The borough became a city in 1816, but the first municipal building of any note was that erected in the eastern half of Market Square in 1854, on the site of the old horseshoe-shaped market house. The old Court House had been abandoned as such in 1841, when the new building on Grant's Hill was completed; the old structure, which had been sold to William Eichbaum, was demolished in 1852, and a new market house, completed in 1855, was erected on the vacated site. Both of these two-story buildings were much alike in shape, size, and appearance, constructed of the same material — brick — and in the same style, an extremely simple and utilitarian version of the mid-nineteenth century Rundbogenstil, a kind of Romanesque Revival.

The municipal offices were on the first floor of the Market Square City Hall, but the much taller second story, with its high arched windows, became a hall for public meetings and the presentation of concerts. During the Civil War, large numbers of soldiers were fed and entertained in this great room.

In 1872, when the new City Hall was opened on Smithfield Street, the first floor of the old building became part of the Market House, while the second floor continued as a meeting place and concert hall. Some of the great musical artists of the late nineteenth and early twentieth centuries were heard here — the young Ignace Paderewski performed on its stage as well as singers like Lillian Nordica. After the Carnegie Music Hall was opened in 1895, the Market Square hall began to decline. The building was finally demolished in 1909, along with the old Market in 1914, to make way for the large new Beaux-Arts City Market which took up the whole area of the Square. This last was also razed in 1963, returning the Square to its open and unencumbered state as donated by the Penn family in 1785.

But to return to Market Square as it must have looked in the late 1860s: the 1854 building would appear to have been rather small for the growing business of a rapidly expanding city. The Square also was constantly crowded with the activities of the Market, and the site must have seemed less and less appropriate for the City Hall. The American scene had also changed considerably since the Civil War. Much more splendour was the municipal order of the day, not only in public buildings but private dwellings as well. Merchants, bankers, hotel keepers, and shop owners, great and small, wanted premises that reflected the wealth and progress of a country that was constantly becoming richer and more prosperous. Onward and upward with the arts and sciences, the new age seemed to say, and this attitude, together with an expanding economy, produced an age, extending from about 1865 to 1900, that evolved an architecture that borrowed from Renaissance Europe suitable forms and styles to express the power and the glory of the late nineteenth century.

All the old architectural graces and simplicities of the Late Georgian, the Greek Revival, and even the Rundbogenstil of the 1840s had either disappeared or were vanishing from the American scene. Gone were the simple Late Georgian or Greek Revival shops; merchants were now building large department stores or other mercantile establishments that looked like French Renaissance chateaux or Italian town palaces — albeit the new versions were something provincial and not infrequently heavy-handed or vulgar. But at this distance in time, the lush ornament and the intricate and elaborate architectural forms have an interest and a glamour that is rather exciting in our own straitened and no-nonsense day.

And in the late 1860s how plain and dingy the old Market Square City Hall must have looked to the city councilmen when they considered the huge building that Philadelphia was planning to erect. Now that the War was over, this kind of bigger-and-better architectural expansiveness was in the air generally. Pittsburgh was ripe for a new City Hall. In those days the City had both a common and a select council, and in 1866, a committee of members from both branches recommended that a parcel of land at Smithfield Street and Virgin Alley (now Oliver Avenue), then adjacent to the United States Post Office and Custom House, be purchased from the owners, Messrs. Lyon, Shorb & Company. On December 31, 1866, announcement of the purchase was made.

Probably the councilmen knew what they wanted in terms of a fairly elaborate building, and at the moment the revived French Renaissance style of the Paris of the Emperor Napoleon III was in the highest favour in this country. Particularly favoured was the work of Louis Visconti (1791-1853) and Hector Lefuel (1818-80), who worked on the Emperor's grandiose extensions to the Louvre. Versions of the architect's Louvre-like pavilions, for about a decade, were scattered the length and breadth of America, and even more ubiquitous was the mansard roof, named for an earlier French architect Francois Mansart (1598-1666) — in fact, the latter became, at the time, a kind of architectural cliché. The mansard was even revived a hundred years later, in our own day, only to become a cliché again.

As architect for the new building the City engaged Joseph W. Kerr, one of Pittsburgh's prominent architects; he was particularly well known as a Gothic Revivalist, but his most important commission was the City Hall, where he acquitted himself very creditably as a designer. The excavations for the building were begun in 1868; the cornerstone was laid in May, 1869. The structure was finished early in 1872 and dedicated on May twenty-third of that year: an occasion of considerable rejoicing for the city. Although the old City Hall has been long since gone, we do know a good deal about it because the City was so proud of its new Hall that it published a book on it in 1874, a slim volume illustrated with handsome lithographs by Otto Krebs. The book, of which numerous copies have survived, was printed by Stevenson & Foster, local printers. It was the proud boast of the builders that the City Hall was entirely a product of Pittsburgh.

It was, for its day, an impressive building. It was a large, cubical construction having a basement, three floors, and an attic, with a frontage of one hundred and twenty feet on Smithfield Street and a depth of one hundred and ten feet from front to rear. The tower pavilion, fronting on Smithfield, had five floors, a convex mansard dome, and a belfry lantern, in all one hundred and seventy five feet high. The main facade of the structure was faced with white sandstone, as were the cornice and trim of the side elevations; the rest was brick. All floors of the building were constructed with wrought-iron beams and brick arching, the public parts being paved with marble tile. The stairs were of stone up to the second floor, beyond which they were of wood. The roof and dome were constructed of wood, as was the clerestoried lantern over the central interior court, but the belfry lantern was constructed entirely of iron.

In the square dome of the pavilion tower was a clock chamber having clock faces, one on each side. From the time of the inauguration of the City Hall, the great clock was supplied with correct time from the Allegheny Observatory. In the belfry overhead was a two-ton bell, cast at Andrew Fulton's local foundry in 1866, which was part of Pittsburgh's fire alarm system from 1872 until 1892. The earliest bell ever cast in Pennsylvania, it also serviced the clock and sounded the hours until 1920, when it was retired to the collection of The Historical Society of Western Pennsylvania. It can still be seen there although it no longer rings the hours.

The formal French Renaissance style of the exterior, even if it was rather loosely and awkwardly interpreted, always seemed to me to impart a certain elegance to Smithfield Street. The symmetrically and formally planned interior, with all the principal rooms ranged around an interior court, was also rather handsomely conceived and, I think, a real asset to the city. The grand staircase had a number of etched and embossed glass windows illustrating the industries of Pittsburgh. These windows are now in the collection of the Pittsburgh History & Landmarks Foundation.

The City, in 1917, moved into even grander and more spacious quarters in the City-County Building on Grant Street. For a number of years the former City Hall lived out a precarious existence as the headquarters of a number of government agencies. It became progressively older and more unfashionable, and the end came in 1953, when it was demolished to make way for a commercial building of crushing mediocrity. At the time of the demolition, mine was the solitary voice raised to save it. It would have made a grand cultural centre for downtown. Certainly, then, I began to realize the real need for a preservation organization in Pittsburgh.

The building erected on the site in 1953 was recently remodeled with neo-Art Deco black glass into the local Saks Fifth Avenue emporium, but this ultra-fashionable shop is no compensation for the loss of that handsome Renaissance courtyard.

Radio script for WQED-FM, circa 1980.

The Ladies of the Post Office

Now that the two identical allegorical groups of statuary have come down from their lofty perches on the crumbling walls of the [Pittsburgh] old Post Office,[1] we can see how astonishingly modern they are. They could easily have been carved by some young American sculptor only last year, but they are seventy years or more old.

Each set consists of three draped female figures, the central one standing and holding her right arm aloft while on either side of her sits another woman. One of these seated figures holds a rudder, perhaps to symbolize navigation, the other probably a mold representing industry; the central statue clasps in the left hand what appears to be a lamp. There is no doubt that these sculptures were intended for Pittsburgh as representative of our rivers and mills, and perhaps the main figure may have been intended to symbolize illumination or even the idea of a gateway to the West.

The old Post Office was designed in the office of the Supervising Architect of the Treasury at Washington, D.C. and a Pittsburgh newspaper of the late 1880s says that the sculptured groups were also designed in Washington, but it is not known at the moment who actually carved them.[2]

Apparently there was, according to old newspaper reports, some dissatisfaction with the Post Office sculptures at the time they were put in place. Ostensibly, this disfavour sprang from the fact that they were not smooth and pretty pieces of academic carving such as were then highly regarded. That they are *not* pretty recommends them strongly to contemporary taste.

The fact that these figures were intended to be seen only at a considerable distance may have had something to do with their lack of academic finish, but even if this be so, one must remember how often nowadays a sketch or a rough study for a nineteenth-century painting or sculpture is preferred to the finished product. During their long stay on the rooftops, the statues have been subject to the past hazards of the Pittsburgh industrial air and a certain amount of erosion from the weather, which would certainly connote some lessening of the earlier "finish."

At any rate, blackened as they are by decades of Pittsburgh smoke, their solemn monumental presence, as they sit now among the broken rubble of the vanishing Post Office, is undeniably memorable.

Power is in them — in their heavy limbs, ponderous hands and feet, and in their formidable, serene heads with their grave, waiting features. These might be "idols," images of stone set up long ago by some forgotten carver who wished to celebrate the forces of nature as personified in woman.

The analogies to primitive sculpture are strong, and it is the primitive element in modern art which often so strongly appeals to the modern sensibility. Here we have something of the mysterious primeval force of the Easter Island sculptures, the stark naïve strength of the folk carving in many early nineteenth-century American cemeteries, or the monumentality and emotional impact of the paintings of Picasso's Classical Period.

In their primitive power and in their "modernity" these sculptures, our almost-lost "ladies" of the old Post Office, are enormously impressive and strangely moving. They call silently to the passer-by in the street to remember his humanity in an increasingly brittle and mechanistic world.[3]

[1] At Fourth Avenue and Smithfield Street in downtown Pittsburgh.

[2] They are now attributed to a Washington sculptor, Eugenio Pedon.

[3] Presently, two of the statues are at the Old Post Office Museum on Pittsburgh's North Side, three at Station Square, and one in the Sunken Courtyard next to the upper station of the Monongahela Incline; all are part of the artifact collection of the Pittsburgh History & Landmarks Foundation.

Manuscript in the collection of the Pittsburgh History & Landmarks Foundation, 1966.

Lions in the Streets
A Sculptural Hunting Party in Pittsburgh

The streets of Pittsburgh, like those of other large cities of the Western World, are guarded and attended by beasts, some fabulous, some real. They do not impede our journeys, nor do they hazard our peace; we can neither hunt nor harry them, and they are food only for contemplation or thought. We cannot, however, avoid them where, in stone or metal, wonderfully or indifferently formed by the sculptor's hand, they are uplifted in crowded public places and solemnly displayed in parks. From pedestal, arch, and cornice, the captive animals gaze down. Regarded affectionately by children and beloved by pigeons, they eminently exist as the surrogates of human vanity, the emblems of our uneasy pride.

Among this animal company of dragons, bison, bears, and others, the lion is the grandest as he is also the most encountered. More honoured in the male rather than the female aspect, the full-grown lion from ancient times has been accounted the King of Beasts. He is the Olympian Zeus, the bearded Pater Familias of the animal world. Thunder and justice reside in his curling mane, majesty inheres in his paws, and his mask is the very face of kingship.

His artistic lineage is long, and he is the familiar of the Assyrian palace, the Roman forum, the medieval cathedral, and the Baroque city square. In Western religious iconography he is omnipresent; as an Old Testament subject he is found in history and proverb, and in the New he is both the devouring Satan and the symbol of Christ as the Lion of Judah. As a heraldic device the lion has no peer — especially for royal coats of arms — and his image has taken many forms on banner and shield. Throughout all literature he has been celebrated in story and song. He was not, nor is he now, any stranger to regal precincts, and the throne of the Byzantine emperors at Constantinople was flanked by golden lions, awesome mechanisms that lashed their tails and roared. Imperial, fierce, and noble, the great beast haunts the whole course of Western history, and his presentment is everywhere.

The slothful man of Holy Writ who spoke of a lion in the way would nowadays be given credence, for the lordly animal is uncrowned king of our streets. Every Pittsburgh reader of this essay will have his own favourite image, even if it be only a mask on a drinking fountain or a doorknocker. Among so much material, it is a hard thing to pick and choose, but the writer aims only to present here some of the more weighty and glamourous figures in local leonine society.

Possibly the most important, certainly the most elegant and mysterious of this maned host are the two large seated beasts that flank the Grant Street entrance arches of the Allegheny County Court House (1884-88), the last work of the great American architect Henry Hobson Richardson. It is appropriate that the portals of Justice be so guarded, and architecturally these symbols are even more apt because the Court House may be spoken of as a lion among Pittsburgh buildings. Since the level of Grant Street was lowered after completion of the building, the statues are rather difficult to see properly, but their lofty position makes them seem even more remote. Of all our carved animals, they are the strangest, the most exotic, and they have the air of not really belonging to the city — of being, rather, distinguished foreign visitors.

It is doubtful if Richardson actually designed these minor details of his masterpiece, since he was a very busy man in his later years, and he died in 1886 while the Court House was building. However, someone in his office or in that of Shepley, Rutan & Coolidge, his successors, may well have done so. At any rate, the carvers of the firm of John Evans & Company of Boston, who executed much of Richardson's ornamental detail, had become, as H. R. Hitchcock asserts, quite skillful in forging Romanesque-Byzantine motifs, using photographs as models. In this light, it is interesting that the Court House figures appear to be lions of the Classical-Renaissance-Academic tradition, done up in Byzantine costume and Milford granite. Whatever their stylistic provenance, how splendid, how subtle are these superbeasts! The curled hieratic animals, haunched elegantly backward, seem to emerge out of the crisp surface of the rock-faced wall like fairy-tale princes from an enchanted wood. Lords of some lost kingdom, imperial *flâneurs,* grand fops, they lower their veiled eyes with an exquisite disdain, a fierce aloof defiance, on the commercial (and political) monotonies of the street below.

Directly across Grant Street, in plate-glass bay windows on either side above the entrance to the Frick Building (D. H. Burnham & Company, 1901-02), is another pair of seated lions. Life-size, massive of mane and paw, they are proud, quietly handsome patricians of our Pittsburgh tribe. Executed at the time of the building's erection by Alexander Phimister Proctor (1862-1950), a talented American academic sculptor of the period, they are very competent

A lion at the Allegheny County Court House.

examples of smooth, naturalistic animal sculpture of the nineteenth century. Unlike their disdainful cousins over the way, these leonine gentlemen, bearded — one might almost say frock-coated — exude an air of prosperous Edwardian complacency: bronze proclamations of financial triumph, powerful symbols of industrial might, they are wrapt in dreams of some business Golden Age. One could not possibly imagine their pouncing on a lamb or an unwary stockbroker.

The financial district of Pittsburgh has, in fact, a not unsurprising affinity for lion sculpture, and one can go hunting with profit in the space of three or four blocks on Fourth Avenue. The lords of this

A lion in the Frick Building.

commercial veldt are the two great couched animals in brownstone to the left and right of the portal of the Dollar Savings Bank (1869-71), whose architect was the Philadelphian Isaac Hobbs, but whose sculpture was done by Max Kohler, a skillful stonecarver of the period. Beneath the Hellenistic cornices, the Baalbek shadows of the looming facade, these heavy representatives of financial probity gaze, like Newfoundland dogs, at the passer-by with a stern domestic majesty. There is no doubt that these hearth-rug champions are the Noble Animals so dear to Victorian sentimentality. Despite their tameness and their bathos, however, they are, perhaps, the Pittsburgh lions that one loves best; they have a gemütlich dignity, a cozy grandeur that is entirely charming. They remind us, somehow, of rich elderly uncles who might, possibly, remember us in their wills.

The careful huntsman continuing his quest may find on other structures in the same area a small multitude of maned heads that verges on monotony. Indeed, the Arrott Building (F. J. Osterling, 1901), at Fourth and Wood, is sprinkled with lion masks thick as raisins on a Lady Baltimore cake. The Keystone Building, on Fourth, sports three leonine heads adorned with fruit and flowers at either side like floral earrings — decorations that add a note of calculated delight to a formal facade. Even more festive are the carved masks on the older section of the Kaufmann Department Store (c. 1892), which hold in their mouths large rings from which depend ribbons and bouquets. In the downtown streets alone there are many more lions, but we have no space in which to track them here.

Further afield in Oakland, there is a small pride of lions gathered in the Hall of Architecture at Carnegie Institute. These are near cousins of the animals already described, since they are plaster casts of the most famous sculptured beasts of the past. Here we resume the chase within this silent menagerie of *moulages,* where we may obtain a comprehensive view of the lion's place in Western art history. From a remote period of Greek civilization come the great beasts — now headless — of the Mycenaean Citadel gate, and from Egypt we have the mask of a lion (30th Dynasty, 376 B.C.), perhaps the most subtle, sensitive, and haunting of all animal portraits. Out of ancient Persia there is a portion of the glazed-tile lion frieze of the Palace of Susa (403-358 B.C.), and in the curley-maned heads of a capital from the Church of Sant' Ambrogio (807) of Milan we may discern the ancestry of the portal guardians of the Pittsburgh Court House.

Continuing our search among the casts, we find in the rich Romanesque forest of the huge St. Gilles facade (twelfth century), lions supporting columns on their backs — a motif also abundantly evident in the thirteenth-century pulpit of Niccolo Pisano at Siena Cathedral. These beasts — some of them devouring other animals — symbolize the Church's victory over Satan, but in the Renaissance they became symbols of secular and kingly power. The elegant tomb (1502-07) of Francis II of Brittany in Nantes Cathedral bears a small, couched, heraldic lion of the latter type; lying at the feet of the Duke's effigy and holding a shield, this little animal has the bright, alert look of a Boy Scout doing a good deed. Other lions lurk in this plaster jungle, but the reader must hunt them out for himself.

In a distant quarter of the city we shall end this sculptural safari with two Lombard lions — couched and, again, supporting columns on their backs — but they quite lack the vitality of their Romanesque prototypes. These modern terra-cotta animals that guard the portal of the Romanesque campanile of the East End's Larimer Avenue School (U. J. L. Peoples, 1904), though they have a certain kindergarten charm, symbolize nothing, and the triviality of their execution heralds the end of the long tradition of lion sculpture and the passing of the Academic sculptural company of gods and beasts.[1] Modern architecture has little use for lions; they are difficult to abstract, and majesty is out of fashion.

Aforetime, as we have seen, lions were the guardians of gates, the lords of entrances, but we hereby admonish them to attend the exit lines of this essay in their praise. The animals of which we have spoken are elderly, but possibly it is not too much to hope that we may yet see young lions in the streets and the return to our modern pedestals and cornices of that majestic and honoured company.

[1]The campanile was demolished in the 1960s, but the portal and the lions are still there.—JVT

Carnegie Magazine, February, 1960.

Temples of Finance
Pittsburgh and a Praise of Pillars[1]

Of all the constituent elements of the Classical architectural tradition, which since the days of ancient Greece has been a powerful and constantly recurring phenomenon in Western civilization, the column has been the most eminent and the most respected. A reminder of man's generative powers, the heir and symbol of all the forests of the world, the chief supporter of the temple image, a commemorative sign of victory and valour, it has become indissolubly associated in the popular mind with the power and the wonder of the Ancient World. The pillar is at once the surrogate of prince, law-giver, and priest, the guardian of treasures, and if nowadays it has been eclipsed by new symbols, its power to evoke the majesty of the past is undiminished. Surely the column as hero of the great Classical theme will one day be honoured among us again.

The elegant porticoed temples of finance, founded and so agreeably erected in Philadelphia at the beginning of the nineteenth century, were reflected in Western Pennsylvania only in the newly-conquered wilderness; the polished shafts of Blodgett, Latrobe, or Strickland [in Philadelphia] were echoed solely by the stalwart trunks of numberless trees. However, civilization was rapidly advancing beyond the Alleghenies, and these primitive forest forms were soon to metamorphose into Classical columns as once they had so changed in Greece long ago. The Greek Revival was to have no minor efflorescence in the opening West of early nineteenth-century America, and Pittsburgh was to be one of the chief centres of the new style.

Prior to 1800 there had been, as well, no bank building in Pittsburgh, but the rapidly-developing frontier town began to feel the need for banking facilities. The directors of the Bank of Pennsylvania at Philadelphia made, in 1803, a formal proposal to the business men of Pittsburgh to establish a branch of that institution in the new city, and on January 4, 1804, the office was opened in a two-story stone house (built in 1787 and destroyed in the Great Fire of 1845) that stood on Second Avenue between Market and Ferry. Thus the initial banking image of Pittsburgh was domestic, but in succeeding decades the shop continued to be the initial headquarters of many a bank that

53

later advanced to grander buildings. Pittsburgh's first financial office was closed in 1818, when government funds on deposit were transferred to the newly-opened Pittsburgh branch of the Second Bank of the United States.

As long as a bank building could be called a temple of finance, the Bank of Pittsburgh (whose foundation in 1810 made it the second such institution to appear on the local scene) provided in its succeeding public versions the grandest and most important symbol of the Classical theme in the western part of the state. Within that tradition the Bank's two buildings, which we will discuss here, eminently reflected changing nineteenth-century taste in temples as well as mutations in the social and business structures of the times.

The same changes occurred in Philadelphia and elsewhere in the nation, but the great Pittsburgh bank provides an especially graphic illustration of the long and honoured eminence of an American temple of finance, and its decline and final ruin is a story which has something of the nobility, the grandeur, and the fateful inevitability of Classical drama. As an account of the rise and fall of columns, as an evidence of public pride in public porticoes, the history of our Bank is of the first interest. Here the pillar is hero; in the pride of his uprightness he was esteemed and praised, and in his fall he was not disdained

The first years of the Bank were hampered by Pennsylvania's restrictive legislation of 1808 and 1810, which acted in favour of chartered rather than incorporated banks; shortly after it was founded, the youthful institution had to change its name to the Pittsburgh Manufacturing Company, under which curious designation it continued its banking activities. The state law was changed, however, and the Bank was also granted a charter in 1814, so it was able to become once more the Bank of Pittsburgh under the presidency of Judge William Wilkins (1779-1865), a prominent early citizen.

As a fully-chartered bank, it began its existence in modest quarters at Third and Market Streets. In 1831 a lot was purchased on Fourth Avenue between Market and Wood. The Bank, which occupied the same site during the course of its existence, thus early occupied a prominent place on that Avenue which had the distinction until recently of being the city's financial district, Pittsburgh's Lombard Street. When the Bank closed its doors in 1931, the street began to decline as well, and now it retains very little of its former eminence.

On March 28, 1834, according to the Bank's records, we are told that "the building committee agreeable to the instructions of the

Chislett's Bank of Pittsburgh, c. 1835.

Board have carefully examined the plans submitted to them for the erection of a banking house on the lot between Third and Fourth avenue, and after mature deliberation, recommend for adoption by the Board, the annexed plans and specifications of Mr. Chislett."

These plans and specifications were the work of John Chislett (1800-69), Pittsburgh's foremost early nineteenth-century architect and the individual who, more than any other, impressed upon Pittsburgh the image of the Greek Revival. He was born in England and received his early training at Bath, but he had come to Pittsburgh as a young man and opened an office in Pittsburgh in 1833. It was he who designed the Allegheny County Court House in 1841, whose dome and handsome Doric portico dominated the city until the building was destroyed by fire in 1882. In 1844 he planned the Allegheny Cemetery, one of America's first Romantic suburban graveyards, and he served as its first superintendent until his death in 1869.

In 1835 he designed Pittsburgh's first office structure, Burke's Building, which is located on Fourth Avenue near the site of the Bank of Pittsburgh. Of all Pittsburgh's many Greek Revival edifices, this is the only important structure that still survives, and the two spalled Doric columns of its porch are the last vestiges of a noble but vanished company of local Greek Revival pillars.

The Bank of Pittsburgh's new building was also gutted by the Great Fire of 1845, although it was considered to be fireproof because it was constructed of brick and cement and its windows were protected by iron shutters. Since the Greek Revival was still fashionable, the structure was rebuilt according to the original design; and for many years to come, the Ionic grace of its Fourth Avenue portico continued the noble Classical image of the temple of finance.

Aesthetically, the most important bank building of the Greek Revival in the western part of the state is the former Erie branch of the Second Bank of the United States, which has been described by C. M. Stotz in his *Early Architecture of Western Pennsylvania.*[2] Built in 1839, after the design of the architect William Kelly, it was, like the parent bank in Philadelphia, patterned after the Parthenon, but as befitted a provincial office, it was of more modest size (being fifty by seventy feet in plan) and hexastyle rather than octastyle. Its front was of Vermont marble, and the side walls were plastered to look like the more expensive material. The Classical garment on buildings of this sort was not always composed completely of the same cloth.

The Erie Branch office had but a brief existence as a bank, and when it failed it was, like the parent institution, sold in 1849 to the United States Government for use as a custom house. It is now very appropriately the headquarters of the Erie County Historical Society.

Meanwhile the bank-shop began, in some instances, to change itself into a palace. Particularly is this evident in those shops that occupied corner sites which were, of course, much preferred by banks inasmuch as they offered more frontage for architectural display. In the later manifestations of the shop-palace type, the old Georgian commercial simplicities of form began to recast themselves — whether in brick, stone, or cast iron — into provincial American adaptations of the Barryesque Cinquecento or the coarse Second Empire Renaissance. In this mutation the principal banking floor (now become a kind of *piano nobile*) was raised on a high basement and approached, at the corner angle, by an elaborate ceremonial staircase which ascended to a richly-ornamented portal. The early premises of the Union National Bank at Fourth Avenue and Market Street illustrates the primal type of corner bank, whereas the 1871 building of the First National Bank at Wood Street and Fifth Avenue displays, in its bouncing *embonpoint* of cast iron, later changes in architectural taste; the directness and simplicity of the old corner bank are quite gone.

Another imported variation of the Second Empire palace theme was the mansarded pavilion so prominent in the design of Napoleon III's New Louvre, an element which was used for many types of American public buildings in the late 1860s and the 1870s. As applied to banking establishments like the Germania National Bank of the early 1870s formerly at Wood and Diamond (now Forbes Avenue), the form and style of the fancy Parisian idiom imparted a phoney-palatial, parvenu air to American financial structures of the period.

An interesting mixture of the temple and palace types of the same period is the brownstone Dollar Savings Bank, which is still located at Fourth Avenue near Smithfield. Established in 1855 as Pittsburgh's first institution devoted to mutual banking — banking solely for the benefit of depositors — the curiously ornate structure was begun in 1868 after the designs of Isaac H. Hobbs & Sons of Philadelphia. The central section was completed in 1871 and the two wings added in 1906. In 1950, the old Boyd Building on Smithfield Street was purchased and remodeled to augment the banking premises.

The use of the colossal Roman Composite order gives a kind of heavy authority to a rather eccentric composition whose debased Classical details recall the solemn caprices of Baalbek or Palmyra. The two lions at either side of the main portal, who seem to be guarding not only the bank's treasures but public morality as well, are completely delightful examples of large-scale Victorian sentimental sculpture.

When the Greek Revival waned in popularity and finally vanished as a vital style-phase in the 1860s, the Classical temple as a model for bank buildings went for a time into eclipse. Much as the medievalistic trend in nineteenth-century architecture culminated at Philadelphia in the work of Frank Furness, so did the very free

Romanesque Revival of H. H. Richardson reach a particularly dense flowering in the Pittsburgh of the late 1880s and the early 1890s.

Pittsburgh possessed only one of the very distinctive bank buildings designed by Frank Furness, but our local example now demolished, the Farmers Deposit National Bank, was discussed at some length by the writer in the January 1964 issue of *The Charette*. On the other hand, the tremendous impact of the Allegheny County Court House and Jail (1884-88) of Richardson practically made Pittsburgh, for a time, a Romanesque city. The fire of 1882 which destroyed Chislett's Court House would seem to have a symbolic significance, since it ushered in locally the Richardsonian reign, which if brief was nonetheless extremely potent while it lasted.

In bank architecture, slim columns and smooth walls disappeared to be replaced by rugged, rusticated surfaces, Syrian arches, and squat pillars with the Byzantine-Romanesque capitals of the new style. In place of Apollo, a kind of medievalized Hercules was now banker, and his muscles, sometimes grotesquely caricatured, were abundantly visible on many a commercial facade.

Of the large number of Pittsburgh bank buildings in the Richardsonian manner one might choose the former German National Bank (now the Granite Building) at Wood Street and Sixth Avenue, which was erected 1889-90 after the designs of the local architectural firm of Bickel & Brennan. Here the banking premises have long since been remodeled into shops, but enough of its wide, Romanesque musculature of wall remains to give us an intense, clear picture of the bank building clothed in revived medieval habiliments.

An almost contemporary example of the type, but much more restrained in detail and form, is the former building of the Pittsburgh Bank of Commerce (1889), also at Wood and Sixth. It has followed in its main outlines the Richardsonian Romanesque style forms, but the building is nicely scaled to its surroundings and generally well proportioned. The local firm of Struthers & Hannah supplied the design. For many years after it had ceased to be a bank it was occupied by a fashionable jeweler and was known as the Grogan Building. Like many small commercial buildings of its vintage it is now largely unoccupied and much fallen in estate.[3]

Although neither of these buildings is of great size, the several stories above the main floor foreshadow locally the appearance of the great skyscraper bank buildings of the period just after the turn of the century.

But it is now time for the temple to emerge again on an even grander scale. During the early 1890s and particularly after the

Chicago World's Fair of 1893, the medieval influence in America, although it always remained popular, took second place in regard to bank construction and continued to do so, as long as the Eclectic period lasted. The new Classicism assumed an imperial and Roman form, and architects were once again haunted by the Pantheon and the great temples of the Forum. In such guise appeared the new shrines dedicated to finance, and the pillar as hero assumed an even grander form.

In Western Pennsylvania it was the Bank of Pittsburgh again which provided the new, grand image and revived the important role of the pillar in the architectural world. The chaste Ionic portico of Chislett's bank now looked a little wraithlike and pale in the city's prosperous Fourth Avenue, and only Roman imperial grandeur could express the temper of the times. The new columns fronting on the Avenue must be triumphant lords of finance, crowned, garlanded, and visible for all to see.

The banker, similarly, was no longer a rough Titan, for now he must be the Roman Apollo leading the Muses — at least those of Sculpture and Painting. Herewith the banking house began to appear as patron of art.

The Bank of Pittsburgh therefore commissioned George B. Post (1837-1913) to design its new building that was erected in 1895-96 on the site of the earlier banking temple. Post, who had also participated in forming the design image of the Chicago Fair, was one of those architects based at New York who had achieved a national reputation for his grandiose contributions to late nineteenth-century American Classicism. His final design for the Pittsburgh bank struck just the right note of Roman splendour, quietly and discreetly presented, with perhaps more than a touch of provincial conservatism. It is a great pity that the Bank could not have been preserved since it expressed so perfectly the Pittsburgh of the late 1890s, and of all buildings of its day in the city, it was certainly the noblest.

Here are the new heroes of the portico, all Roman and magnificent, but what about the fallen Greek champions that had adorned the earlier building? The persistence and the power of the columnar tradition is implicit in the story of the Bank of Pittsburgh pillars.

Many citizens of the city had become attached to the old building, and at the time of its demolition, a movement was initiated to have the Ionic pillars of the portico removed to Schenley Park. According to the *Pittsburgh Dispatch* of June 9, 1895, Edward Bigelow, then Director of Parks, did not approve of the transfer, so the columns vanished. Possibly those who advocated setting up the homeless shafts in the Park were motivated by memories of Classical ruins, but it is more than possible that the would-be preservers simply wished to save these noble symbols of the grand Classical past from degradation.

The exterior of the new building combined the Roman temple porch with the palace front. Inside, the great two-storied banking hall favoured the Pantheon form, with its circular ceiling supported by pendentives. Although additions were made to the Bank in 1917 and 1925, this room remained unchanged.

At either end of the banking hall, between the pendentives, were large lunettes containing murals painted in oil on canvas. One of these, *Pittsburgh Presenting Its Iron and Steel to the World,* was done by Edwin Blashfield (1848-1936), and the other, *Thesmophoria,* was painted by Francis D. Millet (1846-1912). Both of these men, who became well-known academic mural painters, had executed painted decorations at the World's Fair [of 1893], and the Bank of Pittsburgh contributed to their fame by early employing them. The Bank was extremely proud of its two murals, and had them reproduced when occasion offered.

Post's Bank of Pittsburgh, 1896.

For as long as the image of the temple of finance endured, Apollo's painted shrine and the imperial portico presided grandly over Fourth Avenue, ably assisted by the long and honourable history of the institution. For this elegant building, also, the end finally came during the Depression of 1929. The Bank closed its doors in September 1931, although there will always be some doubt that such a final step was absolutely necessary. By the early 1940s, all the Bank's depositors had been paid in full, and since the Bank had ceased to exist, [its building] was demolished in 1944. So perished Pittsburgh's most representative and symbolic temple of finance, and with it vanished the cherished murals of Blashfield and Millet — the demolition contractor, according to a contemporary account in the *Pittsburgh Press,* said that they could not be detached from the walls without damage. It is improbable that anyone tried very hard to save them, and, in any event, they had had their day.

The columns of the portico are another story. History in this instance repeated itself (this time with a "happy ending"), proving that pillars were able to exert their ancient fascination. A local architect, Edward F. Griffith, ransomed the pillars, the condemned captives of an alien day, by paying the owners of the land a sum of money to allow the facade to stand until he could find a use for it. The pillars were finally bought in 1952 for the Jefferson Memorial Park, a local cemetery. During part of its period of decline, Fourth Avenue had a special and authentic ruin that symbolized its own ultimate fate. It is interesting that the reprieved pillars now form part of a large mausoleum (1963) which is a memorial to Thomas Jefferson in the Memorial Park. The columns assumed a new heroic role.

So were the hero pillars saved, but other columns, which are still with us, had come to symbolize the financial might of Pittsburgh. The Mellon National Bank of 1923 is the last great local example of the Classical bank building, but before we consider it we must deal with an interesting mutation of the palace type allied to a skyscraper.

By the early years of the twentieth century, skyscraper bank building had assumed enormous proportions. Perhaps the largest and most ebullient example in Pittsburgh is the twenty-four-floor Farmers Deposit National Bank Building (Alden & Harlow, 1903) at Fifth Avenue and Wood Street (now the Farmers Bank office of the Mellon National Bank and Trust Company) which is like some huge elongated birthday cake, with Baroque layer piled on layer. Among much meretricious terra-cotta ornament on the exterior, some very competent sculpture (now removed) by J. Massey Rhind (1860-1936) continued the image of the bank as art patron.[4]

Across the street rises the slender twenty-six-floor tower of the First National Bank Building (now the Pittsburgh National Bank), which was built in two parts; it began life as a palace and later became a great skyscraper.[5] This structure is of considerable interest because it so graphically illustrates the close connection between the two types at the time of the turn of the century.

In the course of time, the corner-palace office of the First National had become out-moded; it was therefore demolished in 1908 and a new structure designed by D. H. Burnham of Chicago was erected in 1909. Here the Medicean version of the palace type, which we have also seen at Philadelphia, is much in evidence. Tuscan palatial architecture of the Quattrocento provided the stylistic theme, and the fifteenth-century Piccolomini Palace of Siena was the model for adaptation. The great vaulted banking room lined with green and white marble is, however, in its style and amplitude more Edwardian than Italian Renaissance.

This revivified Sienese palace masks the huge foundations of a skyscraper, a feat of architectural sleight of hand not uncharacteristic of the period. In 1912 a great tower of twenty-two stories was added to the palace, and the whole building was treated as if it were an order. The palatial motif was repeated again at the top of the tower and the original building served as the base; the desire for profit dictated the utilitarian, skyscraping layers that made up the shaft.

The Pittsburgh banking firm destined to achieve the widest national and international fame was that of the Mellons. It was the Mellons also who built in the city the last temple of finance when the pillar was hero.

The family's financial eminence evolved from the most modest beginnings. The private banking house which became T. Mellon and Sons was established by Judge Thomas Mellon (1813-1908) on his retirement from the bench at the age of fifty-six. The firm was first located in a small, frame, two-story structure that occupied part of the site of the Oliver Building; after a time the new bank moved to 514 Smithfield Street, a cast-iron-front, mansarded palace-type office erected in 1873.

Judge Mellon's sons, Richard B. and Andrew W., later joined their father, and the Mellon National Bank was incorporated in 1902. Finally the institution bought frontage on the whole block of Smithfield Street between Oliver and Fifth; this range of variegated buildings was demolished to make way for the new Mellon temple of finance erected in 1923-24 after the plans of the New York firm of Trowbridge & Livingston, in association with E. P. Mellon.

As the Mellons have sometimes been compared to the Medici, particularly in regard to the art collecting activities of Andrew W. Mellon (1855-1937) who was largely responsible for the foundation of the National Gallery of Art, it is interesting to examine two minor Mellon buildings that reflect the Medicean architectural image.

One of these was the Forbes National Bank, a Mellon subsidiary, now the Oakland Branch office of the Mellon National Bank and Trust Company. This building, which strongly reflects the style of Florentine fifteenth-century palace architecture, was erected in 1927-28 after the design of E. P. Mellon. The other structure, the Mellon Securities Building formerly at Oliver Avenue and William Penn Place, was a very pleasant remodeling of the printing plant of the old *Pittsburgh Dispatch*. The architect was Roy Hoffman. The structure was opened in 1936 and demolished about ten years later to make way for the Mellon-U.S. Steel Building.

The great granite structure of the main office of the Mellon National Bank and Trust Company, the architectural heir of the Bank of Pittsburgh, is four stories high, with a basement and sub-basement beneath. The colossal order of the main facade is very simply, even severely, treated, and the temple porch has here been reduced to a lofty entrance recess flanked by two huge Doric pillars. Enormous bronze doors open into the great central banking room, which is sixty-two feet high and amply lighted by large windows and a skylight. Basilican in form, this hall is flanked on all four sides by marble Ionic columns. There is much marble and bronze everywhere; a lively touch of elegance is to be found in the sleeves of crimson velvet worn by the railings of the staircase leading into the banking room.

These pillars are the final heroes of the Classical temple of finance and they have a solemn, almost tragic air, befitting the dignity of their pride as the last local representatives of their race.

---

[1]This is the second part of a two-part article. Part I, describing banks in Philadelphia, was published in *The Charette* in March, 1964.

[2]University of Pittsburgh Press, 1936; later reissued under the title *The Architectural Heritage of Western Pennsylvania.* Now out of print.

[3]Demolished in 1967.

[4]This building is now entirely refaced in enameled metal.

[5]Demolished in 1970.

The Charette, May, 1964.

The Abraam Steinberg house.

Architecture and the Pittsburgh Land
The Buildings of Peter Berndtson

A very agreeable and recent segment of Pittsburgh architectural history has been recalled to us with the publication this year of *Organic Vision, the Architecture of Peter Berndtson*, by Donald Miller and Aaron Sheon: the former, the art critic of the *Pittsburgh Post-Gazette*, and the latter, professor of fine arts in the University of Pittsburgh. Peter Berndtson (1909-72) had been a familiar figure in Pittsburgh architectural circles as well as a distinguished disciple of Frank Lloyd Wright (1867-1959), whose theory of organic architecture transformed much American architectural practice in the twentieth century.

According to this theory, the structure, and particularly the house, is conceived of as an organism that proceeds, one almost might say grows, out of the environment in which it is constructed, not only mystically through the perception and ingenuity of the architect but also temporally through the materials used — especially those of the earth itself, brick, wood, and stone — honestly and felicitously used to express concepts of space, proportion, and order.

Organically speaking, Man is a part of nature, and so should his house be, and it is the function of the perceptive architect to express and interpret that relationship while giving form to the individual needs of the client. Peter Berndtson, while thoroughly imbued with Wrightian architectural theory, has notably interpreted it through his own considerable talent; a Berndtson house is a design for living, in which the client and the natural world live together in harmony.

And it was upon our Western Pennsylvania hills and in our valleys that Berndtson, for the most part, constructed his buildings, — or it might be better, in his particular case, to say that he was a poet or an enchanter (one who sings and casts spells) who conjured from the ground and from the air his visions of man's true community with nature. There *are* architects of this sort (alas, rare nowadays) who can design and construct poetically since they are the true philosophers of wood and stone, and it is these men who in the field of building most strongly engage my attention, compel my allegiance. Such a man was Wright, and Berndtson profoundly conveyed his mentor's message to the inhabitants of our own hills. All architects should have disciples as good as Peter.

Possibly it does not matter, in the end, where an architect comes from; if he is a man of vision, his principles and practice can be applied anywhere. Peter Berndtson, of Swedish ancestry, was born in 1909 at Methuen, Massachusetts, son of a prosperous dealer in real estate. He attended the Massachusetts Institute of Technology for two years. During the Depression he lived in New York, where he also married a young actress, Ruth Barstow. When Peter learned of Frank Lloyd Wright, he and his wife joined the Taliesin Fellowship at Spring Green, Wisconsin.

Peter and his first wife were divorced, and he married, *en second noces,* Cornelia Brierly of Pittsburgh, a former architectural student at Carnegie-Mellon University, who was one of the first people to join the Taliesin Fellowship. After their marriage, Peter and Cornelia went to West Mifflin, a suburb of the city, to visit her family, but they stayed to supervise construction of a house that Cornelia had designed for her aunts, the Notz sisters, under the supervision of Frank Lloyd Wright. The Berndtsons' first daughter, Anna, was born in Pittsburgh, but they returned to Taliesin in 1943.

In 1947, they returned to West Mifflin to expand the former domain of the Notz sisters into a community project of eight circular lots called Meadow Circles; but the scheme did not work out.

It would seem that the Berndtsons' marriage did not work out either, although a second daughter, Indira, had been born, as they used to say, "to the union." At any rate, the union was dissolved. The book says only: "but for Cornelia Brierly Berndtson, the call of Taliesin was stronger than the work in Pittsburgh." In 1957 she went to Taliesin, believing in the nobility of that life as a better way for herself and daughters. I cannot say anything about it of my own knowledge, because I did not become friendly with Peter until about 1960 and I never knew Cornelia. They did collaborate closely on most of their architectural projects while they were together, and this might cause problems for architectural historians later. Who did what?

In addition to the abortive Meadow Circles project, the ideas of community discussed at Taliesin were to have another effect on Pittsburgh. Peter's most ambitious community plan was conceived by him and a friend, Emory F. Bacon, then educational director of the United Steelworkers of America. The project was to have been located on the side of Mt. Washington, on the side looking out on Pittsburgh. It was to be an exciting experiment, and had about it something of the futuristic quality of Wright's dream of a "Broadacre

City." The scheme was almost Utopian — far in advance of anything of the kind attempted in Pittsburgh. But again, fate was against it, and nothing came of this unique proposal.

Peter continued to design houses, which were always his forte. It seemed that only in this intensely personal architect-client relationship could he find fulfillment as an artist and as a human being. This rapport had to be a part of all his commitments, or they did not seem to work. Just anybody who needed a house, no matter how prosperous, would not do. The architect *was* special, and the client had to be special too — sensitive, perceptive, understanding, and willing to be guided by the designer in all matters architecturally.

In this, as in his uncompromising attitude toward his art, he was strongly akin to his earlier colleague, Frederick G. Scheibler, Jr. (1872-1958), whose *oeuvre* was proto-Modern, original, quasi-organic, and also regional, i.e., of Pittsburgh: spiritual and artistic brothers. I hold them in special veneration. Both of them held the *house* in special veneration, and they had an almost unearthly sense of the connection between the house and the land. I have sometimes been asked if I have any special favourite among the not-inconsiderable number of houses that Berndtson designed. This is difficult to do, because I like most of them; home-wise, I find them very sympathetic and satisfying.

The house of Dr. and Mrs. Abraam Steinberg (1951) on Morewood Heights, Pittsburgh, was the Berndtson house with which I first became fully acquainted. To me it has always been the "type" of the Berndtson house. It is characterized notably by a pervasive lyricism; indeed it might be called a poetic statement. Peter's notes printed in the book describe it graphically: "The house set on a steeply sloping corner lot grows naturally out of its site. The interior levels rise to meet the grades outside. The brick walls on the street sides slope inward, merging with the sloping site and emphasizing stability."

The few materials, brick, redwood, glass, and concrete, carry through from the exterior to the interior, unifying them as parts of the whole. Spaces within flow into one another, visually and actually, as ramps lead from one level to another. Certain walls are louvred, permitting those rooms to merge with larger spaces. Finally, all the elements in their interweaving create a sculptural whole which contributes a fourth dimension — unobtrusive but pervasive human enrichment.

A good local example of Wright's inexpensive Usonian houses is Cornelia's Notz house (1939) at West Mifflin, already mentioned.

One would like to speak of several other Berndtson houses, but the lack of time forbids. They are all well described and illustrated in the book.

Peter's last years were not easy, and lack of commissions began to take their toll. In 1958 he began a long friendship with the Pittsburgh dancer and teacher Genevieve Jones that was to have a stabilizing influence on his life. At this time he also became a preservationist and restored an old house in Shadyside.

Peter died of complications following a stroke in 1972, but so long as his houses endure he will still be with us — as will his book, which was beautifully designed by Martine Sheon and printed by the Hexagon Press. The book grew out of an exhibition of the Berndtsons' work held at the University of Pittsburgh Art Gallery. Peter's drawings and files are preserved in the architectural drawing collection of the Fine and Rare Book rooms at the Hunt Library of the Carnegie-Mellon University where, also, the book may be obtained.

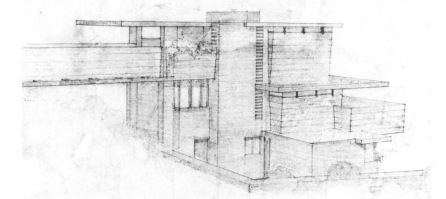

A drawing by Berndtson of the Jack Landis house, Squirrel Hill.

Radio script for WQED-FM, 1981.

Art Deco

Seen by the viewer arriving from the northeast, the great high-rise towers of Pittsburgh's centre rise remotely like castles in a dream. The sun is setting, and against the incandescent west these varied eminences appear merely as forms, silhouettes. The pre-steel-frame turrets and spires are lost in the shadows of the more recent monuments, particularly the great bulk of the United States Steel cyclops which forcibly captures the eye. But even this huge presence cannot cancel the altitudinous grace of those elegant towers of some fifty years ago, the Koppers, Gulf, and Grant Buildings. These were once the giants among the downtown towers, as they were also the largest local examples of the Modernistic "Skyscraper" style — that stylistic manner which we now call Art Deco.

Several miles away to the east of these smooth giants rises the other member of this Modernistic host — the Cathedral of Learning of the University of Pittsburgh, which, in form at least, is also one of the great Deco monuments of the city. Whether it is seen at dawn or sunset, in winter or summer, sun or rain, its variegated, tapering masses make it a Modernistic landmark rising high above the Oakland plateau. In it, as in so much architecture of its time, the past and the present are brought together in a characteristic and fascinating amalgam. The building was intended by its sponsor to be a medieval cathedral devoted to the acquisition of learning; in form it is completely Modern, displaying the fashionable "set-back" silhouette of the 1920s.

It is this compositional form, as distinct from ornament, that the four buildings mentioned above have abundantly in common and which makes them so thoroughly representational of the "Skyscraper" style. The earlier steel-frame high-rise of the turn of the century tended to be a box-like mass, no matter what its size. It is as if builders of the time were fascinated with the mere possession of the technological marvel of the steel cage (not to mention the profits accruing therefrom) and continued to extend the ribbed box skyward. The result was the tower or slab high-rise, which rose straight up from its base. Representative of this type of structure in Pittsburgh are the Frick and Oliver Buildings (1901 and 1908 respectively).

Architects of the period, in decorating the steel-frame, tended to treat the tall box as a Classical order — base, shaft, and entablature — and the emphasis was on verticality. The sheer bulk of these structures was often highly ornamented with stylistic tags from the past, but as a rule architects made no effort to vary the form of these huge new structures, save to provide indentations in the mass for considerations of light and air.

Ironically, it was the matter of light and air which did, after 1910, lead to marked changes in skyscraper form. Large concentrations of these bulky monsters, as in lower Manhattan, tended to engender problems of liveability even in commercial buildings. The problem was solved by the "set-back" system, by which, at certain heights, the mass of the structure could be set back, and gradually the high-rise began to assume a stepped or tapering form. By the early 1920s many American cities had passed laws limiting the bulk of a building in relation to its height. Born as it was, in necessity, the new form quickly became fashionable, and the stage was set for the reformed Modernistic high-rises of the building boom of the late 1920s.

The *élan*, the unbridled optimism, the hectic ebullience of the 'Twenties is now enshrined in legend only a little less expansive than the glittering reality itself. For those of us who did experience that wonderful decade, it was literally a golden time, and nowhere was this glow more eminent than in building. Probably no age has left more monuments than this one, and many of these were erected in the brief period 1924-30. Alas, however, the high-jinx years were riding for a fall, and the Great Depression of 1929 brought an end to all the glamour and the gold.

In September of 1927, the magazine *Greater Pittsburgh* published "a partial list of the major building operations in the city of Pittsburgh," and concluded that "it is generally agreed that the new building construction of the year 1927 will break all records. Major projects, by which is meant those involving the expenditure of $1,000,000 or more, are so much more numerous than at any previous time, that it is probably no exaggeration to say the total cost of buildings of that magnitude either completed in Pittsburgh this year or started in 1927 and to be completed sometime next year, is much greater than the cost of all such buildings erected in Pittsburgh in the previous ten or fifteen years combined." All the skyscrapers discussed here were included in the list save the Gulf Building, which was not begun until 1930.

Possibly New York's Woolworth Building of 1913, with its pointed Gothic tower soaring above the lower bulk of the structure, heralded faintly the new Modernistic style, but the real forerunner of the set-back tower theme was Eliel Saarinen's unexecuted design for the Chicago Tribune Building of 1922, which certainly influenced the architectural form of the Barclay-Vesey Building (1923-26) in New York, which is probably the first of the great Art Deco skyscrapers.

Granted the set-back theme, other historical architectural forms tended to influence the form of the Deco high-rise. Mesopotamian ziggurats, the stepped pyramids of Egypt, Mayan temples, and Southwestern adobe pueblos were suggestive and welcome sources for architects in search of new motifs. The movement even engendered a kind of mystique which is to be seen in the work of the artist Hugh Ferriss (1889-1962), particularly in his book *The Metropolis of Tomorrow* (1929). Here, abstract shapes evolve into buildings that climb into the sky through planes of light.

As far as the "style" of the Deco building was concerned, the two main influences from the Eclectic period were the Gothic and the Classical, and in both cases there was visible in the new skyscrapers not only an abstraction of form, but also an abstraction and simplification of ornament. We shall speak more fully of Art Deco ornament when we discuss the detailing of the Koppers and Gulf Buildings, but in general the two structures which face each other on Seventh Avenue illustrate graphically in the case of Koppers, the reordering of the Gothic style and, in the case of Gulf, a modern adaptation of Classical motifs.

The Koppers Building was designed by Graham, Anderson, Probst & White, a prestigious Chicago architectural firm and the successor of the famous D. H. Burnham & Company, who had been commissioned to design Pittsburgh's Frick Building in 1901. The firm was eminently equipped to purvey the latest fashionable Deco image, and so it is that the city possesses a Modernistic highrise of great *élan* and sophistication. E. P. Mellon was the associate architect, and the contractor was the Mellon-Stuart Company.

Ground-breaking took place in November, 1927, and the building was ready for occupancy in the spring of 1929. Both the silhouette of the mass and the texture of the cladding (or curtain wall) are unmistakably Deco. Influenced by Saarinen's unbuilt tower, prominent stone ribs direct attention vertically to the structure's distinctive summit — a steeply sloping green roof which reaches four hundred and seventy five feet above street level. Those necessary elements of the Deco style, set-backs, occur at the twenty-first and twenty-ninth floors and give the structure its characteristic serrated outline.

The Koppers Building.

A certain amount of surface texture is supplied by the spandrels of the windows between the vertical stone ribs, and these spaces, particularly in the building's upper reaches, are adorned with Modernistic ornament in low relief.

But what was Art Deco ornament — which is so plentifully, and yet so discreetly displayed on the Koppers Building, both on the interior as well as the exterior? As we see it here, it was a modern adaptation of various monumental styles of the past, chiefly the Classical.

Art Deco was a youthful style, at once traditional as well as innovative and dynamic. It created the last ornamental style known to Western art by marrying the machine with the old handicraft tradition. It was new as tomorrow, and yet old as history; it could be quite simple and austere or very intricate and complex. It summed up the past but it announced in no uncertain terms the present and the future.

In the 1920s and the 1930s, of course, we did not call it Art Deco. We spoke of it as "Art Moderne" or the "Modernistic" style, as against the full Modern of the International style which eschewed ornament altogether. The term "Art Deco," first applied to the style in the 1960s, stems from the Exposition des Arts Décoratifs et Industriels Modernes, held in Paris in 1925, where the developing style achieved instant and international renown. Katharine McClinton, who did much to publicize the new stylistic manner, calls Art Deco "a classical, rectilinear, and asymmetrical style" that flourished between 1920 and 1940 and reached its apogee between 1925 and 1935. The lobby of the Koppers Building and the exterior of the Gulf Building display a kind of stripped Classicism, and they are thereby prime documents of Deco.

The earlier Art Deco of the 1920s was often decorative, curvilinear, and graceful (elements also common to the Art Nouveau of 1900), but by 1930 the influence of Cubism and the machine became paramount, and the ever more abstracted, conventionalized, and geometric quality of its ornamental system displayed a new dynamism and a new vocabulary. Gazelles and maidens were replaced by airplanes and lightning bolts. The work of the new industrial designers of the 1930s in constantly streamlining and simplifying their forms has led to the present suppression of all ornament in architecture. But while it lasted, the highly eclectic Deco style, which was also influenced by the Indian cultures of North and South America — Incan, Mayan, and Aztec, to say nothing of Egyptian and African art — has left a variegated and highly interesting record.

Although the general form of the Koppers Building is medieval, extending even to the peaked caps of the dormers just below the green slopes of the culminating "chateau" roof, its exterior ornament is the standard Deco "stripped Classic," albeit of a very suave, sophisticated type. It is however, the three-story lobby of the structure which constitutes the strongest and clearest Deco statement in Pittsburgh.

The walls and columns of this elegant hall are of Italian Cremo, a cream-coloured marble with veins of pale brown and greenish tints used with panels of Red Spanish Rojo Alicante marble. Pink and grey Tennessee marbles in a parquet design form the main floor. Generally, Deco architectural designers were fond of colour, and in addition to the stone itself, the plaster ceiling has ornamental coffers consisting of modernized Classical motifs in gilt, red, and green. A more sober note is to be found in the elaborately-ornamented elevator doors, balustrades, directory panels, clocks, and lobby mailboxes — all in cast bronze with a dull finish. The mailboxes are particularly sumptuous, seeming like miniature cathedrals for letters. Another

A lobby in the Koppers Building.

74

characteristic of Deco ornament appears in the zig-zag motifs of the long, Modernistic light fixtures of bronze and glass.

It is interesting that this supremely fashionable and elegant lobby, with its rich but subdued Modernistic Classicism, has also been influenced by the general architectural tone of Pittsburgh, which has always favoured a rugged simplicity, a spare, quiet strength.

The medieval reminiscences of the Koppers are missing in its neighbour across Seventh Avenue, the Gulf Building, which is entirely dependent on Classical precedent. This is the last great skyscraper in Pittsburgh to wear Classical dress (albeit modernized), as it also wears upon its crown an adaptation of one of the Seven Wonders of the Ancient World, the Mausoleum of Halicarnassus.

The architectural motif of the stepped pyramid (which we have already mentioned as a Deco device) in conjunction with a columned arcade had fascinated architects since the beginning of the Renaissance. Many designers of that period had made reconstructions of the Mausoleum from literary sources, but it was not until archaeological excavations were made at the site of the tomb that some real information was made available to later nineteenth-century architects. From that time the conjectural form of the Mausoleum was often used in actual buildings.

One of the latest and most original of these versions was that used by the well-known New York firm of Trowbridge & Livingston in their Banker's Trust Company Building for J. P. Morgan and Company, in 1914, in lower Manhattan. This recapitulation of the Mausoleum theme is quite Classical, but when in 1929 the same firm was asked to do another version of the same theme for Pittsburgh, they produced for the Gulf Building the Halicarnassian colonnades and the pyramid stripped to their basic forms. Here, also, E. P. Mellon was the associated architect. Like Koppers, the Gulf has the characteristic Deco ribbed texture and the steady recession of forms culminating in a lantern at the top. These limestone flanks, a uniform grey, admitted of no colour relief, but for many years the stepped pyramid served as a weather beacon for the city. Art Deco did rejoice in the new neon tube lighting, and the Gulf pyramid glowed with neon red or blue as the weather was fair or foul. Today only the terminal lantern glows warmly to recall that luminous feast of Deco light.

At forty-four stories, the building was for many years the tallest in Pittsburgh, and it formed a well-scaled and graceful apex to the downtown high-rise population, but now its former glory has been eclipsed.

The Gulf Building (left) and the Koppers Building.

Another large artifact of the building boom of the 1920s is the Grant Building at 330 Grant Street, which was designed by Henry Hornbostel, with Eric Fisher Wood as associate. At forty stories, it is only a little less tall than the Gulf, although its set-back mass (again typically Deco) is more akin to that of the Koppers Building. Hornbostel's early sketches reveal the Deco form adorned with much Beaux-Arts detailing, but as executed the ornamentation also became Deco — proof, certainly, of its desirability in buildings of that period.

In the Cathedral of Learning, designed by Charles Z. Klauder in the early 1920s and executed between 1926 and 1937, the form of the structure, with its carefully calculated set-backs, is unreservedly Deco, but the detailing is traditional Gothic Revival. Probably the conservative character of the University's chancellor, John Bowman, and his desire to recall the medieval past would have served to inhibit any Modernism in ornament. For the most part commercial structures of the period were Deco in both form and style, as proven by the changes in the design of the Grant Building. It was the Modern, the Deco, that rented space.

In one detail of its construction, however, the Cathedral was changed even after the upper reaches of its stonework had been finished. Its top story had been finished by a rather dull traditional balustrade, but this was removed and a more graceful, if only slightly Deco, termination substituted. It is not often that an architect gets an opportunity to rectify his mistakes after construction, but one must assume that it was the desire of Chancellor Bowman for Gothic perfection that carried the day. Here, mere fashion had no place in this ideal Cathedral of Education.

And the Deco was fashionable — the entire world of design from 1925 to 1935 was dominated by it. This "smart" aspect of Deco was most notably found among the more ephemeral departments of architectural design, particularly in the interiors of shops, restaurants, hotels, and theatres. Among Pittsburgh examples of this sort, perhaps the most accomplished were the 1927-30 remodeling of Kaufmann's Department Store (Janssen & Cocken, architects) with its tall piers of black Carrara glass (a favourite Deco material) and its monumental Boardman Robinson murals, and the Reymer Brothers Tea Room and Restaurant (Lamont Button, architect) of 1928 in the Clark Building, with its circular mirrors and silver-leafed walls. Both of these handsome interiors have, alas, vanished, but for those of us who knew them, they linger pleasantly — and Modernistically — in the memory.

Perhaps the grandest of these interiors is the Urban Room which

The Urban Room, William Penn Hotel.

is, *mirabile dictu,* still with us, almost unchanged. Designed by the famous architect and theatre designer Joseph Urban (1872-1933), it was incorporated into Janssen & Cocken's 1928-29 addition to the William Penn Hotel. The Pittsburgh architects' new work followed the traditional design of the older structure, with the result that Urban's huge supper and dancing room is like a fabulous Deco cave in a Renaissance setting. Here black glass and golden fabrics are used in a monumentally austere, almost Modern, way underneath a ceiling mural which has the decorative curvilinear grace of the early Deco of the 1920s. As a theatrical designer (particularly for the Ziegfeld Follies), Joseph Urban was especially interested in the use of light as a design element, and his lighting patterns for this basically rather sombre room were tremendously effective.

Another handsome Deco interior was the banking room of the Pittsburgh Branch of the Federal Reserve Bank of Cleveland, designed by Walker & Weeks of Cleveland and erected in 1931-32 next to the Gulf Building on Grant Street, where it forms a small Deco pendant to its huge neighbour. This elegant, "Moderne" interior in marble and Monel metal, however, has been much changed due to subsequent additions. The central "check" desk and the large Pegasus mural of Glenn M. Shaw were acquired by Duquesne University for Rockwell Hall some years ago. Deco murals have been known to move about — at last report, the Boardman Robinson murals from Kaufmann's were "in storage."[1]

Other minor Deco architectural artifacts have either been changed or have vanished. Typical of the altered variety is the Medical Arts Building at 3700 Fifth Avenue in Oakland — erected 1930-32 after the designs of Maximilian Nirdlinger — an interesting, rather jazzy, Deco composition. Unfortunately, in the last three years the lobby and the shop fronts with their zig-zag ornamentation have been "modernized" — that is, rendered bland and innocuous and unornamented. The real monument of Deco "pizazz" was the Enright Theatre, opened in 1928 on Penn Avenue in East Liberty. All gilt, glitter, and "kitsch" Moderne, this Deco "tent and habitation of a night" was demolished in 1958 — and part of the writer's youth went with it.

"Institutional" structures like club buildings, with their social overtones, tended to use Deco rather conservatively. Definitely Deco in form was the high-rise club house of the Keystone Athletic Club (Janssen & Cocken, architects, 1928-29) but its detailing was strictly medieval of a faintly castellated sort. There are even, high up on the soaring brick walls, Celtic gargoyles. Also the 1930-31 high-rise addition to the Duquesne Club, at 325 Sixth Avenue, was designed by the same architects, in the same style to the same scale.

Hospitals constructed during this period tended to use the same formula. The new building for Allegheny General Hospital (York & Sawyer, architects), constructed 1928-36, has a very striking Deco silhouette, but its detailing is Romanesque. Deco in form, also, is the former Nurses' Home of St. Francis Hospital (now the Community Mental Health Centre) and medieval in detailing. This towering structure was designed by Schmidt, Garden & Erikson of Chicago in 1929.

One local Deco structure for which there was little precedent is the first Allegheny County Airport of 1930-31 in West Mifflin (Stanley Roush, architect), with its addition of 1936 designed by Henry Hornbostel. Here, tradition provided a certain background; the

The Terminal building at the Allegheny County Airport.

general lay-out is that of the formal composition of a small Baroque country palace with its approaches and gardens — save that the radial allées of the latter became runways for planes. The house itself became the rectangular box of the airport with attendant wings and an observation pavilion (control tower) on the roof.

One still approaches the "old" airport through a formal forecourt and enters the building through an elaborate geometrical portal flanked by angular Baroque urns ornamented with propellers, planes, and lightning bolts. The exterior walls are of glazed white brick ornamented with Mayan friezes in black, white, and green. This small aviation "palace" still has a certain "chic," although it has lost its once-extensive traffic and is now used only by corporation and private planes.

Once the beholder's eye has been opened to the all-pervasive presence of Deco in our streets, he will find it everywhere. Many small movie theatres of the 1930s were done in Deco, and numbers of these still survive, some of them now put to other uses. Innumerable shops, their chrome, Carrara glass, and neon tubing now dimmed by time, survive on innumerable "main" or neighbourhood shopping streets. Possibly the best concentration of them in Pittsburgh is to be found on the South Side, on East Carson Street. Glass brick, one of the standard architectural clichés of the 1930s, is still to be found in occasional bars and "grilles." There was even a Deco suburban real-estate development, Swan Acres in the North Hills, which still sports a number of once-modish small villas having ribbon windows and tapestry brick walls.

But the skyscrapers still most grandly announce the Deco theme, and the last large Deco high-rise in Pittsburgh is the Royal York Apartments on Bigelow Boulevard in Oakland. Built in 1937 after the designs of Frederick Stanton of Chicago, the Royal York is unabashedly Deco in both form and ornament. The walls of light brick are richly adorned in cream-coloured terra cotta, and there is an elaborate *porte-cochère* with illuminated columns in glass and metal. The lobby is elaborately decorated with Deco motifs in rich materials, and there is even some graceful Deco furniture that would have been worthy of the Paris Exposition of 1925.

A console table in the Royal York lobby uses swans as its supports, and in this there is something symbolic, because this large high-rise building itself is certainly the swan song of the Art Deco style in Pittsburgh. Shortly after it was finished came the Second World War, and with it the almost complete cessation of construction in the United States. When building was resumed again after 1945, it became apparent that the architectural scene as we had known it before 1940 had almost completely vanished.

Art Deco was, in a sense, a transitional style, and its strength as well as its fascination consisted in its adroit mixture of modernity and the past. It was always interesting even when it was jazzy and meretricious. By 1950, the Modern school of architecture, based on the tenets of the so-called International Style — a concern with form, function, and materials and the complete suppression of ornament as irrelevant to the Modern Age — had completely triumphed. But now, as we move toward 1980, there are signs that the hold of the extreme Modernists is weakening.

Among these signs has been in the last four or five years a renewed interest in the Art Deco period. At first this renewal took on the fervor of a cult, but interest in it still continues at a more quiet and sustained pace. The Art Deco Revival now seems here to stay, and it deserves to stay with us despite the disdain of the Modernists — now something diminished.

As we look at the array of downtown skyscrapers dominated by the huge uncompromising bulk, straight up and down, of the gigantic US Steel Building, perhaps we may hope again for something more akin to the old skyscraper style — something more variegated, more graceful — and more humane.

'The murals are now in the collection of the Pittsburgh History & Landmarks Foundation. Several are to be installed in the Sheraton Hotel at Station Square.

Carnegie Magazine, May, 1977.

The Old Post Office under restoration.

Autumn Wine and Preservation
The Heinz Hall and the
Old Post Office at Pittsburgh

Autumn can be a golden time, not only for humanity but for buildings as well, and it is pleasant to report that this particular season will see in Pittsburgh the occupation and dedication of two aging buildings that have been given new life and a renewed existence in the present uncertain urban climate. They are the Penn Theatre that has metamorphosed into the Heinz Hall for the Performing Arts, and the old North Side Post Office that has become the Pittsburgh History & Landmarks Museum.

That this has been done despite all mischances of fate and hazards of fortune makes the victory for those who love the architecture of the past all the more precious, all the more heartening. Let us be joyful! The Grim Reaper of Architectural Progress has for a season stayed his hand. Death has taken a holiday! This year, the season of the golden leaf has a special sweetness.

Autumn is also the time of the vintage, of the gathered grape. This is the season of new wine, and that we should, architecturally speaking, have our own just-pressed wine in old bottles, adapted vessels, is a special occasion for rejoicing. Let the music sound, and let us praise those who by their perception and munificence have made this miracle possible.

As a miracle, *mirabile dictu,* it is double, but the brighter, the more effulgent, the more beneficent of the two marvels is the Heinz Hall that was dedicated and opened to the public on September 10 and 11 with appropriate ceremonies, with flowers and pageantry, music and wine. Pittsburgh was *en fête,* and the event and the building were much noticed beyond the city.

All this festivity was absent when the building was first completed as the Penn Theatre, one of Loew's movie palaces, in September, 1926. It simply opened for business, for in its existence, the medium was the message — the "silver screen," the core of moving light and shadow — of which the theatre itself was at once the extension and the shrine.

Aside from its prime aspect as a rich document of that great decade of illusionism, the 1920s, the Penn was the chief local representative of the American moving picture palace, possibly — second only to the ever-heightening "skyscrapers" — the most insistent and ebullient architectural image of the period. Publicly, the great "picture" theatre was both the physical and the spiritual heir of the medieval cathedral and the palaces of the Baroque monarchs. That these cinematic chateaux were devoted to fantasy and illusion is not to deny their very real grandeur. To live is sometimes to dream, and rarely has the great American public dreamed more lavishly than in these ornate pleasure castles. Here, for a few coins, every man could be, for a season, a king, and every woman a queen.

That this great company of pleasure domes is now much diminished is an evidence that the temper of our national life has drastically changed. There were many reasons for the vanishment of the picture palace as an institution, but they are familiar to every theatre-goer. Many of these theatres are gone, but many remain. Pittsburgh's own Penn, designed by C. W. & George L. Rapp (who created so many of these castles), after a few years of glory entered a long period of decline. It was abandoned as a picture house in 1964 and, dark and dusty, it was fading toward the inevitable head-ache ball when in 1968 the Heinz Endowment purchased the derelict structure with the idea of using it as an interim concert hall until a new symphony centre could be constructed in the Lower Hill.

Fortunately the idea of new construction was abandoned, as the very real virtues and amenities of the old building became apparent. It was decided finally to recondition the Penn to serve as a new symphony hall and center for the performing arts.

The work was begun in May, 1970, and was completed according to schedule, so that the Pittsburgh Symphony could occupy the reconditioned theatre for the 1971-72 season. Stotz, Hess, MacLachlan & Fosner were the architects for the restoration, and they have done a superb job of transforming the erstwhile movie house into a modern concert hall. It is not easy nowadays to find young men who are adept at drawing period detail, but William Hartlep of the design team was able to supply, where necessary, new work to complement the old.

Nowhere was this more evident than on the front elevation of the building on Sixth Avenue. The Rapps' original design had featured at one side a monumental entrance to the theatre, but for the rest of the frontage, a forebuilding of shops and offices done in beige Classical terra cotta masked the auditorium. In the interest of making a larger entrance into the theatre, the shops were removed and the sash-windows above were replaced by much smaller casements whose ornamental architraves demanded considerable new designing. Firms producing ornamental terra cotta have all but disap-

The lobby and grand stair in Heinz Hall.

peared, and only one company in California now produces it. The new designs were sent thither and duly executed; the old terra cotta was cleaned, and the two now abide very happily together. The new entrance facade, which has a marked flavour of the Viennese Baroque of the eighteenth century, is much superior to the old.

Under the circular copper hoods of the new doors one enters the new wide vestibule. The old grand lobby, with its huge window, has now become a promenade, and part of the grand tier lobby has been floored over to give access to an elegantly-decorated lounge bar that takes the place of the former second-floor offices. A new gallery and reception room has been carved out of former storage cellars in the basement area.

There have been few changes in the auditorium itself, except in its decoration and seating capacity. The original hall seated 3,486 persons, but in the interest of comfort for the audience, the present seats number only 2,729. Acoustically, the entire hall has been renovated, and much of the almost-smothering elaboration of Baroque ornament has been removed to facilitate hearing in the audience. A new shell for the orchestra and a large plaster baffle, or reflector, at the top of the proscenium have been added. Dr. Heinrich Keilholz of Salzburg acted as consultant on the acoustics. Everything has been done to make the stage and the hall as modern — and as handsome — as possible.

When one remembers the heavily "antique" and tenebrous interior of the Penn, one also wonders why the 1920s — a decade that prided itself on its modernity — should have had such a passion for "antiquing" everything. The Penn was no exception, and while tenebrosity was not inappropriate to a picture palace it had no place in a modern concert hall. Accordingly the interior of the entire building was done over in scarlet, white, and gold. Everything glitters, and gleams — visually the new Heinz Hall is a delight to the eye.

Verner S. Purnell of Sewickley was in charge of the new decorative work at the Hall, and the result must be accounted a brilliant success, particularly in replacing the cinematic density of the original decor with the present festive brightness. W. F. Hinchey, Inc., were the contractors for the plaster work. Bill Hinchey, the founder of the firm, worked as a young man on the Penn when it was being constructed — it is not often that you find a *reprise* of this kind.

William Lord of A. J. Vater & Company, Inc., did the gold leafing, murals, and marbleizing. Particularly handsome are his great painted "trophies" that were designed by Verner Purnell on either side of the proscenium arch of the auditorium.

Now officially designated as the Heinz Hall for the Performing Arts, it should very felicitously accommodate the Pittsburgh Symphony Orchestra, the Pittsburgh Opera, the Civic Light Opera, the Pittsburgh Ballet Theatre, and the Pittsburgh Youth Symphony. This autumn has indeed been a golden one for Pittsburgh.

And now to the other half of the miracle. The new Pittsburgh History & Landmarks Museum, just metamorphosed from the old North Side Post Office, once the Post Office of the city of Allegheny, is in its smaller way no less spectacular, no less engaging. Even if the hand of Maecenas has not caressed it lavishly, and it might more appropriately be called silver gilt than golden, it may still serve as an example of what can be done in our inflationary day with relatively small means for preservation.

Where millions of dollars made possible the resurrection of the Penn Theatre, some few hundreds of thousands have been spent on the Old Post Office. The story of its being snatched from the very maw of the new Urban Death would be more appropriate to a Pearl White "cliff hanger" of the early movie days, but there is not space to recount it here. Suffice it to say that its rescue from demolition by the Urban Redevelopment Authority of Pittsburgh has been exciting, even something audacious, and perhaps the building's continuing presence will hearten other young preservationists to joust with the dragons of destruction.

Youthful our building, certainly superlatively, seems now that its pale-grey granite has, as part of the rehabilitation, been cleaned. Stylistically, it belongs to that trim, spare Italian Renaissance of the fifteenth century which was always one of the most beguiling aspects of the Eclectic period in architecture before 1940. In form it follows those churches of the central plan in the Italy of the late fifteenth and early sixteenth centuries that provided the *clou* for later secular buildings. Certainly, even if ours was designed through the eyes and fingers of late nineteenth-century America, the essential purity of its style and form command the eye jaded by modern austerities and banalities. Its tight, compact bulk, the rugged delicacy of its detail-

The Old Post Office Museum, North Side.

ing, its sinewy freshness of spirit enchant the heart when, near or far, it is seen and *felt* as part of the urban landscape.

The building was designed in the office of the Architect to the United States Treasury in 1894, under the supervision of William Martin Aiken. Construction began in 1894, with Frank E. Rutan of Pittsburgh as supervising architect. It was completed late in 1897 and occupied in January, 1898. It solidly and handsomely functioned as a post office until the 1960s, when plans were formulated to annihilate central North Side in the interests of developing Allegheny Center. The Government then erected a new building and sold the old one to the Redevelopment Authority, which scheduled its demolition.

The Pittsburgh History & Landmarks Foundation, already known for restoring houses in inner-city areas, worked for over a year to alter these plans; after complicated negotiations a reprieve for the structure was won from grudging officials who had already begun to smell demolition dust. During the reprieve, the Foundation managed to raise sufficient funds to assure restoration. Accordingly, in the autumn of 1970 work was begun on the building to make it possible to open it as a museum of Pittsburgh and Allegheny County history — an institution badly needed in the area.

Williams/Trebilcock/Whitehead of Pittsburgh were the architects for the work, and Deeter-Ritchey-Sippel, Inc., were named consulting engineers. Since the chief interior feature of the building is the great domed space — in fact the building *is* the dome — the architects were confronted with adaptation problems. (Incidentally, this splendid Renaissance-inspired dome, in contrast to the cramped meagreness of the *present* North Side Post Office, serves as a crushing rebuke to the sorry state of our present public architecture.) Our modern architects, however, knew how to respect a space of the old grand dispensation, and their accommodation of it to the needs of a modern museum has been ingenious and exemplary.

Despite some minor setbacks, the rehabilitation has proceeded, and now it is almost finished. Shortly the Foundation will move into its new quarters, and the Museum will be established and opened like the new Heinz Hall, thereby giving Pittsburgh two major cultural centres in historic buildings that have been creatively adapted to modern use and handsomely restored.

It *has* been this year a golden autumn in Pittsburgh, an effulgent autumn of salvation that promises a silver winter and a golden spring.

The Charette, September-October, 1971.

Fantasy on the Roof
or, Architecture Overhead

I have always been, both by inclination and by temporal position, an admirer of ornament in architecture. I *like* adornment, and I am old enough to remember with pleasure those extensive latitudes of ornamentation current in my youth. I rejoice in the most intricate carving. I am entranced by the most contrived surfaces. A multitude of references to the styles and periods of the past meets with my entire approbation. For me, less is definitely not more. I am as willing as any of the most advanced Moderns to admire a fine space or an adroit use of plane surfaces, to appreciate the just proportions of form and mass, to consider the textures of good materials. But something, in stark modernity of style, always seems lacking. Ah, give me an excellently-detailed Corinthian capital or an elaborately-crocketed Gothic pinnacle and I am filled with joy.

With the development of a new constructional technology in the late nineteenth and early twentieth centuries, particularly in the case of the high-rise, steel-frame building, some interesting mutations and extensions of the old ornamental architectural styles occurred. Ah, the purists of Modernity would say, "Why not let the new construction — the steel frame — express itself without any reference to the ornamental systems of past styles? Let it be," they say, "in all its purity, with only the cladding necessary to protect its interior spaces from the elements." "Very well," I am inclined to reply, "but a little of this goes a long way. It leaves no room for fantasy on the roof or anywhere else in the building." Unfortunately, the unornamented silhouette or surface is now standard architectural fare.

For a time after the steel frame first appeared there was a very interesting marriage of the frame and the ornamentation of past styles. From the late 1880s until about 1940, American cities boasted a fantastic group of towers clothed in the glamourous vesture of the past, now Gothic, now Classical, Byzantine, Romanesque, what you will. It was all very like a gorgeous fancy-dress ball, in which the town seemed to be perpetually *en fête*. While it lasted, it was like a wonderful fantastic dream, and there are still a sufficient number of its monuments left to recall that halcyon era to the searching eye.

All this was brought rather forcefully to my mind when, recently, it was necessary for me to move. I like to live in older buildings, and I like to live in Oakland, the cultural centre of Pittsburgh. Here one can enjoy a sort of perpetual feast of Eclectic architecture in a glamourous parade of styles and periods.

Here, also, is to be found the largest collection of high-rise apartment houses in the late 1920s, local artifacts of possibly the greatest building boom in American history. Oakland is also repository of the most fantastically varied examples of Eclectic architecture in the city. Among all the Eclectic apartment houses my choice fell upon the Fairfax, on Fifth Avenue near Craig Street. This large structure had been built in the mid-'Twenties after the designs of a Washington architect, Philip M. Jullien, in a modified version of the early English Renaissance-Jacobean style. It is huge and commanding and gorgeously adorned.

Quite like a New York apartment house, its enormous facade of brick and stone rises sheer from the Fifth Avenue sidewalk. The archaeology of its design is not too heavy; this is a building, after all, of the Eclectic persuasion, and more than one style is visible here. The multitudinous windows are mostly sashed and multi-paned, and thus Georgian in derivation. The surface of the wall is symmetrically marked-off by bands of Jacobean stone panels carved in low relief. There is a rather narrow central pavilion flanked by similar smaller elements each side of the facade. Most of the flat surface decoration is concentrated here. This richly-textured scheme of decoration culminates at the cornice line in a handsome display of early English Renaissance motifs, all wonderfully carved in stone, that would do credit to an Elizabethan or Jacobean manor house.

With the exception of the superb late Gothic cornice of the Union Trust Building of 1916-17 in downtown Pittsburgh, the Fairfax cornice has the most dazzling display of roof ornaments in the city. Above the three pavilions or architectural projections of the facade, the flat carved-stone panels are ornamented with huge escutcheons, surmounted at the roofline with three-dimensional stone crowns. Arching over these are half-circles of masonry supported by Jacobean scrolls and strapwork. Flanking these arching half-circles are obelisks, and it is these splendid stone monoliths that provide the ultimate touch of fantasy to the Fairfax roofline. Classically they seem to salute the crocketed pinnacles of St. Paul's Cathedral just up the street.

Nine stories up, these scrolls and crowns and obelisks have to be viewed from a little distance to be properly seen and appreciated.

Skyline ornament at the Fairfax.

Although for many years I have looked upon them and admired them distantly, they are now rather eminently my intimates. They are physically very close to me, in fact directly overhead, above my ninth-floor apartment. One windy March day I went up to the roof to see this fantastic garden of ornament, and they did look rather different from the other side although their basic form is the same. Seen from the front, they are the logical culmination of the ascending ornamentation of the facade, but from the back the varied forms have to stand on their own aesthetically. (*Practically*, they do not stand on their own, because they have to be supported from behind by heavy steel struts anchored into the floor of the roof.)

I feel a certain sense of proprietorship in these great stone ornaments, posed in such fantastic majesty on the roof. I was never in real life able to inhabit an Elizabethan or Jacobean manor house, but in this great architectural garden, my constant daily and nightly companion, I have the next best thing. These fine symbols are mine, because I am acutely aware of them and because I have a sure sense of what they represent. Even when I cannot see them (I am, after all, for much of the time underneath them) it pleases me to know that they are there, that they so eminently and gloriously *preside*. And to have these airy castles overhead, all this fantasy, this wonder and this grandeur, I need only pay my rent each month. And, ah, how fortunate — I, in my remote eyrie, I am privy of the kingdoms of this world.

And I have not only my own special rooftop fantasy kingdom, but from my wide windows I can descry others, near and far. Beyond the turrets of St. Paul's Cathedral, I can see the charmingly medieval bulk of the Schenley Arms apartments at Bigelow and Centre, a product of the same great building boom as the Fairfax. Its entire top story is half-timbered, surmounted by steeply-pitched gable roofs. Is this London of the sixteenth century, or is it modern Pittsburgh? To errant fancy it could be either. Near it are the two Tudor turrets of the Bellefield Dwellings of 1902, the first great highrise apartment house in Pittsburgh. I recall once looking directly at the mysterious striped towers, with their peaked caps, from the roof of the Bellefield Dwellings itself.

And, especially at night, distant, distant, ablaze with red and white lights like a Christmas tree ship, the neo-medieval honeycomb of the Mellon Pavilion of the West Penn Hospital. And another Tudor note, the black pepperpot turrets of the Church of the Ascension, their tips just visible. They appear, these turrets, mysteriously Romantic.

There are other areas of rooftop fantasy in Pittsburgh, but I shall speak of them another time. Here I wished merely to introduce the theme and celebrate my own private architectural garden.

Radio script for WQED-FM, 1978.

An Aerial View of Oakland in 1924

Recently, in the course of searching through my files for material for one of my television programs, I came across some aerial photographs of Oakland that apparently had been misfiled. This sort of thing happens more frequently than I care to admit — the misfiling, I mean — but frequently, it is also inadvertent, because sometimes material is moved from one file to another as I am working with it, and I may forget to return it to its original repository. Sometimes, when I consider how I move rapidly over the face of the Pittsburgh region — in television, radio, and the written word — I must admit that it is little short of miraculous that my files retain any semblance of order.

In the case of the Oakland photographs, I quite forgot about my original quest for half an hour in the delight of examining the rather worn eight-by-ten glossies, pictures of my most cherished local neighbourhood (which bore no identifying dates). It is one of my favourite pastimes, to try to date such unmarked Pittsburgh views by noting the presence or absence of various landmarks. In this instance, such is my familiarity with the landscape that it should not have taken half an hour to assign a very close approximate date, but the truth was that this fortuitous encounter had become an antiquarian excursion of such intensity that for a brief period I had lost all sense of time. For some sweet, suspended moments, I seemed by some obscure enchantment to be literally back in that faraway land — Oakland in the mid-1920s. It was Oakland in high summer as well, and summer is always the time for the bravest, the most full-bodied memories. And how many marvelous memories cluster about these streets, these buildings, these hills. Ah, this was the landscape of my youth, a sun-washed map of dreams, a map, how passionately, of love. Here it was always summer, the land possessed beguiling vistas of the past but also of the abounding present, and I was in love with youth, with life. All poetry, then, was mine . . .

Suddenly, I was reminded that this was all very pleasant, even, at seventy, exhilarating, but I still had not found the Late Victorian photograph for which I had been looking. I glanced at the clock on my desk — my youthful memory of Oakland had preoccupied me for

Oakland in 1924 in the Frick Acres area.

half an hour. "When I do count the clock that tells the time . . . ," I quoted Shakespeare to console myself. I did, however, put the Oakland photographs that I found in a special folder, so that in a future moment of leisure I could look at them again.

So here again is the summer of 1924, and here is Oakland as seen from a plane at say, an altitude of two thousand feet. This altitude reminded me also, that a couple of weeks ago, I had gone to Indiana University to give a lecture on recent adaptive usage of old buildings in Pittsburgh. From Indianapolis to Bloomington, a distance of fifty miles, I had traveled by a very small propeller plane which quite took me back to the small planes that I had seen at Rodgers Field in Fox Chapel in the middle 1920s. The kind of view that you got from a plane *then,* when you stayed much closer to the ground, was much more companionable than what you get nowadays way up. In the old plane photographs of 1924, one was able to see the landscape in considerable detail, which made possible a more loving, more intimate sense of identification with it.

And since I have been, for so long, concerned with the adaptive use of old buildings, I shall consider in this discourse the adaptive usage of old photographs. They are very useful in the construction of a kind of continuum of the mutable environment of Oakland, which is also the landscape of my heart.

There is so much material within these two photographs, such an infinity of detail, that I shall probably have to devote more than one discourse to this abundant landscape. And now that I have the glossies before me, where shall I begin? At the top, the bottom, or the middle? Almost dead centre in one of them is the Cathedral of Learning. A photograph of the architect's model(?) scaled to the confines of the glossy has been interpolated. Not only did this help much to date the photograph, but it also demonstrated how Oakland would be changed, Ah, by that great tower it was! This was the first enormous stage of the University's expansion, and nothing in Oakland has ever been the same since.

Inasmuch as we seem to have begun with the centre of our area, perhaps we should best continue that way and radiate outward as time permits or inclination indicates. At least we can see, in the air views, the irregular geometrical shape of the large plot of land bounded by Fifth, Forbes and Bellefield Avenues and Bigelow Boulevard. Here, on its Fifth Avenue frontage, had been erected several largish houses, most of them stylistically of the simple, mid-century Italianate persuasion, a type once common in the half-rural suburban Oakland of the nineteenth century.

In 1900 Henry Clay Frick, who was, like several of Pittsburgh's great industrialists, also an astute and extensive dealer in real estate, had purchased the several lots of the various owners, forming it into one large plot which was still known in the 1920s as Frick Acres. Since the turn of the century, Oakland had become a favoured district for the construction of large apartment houses and, briefly, Henry Frick had considered using his acres as the site of a court of multiple dwellings. In 1916, the well-known local architect Benno Janssen had made sketches for such a scheme which was never executed. In 1921, A. W. and R. B. Mellon made it possible for the University of Pittsburgh to purchase the plot from the Frick Estate.

From that time on, architectural studies were made for new University buildings to be erected in the area, studies which culminated in Charles Z. Klauder's design for the Cathedral of Learning. By way of publicity for it, I am quite sure, one of my photographs — the doctored one of which I have already spoken — was designed. The other glossy, however, shows Frick Acres as it was before the great skyscraper was projected upon the land. Here, in the high sun of the summer of 1924, were the old large suburban houses fronting on Fifth Avenue. At the corner of Bigelow and Fifth, the old Brown house with its wide lawns and its elm trees had, by the early 1920s, quite lost its air of half-rural Victorian establishment and had become known simply as House Number One, Frick Acres. It became a shelter for various University departments. For a time, it housed the offices of the *Pitt News*, when I was a student at the University in the late 'Twenties. I remember being much impressed by the forlorn rooms of the interior, with their handsome white marble Victorian fireplaces. This kind of thing, I recall, was just beginning to be vaguely fashionable again after being so long in aesthetic disfavour. These rooms, with their gracious proportions, quite captured my historical interest, and I kept trying to imagine what they must once have been like.

And, ah, the shadow of the elms which stretched above the sidewalk along Bigelow Boulevard! Two of these were later incorporated into the imported elm population introduced to the Cathedral grounds in the interest of imparting an air of greater antiquity to the general Gothic ambience so ably and suavely provided by Charles Klauder. This Gothicity was established at the behest of the then-chancellor of the University, John G. Bowman. Alas, the elms never flourished at the University, but the Gothic Revival in this magnificent building is still very much with us.

Down toward Forbes Avenue, facing the new Schenley Plaza,

were the tennis courts, usually much populated with moving youthful figures on such a summer day as that of my photographs. And on this day long ago when the picture was taken by the photographer in the plane, surely, surely there must have been someone moving swiftly with flashing arms and legs, gleaming in the sun, golden . . .

As I watched then, I thought that there was never anything so beautiful. And so this rough geometric land became for me a chart, a diagram, a map of love . . . I cannot forego that vision once received. And so it remains — still — as I watch now.

Radio script for WQED-FM, circa 1978.

The Angelic Eye
Bellefield from the Air

Therefore with angels, let us imagine that we are "flying in" by plane, as most of us do nowadays from anywhere, and as the land appears we begin, if the day be clear, to identify the configurations of the city, Pittsburgh, which we know so well. The anonymous skyscape of the flight slowly evolves into the known land, and we become eager in identification. What will appear now?

If we approach the city from the east, the vision of our superior eye sharpens as the enigmatic chart of streets slides into the familiar. Landmarks — a great tower or a hill — emerge, and between them the green grid of spires, roofs, and chimneys. This is the East End of the city, the wide kingdom, the heartland of our daily life.

And now, as the map view narrows down, we see Shadyside, Oakland, and the one particular subdivision of the latter — Bellefield. Here, since we are in command of this plane or our angelic wings, we can stop the action, and for a little time we may remain suspended over Bellefield — this greenness and the moving streets — shops, houses, churches, tall apartment towers . . .

Long known, long loved, long cherished, the district shades off sweetly into other neighbourhoods, also known and loved. It is difficult to set bounds, make limitations. But for the purpose of this chronicle of our view, we must mark off some limits. Here are the boundaries, the named streets — Bellefield of course, Centre Avenue, Neville Street, Forbes Avenue. . .

But before the streets, the land was there. If an angel flying over in prehistoric times, perhaps a million years ago, had looked down, all that would have been visible would have been a lake, seventy-five feet deep, created by the waters of the Old Monongahela, forced back by a great glacier from the north. Where Bellefield now stands would have been the point where the old river flowed back to the present river beds via the ravine of Four Mile Run (Panther Hollow) and that valley now occupied by the B. & O. Railroad. Speak, angel, you who were and are, did you see those long-vanished waves?

In historic times the itinerant angel would have seen the uneven, relatively flat floor of the valley covered with trees. After the middle of the eighteenth century, with the coming of European

99

settlement to the Pittsburgh area, clearings in the forest began to appear.

In the early part of the nineteenth century one of the largest property holders in the Oakland district — of which Bellefield is a part — was an English immigrant from Staffordshire, James Chadwick, who had acquired some thousand acres in Allegheny County by 1820. His homestead and gardens were located in western Oakland, on the hill where Carlow College now stands, but parts of his "farm" extended into the Bellefield area, and even the original campus of Carnegie-Mellon University was once Chadwick property.

The next prominent landowner in Bellefield was Neville B. Craig (1787-1863) — lawyer, editor, and historian who had been born in the redoubt or "blockhouse" of Fort Pitt. If the eye that looked over his acreage was not angelic, at least the regard of the Muse of History attended the mid-century development of Bellefield. Craig, who was proprietor and editor of the *Pittsburgh Gazette* from 1829 until 1841, as well as editor of a well-known historical periodical, *The Olden Time,* wrote several books including the *History of Pittsburgh* (1851). After the death of his wife in 1852, he passed the remaining years of his life with his youngest daughter. He died at his farm, "Bellefield" in Pitt Township, in 1863. It is highly probable that the name of his farm became the name of the district, although there are those who feel that it was just a fancy name given to a rising suburban district. But no matter, the name still lingers sweetly on the tongue and in the heart.

Long ago, how golden with wheat and corn, the angel of the fields flew over, dropping fertility from his fingers on the farms of Craig and Chadwick, to say nothing of the Croghan-Schenley acreage to the north and south. The remaining trees gathered in clumps for protection; beside them cattle and horses pastured. But there was to be, about 1850, another mutation of the landscape as well as a change of the angelic guard. Bellefield became suburban.

About 1850 Messrs. Rice and Dithridge acquired the southern acreage of Neville Craig's farm and laid out a grid of streets with small attendant lots, calling the new development East Pittsburgh (the name, like many real-estate appellations, did not long endure, and it subsided into Bellefield). The streets — Henry (for Henry Lloyd, a local resident), Washington (now Winthrop), and Fillmore (for President Millard Fillmore) — are still there, as are a few of the original houses, most of which were small. The Dithridge family, notable in the early Pittsburgh glass industry, had its name perpetuated in Dithridge Street. Craig Street, the central vertical artery of the district, as well as the companion Neville Street, commemorate Bellefield's illustrious ancestors.

The new angel apparent in the skies even descended to preside in the "elegant" suburban villas that began to appear along Fifth Avenue (shown on mid-century maps as Pennsylvania Avenue in its Oakland reaches) — which along with Forbes was the chief artery to downtown Pittsburgh. Bellefield was not, of course, a railroad suburb, but what it lacked in convenience of transportation it gained in semi-rural seclusion and romantic charm. The Victorian period rather fostered the conception of woman as ministering angel, the established goddess of the Home. The mid-century American suburb rapidly became the focus of the cult, and Bellefield not only was no exception but became a kind of showcase to the new devotion to the "Angel in the House" — to use the title of Coventry Patmore's long poem published in 1858.

This new preoccupation was abundantly demonstrated in the handsome houses of the new suburb. Bellefield in the 1860s and 1870s was a constant client of the Philadelphia architect Isaac Hobbs, whose designs were published during a number of years in *Godey's Lady's Book*, perhaps the best known of all American nineteenth-century women's magazines. These rather ebullient Italianate houses, as we see them now in either Isaac Hobbs' publications containing his designs (*Hobbs' Architecture* in both its 1873 and 1876 editions) or in the files of the *Lady's Book*, constitute a very graphic document of suburban establishments of the 'Sixties and 'Seventies. Towered, bulbous, verandahed, and aggressively bracketed, Bellefield shone forth in several examples, only one of which is now standing, a double house on Neville near Centre. Here the new angel dwelt, but even if she were winged, she had to be well-heeled.

Today, wherever you find a collection of suburban houses you will also find some churches, and this was certainly more true in the nineteenth century. The angel in the house usually went to church, and the children of the house to Sunday school. In the early 1860s in Bellefield, a small Sunday school was established on Henry Street, and this led in 1866 to the establishment of the Bellefield Presbyterian Church at Bellefield and Fifth Avenues. Their first building, a small "carpenter Gothic" structure, was designed by Isaac Hobbs and, of course, published in *Godey's Lady's Book*. The present stone building (Frederick Osterling, architect, 1889) is now the University and City Ministries.

Also established in 1889 was the Episcopal Church of the Ascension, whose great rugged Gothic tower (W. Halsey Wood, architect,

1896-98) at Ellsworth and Neville broods majestically over the eastern boundary of Bellefield and signals, perhaps, to any heavenly angel flying in from the east.

By 1890 the semi-rural, suburban days of Bellefield were definitely over. The great wooded and farmland tract to the southeast was given to the City by the philanthropist-angel Mrs. Mary Schenley in 1889, and Schenley Park was established. When the Carnegie Institute building was constructed at the Forbes Avenue entrance of the Park in 1892-95, the future of Oakland as the Pittsburgh Civic Centre was assured, and with it the future of Bellefield.

With the future of the Civic Centre assured, Franklin Nicola (1859-1938) bought in 1904 the last large tract of open Oakland farmland — the extensive Schenley Farms acreage to the west. Nicola was no angel, but his spirit brooded over the entire Oakland district until his death. It was he more than anyone else who was to establish the grand Oakland image in which that of Bellefield is so gracefully subsumed.

To the eye of any angel of whatever order flying over in the 1890s, houses proliferated in the streets below, houses in all the fashionable styles of the turn of the century. But this decade was essentially one of transition; the population was increasing, and competition for valuable land was inevitable. Multiple dwellings were only a step away and, sure enough, the first high-rise apartment house in Oakland, Bellefield Dwellings (Carlton Strong, architect), appeared in 1904 at Centre and Bellefield. This great, rather sombre pile of stone and brick, with its green Tudor turrets, was essentially a portent and a sign. Since then Bellefield's dwellings are mostly multiple.

After 1890, also, Bellefield had been drawn more tightly into the general net of the city by the traction companies — first the cable and then the electric trolley cars. The streetcars were the final sign of the total integration of the suburb into the metropolis.

A sort of spin-off of the traction age was the amusement park with its mechanical "treats," so dear to city dwellers of the early twentieth century. Usually these popular *pleasances,* fostered by the trolley interests, were located in the far suburbs, but curiously enough there existed on the northern marches of Bellefield, at Baum Boulevard and Craig Street, a peculiarly rococo example of the type — Luna Park. Its existence was brief, 1905-09, but while it lasted, it imparted a garish "show-biz" exoticism to the solid residential phalanxes of "old" Bellefield.

Another, more "integrated," artifact of the trolley age was Duquesne Gardens, which, although it vanished in 1956 (demolished to make way for an apartment house), was, in its curious mutations, an established social fixture of Bellefield — indeed of Oakland and the city. This long, low building was constructed in 1890 as a car barn for the Duquesne Traction Company. In 1896 it was remodeled into a long hall that could be used as a theatre, sports arena, or indoor skating rink. Over the years until its demise, it fulfilled all these functions abundantly, and when it finally bit the dust, it was much lamented by the general populace. If the angel that presided over Luna Park was tinselly, a little raffish, that of the Duquesne Gardens might be called "all-purpose."

Over against these evanescent popular manifestations, the grandest of the Bellefield ecclesiastical images rose in 1903-06 at Fifth and Craig — the Roman Catholic Cathedral of St. Paul (Egan & Prindeville, architects). Here the suave Edwardian bulk of the great church (perhaps a little mechanical and tedious at the edges) achieves a truly monumental quality in the tall stone twin spires of the main facade. They are visible from almost any point in Bellefield, and they lend a variety of vista to the district that is enormously impressive. This monumentality is matched in the neighbourhood by the march-

Bellefield in the 1940s.

ing Ionic columns of the Mellon Institute for Industrial Research (Janssen & Cocken, architects, 1931-37) at Bellefield and Fifth.

All other towers in Bellefield have long since yielded place to the ever-growing collection of high-rise apartment houses. The King Edward Apartments of 1914 at Bayard and Melwood followed the lead of the pioneer Bellefield Dwellings, but it was the stupendous building boom of 1925-30 that produced the largest crop of flat-houses. The Fairfax apartments (Philip Jullien, architect, 1926) on Fifth Avenue and the Cathedral Mansions (John Donn, architect, 1926) were the largest of these in our area, but there were several others, all still extant. Bellefield has one hotel — the Webster Hall (Henry Horn-bostel, architect, 1925) at Fifth and Dithridge, and there is talk of another across Fifth Avenue[1] but perhaps this project will meet the same fate as the elaborate "hostelry" planned by Henry Ives Cobb of Chicago in 1895 to stand on the Schmertz property at Fifth and Craig. It remained a dream. There is some Modern architecture in Bellefield, the best of it being the Neville House apartments (Tasso Katselas, architect, 1958) on Neville Street; the Craig Street branch of the Pittsburgh National Bank (Skidmore, Owings & Merrill, architects, 1966) at Fifth and Craig; and the Scaife Gallery of the Museum of Art, Carnegie Institute (Edward Larrabee Barnes, architect, 1974), on Forbes Avenue. The modern apartment houses and condominia that continue to devour the elder residential amenities of Bellefield are adequate but uninspired, and any domestic angel of today would not be moved to ecstasy by their contemplation.

A modern angel of any persuasion, flying over and competing for sky-space with jets and helicopters, would not find the grid of Bellefield Streets much changed since 1900, however much the mediocre apartment houses and the creeping blacktop of parking lots induce dismay in the terrestrial beholder. Bellefield was studied as part of *A Plan for Pittsburgh's Cultural District Oakland,* published in 1961 by the Pittsburgh Regional Planning Association and the Allegheny Conference on Community Development, but no great physical changes have resulted from it. There is a Bellefield Area Civic Association which keeps a watchful eye on the neighbourhood. Meanwhile, the sun still glows on the familiar streets, the land is green. The writer who lives close to the local trees and towers hopes much for the continued health of his own quarter of the larger City. What is Bellefield's future? Look down, angel, in grace and love, and say . . .

[1]This hotel was never built.

Carnegie Magazine, September, 1975.

The Duquesne Gardens

I sometimes think that present-day preservationists who are so preoccupied with finding new uses for Victorian or Edwardian buildings are simply recapitulating certain problems by no means unfamiliar to our predecessors. Occasionally it was necessary or economical in the old days to find a new use for a building that had been constructed for quite another purpose — a house might become a hotel or vice versa. In the peripatetic America of the nineteenth or early twentieth centuries, buildings were moved about at will or assumed new guises in a rapidly-changing landscape. Rapid change has been a constant characteristic of American history, and in no case was this more true than in the case of urban development.

The Oakland district of Pittsburgh has been no exception to these mutations. Like all areas of local settlement it went from wilderness to farmland to suburb within a time span of little more than fifty years. Even while it was still decidedly suburban much of the district was incorporated into the city of Pittsburgh in the 1860s. The first impetus to the development of Oakland as the local civic and cultural centre came when Mrs. Mary E. Schenley gave to the city the huge tract that became Schenley Park. This trend was accelerated with the establishment, at the park entrance, of the Carnegie Institute (the Carnegie Library, museums of art and natural history, and a music hall) in 1895. Sports also came into the picture with ice skating and hockey at the Casino, built behind the Institute in the early 1890s. In 1909 Forbes Field arrived, and the great days of baseball.

Oakland had evolved as a residential suburb without benefit of the railroads, but its expansion in the 1890s coincided with the development of the street railways. First the cable and then the trolley cars drew the city and its environs into a compact network of cheap and easy transportation. As traction companies proliferated, they vied with one another in their rolling stock, their power houses and their car barns, and the various places of resort such as amusement parks which they provided for their customers. The new trolley lines kept the public traveling night and day, on business or pleasure.

Just as millionaires of the period provided fine stables for their horses and carriages, the traction companies built handsome car houses for their trolley cars. Among them, that of the Duquesne Traction Company on Craig Street near Fifth Avenue was especially handsome, since it was located right in the midst of Oakland's residential district. Constructed in 1890 of brick with sandstone trimmings, it was four hundred feet long by a hundred and forty feet wide. It consisted of a long hall, a single open space with a low-pitched roof supported by trusses, and a two-story forebuilding containing offices and the entries for the cars that were stored in the great hall itself.

This hall form, with its simple trussed roof, was one that could be used for almost any purpose, and during the nineteenth century it not infrequently was. Stretched to its widest limits it could be a mill, factory, or train shed; in smaller versions it could be a school, a church, a store, a house, or even a cow shed. It was an all-purpose form and it could be "styled" in any way that pleased the builder. For industrial or commercial buildings throughout the nineteenth century the Romanesque was favoured in the manner either of the earlier Revival or of the adaptation by H. H. Richardson (1838-86),

The Duquesne Garden, c. 1900.

whose highly personal version of the style was enormously popular during the last two decades of the century.

Stylistically, the Duquesne Traction car house was of the Richardsonian Romanesque persuasion, notably in the large sandstone voussoirs of its windows and car portals. There were probably those who thought the structure too stylish for a mere car barn. It did not so remain for long. Toward the end of the century, as it became possible to manufacture artificial ice, a fad for indoor ice skating developed. To accommodate the devotees of the new ice sport, a large ornamental hall of wood and glass called the Casino had been erected in the early 1890s at the entrance of Schenley Park, where the Frick Fine Arts Building [of the University of Pittsburgh] is now. It was agreeably attired stylistically in the new Second Italianate manner, and it might have become an important addition to the Oakland ambience of pleasure. Unfortunately, it burned in December, 1896.

The new ice-skating public was left forlorn, but not for long. Andrew McSwigan, a former newspaperman who had developed a chain of amusement parks for C. L. Magee, the president of Duquesne Traction, had noticed that the Casino and its ice sports had been very popular. After the fire, McSwigan suggested to Magee that the Oakland car barn could be converted into an ice-skating rink. The traction magnate liked the idea and agreed to provide the funds for the transformation, his only stipulation being that the new arena be "a nice place."

It always *was* a nice place; there was nothing cheap or sleazy about it. The Duquesne Garden Company was formed with McSwigan as general manager. The car barn was purchased from the Consolidated Traction Company for two hundred thousand dollars, and another quarter-million dollars was spent converting it into an ice-skating arena. It was named for Magee's largest streetcar operation, the Duquesne Traction Company. Although the Garden of the original title was singular, many of its hosts of customers knew it in the plural — Gardens. I knew the building for most of my life and I have always used "Gardens." Whether it was singular or plural does not much matter, though. For the span of its life, it was always an important element in Pittsburgh's social and cultural life.

It opened as an ice-skating rink and sports arena on January 23, 1899, and was an instant success. Both the arena and the public rooms of the forebuilding had been elaborately decorated. Skating sessions were held three times daily for twenty-five and thirty-five cents, and trick and fancy skaters were brought in as special attractions. Ice skating became so popular that it was not until 1901 that the arena branched out into other types of entertainment. And even to the very end, the ice sport was the nucleus around which all the other activities revolved and thrived. Hockey, a game which had originated in Canada and which had been played at the Casino during its brief career, was introduced at the Garden the night after the grand opening, and it speedily became one of the attractions of the new pleasure place whose skating surface was billed as the world's largest. The Garden's twenty-six thousand square feet of ice exceeded by eight thousand that of the Paris rink — the most extensive up to that time.

It had been discovered that the acoustics of the arena were good, and McSwigan decided to use the arena as a theatre. On April 15, 1901, Wagner's *Tristan und Isolde,* with Schumann-Heink, Ternina, and Eduard de Reszke of the Metropolitan Opera, was presented to a capacity house: an historic event hailed by the *Pittsburgh Press* as "the first real presentation of Grand Opera in Pittsburgh." After the hockey season, the arena was further altered for theatrical performances. In 1902 another touring company from the "Met," including Enrico Caruso, returned to present four days of opera. Victor Herbert gave a series of "pop" concerts, John Philip Sousa gave band concerts, and a local Civic Light Opera performed at the Garden in these early days. Thus a tradition of musical performances at the Oakland Centre was established that even, to some degree, survived the opening of Syria Mosque in 1915. I remember seeing light opera at the Garden in 1926.

The Garden, although it housed a variety of sporting events — marathon racing, boxing, and bowling — remained mostly devoted to ice skating and hockey until it was converted in 1910 to a roller-skating rink. McSwigan left in 1913 to devote full time to Kennywood Park — which incidentally is the only one of these streetcar pleasure enterprises to survive until today. There occurred a fallow period in the history of the Garden which ended in 1915, when hockey and ice skating returned to the arena. Boxing and hockey, particularly, have had a long and vivid history at the Garden, but speaking of the former, I do not have space here to speak of Harry Greb, the Zivics, or Billy Conn, and in regard to the latter I lack the professional knowledge to discuss the merits of those famous teams — the Hornets, the Yellow Jackets, or the Pirates (not the baseball team). Pittsburgh probably did more in the early days of hockey to develop it as a professional sport from its early amateur Canadian beginnings. Certainly, during the 1920s, the Garden flourished as a sports arena.

The Depression of 1929 brought an end to this tumultuous

period of prosperity, and the old sports palace was in financial trouble again. In 1931, it fell under the sheriff's hammer and passed to the Pittsburgh Railways Company, bondholders, for sixty-two thousand dollars. Fortunately, in 1932 John Harris of the famous Pittsburgh theatrical family took over the Garden lease; he renamed it The Gardens. Harris possessed the same energy and expertise that had belonged to Andrew McSwigan, and he devoted all his ability to bringing the Gardens back into the main stream of city life. He developed his own hockey team, the Hornets. He brought the Norwegian ice-skating star Sonja Henie to the Gardens and to fame in 1936. He organized his own show, the Ice Capades, which flourished mightily in the 1940s and early 1950s. He brought in rodeos, water spectacles, tennis exhibitions, and basketball. A brochure designed in a breezy Art Deco style, now preserved at Carnegie Library, lists all manner of ways in which the arena could be and was used during Harris' regime. Adaptive reuse could go no further. Once more, at the end of its career in the early 1950s, the old building was crowded and prosperous.

However, in 1950 the Pittsburgh Railways Company sold the Gardens to a real-estate "combine" that wanted to erect an apartment house on the site. Concurrently, plans were afoot to erect a new Civic Arena on the "cleared" acres of the Lower Hill. Accordingly the Gardens was demolished in 1956, and with it went a large segment of Oakland's social history.

Looking back, it is good to know that Duquesne Garden died, not in ruin and decay, but in a pyrotechnical blaze of glory. In its end was its beginning.

"Jamie's Journal," *The Pittsburgher,* January, 1979.

The Pittsburgh Athletic Association.

"Yet Once More O Ye Laurels"

The other afternoon, as we were contemplating from a downtown window some of the modern buildings which have changed the face of the city, news was brought to us of the passing of Benno Janssen, who died on October fourteenth at Charlottesville, Virginia. On that still afternoon of silver air and failing sun, it struck us forcibly that he who had been perhaps the most facile and talented of Pittsburgh's Eclectic architects of the earlier twentieth century, who had very abundantly and enormously helped to form the architectural image of the city between 1905 and 1940, had in 1964 left the scene finally, just as that image was being subjected to considerable mutation, if not outright destruction.

Two years ago, in spring, we had made a pilgrimage to Charlottesville to pay our respects to the aging architect in the elegant house that he had designed and built for himself near the Farmington Country Club, outside of Charlottesville. It seemed appropriate that Janssen, who was the very mirror of the fashionable architect, should be passing his last years in the rolling country and the green mountains presided over so earnestly by the ghost of the great gentleman-designer Thomas Jefferson.

"Boxwood," the Janssen house, with its etchings and its Chinese jars, seemed a kind of elegant miniature projection of the suave Pittsburgh buildings he designed, as it was a distillation of the architectural and decorative graces of his milieu and his era. There, in Janssen's own sanctum, the "Pittsburgh Room," which was lined with his sketches and memorabilia of his career, the architect in dressing gown and slippers discoursed of his practice in his salad days.

Janssen, in his time, made notable contributions to the visual and functional aspects of the city, and Pittsburgh may well be proud of him. At a later date we wish to speak further of him and his career, but at the moment we will reprint, with slight revisions, an article originally published in *The Charette* in June, 1959. We wrote it as a celebration of his work while he was still living, and we present it again as a tribute to his memory:

One of the most elegant buildings of the later Eclectic period in this city, the Pittsburgh Athletic Association clubhouse, rears its

111

Italianate limestone, its suave columns, amid the gentle architectural anarchy of Oakland. Anything so Venetian, so opulently European and urban, perched in its then-Victorian and suburban context, seemed a trifle improbable at the time it was built, and its glowing, expansive grandeur still puts its more pedestrian neighbours out of countenance. This slightly-amended version of the High Renaissance is Edwardian "fashionable" architecture *par excellence,* and now that it has been recently cleaned it beguiles us anew with its persuasive glamour. Erected in 1909-11 as an integral part of the then-burgeoning Oakland Civic Centre, it was designed in 1908 by the recently-formed firm of Janssen & Abbott, and constitutes one of the earliest and most agreeable products of their atelier.

Clubhouses, which form a fascinating link between the vast democratic impersonality of the modern hotel and the privacy of the individual home, are well represented in Pittsburgh, and they comprise a not-inconsiderable footnote to the history of Eclectic architecture in this area. A building type evolved from the social needs of the rather fluid and rising middle class of the nineteenth century, the club as an institution took several forms, but only one of them is of interest here — the large metropolitan social club. It must be admitted that the P. A. A. has always been more social than athletic, and the title would indicate on the part of its members a pious regard for, rather than an active participation in, athletics. The architectural form favoured at the turn of the century by the designers of these upper-class social centres was very often that of the Italian urban palace of the Renaissance, and the P. A. A. is not among the least-accomplished versions of the general theme.

Organized club life did not begin in Pittsburgh until the 1870s: the new urban prosperity after the Civil War, an increase of social leisure, and a desire to emulate some of the amenities of upper-class English life caused the founding of two important social organizations — the Duquesne Club in 1873 and the Pittsburgh Club in 1879.

The British, in the search for building types to house the new clubs of the early nineteenth century, first made use of the palatial form. Eighteenth-century clubs, which were still rather near to the tavern, employed what was essentially a domestic scale, but the expanding club land of London — Pall Mall and St. James' — desired and got something more spectacular, more expensive. There is still an element of domestic simplicity in Decimus Burton's Athenaeum Club of 1830, but the Traveler's Club, Pall Mall (1829-32), by Sir Charles Barry inaugurated a new epoch in this type of design. As a model the architect had chosen the Florentine Pandolfini Palace

(Raphael, 1530) and he developed the theme in his Reform Club of 1837, which was modeled after the Farnese Palace (Sangallo, 1534) at Rome. The smaller Italian urban palace was thus established for the next hundred years as the proper model for the better social clubs of both England and America. A good American example of the type is the University Club (McKim, Mead & White, 1900) of New York, which owed its general form to the Riccardi Palace (Michelozzo, 1430) at Florence.

The Pittsburgh Club, as a family organization, had felicitously and appropriately established itself on lower Penn Avenue in the former Shoenberger house, a fine example of the Greek Revival town house which had been built in 1847 and which was very unfortunately destroyed in the name of progress a few years ago. The original Romanesque part of the Duquesne Club (Alden & Harlow, 1887) still rather favoured the domestic scale, but later additions radically changed its early character. Both of these structures were located in the downtown district (the latter has remained there), but the focus of Pittsburgh club land shifted to Oakland with the rapid development of the new Civic Centre after 1900. The University Club (MacClure & Spahr, 1905), among the first of the Oakland institutions, was Georgian in style and more or less domestic in character, but after the advent of the P. A. A., clubhouses tended to follow the grand Classical type, as witness the Masonic Temple (also Janssen & Abbott, 1914).

Both these buildings were located in the new "cultural" quarter which F. F. Nicola, an inspired real-estate operator, and his Schenley Farms Land Co. were busily promoting. The Nicola contribution to our urban development was highly important, and the P. A. A. building is at once a glittering facet and a symbol of the whole project.

The P. A. A. was founded in 1908 by a group of younger well-established business men (whose average age was forty) with the purpose of setting up a social centre for themselves and (to a lesser degree) for their families. It did not differ from similar establishments already functioning in other cities and, like them, it sponsored a variety of athletic activities and other recreational facilities for the membership. Among the founders were the brothers Nicola, and it was hardly fortuitous that when a site was being sought for the new clubhouse, the lot chosen should be located in their "development" at Grant (now Bigelow) Boulevard and Fifth Avenue.

In November 1908, Janssen & Abbott were appointed to furnish designs, and an organization known as the P. A. A. Land Company was chartered to buy the lot and finance the new structure. The land itself cost $309,000, and the building, exclusive of its furnishings, around $300,000. Construction began in the summer of 1909, but the first contractor defaulted on his contract while the foundations were being put in, and it was the firm of Henry Shenk which finished the work. The steel frame, by now a *sine qua non* of all large public buildings, was contracted for by the Brown Ketchum Company of Indianapolis. On April 25, 1911, the new clubhouse, in all its sleek Edwardian glory, was opened for use at a large public reception. No additions were made to the club until 1921, when the P. A. A. purchased the old University Club for its own use and connected the two structures by passageways.

This annex was demolished, and in 1962 new club rooms and a car-park were erected on its site.

The Janssen & Abbott partnership was probably the most important architectural firm of its time in Pittsburgh and it took over the priority of place which Alden & Harlow had so long enjoyed, much as the light, deft Edwardian graces of style which it sponsored replaced the heavier, more bourgeois solemnities of its predecessor in public esteem. The American architect, as well as his public, was becoming more sophisticated, and the now-pervasive influence of French training argued a correspondingly high level of execution. As archaeological knowledge of the past increased, correctitude of style became an important factor in early twentieth-century practice, but a *soignée* elegance and refinement of treatment were also desiderata. The best products of the 1900-14 period have a stylistic correctness and an exuberant yet delicate grace which is quite unmistakeable.

Benno Janssen, an architect of considerable talent if not of genius, was eminently qualified to be the fashionable architect of the day, the accomplished purveyor of taste and elegance, and he was undoubtedly responsible for the general character of the firm's work. He was born in St. Louis, Missouri, in 1874, and studied at the University of Kansas for two years. In 1899, he went to Boston, where he worked for Shepley, Rutan & Coolidge, and later for the firm of Parker & Thomas; at this time he also attended night classes in architecture under a professor from M. I. T. Like many aspiring young architects of the period he studied for two years in Paris (1902-04) and then returned to Boston. He came to Pittsburgh in 1905 to work for MacClure & Spahr, but his stay with them was brief, and late in 1906 he formed a partnership with another young architect, Franklin Abbott, the son of a Pittsburgh banker.

Abbott retired from the partnership later, and Janssen continued the practice under his own name until 1922, when the firm of Janssen & Cocken was formed. William York Cocken, who died in 1958, had been head draughtsman in the office, and it was he who continued the business under his name after Janssen's retirement in 1939. Cocken was also a competent practitioner in the Eclectic field, but after the Second World War the work of the office became progressively more Modern to suit the changing taste of the times.

The monumental Classical building was from the very beginning the most salient aspect of the firm's *oeuvre,* and it continued to be as long as Janssen was associated with it. In 1908, the young partners won the competition for the now demolished Y. W. C. A. Building on Chatham Street — a handsome Italianate-Georgian structure which foreshadowed the stylish Janssenesque graces to come. Their real passport to fashionable favour in Pittsburgh was, however, the P. A. A. clubhouse, and it prepared the way for other large commissions — the Corinthian, but much less inspired, Masonic Temple already mentioned and the late Edwardian-Italianate William Penn Hotel (1914-16), which with its addition (1927-28, Janssen & Cocken) was the largest Pittsburgh structure for which Janssen was responsible. The last of these great buildings with which Janssen was associated was the second Mellon Institute (also Janssen & Cocken, 1933-36), whose stark, stripped Classical exterior and unadorned Ionic order prefigure the near triumph of Modernism.

Over the years, the office also executed a considerable amount of residential work, much of it in the Romantic English Picturesque

"La Tourelle," the house of Edgar J. Kaufmann, Janssen & Cocken.

tradition, especially [of] the country house school of Sir Edwin Lutyens and his contemporaries. These last local manifestations of the Picturesque mode have great charm, even if one feels that they might more appropriately adorn the landscape of a fairy tale or a dream. From the Franklin Abbott residence of 1908 (now demolished) to the E. J. Kaufmann house (1924) and the Long Vue Country Club (1922) Janssen managed to ring, very suavely and competently, all the changes on the Picturesque theme.

Montgomery Schuyler, that most perspicacious of American turn-of-the-century critics, claimed in 1911 that the P. A. A. was perhaps the architectural lion of its day in Pittsburgh. The full-blown High Renaissance manner was not exactly commonplace in the city, and the glamour of this boldly-designed and highly-ornamented composition was a matter for contemporary remark; at any rate, it caused as much comment as had Alden & Harlow's equally rich Carnegie Music Hall foyer in 1907.

Although the design of the P. A. A. owes something to the Ecole des Beaux-Arts, it is most heavily in tribute to Venice. Following Venetian palatial precedent (where, however, only one story to an order was usual), the architect has used two superimposed Corinthian orders, the lower of two stories and the upper of three. The first order, with its arched windows and unfluted pilasters, is heavier and more boldly detailed than the second, which is somewhat lighter in treatment. A further Italianate touch was the addition of a low-pitched roof of tiles, which provides the necessary foil to the abundant ornament below. The exterior was "inspired" (a word essential to the Eclectic vocabulary) by the front of the Venetian Grimiani Palace (Sanmicheli, 1549), and the frieze of Sansovino's Library of St. Mark (1536) provided the model for the wide band of cupids and garlands that adorns the Pittsburgh cornice. One is not conscious, however, of any laborious copying, and the design, albeit an adaptation, a rewording as it were, of some grand Classical passages, has not suffered noticeably in translation.

Schuyler was not uncritical of the general composition, although he praised its palatial quality and the handsomeness of its execution. We may still echo his doubts. Is the *ordonnance* altogether just, are there monotonies and awkwardnesses in the disposition of the elements? The two divisions are possibly a little too similar in treatment, and the lower might have been even more simply handled, leaving the main order for the upper section. The horizontal dimension of the composition is however its main interest, and one must conclude that the architect has handled that element very ably and elegantly, if not according to the strictest Classical canons. In the face of such glowing architectural exuberance these minor criticisms are silenced. The general effect is that of a very handsome Renaissance jewel casket, altogether an affair of nobility or state, expressed in architectural terms.

It is interesting that the facade is composed of both stone and terra-cotta elements, but the two have been so subtly combined that the composition seems to be a homogenous whole. The first two decades of the twentieth century comprise the great age of terra-cotta construction and ornament, and Janssen used it effectively on his addition to the Kaufmann Department Store (c. 1912) and also on the William Penn Hotel.

Possibly Janssen & Cocken's remodeling of the nearby Twentieth Century Club (1929-30) is more Classically correct, more "tasteful," but it entirely lacks the exuberance, monumentality and vigour of our building. Despite its faults the P. A. A. ranks with the best Classical work in Pittsburgh, and it compares very well with other American work of the time.

The rear of the building — so eminently the spot where Eclectic buildings notably fail (who does not remember the "Mary Ann" back?) — has been rather well handled. The stone facades of the building are returned for a couple of bays at each side, but in the centre of the rear elevation a great mass of utilitarian brick projects above the roof line. It is as if the functions of the twentieth-century building were erupting through the top of the sixteenth-century jewel casket, but the eruption is not one of violence. One feels that the architect might have made more of so salient a feature, but failing that, this necessary adjunct is at least unobtrusive.

The Venetian envelope of the building is so eminently appropriate, so representative of the hopes of the men who built it, that it seems unlikely that the architect's choice of style could have been merely fortuitous. Historically, this High Renaissance elegance reflects the Venetian State at the highest point of its power as it also, in a later context, serves to exemplify the apogee of Edwardian prosperity and the noonday of the capitalist world. The P. A. A.'s resplendent facade bespeaks a certain confidence and pride; suggests, one might almost say, a sense of glory which could be either Venetian or Edwardian. The structure is variously symbolic, but it speaks above all of the maturity of the human body, the summer of the flesh, and that moment in the physical cycle of man just before the wrinkles form and the muscles lose their tone. Here, ripeness is all. This glowing stone represents the state toward which the athlete and the younger business man aspired, and it is perhaps the supreme achievement of the architects that they have caught the prime moment and preserved it beyond mutability or decay.

The interior of the building is not of equal interest to the opulent facade, although the outer Italian elegance has, as it were, flowed into the main lobby, encrusting the ceiling and walls with graceful Cinquecento ornament. The handsome coffered ceiling and the Caen stone fireplace, with its arabesques and escutcheons, are obviously pattern-book detail, but it is all well disposed and suavely executed.

Aside from the purely masculine roast-beef-coloured Tudor Bar, with its frowning barrel vault, the other rooms display a quiet club-like good taste.

A word must be said about the swimming pool on the third floor which, with its marble and its green and white terra-cotta decorations, is a Beaux-Arts version of imperial Rome. The Edwardian period was appropriately the era that recovered most extensively the old Roman amenities of bathing, and this pool, which compares in elaboration of treatment with Grosvenor Atterbury's slightly earlier and now-demolished Pittsburgh Natatorium, is a representative "period piece."

The P. A. A. is still a functioning unit in the Oakland Civic Centre, and it is to be hoped that it will continue its career as a handsome clubhouse, particularly since the fate of Janssen & Abbott's tower addition to the Fort Pitt Hotel (1909-11) is uncertain.[1] In the basement of the hotel is the Norse Room (designed by John Dee Wareham), a remarkable period piece entirely decorated with Rookwood tiles. Perhaps the hotel can be saved, but certainly the Club must be preserved to the city as an architectural and social document of the first importance.

But meanwhile the ripe, intricate grace of those Corinthian columns, the festive abundance of its marching garlands, recall to us the bloom on the peach, the flush and fullness of the summer flower, and we are persuaded to remember the glamour of those vanished Augusts — the Venetian sixteenth century and the last bright days before 1914. These elegant facades are, above all, a perpetual reminder of the noontide of life. If the building is not eternal, it suggests eternity, and that is surely the prime purpose of a work of art.

[1] It was demolished in 1967.

The Charette, February, 1965.

On the Terrace II

The Roof of the University Club
in Pittsburgh

Recently, I spoke of the general paucity of true European terraces in Pittsburgh areas where one could drink, or dine, or take tea and talk in those fine open spaces between a building and its garden or its grounds. In this civilized middle ground, one can appreciate the near architecture or the air. Since there is no roof above, the sky above can become a lake of clouds by day, or a map of stars by night. The true or *good* terrace can have the enclosure or the intimacy of a room, but it also should have a limitless sense of space. One is seated in a comfortable chair, there are roses and silver on the table. It is summer; the air is soft . . . Beyond, beyond, there is a view . . . It is of a view that I wish to speak now, of a terrace and towers and a summer evening. If the number of my Pittsburgh terraces has been small, the roof of the University Club would be sufficient to make up a much larger sum. In the last few years, at least, I have, because of the Club roof, had much less cause to lament the local lack of terraces. At the Club I can combine two of my favourite pursuits — *al fresco* social life and the appreciation of the architecture of Oakland.

In January, it is sweet and salutary to speak of summer, and terraces can only be fully enjoyed in summer. In winter the Club roof is, of course, off limits, although I have sometimes entertained the fancy of an elegantly-appointed luncheon party in the snow with everyone in woollen gloves and furs. Surely, with lots of hot coffee in silver pots, one could have as good talk as one could in summer. Well, one can entertain the idea as a fantasy.

Now I would evoke, in January, a summer evening on the University Club roof, and by that I mean the part of its roof that covers the large, high dining room that occupies a separate wing at the front of the building. The Club was constructed in 1923 on Oakland's Natalie Street, which is now University Place. Henry Hornbostel, who designed it, was one of the most talented as well as the most sophisticated and dramatic of Pittsburgh's early twentieth-century architects, and it is probably due to him that we have the terrace with its elaborate cast-iron balustrade, small evergreens in tubs, and, in summer, its flower boxes filled with vari-coloured heliotropes and petunias. The roof used to be floored with red tiles, but this covering began to leak into the dining room below and had to be renewed a couple of years ago. The new waterproofed mixture is coloured green to simulate grass, but I preferred the tiles.

If one arrives early in the evening one can get a good seat at one of the tables near the edge of the raised portion of the roof, just above the walk which is bounded by the balustrade. Next to my chair, the red, white, and purple petunias, those sunset harlequins in all their August flamboyance, spill their sweet slumbrous fragrance into the waiting air.

At eye level one looks out into clouds of leaves, all a little dull and dusty from the long summer hours — clouds of leaves, the great plumage of the plane trees planted so long ago by Franklin Nicola's planners who laid out the Schenley Farms area in the 'Nineties. The planes, once considered so resistant to urban air pollution, have not always survived, and in this case the arboreal frieze is beginning to thin. However, there is enough left to persuade one to believe that one is looking out from a superior tree house, a faintly rustling palace of leaves.

It is seven o'clock, the air is still, there is no breeze; the sun, now all fire, is descending toward the dark green escarpment of Herron Hill. I feel its heat on my back, but even with my sun glasses I do not care to face its burning gaze. I order a martini; its sharp, icy pallor is welcome in the high heat. The passionate abandon of the petunias is at once vaguely disquieting and sensually amusing. I gaze into the intricate leaf spaces before me. I have come here solely to look at the wide sky and its light. And above all, to watch as intently as possible the effect of that light on the buildings of Oakland's cultural centre. I think that there is no more marvelous summer display in the city.

Above the great frieze of green leaves the buildings seem to rise like fabulous palaces, floating serenely on the shifting surface of that magic sea. "Brightnesse falls from the air . . ." The nearest structure is the Soldiers' and Sailors' Memorial Hall, an earlier work of Hornbostel's begun in 1908 and finished in 1910. The University Club is calmer, quieter, more understated, a discreet exercise in good taste, but the Soldiers' Hall, designed in the full tide of the American Beaux-Arts manner, is huge, ornate, passionately exuberant, the somewhat-overblown flower of American imperial patriotism of the early twentieth century. Historically it is much in debt to Classical sources, particularly in its form to the Mausoleum of Halicarnassus, one of the Seven Wonders of the Ancient World.

The Soldiers' and Sailors' Memorial from the University Club roof terrace.

Right now, at sunset, the full tide of the westering sun bathes it in an almost-electric luminance, and its great roof glows in white and gold. A frieze of carved eagles below the square roof seem to shout their approval of American enterprise, the glory of American triumphant arms. In our post-Vietnam day such a building could not possibly be constructed, even if an architect could be found to design it or craftsmen to carve the eagles. Perhaps it is best seen at sunset with a rueful if not a jaundiced eye; it is nice to have it around as a reminder of an earlier and more confident day.

Straight ahead, through a gap in the leafy palace, can be seen the strange, if familiar, facade of the Syria Mosque, the huge Masonic auditorium erected in 1915. Stylistically, it is a curious mixture of

Byzantine and Arabic elements, and its striped, two-toned brown brick walls remind one curiously of both Hagia Sophia, the great sixth-century church at Constantinople, and a large Viennese mocha torte. The confectionery note is much assisted by the frieze of Arabic script that serves as the structure's cornice — it looks rather like spidery white icing. Above the low Byzantine saucer dome projects, aggressively, a flag standard topped by a star and a crescent.

The sunset light is kind to the Mosque, gilding its chocolate flanks and making it seem almost edible. Above the dome the sky in the east, as the sun sinks, has turned to a pale aquamarine colour, against which is revealed in sharp relief the needle silhouette of the *flèche,* or arrow spire, of the First Baptist Church, designed by Bertram G. Goodhue and built in 1909-11. The soaring grace of the spire proclaims that this is the finest Gothic Revival structure in Pittsburgh. The fragile point is topped by a cross, which, as the evening deepens, is lit by electric light. The near juxtaposition of the Star and Crescent with the sparkling Cross, is, in the calm evening air of Oakland, to say the least, startling.

Beyond the Mosque, the tile roof, the suave Classical cornice, and the coupled columns of the Pittsburgh Athletic Association recall the sixteenth-century Grimiani Palace at Venice but, persuasive as is the vision, this is not Venetian architecture but the best Renaissance Revival in Pittsburgh. However, the projecting upper story of the clubhouse, designed by Janssen & Abbott and erected also in 1909-11, can do little more than hint at the beauty of the whole, and the P. A. A. is one of the undoubted beauties of Pittsburgh architecture.

Beyond the clubhouse roof projects another *flèche,* this one the crowning feature of Charles Klauder's Heinz Chapel of 1934-37 on the University of Pittsburgh campus. Seeing two *flèches* in one architectural view is surely unusual, but when one considers the paucity of spires in modern architecture, this duplication can only be counted a blessing.

The great glory of the view from the University Club terrace is that great tower known as the Cathedral of Learning, and its appearance at sunset is so splendid that it must have a radio discourse all to itself.

Until then we will leave the superb Eclectic architectural symphony of Oakland as revealed in the last rosey rays of the sun. As the sunset fades and the dusk on the terrace deepens, we descend to dinner in the dining room.

Radio script for WQED-FM, mid-1970s.

Terrace Life in Pittsburgh III
The Cathedral of Learning from the University Club Roof

Once more, in this monumentally cold and snow-bound winter of 1978, I return again to *al fresco* life in Pittsburgh, to memories of existence in the warm days and hours of summer. Open-air activities in the winter months are possible, for the most part, only for the young; for the aging, lacking southern latitudes, it is necessary, in enforced idleness, to remember the delights of summer or spring. There was a song that in my unheeding youth, I used to sing: *"O doux printemps d'autrefois, vertes saisons . . ."* that returns now to haunt me . . . *"Vous avez fui pour toujours . . ."* How effortlessly the words used to glide outward from my throat to the listening walls and whatever receptive ears there were. It is ironic that in the present day, when there might easily be more listeners, my voice is not what it was.

But as I have said, terraces are not what they were either, and only the University Club preserves the one remaining and shining example of that vanished amenity. Previously, I have spoken of viewing in summer the Eclectic architectural symphony of Oakland from the roof garden, but I largely exempted from my discourse the special qualities of the Cathedral of Learning as the great visual experience from this particular viewpoint. Although the appearance of that great tower at sunset has continued, even as late as last summer, to enthrall me, I find references to it in my journals in the late 1960s and the early 1970s. Of the latter group, I find two rather extended entries one of August 19, 1972 and one, much more complete, of August 29, 1976. Suitably amended and edited, I shall present here the private entries for public hearing as actual quotations. Thus we will have on the air August in February, the two extremes of the year as well as the great wizard of Oakland, in constantly-changing coloured robes. We begin:

Saturday, August 19, 1972: In the evening to the University Club for drinks on the terrace. Despite the early greyness and humid heat of the day, the sky was superbly still and clear. At eight o'clock the light on the Cathedral of Learning was utterly splendid — golden, golden. Surely, this great reaching height is not only a sorcerer, but also a sorcerer's staff — Oh, Aaron's Rod — the golden rod of these urban fields and these days. How satisfying the tapering flanks,

123

The Cathedral of Learning.

rendered so suave and flowing in the evening glow — the ornamental turrets at the corners of the shaft with their dark reticulations of shadow are really masterpieces of intricate design. Now as the light fails, and it fails a little earlier in August than it did in June, the tower fades to a dull grey, waiting for its recession into night.

In the east the sky is the purest muted mother of pearl. All the while, above the old Schenley Apartments, the ghost of the moon has become more and more apparent. Gradually it has disappeared behind the Club, and its evolving effulgence is palely reflected on the Cathedral, which seems more than ever like an enchanter's wand. Right now — at 8:30 — the light is the sheerest enchantment. Above Herron Hill, the sky is an unearthly, frozen lemon-colour, and over against it the great tower rises against a field of luminous gun metal-coloured light. From minute to minute the light changes, deepens into dusk. Magic!

"What voice can my invention find to say?" But even when I am moved almost beyond words, and it's getting too dark to write in my notebook, I can hear at a near table the voice of a suburban matron recounting her misadventures with a recalcitrant garage door in Upper St. Clair, or a male voice holding forth on the state of the stock market . . . I smile, I savour the last drops of my martini. I have no car, and no garage door, I am destitute of stocks, but I have the portals of the night and the tower.

Sunday, August 29, 1976: On the terrace of the University Club, a curiously autumnal evening, very cool, and clear, clear, *clear.* . . . Tonight, under the strong light from the west, the Cathedral of Learning has gone through its colour-changing act as only it can. When I arrived about 6:30 it was a brilliant white-grey, then under cover of a few drifting clouds, mutations of grey and pearl were visible. Now, at 7:00, the entire building is bathed in a brilliant lemon-yellow radiance . . . . The clouds drifting behind it are white and fleecy with grey undersides . . . . A jet glides past with all the clarity of its construction exposed. I have noticed that the colours of the tower are most intense when they are about to change. Due to cloud cover, the upper part of the shaft is in shadow, while another wave of colour seems to mount from the base — the yellow now becomes more brilliant, verging on orange. This mutation lasts only for a moment; as the clouds shift above, the tower now glows dimly brown and a dull apricot. Just as abruptly this phase disappears as the light shifts fabulously, this time from top to bottom to emerge once more as a warm orange-pumpkin colour. It is interesting that the *flèche* of the neighbouring Heinz Chapel has turned to an intriguing green-brown shade . . . . Now one cloud, also pumpkin-coloured, drifts slowly toward the top of the shaft as if to merge with it. The sky behind has faded to a pure aquamarine and against it the great one, still glowing orange, looks almost explosive. . . .

Vaguely, I am reminded of the American dancer Loïe Fuller, who, at the turn of the century, danced with swirling veils under vari-coloured spotlights. And isn't the Cathedral in its own solemn way my dancer of the sunset hour, my prince of the multi-coloured dusk?

Slowly the orange Cathedral faded once more to a warm brown. Since I had watched it so many times before, I knew that, if conditions were right at this sunset, it was about to enter upon its greatest and most momentous colour phase. Near the tower a few Dali-esque Surrealist clouds seemed to be waiting as I waited. Before me, the plane tree tops from which the tower so majestically ascended clustered in agitated worship at this vesperal hour.

At this crucial moment, a rather inebriated middle-aged man came up to me and began to speak weavingly about the view. Fortunately, he wandered away just as the tower started to change colour again. Its superb rose colour seemed to exude from the stone itself until the whole tower glowed like a still flame. I had seen it all rosey before, but never so fully, so intensely. It seemed to vibrate and monumentally to pulsate with some strange life of its own. All the familiar Gothic detailing was muted and subdued, and yet part of that marvelous illumination — the tall tower burned for a moment like a gigantic furnace. Against the aquamarine sky, a group of attendant Baroque clouds, of the same rosey hue but with violet undersides, assisted like choiring hosts in the great drama. All fiery, the sky-reaching tower was no longer a sorcerer but a God, beyond our power to conceive, beyond mortality.

Slowly, slowly, inexorably, as I watched and as dusk advanced, the great tower began to become shadowy at the base, as the rose still wonderfully bloomed at the top. Gradually the light failed all up that glowing shaft — the rose sweetly and ineluctably retreated. I was reminded of some lines of the poet "H.E.": "All comes and goes. The rose blossoms and fades away . . . the rose sleeps into grey."

As the tower retreats grandly into night the great lights, like huge eyes, flash out at its top and once again it becomes the familiar nocturnal sorcerer. The floodlights now bathe the facade of the Soldiers' Hall in white radiance. The leaves of the plane trees rustle companionably. Nocturnal Oakland assumes its usual appearance. But on another evening and at another sunset, the great tower will become a God — hopefully when I can see it. But even that doesn't matter. It will always be there — the splendid harlequin sunset God . . . O Thou . . .

Radio script for WQED-FM, 1978.

At the University Club:
a View of Oakland in Winter

In my last terrace discourse, I was speaking of a summer evening view from the roof of the University Club. In my valedictory sentence, I said that I descended to the dining room, which is just under the roof, for dinner. I did, and behold — in *this* discourse, it is winter. In the realm of the imagination, on the plane of fancy, such transitions are easy. Here exact chronologies are meaningless.

This juxtaposition of winter and summer is now, however, entirely capricious. The other evening I went into the dining room, and by chance was seated just beneath the spot where, last summer, I had watched with such fascination, at sunset, the architectural frieze of Oakland. Having heard my summer discourse on the radio only the day before, I was startled to find myself looking at the exact duplicate of the terrace view, *now*, at night, and under snow. I was reminded of Alice (she of Wonderland) and her sensations as she was falling down the rabbit hole. Wildly, there also flashed through my mind a line from Hart Crane: " 'Til elevators drop us from our day ..."

The dining room beneath the roof is quite large and lofty, and it is adorned with delicately Adamesque ornament and lit by electric sconces and large chandeliers designed by the architect Henry Hornbostel. I was seated by one of the great arched Late Georgian windows, which have glazing bars but with panes large enough that the view was little impeded; in fact the muntins added a piquant sense of antiquity to the dark perspective outside. Here, one was forced to concentrate intensely on the presented visual segment, because this picture lacked the wide spaciousness of that viewed from the terrace. "Picture" is truly the proper word here, because it was so definitely framed by the wonderful arch of the window.

The "picture" was also partly hidden by long, white muslin curtains. Now when I gazed upon the brilliantly-lit facade of the Soldiers' and Sailors' Memorial Hall, I felt as if I were lifting a veil or pulling aside a proscenium curtain. On my table was a shaded candle, and others glowed palely throughout the room. I imagined that these were merely eighteenth-century footlights for my view. The hour was in essence theatrical. Could this *mise en scène* have been what is now called "dinner-theatre"?

I ordered a pleasant soup, meat, and wine. I ate, I drank, but the view was all-absorbing. Its dark poetry seized me, and I moved into it. It was well that I was alone. It would have been difficult to sustain a conversation under the circumstances.

Framed in the presiding arch were the buildings of my erstwhile summer tableau, the Soldiers' Hall, the Syria Mosque, and the Pittsburgh Athletic Clubhouse. Not visible were the *flèches,* the needle spires, of the Baptist Church and the Heinz Chapel, but the Cathedral of Learning, that great robed and tenebrous sorcerer, looming, dark, with blazing eyes presided momentously at one side of the view. The Student Union of the University of Pittsburgh, the erstwhile and much-lamented Schenley Hotel, haunted the vision from the right like a forlorn ghost, and engendered in my mind the wisps of glorious memories.

Extending the illusion of the old proscenium stage, the great plane trees of Frank Nicola's cultural centre, which in summer spread their leafy heads above the terrace, were now seen, lower down and in winter, as bare trunks and branches, looking like canvas flats in a late nineteenth-century stage setting. The brilliant white flare of the flood-lights that illumined the facade of the Soldiers' Hall washed the scene of all colour save black, white, and an infinitude of greys. Light and shadow here were the chief elements in a definitely monochrome composition — the brilliant colours of the summer sunset were now quite gone. The difference in the separate views is that between a pyrotechnical Victorian landscape painting and one of those "artistic" modern photographs that used to turn up in camera annuals of the 1930s.

Here was the still, nocturnal scene, bathed in a luminous calm, which exuded a cold that could almost be felt. January, 1978, had been a month of monumental snow storms, but the snow of this view was that of one of the early premonitory tempests, in which just enough snow fell to redefine the cityscape in winter terms and not overwhelm it — which happened later in the month.

Beyond the pale, blotched trunks of the plane trees stretched the long, white blanket of the Soldiers' Hall lawn. Here one could see the neo-Baroque artistry of Henry Hornbostel in placing the Hall far back at the end of a slowly-rising lot. From my window I watched, as from a theatre stage box, the carved intricacy of Roman-American patriotic display — all the military symbolism muffled by snow. The seated statue of Fame over the main entrance wore a puff of white on her head like an eighteenth-century powdered wig. The heroic figures of a soldier and a sailor that stand on either side of the portal, with their snowy accoutrements, seemed to be defending the Hall against phantom enemies. Would those wintry ghosts advance up the long slope past the half-buried Civil War cannon and the forgotten sun dial? The drama was here a dream.

Not many people were abroad in this frozen scene. A group of muffled and bearded students moved up the powdery pavement of University Place, under the wavering shadows of the plane-tree branches, all of which were edged with white. A girl and a young man in jeans and quilted jackets, their shadows black, in the white light ran up the stepped walk in front of the Hall toward Syria Mosque, although there seemed to be nothing doing at the latter on this wintry night. The Mosque looked rather like a deserted Byzantine barge, foundering in a sea of snow, with only a few riding lights visible. The spidery white Arabic inscriptions at the cornice seemed to echo the snowy tracery of the trees. The people disappeared, and nothing was visible of their passage save their footsteps in the snow.

Further down toward Fifth Avenue, the elegant side elevation of the Pittsburgh Athletic Association glowed in the reflection of the Hall floodlights. From the lower level, and freed from the screen of summer leaves, one can see the architectural composition in all its formality and its purity. The tall windows, the Corinthian pilasters, the garlands, and the reliefs of athletes in the bright light had a sharp clarity that they do not have even by day — and the building looked, from my window, like a Renaissance palace in a Piranesi engraving.

Since it was Saturday night much of the Cathedral of Learning was dark, a great hooded presence, haunted, mysterious, with the great wizard eyes blazing down from the top of the tower, sinister beams revealing carved buttresses and shadowy Gothic arches. The snowy lawns at its base seemed at this distance undisturbed.

Dinner over, I watched the diners, who also dance, circling about in the candlelight. My friend Geoff stopped by my table for a moment to tell me that the night before, when the snow had just fallen, he had looked out of one of the great windows and he had wanted to write a poem. Ah, winter nights do conduce to poetry, even as the nights of spring and summer; and possibly I have written mine here.

As I left the dining room, on my way home, there was in the upper stairhall a large painting by Ciardi — a Venetian lagoon framed by a great arch. The painted sky and sea on the canvas seemed dark and mysterious, but the winter night before me, as I walked out into it, was wonderful and magical. A new visual adventure, the walk home, lay before me.

Radio script for WQED-FM, 1978.

The main corridor in the City-County Building.

Henry Hornbostel (1867-1961)
A Retrospect and a Tribute

To the amateur of the past, the talented men of yesterday will seem a race of giants, and the subtle transmutations of death will cause all memorable persons to seem a little larger than they were in life. In the case of Henry Hornbostel we may justifiably indulge such a romantic after-view, for he fitted the image of the active and colourful artist-architect of the pre-Madison Avenue era of American public life. His death, which occurred in Melbourne Beach, Florida on December fourteenth last, not only put a period to his long and productive life of ninety-four years but it also signaled the vanishing of an earlier, more individualistic, more various era of Pittsburgh's architectural history.

Among the ingredients which go to make up a good architect, a sense of drama is not the least, and Hornbostel, both as artist and public person, acted his part with much vitality and *éclat*. By no means a great design innovator, he did handle with ease, elegance, and a large and masculine originality the standard Beaux-Arts formulae of his time. A forceful and colourful character in his own right, his buildings have both style and guts. Some years before his death he had already become a legend among the members of his own profession as well as the general public. Legends fade, but Pittsburgh, which was the chief theatre of his architectural activity, still possesses the many buildings he designed.

Born in Brooklyn, New York, in 1867, he narrowly missed being apprenticed to a silk merchant because of his inordinate love of colourful neckware — which trait remained with him all his life. His first encounter with architectural practice appears to have occurred in the office of Lemos & Cordes of New York, where he worked summers before his graduation from Columbia University in 1891; in 1890 he had assisted in the studio of Wood & Palmer, a firm he was later to join as a partner. Between 1893 and 1897 he studied at the Ecole des Beaux-Arts in Paris, which was then considered an indispensable part of an architect's education. After his return from Europe in 1897, he became a member of the faculty of the Department of Architecture at Columbia, where he remained until 1903. During these six years he worked at times as a draughtsman for Stan-

131

ford White, and for Carrere & Hastings, who were preparing designs for the Buffalo Exposition of 1901. After he set up for himself as an architect, he was at various times a partner in the firms of Howell, Stokes & Hornbostel; Wood, Palmer & Hornbostel; Palmer & Hornbostel; and Palmer, Hornbostel & Jones, before he established his own Pittsburgh office some time in the second decade of this century.

He first came to Pittsburgh in 1904 as a member of the firm of Palmer & Hornbostel (which had won the competition for the campus of the new Carnegie Institute of Technology) to act as supervising architect to the buildings then being erected.[1] From that time until his retirement, he was very closely identified with Tech, both as resident architect and designer of the original campus as well as professor and first head of the Department of Architecture.

His Central Building Bureau or atelier on the Carnegie Tech campus was the focus of much local architectural activity during a particularly active and colourful period of Pittsburgh's construction history. Long a familiar Tech feature, this chalet-like structure (now demolished) was first built early in the 1900s and then moved to the present site of the Hunt Library, where it eventually became the faculty dining room after the Department of Architecture was established in the College of Fine Arts.

Many architects who later became prominent, both locally and nationally, worked there in its hey-day. From this atelier also issued, in stately progression, the plans for the later building on the Tech campus — Margaret Morrison (1906), the Science Buildings (1908-09), Administration Hall (1912), Machinery Hall (1912-13), and the College of Fine Arts (1912-16). Palmer & Hornbostel also designed, in Pittsburgh, the Soldiers' and Sailors' Memorial Hall (1907), the Rodef Shalom Temple (1906), a grand scheme for the University of Pittsburgh (1908) which was only partially executed and, in association with Edward B. Lee, the City-County Building (1916).

Of these, the most grandiloquent and spectacular is the Soldiers' and Sailors' Memorial, an expansive Beaux-Arts *esquisse* in sandstone. An elegant Edwardian version of the Mausoleum of Halicarnassus, it has recently been cleaned and flood-lighted, and the whole composition has taken on a new drama and vitality. Something of the same power and originality of the design is evident in the roughly contemporary Rodef Shalom Temple, whose massive square dome in cream terra cotta and green tile is a forceful reminder of the architect's talent for creating bold structural masses. Equally powerful, the City-County Building's exterior has been almost stripped of Beaux-Arts ornament, and it has something of the stark Classical

Rodef Shalom Temple.

monumentality of French late eighteenth-century "Revolutionary" architecture. Its design anticipates much modern practice, but it is carved essentially of the same rock that produced the neighbouring Allegheny County Court House and Jail. The magnificent great hall of this building is more nearly allied to the Beaux-Arts theme, but its originality and compelling decorative quality are a tribute to the designer's ability.

The masterpiece of this group of buildings is undoubtedly the tower of Carnegie Tech's Machinery Hall, whose dramatic siting and powerful conception still make it the *clou* of the Tech campus.

That the firm of Palmer & Hornbostel also executed large commissions in other parts of the country, notably the architectural adjuncts to New York's Williamsburg, Queensboro, and Hell Gate bridges — the latter especially a wonder in its day (the middle 'Teens of this century) has been unjustifiably forgotten. Hornbostel, with his instinct for creating large and bold forms, was able to work closely and effectively with engineers on this type of commission. The firm was also responsible for several large public buildings, notably city halls for Wilmington, Delaware, and Oakland, California.

After the dissolution of the partnership with Palmer, Hornbostel was concerned with several important Pittsburgh buildings — the Schenley Apartments (1922), the University Club (1924), the Grant Building (1927-29), and the Webster Hall Hotel (1926): the latter in association with Eric Fisher Wood, who also collaborated in the design of the George Westinghouse Memorial (1928) in Schenley Park. In 1925, Hornbostel won the competition for the design of the Warren G. Harding Memorial at Marion, Ohio.

Aside from his active practice and his connection with Carnegie Tech, he filled many other posts during his long career. He was the first chairman of Pittsburgh's Art Commission and served as supervising architect for the Pennsylvania State Planning Commission. As director of Allegheny County Parks from 1935 to 1939, he was instrumental in the development of North and South Parks, and he was as well a moving spirit in the creation of the Allegheny County Fair. He served as a commissioned officer in the First World War, where he gained the title [of Major] by which he was afterward known.

He was married first to Martha Armitage of New York in 1899, and second to Maybelle Weston in 1932. He had two sons, Lloyd of Melbourne Beach and Caleb of New York. The latter is a well-known architect in his own right.

After his retirement, Major Hornbostel moved to his summer home in Connecticut and later to Melbourne Beach, where the second Mrs. Hornbostel died last October.

Aside from the larger creative aspects of his work, he was an exceptionally talented, a persuasive, an almost miraculous, draughtsman, and many of his published drawings testify to his very real pictorial gifts. . . .

The long span of his life has enforced, by default, the silence of his architectural contemporaries, but his former students will recall him as a vivid personality and an inspiring teacher. At his best, he generated a dynamic and creative force in the drafting room, and life there was, from all accounts, far from dull. For a time his architecture was in eclipse, but there are signs now that his buildings are coming to be appreciated at their true worth. We herewith, both architect and layman alike, make our formal valediction to the man, but his buildings, which are the sum of his manhood and his architectural ability, will remain in our streets as his abiding monuments.

[1]Carnegie Institute of Technology is now Carnegie-Mellon University.

The Charette, February, 1962.

Of Temples and Technology[1]
The Drama of Henry Hornbostel's Buildings at Carnegie Institute of Technology, Pittsburgh

The plan of the original Tech complex, however often it may have changed, imposed on its constituent buildings the basic Beaux-Arts formulae of *order and symmetry*. Unlike many American campuses, which in their diversity of styles are very often small conglomerates of our whole national architectural history, the Hornbostel group is remarkably homogeneous without lacking drama. In contrast to the general subdued prose of most of the structures, there are passages of almost poetic fancy (at once belying and emphasizing the Classical framework) that provide abundantly the Romantic note.

To both student and layman, a description of the buildings (especially the College of Fine Arts and Machinery Hall) . . . may reveal the extent to which a Master Plan was here effective, uniting in unusual harmony the humanities and the emerging age of technology.

The College of Fine Arts is, after Machinery Hall, the most striking and original of Hornbostel's buildings on the Tech campus, and possibly the one in which he took the most interest. The central portion was erected in 1911-12 and the two wings in 1915-16, making it in point of time the last of the original complex of structures to be completed. Hornbostel had, in this instance, the problem of designing a school building in which five of the major arts were to be taught, and in which studios, drafting rooms, and rehearsal halls had to be included as well as classrooms. It is, therefore, of interest as a building type, and it has a certain importance as an example of its genre. One can compare it, and certainly not to its disadvantage, with an earlier structure nearby — the Carnegie Institute (Alden & Harlow), in which four functions of a roughly similar cultural nature had to be accommodated. In the College of Fine Arts the student has the advantage of studying in a completely artistic milieu, and the worker in one art may profit by contact with those working in several others. As the Carnegie Tech guidebook of 1915 says, "The predominant architectural motive in the design and construction of this building was the thought that the best way to teach a knowledge and appreciation of art, is to let the student see, in his immediate environment, to what degree of excellence art itself can attain." This building is, again, of brick and terra cotta with some stone detail.

The flat-roofed portion between the two wings suggests most strongly nineteenth-century academies of art, notably in the five niches of the facade; and the labels of the five arts above them symbolize the purpose of the building. The broad simplicity of the wall itself and the arch moldings recall North Italian brick architecture of the Quattrocento, and the disposition of the arches is reminiscent of certain Florentine palace facades, notably Giuliano da Sangallo's Palazzo Gondi and Brunelleschi's Palazzo Parte Guelfa. Elaborate sculptural treatments were planned for the semi-circular niches, each one to represent a separate period of art (Gothic, Greek, Roman, Renaissance, and Moorish). Unfortunately, only one of the bays, that next to the central Roman alcove which serves as the main entrance, was brought near completion. This bay, representing the Renaissance period, was executed by an Italian craftsman, Giammartini, and cost $50,000, a sizeable sum even for that day when period detail was cheaper. It is a pity that the gold of our industrial Maecenas did not extend to the further adornment of the facade and that the uncarven blocks remain as a sort of epitaph for that vanished architectural season. But even to entertain in the imagination those sculptured niches as they might have been warms the heart frozen by too much modernity.

The central, Roman, entry niche, with its Doric severity of treatment, forms an appropriate portal to the neo-Classical majesty of the great entrance hall with its grey limestone walls and its colossal order. The vaults of the hall and the stair, frescoed by J. M. Hewlett, form a sort of celestial atlas of art history, providing for the student a plentitude of reference and example in both word and picture. The floor plans of great buildings inlaid in the marble pavements complete the architectural reference in the most intriguing manner.

A staircase of Baroque amplitude and intention ascends grandly to the upper transverse corridor, whose groined Roman vault continues the largeness of conception and tone in the lower hall. At the top of this stair, the doorway to the Dean's office is monumentally enclosed by a large plaster cast of Puget's portal for the Hôtel de Ville at Toulon, a seventeenth-century sculptural tour de force. The use of this cast is characteristic of the period, since the Eclectic architect, like his Baroque forerunner, did not scruple to use such material, either for decoration or didactic purposes, if it served as a means to an end.

At either end of the building, the transverse corridor ends in

The entrance corridor of the Fine Arts Building.

a raised landing partially screened by columns — all tastefully Louis XVI — and these platforms, which connect with the main staircases, illustrate brilliantly the architect's contrived use of inner space to create an effect of drama. Here one is particularly conscious of the familiar Hornbostel trademark — the constant change of level to vary and enliven his interior composition. This device contributes to the Fine Arts building a variety of vista and point of view at once Classical and Romantic, ordered and yet oblique and irregular. These looming, tenebrous halls are akin to the vaulted visions of Piranesi and Hubert Robert and they suggest, acceptably and with some modern improvements, an imperial and ancient past.

The presence of so much architectural drama prepares one, like a fanfare of trumpets, for the elegance of the theatre, which is the most richly adorned room in the building. Elliptical in shape, it is a more refined, a more chastely decorated version of the oval court which prefaces Margaret Morrison. The rather delicate decorative scheme is basically Louis XVI, rather freely treated and seen through the eyes of 1900. The colour of the place is muted, possibly a little drab, but the lightly-stained oak, the pallors of the leaded glass skylight,[2] the painted panels *en grisaille* contribute particularly to the general effect of subdued, intricate extravagance, the tone of one of Hornbostel's own finely-executed *esquisses*.

The seven painted panels, one of which is the stage curtain itself, illustrate abundantly the chief features of the Egyptian, Assyrian, Greek, Roman, Byzantine, Medieval, and Renaissance stylistic periods. These paintings, executed by J. M. Hewlett, Charles Basing, and A. T. Hewlett of New York, have darkened with age, and they now look like under-ocean visions — the plunder and the ruin of the past submerged in a sea of shadows.[3]

Andrew Carnegie had not wanted a theatre in the building, but Hornbostel, according to his own account, talked him into it. Functionally, the room cannot be considered a good theatre because of its shape, which is rather unusual in theatrical construction. The writers [of these two articles] have been able to find only one prototype of the Carnegie auditorium — an unexecuted design by the French eighteenth-century architect Potain, in which, however, the stage projects widely into the pit. At Carnegie, it is possible to see all of the stage only from the central block of seats, and the problem of general visibility is not assisted by the great cabled columns of oak which flank the proscenium. This rather intimate auditorium — it holds but four hundred people — is definitely in the Renaissance courtly tradition, and possibly it is a little too *grand* for some of the dramatic fare presented there today. A new theatre has been included among the projected amenities of the current Tech building program, and perhaps this is as it should be, but Hornbostel's theatre, which is a beautiful room in its own right, could be used even more advantageously as a concert hall.[4]

Another handsome room in the College of Fine Arts is the library, a noble hall whose bland elegance, even its present, deplorably over-crowded, condition, cannot spoil.

Although it was not part of the original plan, Machinery Hall[5] with its commanding tower, is the *clou*, the dominating vertical element, in the Carnegie complex, accenting precisely but not over-emphatically the spreading horizontals of the general composition. It is also the apex and measure of the talents of its architect. Built in 1912-13, it does rather plentifully show forth the maturity of the Hornbostel manner. The central focus of his competition design had lain in the large towered building[6] at the other end of the campus, and in this latest development it would seem as if the logical climax of the scheme had shifted and flowed down the hill to lodge above the ailanthus trees and the railroad tracks.[7] It did so at some disadvantage to the Classical unity of the overall composition, since the tower tends to "sink" too much when seen from the upper campus. The aggrandizement by its agency of the outer and distant view of the building cannot, however, be doubted or gainsaid. The daring, declamatory mass so boldly sited above the wooded ravine, the fantastic solid silhouette, so Classical and yet so connotative of the new technology, is, after Burnham's rotunda for the Pennsylvania Station, the most fantastic and original Beaux-Arts "bit" in Pittsburgh and one of the best things of its kind in America. Henry Hornbostel never did anything better, and it remains his masterpiece and his monument.

The present Machinery Hall is merely an augmentation of an earlier undistinguished structure, erected in 1906, which housed the school's power plant. Since the building was intended to house also the departments of mechanical and electrical engineering, the central structure which masks the smokestack of the plant is preceded by an entrance wing and flanked by two pavilions. The materials are the familiar brick and terra cotta, and there are large areas of glass to admit the maximum of light into the pavilions. In the placing and composition of the building, Hornbostel has again made use of the Baroque device of the changing level to create a dramatic effect. The first floor is placed below the end of the Mall, so that one approaches the main entrance (which is in the second floor) by an ascending stair-

Machinery (now Hammerschlag) Hall.

case flung over a moat of space. The Quattrocento note is eminently to the fore in the grand Albertian arch, with its superincumbent pediment, under which the stair continues to ascend into a semi-circular niche (a larger version of those on the Fine Arts Building) framing the main portal. High above the Classical roof looms the fantastic rotundity of the tower, with its omnipresent plume of smoke, looking like a giant spool or a celestial dynamo. This tower is the very apotheosis of the machine, and appropriately crowns the building which somehow suggests early fantasy fiction of H. G. Wells.

The very name "Machinery Hall" suggests the great expositions which were so much a part of the nineteenth- and early twentieth-century scene. The Beaux-Arts formula was particularly well adapted to buildings erected for exhibition or show, and Hornbostel's structure would have been equally at home on any fairground of the time. One remembers in this connection that he had made perspective drawings for the Paris Exposition of 1900 while he was in France. Hornbostel's tower is more original than much contemporary exposition architecture, say the Tower of Jewels at the Panama-Pacific Exposition of 1915 in San Francisco.

140

Several studies were made for this tower, and among the working drawings in the Operations Department at Tech is to be found a preliminary study dated May, 1912, which is weak and trivial — resembling the cover of a not particularly good Louis XVI vase. No one can, however, quarrel with the effectiveness of the executed version. The circular portion is firmly placed on the huge square base with the truncated corners (a form used earlier by Hornbostel in the Rodef Shalom Temple in Pittsburgh). On the side of the base, facing Junction Hollow, there is another great Albertian arch which carves a deep niche of shadow under the rather thunderous cornice (heavy detailing was, however, needed here so that the ornament would be seen at a distance). The circular turret most particularly suggests late eighteenth-century practice, and it bears some similarity in form to that of the little Dairy of Marie-Antoinette at Versailles. Should we seek further for stylistic influences, it may be said that the monumental, stark arcade surrounding the brick core shows a close resemblance to the work of the so-called Rationalist architects, Boullée, Ledoux, and Lequeu. Ultimately, the ancestry of circular buildings of this sort is probably to be found in Roman temples like that at Tivoli, and this motive is also to be noted in the landscape background of French Classical painting from Poussin to Hubert Robert. The Tech tower combines, not only in its style but also in its essence, both Romantic and Classical elements common to late French eighteenth-century art.

Here the glamour of the French Classical past consorts admirably with the rigours of the industrial present. If the machinery and the smokestack are hidden, one can only applaud the concealment as necessary and seemly. The Dantean perspectives of the Pittsburgh industrial landscape often need some mitigation, and that provided by Hornbostel has not been the least effective contribution to our municipal scene. Whatever the faults of Machinery Hall may be, the whole conception does have a grandeur and a beauty, a dramatic impact, missing in much modern work, and the fantastic tower seems like a structure encountered in a dream.

Like the shrine at Tivoli, it recalls an altar or a temple. Henry Hornbostel once recollected that, when the Building Committee asked him why he had built this circular temple to house machinery and a smokestack, he told them that "this motive was used in the past as an expression of love." *Amor vincit omnia* — love conquers all — and Aphrodite rises superior to the forge and encloses it.

Near the end of his *Architecture of Humanism*, Geoffrey Scott recalls a deserted church on the Abruzzi coast built on the site of a former shrine to the ancient Goddess of Love, and the name of the building was San Giovanni in Venere — or, St. John lodged with Venus. In the case of Machinery Hall we have an analogous situation — the foundry surrounded by a temple of love, the present within the past, Industry in the embrace of Art, Venus lodged with Vulcan in that just marriage of the masculine and feminine which is the secret of all great art and even of life itself.

In the past, the tower of Machinery Hall has served as the symbol of Carnegie Tech, and it is to be hoped that it will continue to do so in the future, although it is rumoured that a new emblem[8] is to be sought among the projected buildings of the "New Tech." This is not well advised; it is foolish, surely, to push the achievements of the past into the background in the interest of looking forward. We predict no success for this movement inasmuch as Machinery Hall, whether one likes it or not, is difficult to minimize. Howsoever unfashionable, Henry Hornbostel's tower, Technology's Temple of Love, will still dominate the Carnegie campus.

[1]This is the second part of a two-part article. The first part, by Barry B. Hannegan, was published in *The Charette*, September, 1958.

[2]Since replaced or concealed by a bare, utilitarian lighting grid.

[3]In recent years, the painted panels have been removed, save for the stage curtain itself.—JVT

[4]As yet, a new theatre has not been built.—JVT

[5]Now called Hammerschlag Hall.

[6]Not built.

[7]The tracks are in a ravine, Junction Hollow, that separates the campus from the Carnegie Institute.

[8]Not yet achieved.

The Charette, November, 1958.

Henry Hornbostel: the New Brutalism

Hercules is not only known by his foot.
—Sir Thomas Browne

The New Brutalism is not exactly new; it is merely one of the more potent architectural catch phrases current today. Like all catch phrases, it has a certain pertinence to the present time, it speaks of the spirit of the age, but, in this case, of an age that was a long time forming. Always, the phrase in the air is useful, and we use it here advisedly. We merely wish to add our own emendations, some historical echoes to the words already formed.

We wish to examine some bold and insistent architectural forms and details that emerged within the old Classical tradition. The geometric rationalism of some late eighteenth-century French architects foreshadows later utilitarian developments consequent upon the expanding Industrial Revolution of the nineteenth century. Claude-Nicholas Ledoux's design for a salt works or a gun foundry would seem to anticipate the cult of brutalism, of emerging ugliness, which is nowadays considered to be a kind of beauty. Now we have Hercules entire, not merely his foot.

Is the brutal ugly — or beautiful? Is it the harsh word that commands respect — or the soft? Certainly, since the beginning of the Industrial Revolution we have been hearing more of the harsh words, we have contemplated increasingly the heavy muscles of Hercules as the old Apollonian graces of the "styles" (often used until recently to mitigate the rigours of the new forms) vanished and left us face to face with the unadorned brute.

Great works of nineteenth-century engineering have their devotees, and the mill and factory architecture of the same period is beginning to be appreciated. We admire as well today those architects like Frank Furness and William Butterfield who made a cult out of harshness and a virtue out of ugliness.

There were other architects who met the facts of the new industrial age halfway, who enclosed the stark realities in a stylish framework, but who, even so, could make on occasion amazingly frank statements. Among these were Henry Hornbostel (1867-1961). Salient examples of the brute held within bounds may be seen in his work at Carnegie Tech in Pittsburgh, executed between 1905 and 1915.

Hornbostel, who had spent some years at the Ecole des Beaux-Arts just before the turn of the century, never deserted the principles, the practice, or the style of the mentor institution, although he was an architect of considerable originality. He departed from it most widely in certain portions of his Carnegie Tech buildings.

The New York firm of Palmer & Hornbostel had won the competition for Andrew Carnegie's new school of technology in 1904, and Hornbostel, who had come to Pittsburgh to supervise the construction, found himself establishing a new school of architecture at the institution. For the next ten years, as he gradually revised the original scheme for the campus, new elements were added to the design.

The general *parti* of the Tech campus adhered always to the formal principles of Beaux-Arts planning, and since most of the original layout was executed within a decade and under Hornbostel's active direction, it has a remarkable homogeneity. However, it is to certain unadorned elements, factors nakedly expressive of a technological age, that we turn our attention here. How Hornbostel met Hercules is the burden of our essay.

Inasmuch as he had to design buildings for a technical or trade school, the hand of the architect was to a degree forced, but this was a problem common to many architects of the time. New functions had often to be fitted into old forms, and much would depend on the ingenuity of the architect; but to what extent was he willing to let his forms or even his details speak for themselves as evidences of the emerging age?

There was nothing original in Hornbostel's use of Renaissance pavilions, with their tall, round-arched windows and low-pitched roofs. They had become almost a cliché among architects of the Beaux-Arts persuasion, useful for everything from hospitals to pumping stations. They were also useful at Tech, where mechanical trades were to be taught, and they were connected by long, ramped corridors through which machinery and materials could be moved about easily.

In the iron-bound arches and doorways of these corridors, it can be seen that the materials with which some of the students worked had begun not only to encrust but to define the walls. In the pipe balustrades of the staircases a utilitarian article of common use has achieved a new dignity: although, true to his Beaux-Arts training, Hornbostel could not resist finishing them off with more conventional ornamental finials. Even so, in the stark use of these materials no modern architect could have been more forthright or more explicit.

We have already spoken much, in this magazine and elsewhere, of Hornbostel's "centrepiece" for the campus — Machinery (now Hammerschlag) Hall (1912-13), with its great pivotal tower which is a masked smokestack. One wonders what Boullée or Ledoux would have done with such a problem, but it is doubtful if they could have solved it any more dramatically. Here in the great arched structure that boldly surrounds the stack, an eighteenth-century "temple of love" has been abstracted, or metamorphosed, into a piece of machinery. Lifted high above the Beaux-Arts pavilions, it not only continues but transcends the mechanistic theme; it is the focus around which all the other elements of the campus revolve — the very apotheosis of Technology.

Here is also the powerful torso of Hercules, but his muscles are still surrounded by his classical attributes.

In the nearby U.S. Bureau of Mines on Forbes Avenue, which was erected in 1915-16 and which, although not a part of the Carnegie Tech complex, is very closely related to it stylistically, Hornbostel used the tall smokestack again, this time unadorned, but in deference to his Beaux-Arts training he used a pair of them balanced on either side of the Bureau powerhouse (1918).[1] In the general design of the Bureau the pavilions are once more much in evidence, as well as the pipe railings and the stark brick interior surfaces.

This building was also the last to be designed in Hornbostel's campus Building Bureau before it was disbanded late in 1914.

The Hornbostel formula of containment had been used by him in a rather different way in his architectural embellishments for Hell Gate Bridge (built 1915-17, but designed earlier) across a channel of the East River near New York City. This, at the time that it was built, was the longest and heaviest steel-arch bridge ever attempted by the engineers. Here the ponderous leap of the steel trusses is firmly clamped between Hornbostel's granite-covered Classical pavilions. We could not ask for a better illustration of the architect's control of the situation. The powerful brute stretches himself from bank to bank — a long distance over a turbulent channel — but he is firmly kept in his place by the muscular and graceful sentinels at either end.

The most forceful demonstration of Hornbostel's special treatment of the brutalism of his time is to be found in the staircase of Baker Hall (1913-14). Another product of Carnegie Tech's Central Building Bureau, this structure was designed as the terminal feature or head-house of the long range of corridor and pavilions begun in 1905. It was known at first as the Central Building and later as Administration Hall.

Here again we have the pavilion with the low-pitched roof, but since this structure had a special significance, the architect used the triumphal arch motif and the great Albertian arch which he had employed with such success in Machinery Hall. In the latter, however, the architectural drama is external, but at Baker the huge arch merely serves as a preface for the superbly contrived staircase and the descending sweep of the ramped corridor (an eighth of a mile in length) that runs completely through the long range of buildings.

The staircase is a tour de force in the Guastavino tile system as well as a demonstration of Hornbostel's talents as an engineer-architect. In the squared helix of the stairway, the treads are so designed that those on the corners are approximately equal to the others, rather than the small and treacherous wedges usually found in such construction. The graceful, ascending shell contains no beams, only a small amount of steel reinforcing. As D. L. Hendersen said in a recent article in *Carnegie Technical*, "The curving tile under-surfaces are structural, acting as a monolithic unit held rigid at the wall and stiffened on its outer edge by the balustrade." The staircase was constructed by the workmen of the R. Guastavino Company under a special contract.

Rafael Guastavino (1842-1908) was a Catalan architect who adapted a method of tile construction, long known in the western Mediterranean region, into a system which bears his name. His manner of using cohesive tiles is well illustrated in the Carnegie Tech staircase; it was well known and extensively used by architects and builders in this country, where Guastavino had established himself in the early 1880s. His first important commission was that for the Boston Public Library (1888-95), where his structural system was amply illustrated. He formed a company for the manufacture and in-stallation of the tiles, and his son and grandson carried on the business until a few years ago, when it was disbanded. The Guastavino tile system has been replaced today by the concrete shell.

The archives of the company are now in the possession of Pro-fessor George R. Collins of Columbia University, and it was he who first called our attention to the special quality of the Tech staircase.

The Guastavino Company made various types of tile, some of them highly finished, but that used at Baker Hall was a basic con-struction tile, not intended to be seen and usually covered by another more decorative material. The entrance niche at Machinery Hall is partially faced with these tiles, which are a light reddish-brown colour, and the same procedure was followed in the reveals of the entry arch at Baker. They are also used to line the overhanging eaves of the older Tech buildings.

The same tiles constitute the barrel vault of the Baker Hall

The stair of Guastavino tile, Baker Hall.

entrance lobby, which is two stories high and which bears a marked resemblance to the main hall of the Bureau of Mines, except that the vault of the latter is more highly finished. The vaults of the Baker Hall lobby intersect that of the second floor landing of the staircase through an opening that converts the landing into a balcony. The flow of space in this interior is exceptionally interesting.

That flow is climaxed in the slow, forceful, curving ascension of the stair. Here all historical ornament has been eschewed, and all amenity of concealment or covering has been foregone. One might call this organic architecture, since it flows so naturally that it seems almost to have grown in its place. This flight of stairs is pure structure, a naked fact of construction.

One is reminded irresistibly of a flayed human body, with all the muscles exposed to view, and the red-brown colour of the raw tiles themselves reinforces this impression. There is something disquieting and yet fascinating about these almost-bleeding loops of architectural flesh. One is conscious also of a strange consonance between this staircase and those coloured drawings and engravings illustrating old anatomical treatises. In these stairs we can see Hercules without his skin.

But even here, one is conscious of Hornbostel's ameliorating hand in dealing with the raw brutality of his material. The curving arcs of the staircase are so graceful that one is reminded of French eighteenth-century staircases. The architect has also very sensitively made smooth the *inner* side of his balustrade so that the user of the stair will suffer no abrasion, which is more than can be said of the works of some contemporary architects.

The Hercules of Hornbostel, with or without his skin, still testifies to his Classical origin.

---

[1]The U.S. Bureau of Mines has been recently sold to Carnegie-Mellon University.—JVT

The Charette, May, 1966.

Die Heimkehr aus dem Fremde
A Return to the Home Place

Recently there have been running through my mind musical fragments from an opera by Felix Mendelssohn, *Heimkehr aus dem Fremde* — the homecoming from foreign parts. The title always seemed to me to be properly Romantic, suggestive of a rich nineteenth-century nostalgia. At any rate, the title and the bits of music were ornamental to the grey, indifferent summer day, laced with intermittent showers of rain, on which I returned home after a sojourn of some months in a hospital and then a nursing home. Although I have always been fond of motoring, it was a motor car driven by a youthful disciple of speed which struck me down in my own home territory, wafting me hence to one of the great multi-celled hospitals that are so much a part of the landscape of Oakland. Physically so near to my apartment house, the place of my lengthy incarceration seemed to exist in some distant antiseptic world dominated by the sorrow and the malaise of the body. Home, even Pittsburgh itself, might as well have been as far away as Timbuctoo. This huge hive of illness might be anywhere. Remote, it was alien to the everyday round of heart and hand.

Immured in these painful latitudes, I thought of that phrase from John Donne's *Devotions* encountered long ago in my youth and which I had used as a title some years ago for a series of articles on hospitals: "But yet as long as I remain in this great hospital, this sick, this diseaseful world . . ." In those days, when I did not know much about hospitals, Donne's phrase was little more to me than a convenient literary device. Now it became immediate and pertinent. As one gets older, the image of the hospital begins to loom larger on the horizon of the "senior citizen." Until the end of the nineteenth century, the hospital was a slightly sinister building to which one went only *in extremis,* a place of last resort. In the old view, one was born, lived, and died at home. Gradually, the hospital took over the major stations of life, and home became of secondary importance. Nowadays, the hospital is becoming so crowded and expensive that home appears likely to be, once again, the last refuge for the person who is ill or incapacitated.

I have known in hospital many fine people who have done all they could to assist my recovery on more than one occasion, but the

149

hospital remains for me an alien place, a foreign strand which one leaves with a sigh of relief. So, on this grey, peripherally rainy day of early July, I returned in my wheelchair to my own apartment, which I regard as an extension of myself — a kind of summation and mirror of my life. Thus, my homecoming from foreign shores was a return to myself, to that part of me that is at once most private and most public — the rooms, the furniture, the objects that surround me like an exotic hedge or an enchanted wall.

Directly on my entrance, I am aware of the white walls and the thick beige carpet, which even on this grey day seem to glow and shine with welcome. At one side of the living room, bookcases climb toward the ceiling, creating a great tapestry of books with their bright bindings and colourful dust jackets. Here are the volumes that I have collected of late years, making the books a chronicle of my recent intellectual life inasmuch as I gave the library collected in my earlier years to the Pittsburgh History & Landmarks Foundation. I have often said that I do not collect books, they just collect around me. My earlier library had by constant accretion become too large to be quartered privately, so now they exist publicly and are thus used by a number of people. My home library is highly eclectic. In it are to be found modern and Victorian poetry; biographies of unusual people of the nineteenth century; studies of Victorian and modern cities; the *Journals of Sir Walter Scott; Society As I Found It* by Ward McAllister; *Ancient Devotions to the Sacred Heart of Jesus; Fashions in Church Furnishings; Dreamthorpe* by Alexander Smith; the *Letters of Madame de Sévigné; The Hill of Dreams* by Arthur Machen; early detective novels; and the *Facetious Nights of Straparola.* What a patchwork of the hap-hazard and the esoteric! Is this a private collection of books or a shop devoted to high-minded curios and glamourous ephemera? "Never mind," I said to myself on seeing them again, "it is all mine, and I shall have the pleasure of browsing here as I please."

And the pictures gradually unfolding to view on the walls as my questing eye seeks them — the Joseph Pennell drawing given to me long ago by Cousin Lally; the Alinari reproduction of Pisanello's pale drawing of Quattrocento costumes; the Rockwell Kent lithograph with its presentation inscription to John O'Connor; the embroidered pictures of the eighteenth and nineteenth centuries; etchings by Paul Cadmus and Martin Lewis; photographs of my mother in 1904 and my grandfather in 1875; the reproductions of sixteenth-century French album drawings of Anne de Joyeuse, Admiral of France, and the Cardinal de Chatillon; Ruth Covert's oil painting, dark, sinister,

150

and sombre, called *North Atlantic,* in its enormous Victorian gilt frame; the little Russian icon; the fancy Victorian plates painted with orchids and icebergs; the corbel of a young man's head from a Polish castle; the nineteenth-century costume prints — are all on parade to be reexamined once more, all of them so many windows on my past life. How and when had they been acquired? So many reminiscences, all crowded into the first ecstatic minutes of homecoming.

The furniture arranged solemnly around the room seems also to be a chorus of welcome. I have long lived in the compact, modern manner; my apartment is "studio," and therefore my living room is also my bedroom. My sofa, covered with great heaps of multi-coloured cushions, has been for years my bed. It has been an elegant social adjunct whereon I have fashionably conversed, often laughed and sometimes wept, in ecstatic moments; thereon I have made love, and in disillusionment just as passionately quarreled. I have read there much, and even written. My bed has been a long-time companion. I was pleased to get back to it after so many foreign beds. It knows me and has the shape of my body now. Second to it in importance is my wing chair, in the opposite corner of the living room near the front windows. This stately eighteenth-century presence was a newcomer to my possessions when I moved into my present apartment two years ago. As a writer, I do not like to sit at a desk; I prefer to write in my lap, usually on a tablet propped on a large book — an atlas, for instance, makes a good desk. I am not modern and never really learned to use a typewriter. Also in my big chair, I have plenty of light — another pre-requisite for a literary career — from my three windows facing toward the northwest with its clear, cool light, which is also reflected with a still intensity from the white walls of the room. The windows are high and wide with Georgian sashes, each divided by glazing bars into six lights (it is another of the charming vagaries of the Eclectic period in architecture that although the general style of building is Tudor, the windows are Georgian). The glazing bars separate the presented Oakland panorama into convenient vignettes without interfering with the general view. There is for instance, a square of glass devoted to the east-transept gargoyles of St. Paul's Cathedral. My windows, innocent of blinds or curtains, in all their architectural starkness frame the wide skies over Oakland both by day and night. Perhaps the mysterious night view is the most spectacular, with the sprinkling of lights on Herron Hill, and more distantly, Garfield Heights and sometimes the orange glow over East Liberty.

Across the room is the large wicker chair whose back is like the spread tail of a peacock, and I like to sit in it when I want to feel important. Facing it, at the room's centre, is a Second Empire armchair of carved walnut upholstered in purple damask. It recalls very forcibly the 1860s, as does the Gothic Revival side chair near it — both of them seem to be asking for crinolines and chignons and flowing side whiskers; about them seem to hover the ghosts of decorous conversations of long ago. Near me as I write are two silver (mercury glass?) gazing globes, large and small, which reflect the room and the windows in a sorcerer's perspective, removing my enchanted eyrie to some far and distant land. At any hour of the day or night this is my own wizard's castle.

In the centre of one long wall is the tall Biedermeier chest with its simple Classical colonette-pilasters and coved cornices, really an architectural construction in the guise of furniture. It is intriguing to keep my shirts and socks behind what looks like a Renaissance town palace. Above it loom the misty grey-green globes of my Venetian jars, whose highlights echo those of a glass eighteenth-century wig stand, with its red and amber tones, that glistens on the sill of the central window.

A didactic note is not missing from the walls as I look across the room. Above the stereo hangs a reproduction of one of the Ajanta frescoes of the sixth century in India — the Bodhisattva Padmapani, "He who holds the lotus." Here the Bodhisattva is represented as a beautiful youth crowned with jewels and flowers, looking down in mercy on a suffering world. When Buddhism was transplanted to China and Japan, Padmapani also made the journey, but in so doing he changed his sex and became Kwan Yin, the All-merciful Mother; in Japan she is known as Kwannon. By my working chair I have a large statuette in Blanc de Chine porcelain of Kwan Yin, still bravely holding the lotus: "O thou treasure."

So I returned from foreign latitudes to my home place in a wheelchair, bewailing my shattered but now-healing leg. I complain, but still I hope the wheelchair is not permanent, and I rejoice in the treasures of the world, of which my own treasure house is perhaps the least: but it is mine. In conclusion I will quote a few lines from one of George Herbert's poems which I read someplace recently:

> I will complain, yet praise;
> I will bewail, approve;
> And all my sour-sweet days
> I will lament and love . . .
> Less than the least of all God's mercies, is my posey still.

Radio script for WQED-FM, 1979.

The Last of Webster Hall
The Passing of a Famous Oakland Hotel

The grand corridor of Webster Hall in its hotel days.

There are times when one considers that in America, at least, there is no building type more ephemeral than the hotel, although perhaps the shop or store building is equally transitory. Sometimes, when a hotel is closed, the shops or bars or restaurants contained within it disappear as well, and we are faced with a multiplicity of vanishment. With the advancement in technology during the last hundred years, even a relatively recent caravansary may be outmoded in three decades, and a fifty-year-old hotel is often a sure candidate for oblivion. Pittsburgh's Monongahela House, first constructed in 1839, was more fortunate than most, inasmuch as it was demolished a century later, but in its last years it retained scarcely a vestige of its former state. Of all Pittsburgh's well-known older hotels, only the William Penn, opened in 1916, is still with us in a fully-functioning state.[1] Perhaps the most glamourous, the Schenley, opened in 1898, is still with us as a mere shell of its former splendour, but as the Student Union of the University of Pittsburgh it retains nothing of its once-proud state.

The latest local candidate for "phasing out" is the Hotel Webster Hall, at 4415 Fifth Avenue, which for fifty years had been one of the landmarks of Oakland. It is to be remodeled in the near future into an apartment house. Not all landmarks remain, and this one is to be changed drastically. This discourse is a nostalgic excursion into the past.

Erected on a tract of vacant land on the northwest corner of Fifth and Dithridge, Webster Hall was among the first of the high-rise structures of the late 1920s to be built in the Bellefield district of Oakland. All the rest of these structures, devoted to multiple occupancy, were apartment houses, but the Webster Hall was both a hotel and a men's club — a combination that could only have occurred in the rich, inventive climate of the 'Twenties. In a list of building projects undertaken in Pittsburgh in 1926-27, a list published in the September, 1927, issue of *Greater Pittsburgh* (the magazine of the Pittsburgh Chamber of Commerce), the building, then just completed, was called the Mayflower Hotel and, in parentheses, the Webster Hall Annex.

"Annex" sounds like a strange term for a building that was envisioned as part of a chain of five such club-hotels for men. The original Webster Hall had been built in 1924-25 in Detroit by the Webster Hall Corporation, whose president was a Detroit lawyer, Peter Miller, who wished to provide pleasant, agreeably elegant living quarters for young unmarried men at a democratic, but not too democratic, price. The hotel was to have all the amenities of the club, but without the exclusiveness and the expense. Miller had established the corporation with the idea of providing such accommodation for young men. The hotels were named for a Judge Webster of Detroit who had helped Miller when he was young. The corporation, and the only two hotels ever completed, were thus a combination of Victorian idealism and 'Twenties materialism. It seemed, the incorporators thought, like a good, worthy idea — so let's try to make some money out of it!

Apparently the idea had worked in Detroit, so the corporation decided to recapitulate in Pittsburgh. They asked the well-known Pittsburgh architect Henry Hornbostel to design a large twelve-story building with elaborate public rooms on the first floor and extensive athletic facilities — a swimming pool, gymnasium, and handball courts — on the two top floors. In between were four hundred bedrooms for the clientele. All of it was a highly-decorated dream that only the 'Twenties could have engendered, and for a brief period it blossomed like the rose.

Ground was broken for the Pittsburgh Webster Hall in August, 1925, and it was opened on October 15, 1926, when the *Pittsburgh Post* ran a special section on it, extolling its amenities and its wonders. One entered the building through a lofty portal ornamented in a restrained Baroque style (this long ago succumbed to a more Modern entry which completely lacked the glamour of the original). Within was a vaulted lobby thirty-two feet high which led to a long transverse hall. The *Post* described the decor of the lobby and hall as "Byzantine." At the Dithridge Street end was a motor entrance and a drugstore, and at the other end of the hall the vaulted coffee shop, whose walls were lined with tiles. According to the *Post*, it was Gothic in style. The ladies' reception room was French, the men's, Spanish,

The coffee shop in the late 1940s.

155

and there were also Empire and Victorian reception rooms. In the centre of the building was the grandest space of all, the Georgian Dining Room, which was a rectangular columned hall with segmental aspidal ends. Hornbostel had a special flair for creating this type of grand space. It still exists, almost unchanged in form, whereas all the other rooms have been completely modernized. Great windows, now gone, opened on one side to a tiled garden court. All this decoration was in the best Eclectic tradition of the early twentieth-century American hotel.

What a brave show it made when it was first opened and when I was young! Since this hotel-club-dream palace had been built for young men, I thought that it was peculiarly and particularly mine, although I never lived there. Now, in this distant nostalgic day, memories return to me, fragmentary and sweet — long, earnest colloquies on poetry, painting, and love in the coffee shop (which in those days was open all night), cokes and cigarettes in the drugstore, the splash of water in the swimming pool, and on some lost morning of spring, the sound of my voice singing in one of the rooms high up:

> Wie im Morgenglanze
> Du rings mich anglühst,
> Frühling, Geliebter.

How long ago it was! Unfortunately there were not enough unattached men, young or otherwise, who were affluent enough to fill the four hundred rooms, and the great Depression of 1929 did not help the situation. Already in 1928 one floor of the building had been thrown open to women, and in 1931 the management decided to abandon the men's-club idea and open the hotel to transient trade. From then on the rate of change in the fabric of the building was constant, and it is difficult to remember when any particular changes were made.

In 1934, after the repeal of Prohibition, the drugstore became a bar called the Boot and Saddle, which engendered for me such a collection of memories that it is difficult to choose among them. Last week, in a specially-nostalgic excursion, I sat at the bar with a friend and we drank a toast to Webster Hall. All that horsey decoration will disappear along with the bar. It is to be replaced by banking premises under the new dispensation. O dolor!

The coffee shop and dining room as now constituted will be closed, but there are rumours that the new apartment building will have a restaurant. It is to be hoped that the Georgian Room, which of late years had chiefly been used for dancing, can be preserved, since it is one of Hornbostel's finest interior spaces. We at the Landmarks

156

The Georgian Room.

Foundation intend to keep an eye on it.[2] Possibly it could well be returned to its original function. I dined there fifty years ago, and I would like to dine there again. With a little imaginative redecoration it could be changed into a fabulous restaurant.

I shall regret the coffee shop, although it has changed so much — except for the vaulted ceiling — that it hardly seems the same room that I once knew. However, it is sacred to the memory of so many friends now gone that I almost feel like placing a wreath in it. Even in the 1960s, it was such a pleasant place to go after a concert to drink tea and consume the famous Webster Hall coffee cake. Since the opening of Heinz Hall, the coffee shop has not been the same, but at least I have half a century of memories.

The swimming pool and the athletic facilities are long since gone, making way long ago for more hotel bedrooms. I do remember dimly the high, watery hall of the swimming pool, the calling and the laughter, and the waving, plunging blue-green water and ah, a fine moment when one streaming beloved head, with eyes alight and gleaming lips, rose from the bright pool to smile at me. Once more I hear the echo of my voice singing:

> *Dass ich dich fassen möcht,*
> *In diesen Arm.*

And now, as I say a long farewell to the Webster Hall that I once knew, *that smile,* so wonderful, seems to spread and glow all about me. "Nothing is lost," it seems to say, that smile, "Pray you, love, remember . . . remember . . . remember . . ."

---

[1]The William Penn has been taken over by Alcoa, and it has been brought back to its former glory.—JVT

[2]There is indeed a new restaurant called Tiffany's which also consumed the old tile-vaulted ceiling of the coffee shop. The Georgian Room, now part of Tiffany's Restaurant, is used for special functions and is largely intact.—JVT

Radio script for WQED-FM, 1977.

The Church Beyond Fashion
A Discussion of Henry Hobson Richardson's Emmanuel Episcopal Church, Pittsburgh, Pa.

Massive and rugged, Emmanuel Episcopal Church lifts its great gable, its dramatic roof, against the industrial sky of Pittsburgh — a memorial to certain immemorial usages in architecture and a portent of the structural climate of our own day. Medieval builders might have rejoiced in its rigourous honesty, its forthright functional vigour, and modern church builders will find it no less interesting. The architect of the mid-twentieth century is hereby invited to inspect its history, its sinew and its enduring bone.

Although H. H. Richardson (1838-86), one of America's great architects, designed several church buildings — the most famous of which is Trinity in Boston — the small and inexpensive Emmanuel is not only one of his best ecclesiastical structures, but also it ranks only a little below the Allegheny County Buildings (1884-88) at Pittsburgh and the Field Store (1885-87) in Chicago — among the most forceful and interesting works of his later career. This largely-unadorned structure has an elemental grandeur, a monumental simplicity, which was not eminently characteristic of the Eclectic age which produced it but which today commends it highly to the modern aesthetic view. Beyond Fashion and beyond the caprices of the changing stylistic seasons, it seems to possess a curious timeless serenity, more than a hint of architectural immortality.

The basic form of Emmanuel is as architecturally elemental as a hill or mountain; it has the inevitable taken-for-granted quality of a natural object. One has the sense that it may be, in a solid terrestrial way, that "house not made with hands" of which St. Paul spoke, for it appears not so much to have been built as to have *emerged* from the earth on which it stands. When a small child draws a house, it is very often the primitive gabled cube or oblong which takes shape under his hand. When the local builders of northern European countries wanted a house or barn or chapel, it was the same shape which looked right to them and which satisfied best their simple needs. Certain medieval English farm structures may be cited, such as the large early thirteenth-century Tithe Barn at Great Coxwell, Berkshire, with its huge sloping roof, which is similar both in spirit and form to Richardson's structure. Emmanuel is often called the

Emmanuel Episcopal Church.

"bake-oven" church, and this homely simile, this likening of the building to such an ancient and common object of *use*, underscores again the elemental nature of the work. No matter how Emmanuel may look to us — like a hill or an oven or even a loaf of bread — it speaks insistently of the earth and the ultimate simplicities of life.

The church is, however, no gaunt, awkward meeting house — the sort of structure a new congregation might build in a developing neighbourhood until something more elaborate could be financed. During the Eclectic period the fitness or the beauty of a building was, all too frequently, in inverse ratio to the amount of money spent upon it. One may see notable examples of bad and undistinguished architecture in the vicinity of Emmanuel, and the same might be said of any large American city. The generally gilded character of the age cannot be held entirely responsible for all of the dreary stuff, but it was assuredly the lack of the Victorian Midas touch which produced the austere beauty of Emmanuel. This parish, in the early 'Eighties, was moderately well-to-do, up-and-coming, smart and sophisticated enough to apply to the then-fashionable Richardson for a design, much as its later counterpart might have waited upon Cram or Goodhue. The fact that Richardson was being considered at the very same period — August and September of 1883 — as one of the architects to submit designs for the proposed Allegheny County Buildings may have been an influence upon the Emmanuel commission. Richardson was, so to speak, "in the air" — Pittsburgh's architectural Man of the Hour.

Emmanuel parish, which had been founded in 1869 in Allegheny (now Pittsburgh's North Side), had acquired in 1882 a lot at the corner of Allegheny and North Avenues, then a fashionable and still-developing residential section. Blighted now and mortally decayed, the district is a neglected Eclectic garden, running completely to ruin, although it keeps still a kind of doomed dignity, a raddled stateliness which provides the proper historical setting for the Church.[1] In the hey-day of the quarter, though, Emmanuel must have looked a bit strange, huge and uncharacteristic — set among the more archaeological forms and styles. The building committee of the church might have been expected to procure a design somewhat nearer in spirit to that of their own houses — something more impressive and much fancier. Like other church building committees before and since, they *did* try.

Richardson's office in the latter part of 1883 was very busy with the competition designs for the Allegheny County Buildings, but even so the first set of plans for Emmanuel were sent to the vestry sometime early in 1884. This first project was much nearer the standard Eclectic norm of the period than the executed church, but it was still a very creditable design and would undoubtedly have added another interesting item to the Richardsonian canon had it been erected. Although it was archaeologically quite derivative, it is, for that very reason, of great interest, since it belongs to the same period as the first studies for the Pittsburgh Court House.

Although no dimensions are given on the plans (which are preserved among the Richardson papers in the Houghton Library at Harvard), the building would have been approximately the size of the present church. It was to have been constructed of stone, instead of brick — the notably cheaper material of the actual structure. It incorporated a later development of the central tower theme which Richardson had first used at Trinity Church in Boston (1876), the basic concept strongly influenced by the Spanish Romanesque lantern churches of the twelfth century. The southern French Romanesque detailing of the exterior plan echoed that of the Court House, but the central tower (which constituted — with its four brief subsidiary arms — the body of the church) had obviously been copied from that of the twelfth-century church of Montmoreau (Charente). The general form of the first Emmanuel project anticipates that of Shepley, Rutan & Coolidge's Shadyside Presbyterian Church (1889-90) — a building which had a profound influence on the development of later Protestant churches of the auditorium type in Pittsburgh. The heavy domed mass of the first scheme, with its Romantic detailing, was eminently the desired architectural image of its period, and certainly the congregation and vestry of Emmanuel would have preferred it if they could have afforded it.

Could the parish manage to build this domed church in stone or even in brick trimmed with stone? There was much discussion, but the lowest contractor's bid came in at $48,000. Finally, in July, 1884, the Rector suggested to the vestry that plans be procured for a less pretentious structure to cost around $12,000. A motion was then adopted "directing the building committee to communicate with Mr. Richardson and inform him that the means obtainable were inadequate to build after his plans and to ask him if he desired to furnish other plans for a much plainer church building to cost say $12,000 or $15,000 complete and ready for use, but so constructed as to permit an enlargement." The plans for the first project were returned to Richardson's office, where they may have been re-worked and used in the design of the Baptist Church at Newton, Massachusetts, which was commissioned in October, 1884.[2] The Newton building has roughly the same form as the first Emmanuel scheme, but the detail is generally inferior and the floor plan different.

The new plans for Emmanuel must have arrived early in 1885, since the Rector exhibited them to the Vestry in February of that year. In the Minute Books there is no indication of the Vestry's reactions to the aesthetic merits of the drawings, but the new set did meet one important requirement inasmuch as the Rector announced at the same meeting that a bid had been received from a Mr. Henry Shenk to construct the building complete for $12,300. In April, 1885, the bid was accepted and the foundation begun. The church was finally completed early in 1886 and dedicated on March seventh of that year. Reports published in the Pittsburgh newspapers at the time state that the ultimate cost of the church, with all its furnishings including the organ, was about $25,000.

The church is a simple rectangle covered by a huge roof whose sharply sloping exterior descends to relatively low side walls, the battered bases of which continue the slope of the roof. On both sides, the great expanses of slate are relieved by three low, stunted dormers which help to light the cavernous interior. The entrance-facade is a high, plain gable, completely unadorned save for the patterning of the brickwork, especially the brick banding of the voussoirs of the loggia arches and the three windows above. These flat walls, so intricately and delicately incised, seem, in full sunlight, like the rippling surfaces of a stream touched by the wind, and they form a dramatic contrast to the intense, mysterious shadows of the entrance arches, which are hollowed out like caves at the base of a cliff. The semicircular apse at the other end of the building continues the line of the exterior walls, and the sloping roof falls in a wide, sweeping curve to meet them, giving the chancel a flowing, molded simplicity of form. There is no carved ornament anywhere; the building materials themselves provide such simple decorative effects as are evident. All the elements of the structure express in the simplest terms its function.

The working plans for the church are apparently no longer extant, but two sheets of studies for the building still exist among the Richardson papers in the Houghton Library. For the second project there were two versions made, similar in form but differing in details. In the first of these studies there is only a single arched door, flanked on either side by a large window, in the centre of the facade, but this arrangement was (fortunately) not used, since it is quite lacking in the dramatic impact of the arches in the executed version.

The interior is quite as effective as the exterior. Dominant there is the great roof, with its exposed rafters and unadorned beams. Pairs of great trussed rafters are connected by collars which are supported by curved arched braces composed of laminated planks; between the collars and the ridge beam are king posts. This structural woodwork can be admired by the most Modern functionalist, yet it also gives the sense of walking adventurously under the over-turned hull of a great ship. Against the blackened beams of the apse, the white marble and mosaic work of the Cosmati-esque reredos and altar stand out with almost-startling vividness. This glistening chancel adjunct, with its Byzantine and Quattrocento detailing and its Gibson Girl angels — similar to contemporary Tiffany work in the East — was designed and executed by the Pittsburgh firm of Lake & Green in 1898 as a memorial to William Thaw. Banks of organ pipes separate the chancel from the rest of the church, but these were not structural elements designed by Richardson. The stained glass of the small side windows is properly "Romanesque" in design and pleasing in colour; above the gallery (constructed over the entrance loggia) the large triplet of lights is, again, properly filled with glass by Tiffany, which has the glimmer and sheen of peacock feathers.

In 1887, Frank E. Alden, who had been Richardson's supervising architect on the Court House, was called in to give his opinion concerning the church wall on the Allegheny Avenue side, which had begun to lean outward. Probably due to some fault in the site, the footings of the walls had tipped toward the street as a result of the thrust of the roof beams. This Leaning Wall of Pittsburgh has become a small local joke — certainly never intended by Richardson. But perhaps even it serves a function — enabling lesser architects to scoff their way toward intimacy with this noble structure. Alden could do nothing about the wall, but he probably designed the parish house of the church, which was erected in 1888.

To sum up, Emmanuel illustrates most forcibly the power of a really great creative talent to break through the uncertainties and the historic gestures of contemporary Eclecticism. In the context of its time and neighbourhood, it looks like a mastodon at a fancy-dress party. To what degree Richardson was responsible for the first (discarded) Emmanuel design it is difficult to say, since he was a very busy man in his last years and could not attend to the details of every commission; it is quite possible that it was a job "turned out" by the office, subject, of course, to his final approval. One feels, however, that the *executed* church is Richardson's own conception, and one is in full agreement with Professor H. R. Hitchcock, the authority on Richardson, when he says that Emmanuel is wholly characteristic of the architect at his best.

Professor Hitchcock feels also that Richardson's inspiration came not only from his wide knowledge of the architecture of the past but also from his acquaintance with the work of his English contemporaries of the 1860s and 1870s. In proof of the latter, Mr. Hitchcock cites, in a letter to the writer, the case of two churches by William Burges (1827-81), one of which was, like the first Emmanuel project, never executed. The first of these churches, St. Faith's, Stoke Newington, London (built in 1872 and completed later by James Brooks), is rather similar in feeling to Emmanuel, although the proportions and much of the detailing of both are quite different. It is possible that Richardson may have seen this church on his visit to England in 1882, but it is doubtful if he could have known about Burges' design for a projected church at Brighton which bears a marked resemblance to Emmanuel as executed. (The Burges drawing was discovered in an English collection by Professor Hitchcock, who has kindly lent it to the writer.) When all the evidence of influences has been examined, one is justified merely in saying that there exists a definite parallelism of approach to contemporary architectural problems which proves Richardson's innate kinship with his English contemporaries. It may be noted, however, that Emmanuel is much freer of medieval historicisms and period detailing than Burges' project.

Similarly, although there is no proven evidence of the direct influence of Emmanuel on modern ecclesiastical building, it certainly illustrates Richardson's anticipation of and relation to contemporary functional practice.

The heirs and assigns of the Vestrymen, the good burghers of the 'Eighties, who built Emmanuel have long since fled to the suburbs, and their Eclectic mansions now crumble in the stagnant streets. Commerce and light industry have eaten up many of these fugitive domestic castles, so that Victorian decay and the harshest of modernity now ring the church around. But Emmanuel, an indissoluble tabernacle, still sits calmly in the interdeterminate streets, and — like a hill or an oven or a loaf of solid bread — it seems to exist beyond the vagaries of our changing city in this our uncertain season. For Henry Hobson Richardson, it is not the least memorial to his talent and for us it remains an embodiment and a reminder of eternal architectural verities.

¹This area of Pittsburgh, Manchester, is now the setting of an active rehabilitation campaign.

²Recent scholarship suggests that the Newton Church was not by Richardson's office.

The Charette, April, 1958.

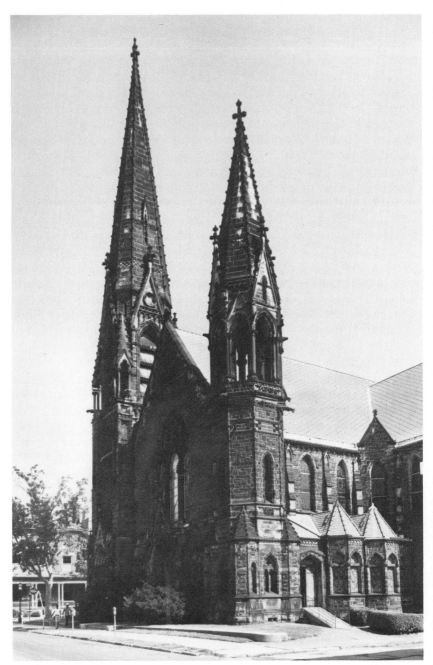

Calvary Methodist Church.

Texas—Gargoyles and Preservation
Calvary Methodist Church on Pittsburgh's North Side

"Over in Allegheny," wrote Montgomery Schuyler, the great American architectural critic, in the *Architectural Record* of September, 1911, "one comes with some pleasure, and even more astonishment, upon a Methodist Church in Beech Avenue, perhaps of no very special interest in design, but of a very special interest for the liberality and richness with which the elaborate design has been executed." Schuyler's Henry Jamesian prose, which adds flavour to the sharpness of his architectural judgment, expresses rather perfectly the reactions of the present-day amateur of architecture to Calvary Methodist Church, which is located on the corner of Allegheny and Beech Avenues on the edge of the preservation district known as Allegheny West. Now a group of preservationists are trying to save the Church. Even at the time Schuyler wrote, this kind of Late Victorian provincial Gothic Revivalism had begun to look a little old-fashioned in the face of the smooth, archaeological contemporary work of such experts as Ralph Adams Cram and Bertram Goodhue. In the 1920s it had reached the very nadir of critical favour, but by mid-century it had once again begun to be appreciated. Calvary's awkward towers, soaring above the strident avenues of its half-commercial, half-residential environs, have an uncertain but quite viable grandeur that readily appeals to us in spite of small aesthetic reservations; its high-placed pinnacles, all abristle with gargoyles and Gothic incrustations, have a fantastic exuberance, a sort of wild dignity that still cannot fail to astonish us — although the astonishment is not unmixed with amusement. Will those gargoyles bite? The sculpture of the very ornate main facade has an odd, crisp vigour, a crude provincial elegance, that pleases the eye grown weary in contemplating the austerities of many modern buildings.

The church was designed by the Kansas City firm of Vrydaugh & Shepherd in 1892. Martin Vrydaugh, the son of an immigrant Flemish architect and the chief designer of the church, eventually came to Pittsburgh and went into partnership locally with T. B. Wolfe, who had been the supervising architect on Calvary while it was building.

This, the most ornate and luxurious Protestant auditorium church ever built in old Allegheny, now Pittsburgh's North Side, came about as a result of a congregational division after Christ Methodist Church in downtown Pittsburgh was destroyed by fire in 1891. One contingent went to the East End where it built a great Richardsonian Romanesque building (1893) called Christ (now the First Methodist) Church, while the other moved to the North Side (and became Calvary Church). The congregational assets were also divided, and since both groups contained a number of affluent members there was much to divide. In the case of the building of Calvary Church, a great deal of money was expended; the wealthy industrial and mercantile class, then near the apogee of its power, wished to see its affluence mirrored in the religious architecture it sponsored. Among the important members of Calvary were Joseph Horne and J. B. Shea, of the Horne Department Store, and Charles Scaife. In this connection one is reminded of similar religious structures of the late Middle Ages in Flanders and England, and particularly of the great cloth merchants' churches of the fifteenth century. The first service in the new church was held on Christmas, 1893, but it was not dedicated until May, 1895.

Basically, judged by any standards, the design of Calvary has neither integrity nor coherence; it is actually a pastiche of medieval features. However, it is pre-eminently a document of its own day, and it seems to be the religious counterpart of the millionaire mansions that once were its near neighbours. Adjacent to the structure are two or three streets of smaller houses that have managed to survive and which are now being restored, and they presently flourish as a part of the preservation district of Allegheny West.

Calvary is the standard Protestant auditorium church, such as might be found in any large American city, but its elegance of execution lifts it to a higher plane. It is, as it were, the apotheosis of the type. There is nothing else quite like it in Pittsburgh.

In dealing with a building of this sort, the architectural critic often finds himself involved in a guessing game as to the architect's sources. The spire of the main tower may have been modeled after — rather far after — the southwest spire of Chartres Cathedral; the stage of the tower just below the belfry, with its blind arcading, resembles those of certain Norman churches, notably St. Pierre at Caen. The outsize spirelet that flanks the other side of the facade is vaguely reminiscent of a gable pinnacle on Peterborough Cathedral in England. In all, the exterior resembles those of certain buildings to be found in countries on the periphery of Europe — structures like

Rosslyn Chapel in Scotland or Trondheim Cathedral in Norway, where the craftsmen, far from the centres of style and culture, followed their own bent and produced buildings that are stylistically uncertain but which have a subtle and off-beat charm.

It is the execution of the exterior stone carving that gives Calvary *its* peculiar charm. The facade does not, in the last analysis, rise above the quality of a rather sophisticated folk art; there are affinities with monumental work done for graveyards and the decoration of county court houses. But the Calvary sculpture, with its rough vitality, is comparable, at its best, to that which some minor fourteenth-century craftsman might have executed for an English parish church.

There is a story that the carving was done by a Texan; this was related to me twenty-five years ago by the last surviving member of the stone contractor's family. The late Mrs. Jackman, one of Martin Vrydaugh's daughters, said that it was done by Italian stone carvers, but there is no corroborative documentary evidence one way or the other. I am inclined to credit the story of the Texan, who also wore a ten-gallon hat, because he is also a tradition in the church. Nobody can remember his name, however.

Much American Gothic Revival sculpture, even that done for archaeologically more correct buildings, has often a certain mechanical quality — it is too obviously a merely reproduced art. No matter how perfectly done, the effect of such work is dry and uninspired. At Calvary, however, the sculpture does have, despite its crudeness, a native vigour and liveliness; the facade seems to ripple and undulate with a coarse, highly-decorated life of its own. The Texan carver, whatever his training, seems to have brought some of the breeziness of his home state into his efforts. He possessed sufficient skill to carve whatever the architects gave him as a model, but he did it with a verve and gusto all his own.

The cusped moldings of the reveals of the two main tower portals and the central doorway are possibly modeled after those of the twelfth-century church of Souterraine (Creuse), illustrated by Viollet-le-Duc in his *Dictionnaire Raisonnée.* Here the play of light on the carved surfaces is an important element in the total effect: formal, almost geometrical, patterns of lightened shade are created, and they shift and vanish as the day wanes. Except for a few masks and faces in relief there is no figure sculpture on the facade, and one recalls the rigourous Mosaic proscription against images that was for so long a part of the Protestant aesthetic outlook.

A stringcourse just below the large central window has inset medallions of female heads, carved with a sort of heavy intensity, that have a haunted, doomed quality reminiscent of Hellenistic sculpture.

But it is the gargoyles, quite freed here of any function in carrying off rain water and poised as if to spring from the canopied niches or the upper stringcourses, that all-pervasively provide the note of vibrant restlessness. The ominous, narrow beasts — done possibly in emulation of the oxen of Laon Cathedral — that thrust themselves outward from the niches at the base of the spire are the largest of this fantastic host, and they preside over the abortive flights of their lesser brethren. The Texan used all his skill on them, and they do give a note of rather *distrait* unity to this potpourri of Gothic reminiscences. How eminently must they have recalled to the late nineteenth-century church-goer the Romantic medieval past, and how justly they constitute for us, today, an intriguing footnote in the aesthetic history of the Victorian Age. . . .

A gargoyle from Calvary Methodist Church.

Radio script for WQED-FM, 1981.

Pittsburgh's Church of the Ascension

We, who are so far from the nineteenth century's architectural preoccupation with the medieval past, may be inclined no longer to notice the darkly Romantic aspect of the Church of the Ascension, which has stood since 1897 on the edge of the Oakland district in Pittsburgh. Even the casual passer-by, however, cannot entirely escape the powerful looming impact of this mass of masonry, which insists upon competing for attention with the more modern silhouettes of the apartment buildings gradually surrounding it. Probably few Pittsburghers know that this church is one of the last designs of an almost-forgotten architect — William Halsey Wood — who, had he not died in 1897 at the untimely age of forty-two, might have left a more notable impress on the history of American architecture.

The knowing observer will not fail to notice that the church has a certain affinity, both in tone and feeling, with the work of H. H. Richardson. Hardly surprising, since Wood (like so many young architects of the period) began his career under the influence of this Master Architect, the towering genius of nineteenth-century American architecture. The details of the Ascension are Gothic and the tower is Perpendicular Gothic (almost Tudor) in form, but the generally massive proportions of the building recall Norman work and more specifically the Romanesque of Richardson. The more creative artists of the nineteenth century sometimes used two or three styles in one composition, blending them — with a greater or lesser degree of harmony, according to their ability — to produce a new effect. Wood was sufficiently the artist not to be held too closely to the copy books.

Wood, who was a member of that group of High Church Episcopal or Anglo-Catholic architects whose first famous exponent in America was Richard Upjohn and the last Ralph Adams Cram, was primarily a church architect, although he executed commissions in other fields of practice. He got his early training as an apprentice (a method still fairly common at the time), and was, for a brief period, a partner in a firm in Newark, New Jersey. At the age of twenty-four, he opened an office of his own in the same city and early received

171

some important domestic commissions, as his wife records in a memoir of her husband.

Two of his most interesting houses were "Winmarleigh," which he built for himself in 1889, shortly after his marriage, and a country house designed for Spencer Trask of Saratoga, New York, which was an arresting variation on the Richardsonian theme. "Winmarleigh" itself, a rambling construction in half-timber and over-burnt brick, might be considered a precursor of Frank Lloyd Wright's "Taliesin," but Wood's dependence on medieval precedent was too evident and he did not possess Wright's genius.

The latter part of the nineteenth century (when competitions for large public commissions were the rule) was a period when the architect could cultivate large horizons, and Wood was not lacking in his own grandiose visions. He competed both for the Carnegie Library of Allegheny in 1887 and the Carnegie Library of Pittsburgh in 1891. His design for the Allegheny building was highly original, with a flowing interior plan based on circular motifs. In both the Pittsburgh Carnegie Library competition drawings and in those for the Cathedral of St. John the Divine in New York City (1888-90), his rather turgid medievalism and his grandiosity got the better of him, and he produced, in both cases, ingenious fantasies which remind one of Wagnerian stage scenery of the period. These dream palaces, which have for us today a rather horrid fascination, have something in common with Breughel's *Tower of Babel* and Antonio Gaudi's Sagrada Familia at Barcelona. At least Gaudi's church got partially built! The only one of Wood's designs for Pittsburgh district libraries which was actually constructed was that for the Carnegie Library of Braddock, a rather dull building.[1]

Aside from these abortive projects, Wood was much occupied with the design of smaller churches. One of his earliest ecclesiastical commissions is his most original and his most interesting design — the Peddie Memorial Baptist Church of Newark, which was begun in 1888. This strange building has all of Wood's fumbling power and breadth of treatment as well as a definite originality of a startling uneasy sort. The Richardsonian elements, including the Norman turrets, have been abstracted, as it were, and reduced to their simplest forms, but unfortunately the effect is that of some fabulous fantastic sundae about to melt. A critic writing in *The Architectural Record* (1892) called it an "architectural aberration," but only in the sense that it departed from the usual. It certainly does that, and the modern beholder is possessed by a mixture of both admiration and dismay. There is a definite similarity of feeling between this building and

Wood's unsuccessful competition design for the Allegheny Carnegie Library, which is however a simpler and more forthright conception than the Newark church. The Allegheny design, with its plain rock-faced walls, is infinitely superior to the building actually erected (a pedestrian Richardsonian design by Smithmeyer and Peltz, who had just designed the Library of Congress in Washington). Had Wood's project been accepted, Pittsburgh might have possessed a not-unworthy pendant to Richardson's great County Buildings.

In the Peddie Church and the Allegheny Library, Wood reached the peak of his originality as a designer. Had he been able to develop the trends evident in these buildings, he might have become a really creative artist akin to Louis Sullivan. But he could not, and such glory was not to be vouchsafed to him. The reasons for his failure constitute an interesting psychological problem, not only in regard to Wood himself, but in the relation to the nineteenth-century American artist in general. Was it (as was suggested in an obituary notice at the time of his death) that he lacked sufficient education or a properly rigorous training in his profession? Did he suffer because there was not in America a broad and deep cultural background in which he could base his own experiments? He was successful early in life, so there arises the question: was he the victim of the American cult of success at any price, which might include the dilution of his own ideals to suit popular fancy? Did he simply lack sufficient physical vigour (he died of tuberculosis) to meet the exactions of his profession? Was he, above all, one of those whom Genius has brushed only slightly and made the tragic heir of unfulfilled promise? The answers to all these questions must, with some qualifications, be in the affirmative. But confronted by the buildings themselves, the inevitable question arises — how could he, with his unquestionable ability, have gone *quite* so wrong?

And wrong he could certainly go! The not-inconsiderable number of his churches, whether they be in the Romanesque or Gothic style, have certain characteristics in common. There is pre-eminently the constant striving for a certain rude originality, which often produces highly interesting results but which may descend into crudeness or awkward fantasy. And no matter how successful he may have been in some feature, the parts rarely add up to any complete whole. His compositions, no matter how arresting, have finally a certain abortive quality; we are too conscious of some protrusive or intrusive elements, the malapropos molding or the inept turret. His ornament, when he follows historic precedent, is tame — as in the Perpendicular windows of the Church of the Ascension or St. John's, Youngstown, which are effective only in contrast to the surfaces they punctuate. When he attempts to be original he is apt to be uncertain and heavy-handed, as in the choir stalls of the Church of the Ascension. The Richardsonian ornamental tendrils that blossomed so luxuriantly for Louis Sullivan withered away in the hands of Wood. And yet when all these things have been said, there is always something interesting in his work, something obliquely attractive, something harsh and vital that captures and holds the attention. His buildings have, at their best, an impact and a curious bleak charm that is lacking in many of the more correct Eclectic compositions of the period.

There is no doubt that he was in some demand as a church architect, since he was included among the architects asked to compete for the Ascension design. All material relative to the design and construction of the church is contained in two large scrapbooks preserved in the church archives, and they constitute a very interesting record of a construction job of the time.

The building committee, in 1896, asked several prominent architectural firms to compete, among them Cram, Wentworth & Goodhue; Shepley, Rutan & Coolidge; D. H. Burnham & Company; McKim, Mead & White; Peabody & Stearns; Alden & Harlow; Wilson Eyre; and Halsey Wood. All firms submitting plans were to be paid $150.00, and most of them accepted. McKim, Mead & White declined to compete because of press of business. The church was not to cost more than $60,000. The rector of the church favoured the plans submitted by Wood, seemingly because Wood was such a strong churchman and understood the needs of an Episcopal church. Wood was finally given the commission in October, 1896, but the contract for the actual construction had hardly been signed when Wood died in March of 1897. After some negotiations, the plans were secured from his estate, and F. E. Alden of Alden & Harlow was appointed to supervise the construction. There is no evidence, however, that any major changes were made subsequent to Wood's death, so the church is built as he planned it.

It cannot be claimed that the Church of the Ascension is in any way an exceptional example of Wood's work; it is quite typical of his later churches. As a rule, he tended toward massiveness in his towers, and they are the focal points of his compositions. One thinks of his powerful Romanesque campanili for St. Michael and All Angels at Anniston, Alabama (consecrated 1890) and St. Paul's, Chattanooga (1888), but these are, comparatively speaking, slenderer and form more definitely vertical accents. His great central lantern for Christ Church, Bloomfield, New Jersey (1893), is a Gothic echo of Richard-

The Church of the Ascension.

son's Trinity Church, Boston. The square tower at the end of the nave is a marked feature of some English medieval parish churches, and Wood had used this type at St. John's, New Haven (1895), but not so powerfully as at the Church of the Ascension. The Pittsburgh tower bears a marked resemblance to that of the Welsh parish church of Wrexham, Denbigh, which is very late Gothic (1506), but Wood's model quite lacks the brutal assertiveness that he gave his own creation, which broods over the church like a thunderhead and seems to proclaim unequivocally the power and majesty of God. Montgomery Schuyler, the great American architectural critic, writing in 1911, called it one of the best things in Pittsburgh. The rest of the exterior of the building appears anti-climactic, even uninteresting, and the rather gaunt vestibule building, with its unnecessary turret, serves merely to buttress the tower. Whatever failure there may be in the several parts, however, the whole composition has a certain verve and sweep that just misses a satisfying coherence.

The same breadth and freedom of handling are evident in the interior. Both nave and chancel are generally broad and low in their proportions, but the feature which sets most eminently the tone of the interior is the wall finish of the buff brick, which has aged to a rather unpleasant colour.[2] A series of plain brick arches carried on octagonal stone pillars separate the side aisles (here mere passageways) from the nave, and they serve to announce major themes in the composition — the great reticulated brick arch at the entrance of the chancel, which is matched at the other end of the nave by an unadorned arch marking off the space under the tower. Similar plain arches demarcate the transepts from the crossing. An interesting note is supplied by the bold foliated caps of the nave piers, which have no abaci and which project sharply directly beneath the springing of the arches. There is a low-pitched beamed ceiling of no particular interest, with its tie-beams supported on wooden corbels. The general effect of the interior is that of the north Italian brick Gothic architecture of the thirteenth and fourteenth centuries, which introduces yet another stylistic note and which may be, perhaps, an echo of Ruskinian precept. It is a tribute to Wood's power of synthesis that none of his styles clashes too violently.

Minor details of the interior are generally not too successful. The mural of the Ascension over the High Altar, done in emulation of LaFarge's similar decoration in New York, is too pale and delicate for such a rugged architectural setting. The brick embrasures of the clerestory windows are poorly designed, and the English rectilinear tracery in most of the church windows accords ill with the Italianate interior. Attempts have been made, on the advice of Ralph Adams Cram, to lighten the pervading gloom by plastering and painting the walls of the chancel, but the resulting gaunt whiteness has a deadening effect. It would be better, possibly, if all the walls were painted some pale tone, thus permitting them to retain the texture of the brickwork. The small side chapel, with its elegant entrance grille, is quite handsome, but its decorative scheme is later in date. Although the structure is basically Wood's, the general effect owes a good deal to Cram. Again, after we have admired the boldness of Wood's conception, so evident in the whole church interior, we are left to discount the darkness and the gauntness.

Wood must remain a puzzling figure, since the impress of his work is, in the last analysis, so equivocal. Even if his work is often aesthetically bad, it could sometimes often be very good, but alas not good enough for really memorable results. He failed to be an outstanding figure in our architectural history but he failed rather grandly. What he *did* achieve as an artist merits, nonetheless, our interest and our respect.

[1]Another Wood design in the Pittsburgh area is the tiny but very picturesque Church of the Good Shepherd in Hazelwood (1893).

[2]It is now painted white.—JVT

The Charette, June, 1956.

The Gothic Revival in Pittsburgh

The Picturesque and Romantic Phase

There are those who have rejoiced to inform us that the age of Revivals is past — a statement which the examination of contemporary building does nothing to refute — and if this state of affairs be not a cause for lamentation, it may be, at least for some of us who were born and received our architectural upbringing during the Eclectic period, an occasion for the rueful backward glance.

This study of the Gothic Revival is a rather unfashionable and minority report undertaken by one who likes Revivals and who finds pleasure in Eclecticism. A predilection of this sort is sure to be frowned upon by the judicious, who assert that much of the nineteenth and the early twentieth centuries was, architecturally speaking, anarchic, confused, and imitative — and that the period was redeemed only by the work of a few architects who pointed the way to our own modern style. For Eclecticism itself there are still few good words.[1]

The judicious are, to a degree, right — the period *was* anarchic, confused, imitative; but it was also wonderful! In those days we lived adventurously. We cashed our checks (or clipped coupons) in Roman basilicas, we lunched in Basque villages, we dined in Adam dining rooms; under Cinquecento balconies we danced, and Gothic arcades attended our devotions. The castles of Spain and the bazaars of the Orient environed us in a kaleidoscopic dream.

All history and the centuries were ransacked to provide the multitudinous variety of our habitations and places of resort. History, alas, attends us no longer, for there is but one admissible style, the ubiquitous Modern. Romance, it is true, is to be found in the architecture of our own day, but it appears niggardly and unvarious — to catch the full flavour of Romanticism we must look back.

The Gothic Revival constituted one of the main streams of the period of Revivals. Its first appearance was coeval with the rise of Romanticism in England during the eighteenth century, and it was an early manifestation of that new interest in the medieval past which was largely to replace the Renaissance orientation toward the Classical period. From the first, the revived Gothic architecture was closely linked with literature, and the importance of the word in

177

disseminating the Gothic Revival beyond England cannot be underestimated.

Two of the men who were most responsible for popularizing the Revival — Horace Walpole and William Beckford — were writers, and there is no inconsiderable connection between the *Castle of Otranto* and *Vathek,* their respective novels, and Strawberry Hill and Fonthill Abbey, their respective houses. Many of the most influential architects of the later Revival were also writers — notably A. W. Pugin, G. E. Street, G. G. Scott, and R. A. Cram — and what they wrote was often as important as what they built.

Another facet of Romanticism was the cult of the Picturesque, which was of such importance both in architecture and in landscape gardening. For the devotee of the Picturesque, the sole purpose of a building or of a landscaped garden was that the two should compose themselves to form a picture or an effect which would arouse certain emotions of pleasure or disquiet in the beholder. Certainly this viewpoint is open to censure, for there are other criteria by which the art of building may be judged, but in its limited way it may still have some validity for us. It was one of the more unfortunate aspects of this new interest in "the View" that architecture as *structure* was quite lost sight of in the search for pictorial effect. And even more unfortunate was the fact that architecture tended to become more and more the handmaiden of literature and painting, rather than an end in itself. Under these circumstances the revived Gothic of the eighteenth and the early nineteenth centuries was apt to be thin, superficial, and lacking in firm structural qualities. Strawberry Hill, however charming, and Fonthill Abbey, however dramatic, are cases in point. This striving for the associative and the pictorial can, however, in minor subsidiary architecture such as the gatehouse of the Allegheny Cemetery at Pittsburgh, have a most pleasant and effective result. Possibly our appreciation of these Romantic effects, these "staged" compositions, has a certain antiquarian flavour, but it is, nonetheless, genuine.

In eighteenth-century America, the reflection of the English Romantic craze for Gothic was feeble and vague. It is interesting that the Gothic novel appeared at Philadelphia in the work of Charles Brockden Brown (1771-1810) whose *Wieland* (1798) is in the same vein as the *Castle of Otranto* and Mrs. Radcliffe's *Mysteries of Udolpho.* Brown also interested himself in architecture, and scattered through his unpublished diaries are many architectural drawings, some of them, possibly, the products of the fervid imagination which produced his novels. Rudimentary Gothic detailing had crept into such

178

buildings as the second Trinity Church in New York (1788-90), but the first conscious attempt to use the Gothic mode occurred, again, in Philadelphia where B. H. Latrobe (who was later to make designs for the Arsenal in Pittsburgh) designed what is generally conceded to be the first Gothic Revival house in America — "Sedgeley." This house, no longer standing, was an essay in the thin "applied" Gothic of the eighteenth century, and it is not nearly so effective as Latrobe's Classical work. Latrobe also executed the Philadelphia Bank (1807-08 — demolished c. 1830) in the Gothic style, and William Strickland, in the same city, was responsible for one of the earliest important American revived Gothic buildings in his Masonic Hall (1809-11). Maximilien Godefroy had designed St. Mary's Chapel, Baltimore (1807) in a curiously personal, slightly fantastic, version of the Gothic, and Latrobe had made an alternate Gothic project for his Baltimore Cathedral (1805). By the end of the first quarter of the nineteenth century, the revived Gothic was rather well established as one of the important American style trends and also as the chief rival of the Greek Revival.

Although Gothic was not unknown in the cities of the Eastern seaboard, it was much later in making its appearance at the semi-frontier town of Pittsburgh, and when it did it was sponsored by a person who was of considerable importance in the history of the American Gothic Revival — John Henry Hopkins. Hopkins, with his intellectual and artistic brilliance and his many-faceted personality, was an early nineteenth-century re-incarnation of the "complete" man of the Renaissance who was at home in many fields of knowledge and active in various endeavours. He was a type that is, alas, rarely met with in our own day of extreme specialization. Born in Dublin, Ireland, in 1792, he came to America in 1800 with his parents. His education in boarding schools and at Princeton (where he spent a brief period) would be considered meagre by present-day standards, but he became very proficient in Latin, Greek, French, drawing, and music; he also learned fencing and dancing from a French émigré. He was a talented water colourist and helped colour the plates for Wilson's *Birds of America* while he was living in Philadelphia during his early youth. He studied iron manufacturing for three years, and during the War of 1812 superintended a furnace at Bassenheim near Harmony. Meanwhile, he had met James O'Hara, the early Pittsburgh "tycoon," who, after the failure of the Bassenheim venture, set Hopkins up as superintendent of an iron furnace in the Ligonier Valley. This project also failed, and Hopkins then studied law in Pittsburgh, was admitted to the Bar in 1818, and became a very successful lawyer. After he began to play the organ at Trinity Church, he became interested in the Episcopal Church, took Orders, and became Rector of Trinity in 1823. In 1832 he was elected Bishop of Vermont, and his abilities were thereafter manifested in a wider field. Full of years and honours, he died at Burlington, Vermont, in 1868. He had thirteen children and he wrote more than fifty books. There were giants in those days.

All through his ecclesiastical career, Hopkins took a great interest in the arts of the Church — music, painting, and architecture — and as a true child of his time, he was particularly enamoured of the Gothic. For him, as for so many of his contemporaries, it was the only *true* religious architecture.

Among the first, and architecturally the most important, of his books was his *Essay on Gothic Architecture,* published in Vermont in 1836. Hopkins' knowledge of Gothic was never very sound, and the book shows his dependence on various English literary sources and the engraved plates of Britton and the elder Pugin. He was by no means a professional architect, and he was more nearly an amateur in the eighteenth-century sense. In designing the second Trinity Church (1824) he had to serve as his own architect because he could not find any professional man in Pittsburgh competent to handle the Gothic style. In preparation for his Trinity project, he had copied engravings of English cathedrals and studied Britton's *Antiquities,* which a European architect, John Behan, then resident in the city, had lent him. Despite his lack of training, however, Trinity was a great success, and many other churchmen applied to him for plans. The *Essay* was issued in response to this demand — in fact, the volume is really an early nineteenth-century "how to" book. The prospective builder who was without benefit of architectural advice was told how he might have a church or chapel in the latest mode, and what he lacked in money, taste, or knowledge could be made up for by the use of a little ingenuity and Hopkins' handbook. Most of the designs, which are not very well served by the crudity of the lithographic plates, are pale reflections of the late eighteenth- and early nineteenth-century revived Gothic — the prevailing manner being Tudor or Perpendicular, which was quite in keeping with the style trend of the time.

Trinity itself was little more than the standard Protestant meeting house of the period, Gothicized with some "features" from Britton. According to Hopkins himself, the best part of the exterior was the tower, "which exhibits an example of the flying buttress taken from Henry the Seventh's Chapel."[2] The exterior walls were

The second Trinity Church, by John Henry Hopkins.

of brick covered with stucco in imitation of stone. Galleries flanked
the nave of the church, which was little more than a long hall with
a niche at the end which did duty as a chancel, where the pulpit all
but overwhelmed the altar. The flat ceiling was painted to represent
fan vaulting -- a scheme which was designed and partly executed by
Hopkins. In its thinness, its imitativeness, and its lack of structural
honesty, the building was typical of much eighteenth-century Gothic,
but it aroused religious emotions in the breasts of good Pittsburghers
of the day and it was undoubtedly Picturesque. As seen in old prints,
it has a lithogenic and tenuous charm.

Much less successful was the first St. Paul's Roman Catholic
Cathedral (built 1829-34 and destroyed in 1851), a large brick
structure noted for its size — indeed it was one of the largest churches
of its time in the United States. Its attenuated masses and spiky tower
had a meagre, insubstantial air, although it did not lack a certain
awkward if "phoney" grandeur.

We must leave architecture, for the moment, to consider another
prime manifestation of the English Romantic movement, which is
important because of its close connection with building — the quasi-
naturalistic landscaped park. Although these informal landscapes
could be created on a small scale, they were mostly the concomitants

of the great aristocratic country houses. The Classic formalism of the Renaissance garden, with its ceremonial vistas and rigid parterres, vanished away before these new "natural" arrangements of the landscape — the gently rolling hills, the artful glades, the contrived lakes, the carefully-disposed clumps of trees. Nature was taken up and made the "presented," "placed." The landscaped park had also considerable municipal development in America (Philadelphia opened the first park of this sort in 1855), but with that we are not primarily concerned.

The English park was late in coming to America, considerably later than the Gothic Revival itself, and when it did it was subject to further changes and put to new uses. Aside from its use in the development of the American municipal park, this type of landscape art may also be seen in two other strangely parallel manifestations of the flight from the rigours of the rising industrial age — the Romantic suburb and the Romantic "rural" cemetery — and Pittsburgh has excellent examples of both. The elegantly-arranged landscape as an aristocratic preserve was uncongenial to the American temper, and the variations allowable on that theme had to be of a practical or a useful nature. That the English park style was first used (on any large scale) in the lay-out of "rural" cemeteries may seem a just if rather strange comment on American practicality, but that it was also an attempt to screen pleasantly the Romantic preoccupation with Death cannot be denied. Environed by Gothic turrets, willow trees, and bosky glades, the grief-stricken could confront with equanimity, even with a certain mournful pleasure, the inevitable and ultimate Bone. The dead, released from the crowded tenements of the city graveyards, were splendidly and variously domiciled on these new Romantic hills! A tomb with a view became one of the goals of the new bourgeoisie, and the sepulchre, howsoever whited, was carven and adorned with all the devices of Eclectic grace. The first American cemetery of this type was Mount Auburn in Boston (1831) which was followed by Laurel Hill, Philadelphia, in 1836 and Greenwood, Brooklyn, in 1838. By 1840, the park-cemetery, a type still with us today, was well established.

Pittsburgh was not far behind these Eastern cities in establishing its own Romantic necropolis; in 1844 Allegheny Cemetery, located on a tract of rolling land between Butler Street and Penn Avenue, some three miles from the centre of the city, was chartered and established. For a private citizen to have created such an extensive park would have been considered ostentatious in the last degree, but, according to contemporary opinion, it was eminently suitable for the dead. John Chislett (1800-69), a local architect who had been born in England and who had received some of his early training at Bath, was appointed the first superintendent, and it was he who was responsible for the lay-out of the grounds. Probably he was familiar with the work of the Philadelphia architect John Notman (1810-65) at Laurel Hill, and the earlier project must have influenced his own design. Notman's Laurel Hill mortuary chapel (1838 — now destroyed) was in the fashionable Perpendicular style, and Chislett followed suit in using the same late manner for his entrance gate at Allegheny. The structure, little more than a Gothic screen with a small lodge at one side, is pierced in the centre by a Tudor arched gateway. It is difficult to date with exactitude; it may have been designed as early as 1844, but the historical volume on the cemetery (1873) says that it was still in construction in 1848. However that may be, the general effect is charming — the sober, tasteful massing and the chaste detailing, which quite lacks the thin exuberance of that of Notman's chapel, constitute a delightful architectural *morceau* quite as effective in its way as some of Chislett's better-known Greek Revival buildings. Chislett's receiving vault of 1857 (which has since been rebuilt on the original plan) is not nearly so successful, and one has the uneasy sense that it is merely a collection of "features" from the copy books, thrown together to form a design, albeit a symmetrical one. In these small buildings of Chislett's, as also in some of Latrobe's Gothic work, one has pervasively the sense of Classical mass underlying the Gothic detail; these men could not help thinking Classically even when trying to be fashionably medieval.

Chislett, echoing John Henry Hopkins, asserted in the aforementioned historical volume that Gothic was chosen for the Allegheny buildings because it seemed to be the appropriate style for a place of Christian burial. Pugin would certainly have approved, and the Ecclesiologists of the 1840s have given their blessing to these sentiments. Notman at Laurel Hill was much more Eclectic in outlook — he designed a Greek gatehouse as well as a Gothic chapel. The architecture of the Romantic cemetery tended to become increasingly Eclectic as the nineteenth century continued (Allegheny has a Richardsonian Romanesque gateway at Penn Avenue, erected in 1886-87), and many were the styles employed in the larger mausoleums as well as the smaller monuments. The Moorhead mausoleum is a strange domed structure with vaguely Gothic detailing.

Chislett's gatehouse was enlarged (1868-70) by the addition of a building containing the offices and a chapel, after the designs

The Butler Street entrance of Allegheny Cemetery, with Chislett's gate to the left and Barr & Moser's administration building to the right.

of H. Moser of the Pittsburgh firm of Barr & Moser. The Picturesque effect of the earlier structure is considerably augmented by the new work, especially when one considers that the basic mass of the later work, with its drip-molded windows, machicolated cornices, and thin corner turrets, is essentially that of the late eighteenth- and early nineteenth-century English residential Gothic, and thus may be considered as a late survival of the Picturesque in its historical sense. However, the general elongation of the forms and the coarseness of the detail are characteristic of American provincial work of the 1860s and 1870s. The arcade of five bays, rather resembling a segment of a cloister, that flanks the side of the chapel and connects with the gate screen is an exception to the prevailing heavy-handed detailing; this open passage, with its groined vaults, is designed and executed with a crisp competence that is rather admirable when one considers the whole state of Gothic Revival work in Pittsburgh at the time. Here again the literary reference is not lacking — there is something about the shadowed angularity of this arcade, a curiously graphic quality, which reminds one of the work of the English book illustrators of the 1860s.

The eighty-foot octagonal tower at the other side of the building, with its battlemented top, provided a definitely vertical as well as a Romantically castellated note to the composition. Strangely enough, the rod-like turrets that ring the top recall those of the gaunt English Baroque tower of Hawksmoor's St. George's in the East (1715-23), a London church burned out in the Blitz but whose ruin is more interesting than its prime state. There could obviously be no connection historically between the two buildings, but here one is forcibly brought face to face with that love of fantasy, that yearning for the original and unusual, something quite beyond style or period, which is essential in the human spirit, and which has haunted the whole course and range of architecture; unbidden, unforeseen, it may emerge and be bodied forth in stone or wood, in strangely similar forms, at various times and places.

To sum up, this charming little composition of gate, chapel, and tower, nothing really very wonderful in itself, may be taken as the very type of Romantic Picturesque architecture. It abides in our midst and may be studied and looked upon at length. It is its purpose, and perhaps its virtue, to suggest, to recall, to stir a little the softer emotions and superlatively to present itself as the dominant element in a picture. We do not require of such a building that it be well founded; all that we ask is that the structure be put together well enough to support its role in the pictorial effect. This is the architecture of drama and of the world of dreams. As we approach the gate from Butler Street, it "composes" wonderfully with the landscape to form a "backdrop"; one almost expects the house lights to go down, to hear a few muted bars of Mendelssohn or Tchaikovsky, and to see characters in costume emerge from the Tudor arch.

[1]Now in the early 1980s, there does seem to be an interest in both Eclecticism and the Gothic Revival. The Old Master of the International Style (the very essence of Modernism), Philip Johnson, has recently designed for Pittsburgh a glass Gothic skyscraper, PPG Place, which is now in course of construction.—JVT

[2]Henry the Seventh's Chapel is a late Perpendicular Gothic addition to London's Westminster Abbey.—JVT

The Charette, March, 1957.

Evergreen Hamlet:
the First American Romantic Suburb

We must not assume that in this country the dead were the only denizens of the Romantic English park. The living citizens of the new industrial cities, when they could afford it, fled to the new Picturesque suburbs. The first significant American development of the landscaped park for suburban or residential use occurred under the aegis of Andrew Jackson Downing (1815-52) the horticulturist of the Hudson Valley and, for a time, the "house and garden" *arbiter elegantiarum* of the Western Democratic world. His *Treatise on the Theory and Practice of Landscape Gardening Adapted to North America* (1841) is, in its several editions, a minor landmark in the history of American taste. Here again we are conscious of the Word in disseminating a new idea among the rising American Middle Class. The aristocratic origins of the English park were played down, and the book, a near cousin to Hopkins' *Essay,* conveyed the message that every house holder with a little land and a small expenditure of taste and means could have a miniature English landscape garden "tailored" to meet the conditions of American life. This origin of the "you, too, can have" philosophy brought quiet rejoicing to the infant suburbs wherever two or three business men and their wives were gathered together. As a devotee of the Picturesque, Downing was also interested in the houses about which the landscapes were arranged, and two of his other books, *Cottage Residences* (1842) and *The Architecture of Country Houses* (1850), illustrate abundantly his preoccupation with Romantic architecture. Given such an impetus, the Moorish and the Gothic and the Tuscan villas proliferated among the winding paths and the "composed" shrubberies of the Downing landscape. They have proliferated, with variations on their several themes, down to our own day, and if the villas be no longer Eclectic in treatment (they are now all modern) the general suburban lay-out is still Romantic, however modified by present-day conditions.

The first of these early suburbs was Llewelyn Park in New Jersey (1852), which was laid out, for the most part, by the architect A. J. Davis, who was much influenced by the theories of his friend A. J. Downing. For this development, Davis also designed villas in assorted styles, most of which have now vanished. The moving spirit of this enterprise was a business man, Llewelyn Haskell, who wished to create a residential park for business men and "intellectuals" who could afford to live there. The men of business and the "intellectuals" did not get on, however. There were rumoured "goings on" among the latter group which excited something less than approval among the respectable, so Business finally took over. The suburb still survives, but except for the central strip of landscaped ground, much of its original Picturesque aspect has disappeared.

Although not so elegantly planned or executed (it was laid out in 1851 on vaguely Romantic principles by Hastings & Preiser, a local firm of surveyors), Evergreen Hamlet near Pittsburgh is of great interest because it is almost exactly contemporary with the New Jersey preserve; in fact, it might more properly be called the first American Romantic suburb. Definitely no "plan of lots" was Evergreen Hamlet, and even the very name prepares us for Romance! The Hamlet was intended to be the abode of remote and respectable, but also Romantic, domesticity. There were no "intellectuals" here. A rural refuge from the smoke and clangour of industrial Pittsburgh, it was founded by a local lawyer, William Shinn, who, with a group of other well-to-do citizens, formed a community with the purpose of securing to themselves the advantages of both city and country living. *Rus in urbe,* or its reverse, was the desired goal. The charter drawn up for the community contains the rights, privileges, and duties of the members, and it is a most interesting document, reflecting as it does some of the idealism of those Utopian communal societies which were so much a part of the American social scene before the middle of the nineteenth century, all of which have vanished as the dews of the morning. This was definitely a middle-class community, however, and the members retained their property and owned their own houses in the settlement, although there was a communal schoolhouse where the children of the associates were taught by a communal teacher. In retrospect this venture has a little the aspect of one of the large social experiments of the century (such as Economy only a few miles away), "watered down," as it were, into a middle-class private paradise — J. P. Marquand in hoop skirts and side whiskers. The truth is, however, as Christopher Tunnard has remarked, that these planned Romantic suburbs were sponsored by business men and only business men could make them work — as long as they were not too closely associated as a group.

The Evergreen Association, belying its name, disintegrated in 1866, although the Hamlet continued to be inhabited by city dwellers who yearned for the country. Vaguely Utopian as it was, the association was doomed from the start, since we may hope for a perfect community only in Heaven. Evergreen, well preserved as it is, has retained its original aspect better than Llewelyn Park, and four out of the five houses of the group are still extant. The place has a charm and a faded provincial elegance that induce in the observer a pervasive, if rather half-hearted, nostalgia.

One or two of the houses are interesting as pleasant local examples of the mid-century residential Gothic — sometimes referred to as "steamboat Gothic," a term which, if not strictly accurate, has a certain pungent and *gemütlich* quality. All the houses in the settlement were, except one, built of wood, with batten-board walls and wooden detailing, and it is probably the woodenness of this type of building which recalls the Middle Western steamboat so vividly.

The Hill-McCallam-Davies House was designed in 1852 by J. W. Kerr, a local architect very active at mid-century in Pittsburgh. With its pointed windows, Tudor verandahs, and barge boards, it might be described as vernacular — vernacular Gothic — a Middle Western provincial version of the more sophisticated late Medieval *cum* Tudor *cum* Jacobean house which had been Americanized by Downing and Davis from the original English Picturesque *cottage ornée* and ornamental villa.

The Davies house, Evergreen Hamlet, 1852, by J. W. Kerr.

The Shinn-Beall house (also 1852), with its Gothic "lattices" harks back again to the eighteenth-century Gothic in its detailing. There is something nondescript about the general massing of these houses, and one feels that the Gothic elements have only been "laid on" as it were, a feeling that is also most apparent at St. Luke's Episcopal Church, Woodville (1851), where a rectangular meeting house has been enlivened by pointed windows. This is real American "folk-Gothic." These Evergreen house types were once legion in the Middle West and they are still numerous in small towns, where they have managed best to survive the rigours of time. Simple, unassuming, these well-preserved Evergreen villas, whose white walls contrast so admirably with the verdure about them, appeal to something deep within the American heart; this architecture has a morning and youthful freshness that is absent from later suburban construction.

It seems almost overwhelmingly appropriate that William Shinn, the prime mover in the Evergreen community, should rest finally in another chartered suburb — that ante-chamber of Eternity of which we have spoken — Allegheny Cemetery. One has the sense that the suburban cycle has come full circle and that the winding roads of the Romantic suburb undulate imperceptibly into the Romantic cemetery. There is a certain horrid consonance between the artfully-disposed Eclectic villas — Gothic or Renaissance — of the one and the carefully-placed Greek or Egyptian mausoleums of the other. And when one considers the deathly gimcrack Romanticism of many later Romantic suburbs, who shall say that the dead have not, very often, been more felicitously housed?

There is another type of minor Romantic structure — "the sham castle" — of which two small Pittsburgh examples may be worth noting. The history of the nineteenth-century crenellation and pseudo-medieval fortification is a fascinating study in itself, but we have space to touch on it only briefly. Not far from Allegheny Cemetery, at the Arsenal on Butler Street, there was another late Gothic gateway of the castellated type. This was not part of Latrobe's plan for the Arsenal; and it appears, according to Stotz, to have been erected sometime between 1830 and the Civil War. Although efforts were made to preserve it, it was demolished some years ago. With its innocuous battlements and fake vault, it belonged definitely to the "sham castle" genre.

To this same type of mock fortification belongs a much later construction, the so-called English Parapet (1898) at the King estate, now a part of Highland Park. This utterly delightful bit of architectural whimsy, this most bogus of "sham" castles, all "run up" as an

189

ornament to a Presbyterian garden, is as charming as it is little known. It is the sole example in Pittsburgh of the Romantic English "folly" of the Picturesque period — in fact it is probably one of the few specimens of its type in America. Constructed so late in the century, at a time when the designers of millionaire estates in the East were imitating the great Italian Cardinalesque gardens and the parterres of Le Nôtre, the King "folly" has a peculiarly remote *retardataire* quality which contributes materially to its poetic charm. These pseudo-battlements and fake turrets, all constructed, however, in solid stone, have no other purpose than that of adorning a view or providing the background for the pastime of a summer day.

Not alone in our vernacular *cottages ornées* did the Gothic Revival appear, but also in large residences, the family "homesteads" which in one or two cases had almost the status of country houses in the English or Hudson Valley sense. In this type of house, which was little more than a not very subtle expansion of the English ornamental villa, the gables were sharp and pointed, the sashed Gothic windows were high and narrow, and the barge boards and Tudor chimneys ubiquitous. The spirit of Romance continued to breathe through the smoky Victorian air, and probably the owners of these mansions fondly imagined them to be noble but "improved" descendants of English late Gothic manors — a resemblance more apparent in fancy than in fact. The type vied for popularity with the Italian villa and the French Second Empire *maison particulière*. Sometimes, such was the growing Eclecticism of taste of the period, elements of all three might be found in one building — mixed perhaps with a debased Barryesque Classicism from England or remnants of the American Greek Revival. The books of specimen houses which began to be published in greater numbers illustrate the growing complexity of architectural styles.

Certainly the most elaborate of the Gothic manor houses of the mid-nineteenth-century still in this area is the Singer house in Wilkinsburg, which was built by the Pittsburgh iron master John F. Singer, c. 1865-69, which would make it roughly contemporary with the Allegheny Cemetery administration building. Situated half way up a hillside, it was once surrounded by landscaped grounds, containing a lake and Romantic shrubberies, but now deserted by its former glory, it looms with a sort of forlorn elegance among the wayward and desiccated streets of an aging real-estate development. It looms, it cuts the sky with the sharpness of its roofings and gables, it vaguely *aspires,* but one is not sure to *what* — there is something fruitlessly excessive about the desire for mere height apparent in all

The Singer house, Wilkinsburg: detail.

the buildings of this period. Of the period, again, is the rather heavy asymmetrical massing, the Tudor verandahs, the flattened Tudor arches of the windows, the elaborate barge boards, and the molded chimneys. Some of the windows have elaborately-carved hoods (a feature which seems to have been developed as a concomitant of the Italian Villa type), and the barge boards seem to be less architectural adjuncts than finely-executed lace "edgings." The crude richness of the French Second Empire seems to inform all this intricate detailing, and one is reminded of very late Gothic sculpture, Flamboyant, Perpendicular, or Plateresque, where both Gothic and Renaissance forms mingle. The effect of this filigree work against the surfaces of the dark stone walls is incongruous and startling in the extreme. As a final Romantic note, the house possesses a small detached chapel at one side[1] which was once crowned with a small arrowlike *flèche* — probably the first use of the *flèche* in Pittsburgh. The house and the chapel together, even in their present raddled state, seem to compose as the chief elements of some Romantic engraved vignette or an illustration for a "Keepsake" or book of "Views."[2]

This Romantic Picturesque architecture on a larger scale was not nearly so successful. The small architectural "idea," the effective and charming *morceau*, when "blown up," as one might say of a photographic enlargement, into something bigger, often produced a drawing-out and elongation of the compositional elements, an attenuation of mass and thinning of detail.

The Singer house design contains just a suggestion of this sort of thing, but the second St. Paul's Cathedral, a large brick building erected 1853-70 after the first church had been destroyed by fire, illustrates only too vividly that tendency of the outsize Romantic vision to become nightmarish. Charles Bartberger (1823-96), the architect, was a German immigrant who had received part of his technical training at Karlsruhe in Baden before coming to Pittsburgh.[3] St. Paul's is reminiscent, to some degree, of German Gothic brick architecture of the fourteenth and fifteenth centuries, but the octagonal dome over the crossing recalls the Rhenish Romanesque. The two tall turrets on either side of the facade were probably modelled after the fifteenth-century tower of Landshut Cathedral in southern Bavaria, but they were so thin and spiky as to be entirely out of scale with the rest of the structure. The detailing of the exterior was standard pattern-book Gothic, mostly fourteenth-century English, and mostly as pedestrian and uninspired as similar mid-century work, as witness the second First Presbyterian Church (1851), also by Bartberger, which because of its smaller size is a more successful building. St. Paul's proved all too abundantly that mere physical grandiosity was fatal to the literary and Picturesque Gothic as it was literally fatal to Wyatt's Fonthill Abbey. The Cathedral may have been quite sound structurally, but it did not look sound and it seemed always to be inviting the wrath of the winds of heaven.

The Picturesque Gothic, to a degree, remained with us until the end of the Eclectic period, but in its historical late eighteenth- and early nineteenth-century sense, it was but a waning star after the mid-century. The archaeological and the High Victorian phases of the Revival were to introduce new methods of approach to Gothic and new concepts of design.

---

[1]The chapel was destroyed by fire in 1976.

[2]More about the Singer house will be found in "Medieval Pittsburgh: the Singer House, Wilkinsburg."

[3]Charles Bartberger has been credited as architect, but perhaps he acted only in a supervisory capacity, as the design has been ascribed to John Walsh of New York.—JVT

The Charette, April, 1957.

The Archaeological Phase:
Two Churches by John Notman

The evolution of architectural styles is a perennially fascinating subject, and the mutations within a style itself are fruitful points of enquiry. One phase of the Gothic Revival in America — the archaeological — may be illustrated by considering the two churches of St. Mark in Philadelphia and St. Peter in Pittsburgh, since they are probably the two best examples of the type in this country, being little inferior to English work of the time. The two buildings, remarkably similar in form and style, are also rather dissimilar in tone and execution, and they demonstrate, in a most interesting manner, the influence of local cultural factors on architectural style. However, it is necessary first to give some consideration to the development of the new style phase in Europe.

Toward the middle of the nineteenth century, a much sounder and more archaeological approach to the revived Gothic was apparent on the part of some scholars and architects. The new attitude is hardly surprising in view of the fact that antiquaries as well as members of the architectural profession had been studying and measuring the ancient monuments for more than a century. Although the desire for the Romantic and the Picturesque still persisted (indeed, these elements were to be important all during the course of the Revival), there was a new interest in Gothic, per se, as a definite historical style with a logic and structure of its own that could be analyzed and imitated. As the wealth of documents, the fruits of constant research, accumulated, it was only natural that mid-century buildings, in scale, plan, and detail, should be expected to conform to the best medieval examples.

The archaeological phase of the Revival was, one might say, a time of "settling down," of "taking stock" after the irresponsibilities of youth, and pre-eminently of providing a sound background against which the later High Victorian architects could work. Such a period of archaeological painstaking resulted at best in buildings of great correctitude of style, and at worst in imitations that are dull and tedious. It was not a very creative phase of the style, it did not produce any architects of originality, and like other periods of the Revival it was fed copiously from literary sources. The influence of literature on architecture was just as apparent as it had been in the Romantic period, and architectural construction was elaborately surrounded and buttressed with theories — historical, ethical, philosophical, and religious. The Word resounded, often with considerable force, through two continents, and everybody who had any interest in architecture at all *read* about it — the patron as well as the architect.

Two very important influences, both of them literary to a marked degree, inform this period and set most eminently its tone. The first was the work of the architect Augustus Welby Northmore Pugin (1812-52) who built a whole philosophy of life on his interest in Gothic architecture and who laboured so assiduously to advance his views that he fell ill and died at an early age. The other influential element was the Ecclesiological Movement which, beginning in 1839 with a group of dedicated undergraduates at Cambridge University, produced the all-powerful Ecclesiological Society of London. Closely connected with the Anglo-Catholic Movement in the English Church and dedicated to its tenets, the Society was also much preoccupied with liturgical and theological matters. Both Pugin and the Ecclesiologists believed the Gothic to be the only Christian style and the "Middle Pointed" or Decorated Gothic of the fourteenth century in England to be the purest and most "correct" of all the phases of that style. The Ecclesiologists succeeded in erecting this preference into an architectural dogma and the fourteenth-century "Decorated" became *de rigueur,* the approved style for archaeological imitation. It may be said that this period of enforced, and sometimes inspired, copying did the art of architecture no harm, although the ethical and religious preoccupations of these protagonists of the Revival may seem today to be rather beside the point.

It did not take long for the new influences and the new writings to cross the Atlantic to America, where, mostly in the cities of the Eastern Seaboard, they found a limited if receptive audience. Richard Upjohn (1802-78), the most famous of the early Gothic Revival architects in the United States, was strongly impressed by the Anglo Catholic movement and became himself a High Church Episcopalian. His Trinity Church in New York (1841-46), the building which established his fame, belongs to the earlier, Perpendicular, style phase of the Revival, but his mid-century work shows the influence of Pugin and the Ecclesiologists. Upjohn was quite representative of his time in his earnest devotion to religious ideals, and the Anglo-Catholic architect became a typical and influential figure of the Gothic Revival.

Aside from Upjohn, the American architect who used the mid-century archaeological Gothic with the most assurance and the most success was John Notman (1810-65) of Philadelphia, who has already been mentioned in connection with Laurel Hill Cemetery. Apparently he was not an Anglo-Catholic, and he seems not to have had any predilections in that direction, but he was well equipped to purvey the fashionable architectural idiom of the moment. Although not so well known as Upjohn, his work compares favourably with that of the more famous architect, and in the case of the two churches we are about to discuss, surpasses it. St Peter's, Pittsburgh, was almost unknown until the present writer published a study of the building, but St. Mark's has always had a certain architectural fame.

The Episcopal parish of St. Mark in Philadelphia was founded in 1847 by a group of devout laymen who wished to revive what they considered a more Catholic form of worship; this group was also familiar with the work of the Ecclesiological Society. Notman was asked to prepare plans for a church, but even after these had been completed the Vestry decided, early in 1848, to apply to the Society itself for another set of plans. These drawings, executed by R. C. Carpenter (1812-55), who was then the favourite architect of the Society, were duly dispatched to Philadelphia, but they were not used owing to "certain peculiarities," as the Vestry Minutes state. Notman's final plan, adopted in February, 1848 and including some "improvements" from the English one, was largely his own, and consequently the church as erected differed only in minor details from his first plan of 1847. Notman's design shows a really astonishing degree of sophistication in the use of the archaeological manner, considering that he must have known the correct models only through literary sources.

Notman's career has been extensively recorded by Robert C. Smith of the University of Pennsylvania, and there is also a brief sketch of his life in Joseph Jackson's *Early Philadelphia Architects and Engineers,* which is not, however, always accurate. He was born in Edinburgh, Scotland, and came to this country about 1831; he settled in Philadelphia, where he first worked as a carpenter before he undertook to design any buildings. Apparently he had received some architectural training in Scotland, and he may also have attended the classes in architecture given at the Franklin Institute of Philadelphia, possibly receiving instruction from William Strickland. In 1830, he received his first commission, Laurel Hill Cemetery, but his next projects were a group of residences in New Jersey, mostly in the Italian Villa style. Throughout his career, he showed a preference for Italian architecture of various types, particularly in his elegant Barryesque plan for the Athenaeum of Philadelphia (1845); the rebuilding of

Nassau Hall at Princeton (1855); the Church of the Ascension at Philadelphia (1846), which was modeled after S. Ambrogio in Milan; and his facade for the Cathedral of SS. Peter and Paul, Philadelphia (1846-64), which has as its inspiration the Baroque church of S. Carlo al Corso at Rome. For his churches he usually used either the Romanesque or the Gothic — in the former style there are the Philadelphia churches of the Holy Trinity (1856) and St. Clement's (1855). If Notman's handling of the revival Gothic, as exemplified in his best churches, was refined and temperate to a degree, the same cannot be said of his personal life, since it is recorded that he died of drink.

St. Mark's is a brownstone building of considerable size in the "Decorated" style, with a clerestoried nave of seven bays, side aisles, a chancel, and a tower with a stone broach spire; with its refined purity of style, it had all the elements which an Ecclesiologist of the period would have found necessary for architectural salvation. So that the church might be oriented liturgically, it was placed on the site with the south side facing Locust Street, and the tower, which abuts against the outer wall of the second bay of the south aisle, serves as the main entrance. At the east end there is a deep chancel (a *sine qua non* of the nineteenth-century ritualistic church), enlarged in 1901 by the addition on its southern flank of a Lady Chapel, designed by Cope and Stewardson in a more elaborate version of the "Decorated." Other than the Geometric tracery of the windows and some simple mouldings and ornamental bands, there is little ornament on the exterior, and the church relies for its monumental effect solely on its nicely calculated scale and broad, simple massing, so characteristic of Notman's best work.

The same quietness and regard for correct proportion are evident in the architect's treatment of the interior, which consists of a nave separated from its flanking aisles by arcades of great simplicity and refinement of detail. Following the example of fourteenth-century models, Notman covered his nave with a simply-treated hammer-beam roof. The chancel, which is basically the standard "Decorated" structure of the time, has been adorned with such a wealth of later fittings that its essential purity of line has been rather "snowed under." The whole interior, with its carven furniture, rich ornaments, and stained glass windows shedding "a dim religious light," is splendidly representative of the wealthy Anglo-Catholic church of the late nineteenth and early twentieth centuries.

Today the sensitive observer, coming upon St. Mark's and its attendant parish buildings set amid the towering skyscrapers, has the sense of having wandered into a little pocket of the past — at once medieval and Victorian — miraculously preserved against the encroachments of the modern world. One needs no reminder here of the persistence of the Romantic spirit; the place seems to cast a spell on the beholder more subtle than that induced by historical memories. The Christmas-card remoteness of these delightful structures conjures up a vision of lost innocence, some half-forgotten dream of childhood, because the little group has the minute and heart-rending perfection of a "village" under a Christmas tree.

St. Peter's, Pittsburgh (1851-52) is a little later in date than St. Mark's, and it resembles the Philadelphia church to a marked degree in plan, mass, and detail, although there are certain differences. Again we have the clerestoried nave with side aisles, the chancel, and the tower with its stone broach spire placed at the side of the structure. At St. Peter's, however, the tower lies within the plane of the main facade, occupying the first bay of the aisle and with its second story abutting against the clerestory wall. The Pittsburgh church is also smaller, having a nave of only six bays instead of seven; the proportions are slenderer than those of St. Mark's, and the treatment a little less sophisticated. The marked accent on verticality and the slender massing of St. Peter's produce an impression of wiry compactness and elegance of form which is quite as handsome in its way as the more solid bulk of St. Mark's.

The church was projected in 1850 as a "chapel of ease" for Trinity Episcopal Church, the "mother" parish of Pittsburgh, to take care of the congregational overflow from the older building. That congregation was decidedly not High Church, and it would have had no sympathy with the religious ideas which gave rise to St. Mark's. It did, however, want the best type of architectural design available at the time, and the Vestry of Trinity applied to Notman, whose fame as a church architect was well known in Pittsburgh. It is possible that Notman had also contemplated publishing a book of plans since he submitted to the Vestry three numbered sets of drawings of which number two was chosen, with the stipulation that the architect make some minor changes. The cornerstone was laid in April, 1851, and the church was opened for services in December, 1852. In 1901, St. Peter's was moved stone by stone from its downtown site at Grant and Diamond Streets to its present location at Forbes Street and Craft Avenue. At that time a vestibule was added to the facade and a parish building erected to the rear of the church, after the designs of the local firm of Vrydaugh & Wolfe.

Except for these structures, which rather spoil the mid-century

St. Peter's, as rebuilt in Oakland.

aspect of the church, the exterior has been little changed since it was erected, although the sandstone walls are now a uniform sooty black — a colour common to old buildings in Pittsburgh. Again, as at St. Mark's, there is very little ornament, and that little is quite simple and restrained. To complement the Geometric tracery of the windows there is a very fine fourteenth-century doorway in the side of the tower (which, as is still the case at St. Mark's, was the main entrance on the Grant Street site). The two corbels terminating the drip moulds of this portal constitute an amusing note, since they represent the heads of well-nourished mid-century gentlemen with side whiskers. One wonders if they were intended as portraits of the architect.

The interior of the church shows even less evidence of change than does the exterior. The general sparseness of decoration (in marked contrast to St. Mark's), the cool off-white colour of the plastered walls give the nave a bare, almost puritanical tone (quite in keeping with the spirit of Pittsburgh Protestant churches at the time), which makes it easier to assess its fine architectural qualities. The simplicity of the mouldings and pier shafts of the nave arcade emphasizes the large opening of the arches, and there is no sense of sharp division between nave and aisles. The smaller spatial volumes of the aisles merge easily into the greater height of the nave with its fine overarching hammer-beam roof, which is similar to that of St. Mark's. Here again the general slenderness of the members and the lack of carved detail save the roof from the feeling of confused fussiness which characterizes several of Upjohn's beamed roofs of the 'Forties — notably in Grace Church, Brooklyn (1847-48). This straightforward solution of a structural problem is a far cry from Bishop Hopkins' painted fan vaults in the second Trinity Church.

There is a starkness and forthrightness about St. Peter's Church which does not lend itself to nostalgic or Romantic reverie. In the present setting, that of an old residential district which has faded into a dreary nondescript quasi-industrial quarter, the building does not have the air of a small ecclesiastical pocket of resistance, but rather the politely deprecatory air of a city church which has "lost out." It was, however, a lion in its day. When the church was opened for services in 1852 the *Pittsburgh Journal* observed: "We believe that Pittsburgh can now boast the most beautiful church building of the western country and even at the East, while we have seen buildings far more costly and decorated with much more elaborate ornament, we have seen none which for majesty and imposing grandeur and simplicity can be entitled to rank before it." Even when one has discounted the local journalistic hyperbole, one would not, even today, wish to contradict the statement. With the exception of Cram's Calvary Church (1906-07) and Goodhue's First Baptist Church (1911), St. Peter's is probably the best thing produced by the Gothic Revival in Pittsburgh, and it exemplifies most clearly that simplicity, sobriety, and coolness of tone which have always been notable characteristics of Pittsburgh architecture.

In a study of limited scope such as this, the writer has felt justified in giving extended treatment to the churches of St. Mark and St. Peter, not only because they are important monuments of the American Gothic Revival but also because of the light that they shed on the part that local conditions may exert on architecture. These two buildings, almost contemporary, designed by the same architect in the same style and so similar in general form, are yet completely different in feeling and "tone." There is implicit in the fabric of St. Mark's a sense of the whole cultural milieu of Philadelphia, with its relatively old tradition and the urbanity and sophistication, faintly provincial and quiet though they are, of a city near the sea, a port not only for commerce but for new ideas from abroad. The architectural "idea" which had found so ready a haven at Philadelphia was transported by Notman almost bodily to Pittsburgh, but in that passage the original conception underwent something more than a sea change. When St. Mark's became St. Peter's, what happened? The "idea" was the same, and there was not much difference in the materials that bodied it forth, but St. Peter's, in its starkness and simplicity, exemplifies forcibly the qualities of the pioneers who had established Pittsburgh — the forthrightness, the hearty quietude, the sobriety, the sturdy Protestantism, and the dislike of new doctrine and undue display. No matter what the style of the building, the treatment of the same theme may vary widely. Beyond the idea and the stone, there abides the "spirit of the place" — the formed earth and the eternal hand of man emerging from that earth — which fashions the idea into the desired usage.

The Charette, May, 1957.

Modern Gothic in Pittsburgh

In lamenting the many mansions of that Eclectic paradise so lately and unfortunately sunken from the Modern view, we must take into account the last, and in many ways the most exceptional, productions of the Gothic Revival in Pittsburgh.

The Revival continued to be a favoured style throughout the nineteenth century and the early twentieth centuries, reaching a peak of explosive grandeur in some magnificent churches and great skyscrapers constructed within the first forty years of this century.

The Gothic of the twentieth century might be described as neo-Archaeological since, in the hands of men like Ralph A. Cram (1863-1942) and Bertram G. Goodhue (1869-1924), considerable emphasis was placed on purity of style and a wide knowledge of Gothic construction methods, although these architects were able to manipulate the elements of the style so creatively that their best work has a vigour and originality all its own. However, this final flowering of archaeological correctitude was, to some degree, the result of the ideals of the first archaeological period, which had a continuing influence through the rest of the nineteenth century, notably in the work of Sir George Gilbert Scott (1811-78) whose buildings had a reputation for stylistic propriety if they were not very original.

After the middle of the nineteenth century, during the High Victorian era in England, some really creative architects emerged. Among others, William Butterfield (1841-1900), George E. Street (1824-81) and J. L. Pearson (1817-98) tried to adapt the Gothic to the new forms and functions of the century and to construct their buildings freely and creatively. The most interesting of this group is Butterfield, whose forceful, masculine, highly personal work is characterized by an almost brutal directness and a very free handling of the Gothic style. Among contemporary Americans, the work of the Philadelphian Frank Furness (1839-1912) — in whose office Louis Sullivan worked as a young man — is most similar to that of Butterfield in its powerful and fascinating ugliness, its vigour and its "punch." The Pennsylvania Academy of Fine Arts, Philadelphia (1872), his most representative work, is only ostensibly Gothic — it is almost pure Furness. A very bulldog of a building, it seems to lunge aggressively at one, displaying all its fierce variety of materials, its rude massing and coarse unconventional detail. This is no architecture for those of tender taste, but in its blunt, creative way it is more effective and more important than the tidy Gothic pastiches run up by the Scott school.

The High Victorian Gothic manner was never very important in Pittsburgh, probably because the Richardsonian Romanesque so completely possessed the architectural field in this city for some years that there was little chance of another style gaining wide popularity. In odd corners of Pittsburgh, however, a few bits of the High Victorian style have survived, such as the double house at 233-35 Sheffield Street, whose aggressive hardness and crisp coarse detailing gives the appearance of having been cut from sheet metal. A felicitous combination of the earlier "Decorated" archaeological manner and the High Victorian may be seen in Trinity Cathedral (1870-71), by the Detroit architect Gordon W. Lloyd (1832-1904), where the fourteenth-century spired tower and the broad, sprawling nave combine the two types in a most interesting manner. The charming Picturesque folk Gothic, as exemplified in the first Calvary Episcopal Church (1861-71) by Joseph W. Kerr (1815-88), steadily lost out to the more complicated, exuberant (and often inept) massing and detail of such buildings as the First Lutheran Church (1886-88) of Andrew Peebles. The Ruskinian Italianate Gothic made its appearance rather belatedly, but competently, in the Fifth Avenue High School (1894) by Edward Stotz, and the Parish House of the first Calvary Church (1893). Around the turn of the century, at the beginning of the Edwardian period, a rather dry, wiry Gothic became fashionable. A good example of this type is T. P. Chandler's Third Presbyterian Church (1901-03) whose basic Sir G. Scott Decorated mass is enlivened by detailing of a Curvilinear sinuosity which seems nearly allied to the Art Nouveau.

But structures like the Third Church, Egan & Prindeville's third St. Paul's Cathedral (1904-05), and Chandler's First Presbyterian Church (1903-05) were as shadows before the superior effulgence of the work of Cram, Goodhue & Ferguson. Both [Ralph Adams] Cram and [Bertram Grosvenor] Goodhue (Ferguson seems to have been a "sleeping" partner in the firm) were most pre-eminently the heirs of the archaeologists of the nineteenth century, and they possessed talents of the first order which enabled them to work freely and often to compose in a most masterly fashion within the style that they thought was most sympathetic to them. Like other big firms of the time, they worked competently in several styles, but the Gothic was particularly their field — and they were *the* Gothic firm *par excellence.* Even after the two principal partners went (as is the wont of many

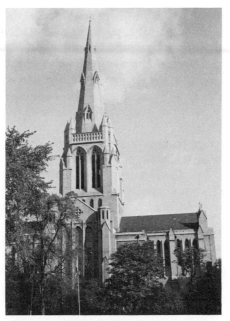

Calvary Episcopal Church.

such partners) their separate ways in 1914, they continued to be eminent Gothicists. However, during the time that they were associated, it is still possible to differentiate between the work of the two men, since the firm possessed two offices — one at Boston in the charge of Cram and the other headed by Goodhue in New York. The *oeuvre* of both architects is marked by the utmost knowledge, suavity, and good taste, but Goodhue undoubtedly had more originality and creative force than Cram.

Pittsburgh possesses one of the finest of Cram's early works in the second Calvary Episcopal Church (1906-07), which is an elegant and accomplished exercise in the Early English Gothic, although Montgomery Schuyler, with his accustomed perspicacity, noticed certain affinities with the early French version of the same style. The long, narrow lancets of the transepts are most effective, although the west front, with its dramatic arcading of the nave windows, is superior as an architectural composition. The tower with its octagonal stone spire is superb; it seems to gather itself magnificently from the crossing to ascend in masses of the most exquisitely adjusted proportions against the sky. Cram himself was very proud of this tower, and justifiably so — certainly nothing finer was produced by the architects of the English Gothic Revival.

The interior of the church, especially the nave, shows a nice regard for scale and proportion, but the general effect is austere and chilly, sometimes to the point of dullness — a dullness which is not redeemed by the elaborate complexity of the late English Gothic rood screen. The whole building, so obviously and ultimately the Church in Good Taste, has a sort of refrigerated elegance, a notable *preserved* suavity, which constitutes a monument to the well-bred austerities of a vanished era.

Goodhue's First Baptist Church (1909-11) is quite another cup of tea — the general style is that of the Late English Gothic informed with touches of French grace, as witness the very handsome *flèche* — but the architect's dependence on historical precedent is much less evident and his handling of the style is pliable, light, and free. The general mass has a moulded sculptural quality — always a notable characteristic of Goodhue's best work — and the well-calculated relationship between the large area of glass and the solids makes for a composition of great airiness, liveliness, and verve. The interior shows how cleverly the Gothic cruciform plan has been adapted to the needs of a particular Protestant sect without sacrificing the integrity of the Gothic style, and the whole great space — so little broken up — is infused with colour and warmth. From the standpoint of originality and effectiveness, it is altogether a better job than Cram's church.

The First Baptist Church.

204

The East Liberty Presbyterian Church.

Cram had, however, the last, if not the best, word in his two East Liberty churches — Holy Rosary (1929-30) and the East Liberty Presbyterian Church (1931-35). It is interesting that Cram, like Richardson before him, had been attracted to Spain, and his later manner was much influenced by the Spanish Gothic. The interior of Holy Rosary shows particularly the influence of the great Catalonian Gothic churches, and there is much minor detailing of Spanish origin. The handling of the transepts and central tower of the East Liberty Presbyterian Church shows an obvious debt to Spain, although the general treatment of the mass of the church is rather more free than in his earlier work. These late churches are accomplished, dramatic, and handsome, but there is in their execution a certain tired, mechanical quality which detracts from their ultimate effect and which heralds the end of the Gothic Revival.

It was given to Pittsburgh to build, if not the largest, at least the last and the most fantastic monument of the Revival — the so-called Cathedral of Learning (1926-37) of the University of Pittsburgh. Here is the out-size Romantic vision, allied to the steel frame, soaring almost out of control; this is essentially Wyatt's Fonthill Abbey

205

on an undreamt-of scale. In this connection it is interesting to speculate what Wyatt would have done if he had had the steel frame. Education has never been really at home in this monstrous tower, and the Cathedral promises to remain the silliest and one of the most splendid of all the architectural follies of the 'Twenties.

The idea of a "cathedral" devoted to education had apparently been conceived as early as 1921, and such a conception was quite in keeping with the Romantic ebullience, the still-expansive *élan* of the capitalist world during the 'Twenties — a period which saw the last most hectic flowering of that world. In those days a rising stock market begot more towers, and there was no inconsiderable connection between the state of a corporation's stock and the number of floors in the building it occupied. The business world had become the fountain of Grace and the source of Light, and if Cass Gilbert had designed a "cathedral of commerce" in the Woolworth Building at New York, why should not education, by now also an expanding industry, be similarly housed? Onward, and especially upward, with the arts and sciences (following, of course, the celestial ascent of the stock market) was the watchword of the day, and how could education be more suitably enshrined than in fifty-two (count 'em!) stories of steel and stone?

It must be concluded that Pittsburgh has kept, architecturally speaking, a weather eye on Philadelphia, for to Charles Z. Klauder of that city was given the task of making the Pittsburgh vision a reality. It was the period of the Chicago Tribune Tower competition (1922-23) in which Eliel Saarinen lost out to Hood and Howells' dramatic re-hash of the Tour de Beurre at Rouen. From the time of the Woolworth Building (1911-13), the North French and Flemish Late Gothic had had a certain number of adherents among architects of skyscrapers. F. J. Osterling, in his handsome Union Arcade [Union Trust] Building (1915) at Pittsburgh, had frankly and very tastefully imitated the style of the New York prototype, although the Pittsburgh structure more nearly approximated its European models owing to its smaller size. The only other Gothic skyscraper in Pittsburgh, the former Keystone Athletic Club (1928) by Janssen & Cocken, is contemporary with the Cathedral of Learning. Following roughly the theme set by Arthur Harmon in the Shelton Hotel at New York (1923), the Pittsburgh building (now the Sherwyn Hotel)[1] is an interesting essay in the Italian brick Gothic of the fourteenth and fifteenth centuries as interpreted by the 'Twenties.

Aside from these two excursions into the Gothic, the design of Pittsburgh skyscrapers was much dominated by the neo-Classicism of D. H. Burnham (which proved so attractive to Pittsburghers after the Richardsonian Romanesque ceased to be fashionable) and various aspects of the French and Italian Renaissance. Probably the very paucity of Gothic tall buildings in Pittsburgh whetted the public appetite for novelty (so prominent a characteristic of the 'Twenties) and contributed to the advance publicity and the financial campaign which preceded the actual construction. The Cathedral was to be the ultimate monument to the progress of learning as well as a symbol of the aspirations of the chicken-in-every-pot school of thought.

All the augurs being auspicious, the excavation for the building was begun in September, 1926, on a plot in the cultural centre of Oakland, but unfortunately the period of financial prosperity came to an end in 1929 and the work lagged. The height of the tower, after some fluctuations of opinion, was finally fixed at forty stories, and although the structure is now substantially complete, some parts of the interior have never been finished to this day.[2] No matter what the extreme Modernists may say, the building is striking, very handsome and, at times, beautiful — if one is to consider only its appearance. These soaring structural masses, with their accent on verticality, compose well, and the transition to the smaller upper volumes of the general mass is managed very neatly with the assistance of the finely detailed corner turrets. The tremendously elongated Gothic windows (or one might rather say, the "idea" of such windows) sweeping up the outer faces of the tower are effective and interesting, although the traceried tops cut off light from some of the upper floors. In this last monument of the Revival, the Romantic spirit has produced the final and not the least grandiloquent statement of the Picturesque in architecture. By day it is a castle quite beyond the resources of Spain or Thule; on a night of storm, or fog, or even on a fine Spring evening, ablaze with light, it will be a sorcerer's staff, Merlin's very tower, rising above the erstwhile farmlands of Oakland.

One cannot abide with ease in Thule, however, and one attends classes in Merlin's tower only at one's peril. As a "stunt" of the 'Twenties the Cathedral now seems rather *vieux jeu*, more than a little *demodée*; as a functioning building it is an almost unmitigated architectural disaster. Commerce still is well accommodated in the Woolworth Building, but education, since the student body of the University has grown to huge proportions, has become hideously cramped in her "Cathedral." Problems of traffic inside the structure are particularly acute, and anyone who tries to get about the place when classes are changing will find the experience, if not infernal, at least purgatorial. Unfortunately, the designers worked from the

The Heinz Chapel, with the Cathedral of Learning beyond.

outside in — a formula nearly always fatal to sound architecture — and the functions of the building were simply stuffed into the outer envelope like groceries into a sack. At the present time, the sack is bulging dangerously, and some method, possibly the erection of smaller buildings about the base of the tower as has already been considered, will have to be found to relieve the congestion.[3]

The great Commons Room (1937), with its Gothic groined vaults rising some sixty feet from the floor, is the best feature of the interior and a *coup de théâtre* of the first order. This again is dramatic architecture, and it is related surely to the work of Baroque and Romantic scene designers and to the *Carceri* of Piranesi in its involved compositional complexity. The artfully-broken great central spatial volumes of the room are enlivened and embroidered by the smaller recessional spaces of the surrounding galleries. During the 'Thirties it was hoped that the place might prove an "inspiration" to the student body, but it is doubtful if this stagey hall has ever inspired anybody to anything. No doubt, however, the students have over the years found it all rather fun.

This great hall is surrounded by the "Nationality" classrooms (related to the "display" rooms of department stores and the historical installations in museums) which, with their variety of styles, constitute almost a minor summation of the Eclectic period. These late fantastic manifestations of the Eclectic spirit, these magpie accumulations and cultural hoardings, have a bizarre, portentous charm which proclaim the imminence of 1939 and the end of our period.

The Gothic architecture of the Heinz Chapel (1934-38) and the Stephen Foster Memorial (1935-37), subsidiary buildings on the University campus and both by Klauder, is characterized by a sort of bored ineptitude, uneasily relieved by flashes of inspiration. The chapel, although its design has a few good "passages," is nothing but a weary echo of Goodhue's Baptist Church, and some of the detail of both buildings is perilously similar to the earliest "cardboard" Gothic, but without its engaging charm. In the end of the Gothic Revival was its beginning.

The mansions of Eclecticism have been desolate for some time now, and Gothic arches and Renaissance columns are looked upon, if not with dismay, at least with suspicion. Modernism has completely triumphed, and when we consider the rather senile architectural doodling of the Heinz Chapel and the Foster Memorial, it seems only just that it should have done so. But one misses the earlier and more accomplished graces of that vanished time before the Second World War, and it is a hard thing that we should be so utterly denied them today. However, *tout change, tout passe,* and it is possible that instead of looking back we can look forward again, into the cloudy future of the Modern style, where there may be some new mutation of the Gothic, a farther Revival, which could be more interesting than that we have just considered.

[1]Presently part of Point Park College.

[2]This, in 1983, is still true to a small extent.

[3]This has still not happened.

The Charette, August, 1957.

The fourth Union Station of the Pennsylvania Railroad in 1905.

210

Pittsburgh Railroad Stations
Past and Present
An Architectural Excursion
with Stopovers at Philadelphia

Part I

There are buildings like gardens in this prosaic world which
have a special glamour, a weighted importance in the course of our
days, and which linger pervasively in the memory even beyond their
departure.

Let us now praise railroad stations, which have for many of us
a beguiling attraction induced by youthful memories of their glorious
and exciting past. The nineteenth century was prodigal of new
building types — libraries, factories, exhibition halls, and hotels —
and fascinating as many of them are, none can compare in interest
with the structures developed to serve the railroad.

By the end of the century, the continents were covered with nets
of steel — new roads which coursed with the multitudinous, quasi-
nomadic life of the age — for travel had become possible for almost
everyone. These running tracks were punctuated and adorned by
thousands of stations, an overwhelming variety of buildings — from
the village "depot," which often became the centre of town life, to
the great vaulted or towered palaces in the cities where the
kaleidoscopic social existence of the time could be seen in all its
density and variety.

As the fragmented, static society of the pre-mechanistic age was
changed by the new technology into a more fluid body of larger units,
the building types suitable to the needs of the old order were no longer
adequate. A king's palace might serve as a library or picture gallery,
but it would not do as a hospital or a hotel, and churches and theatres
which had accommodated relatively large groups of people in the past
provided no proper models for huge exhibition halls or department
stores. Coaching inns, similarly, could not accommodate the huge new
traveling public, so that railroad engineers and architects had to
invent entirely new structures such as the station, the train shed,
and the railroad hotel.

Among this plethora of novel constructions, the railroad station
was a very special creation, because it had to serve as a bridge
between the relatively stable, stay-at-home world and the peripatetic,

changing world of movement. The two modes of life intersected and intermingled at the depot in a dramatic confrontation unknown even in the ancient bazaars of the Orient. Everyone came, everyone went, and at some time everyone met at the station. The great metropolitan termini, where everything was provided for the ease of the traveler, became little microcosms of the cities in which they stood and, in retrospect, they seem the abodes of adventure and romance, palaces of smoke and light.

The development of the station also coincided with the widest amplitude of nineteenth-century architectural Eclecticism, and all previous history was ransacked to provide habiliments for the new constructions. The baths of Rome and the turrets of the Middle Ages soared above the iron sheds, providing for the bemused traveler a steadily larger atmosphere of wonderment and fantasy. So, even a "whistle stop" might be adorned with a "Gothic" cottage or a miniature Hindu temple, and there was no minor country depot which might not have its exotic adornments. The architectural realm no longer seemed to stay at home; it was almost as if the "styles" flowed along the tracks, stopping now here, now there, until our railroad lines became very compendia of the history of building. Babylon and Egypt attended our smallest journeys, and the towers of Venice and Antwerp enlivened the unsubtle perspectives of America's Middle West. If nineteenth-century Eclecticism had no other monument than the railroad station, the chronicle would still be sufficient.

Above all, railroad stations were, very often, buildings that one *remembered* — there was about them a charm, a grandeur or a "tone" that stayed in the mind. Nowadays, when the grey cloak of modern conformity has spread over so much of contemporary life, when variety and delight have departed from us and a monotonous sameness informs our public architecture, we may recall with gratitude these relics of an elder and more spacious day. Whatever their architectural shortcomings, and there were many dull and dreary depots, it must be admitted that the station as a type had an individuality all its own in an age when individuality was still valued.

The railroad station was not an unfamiliar *mise-en-scène* in the literature and art of the nineteenth century, and one remembers most poignantly that place where Anna Karenina threw herself under a train. In painting, W. P. Frith's anecdotal Paddington Station canvas was one of the most popular, if not "artistic," pictures of the Victorian era. References to our buildings abound everywhere, but the type had no historian until recently, when it was thoroughly studied and documented by C. L. V. Meeks, whose *The Railroad Station* is the

212

authority in its field. For the depot *aficionado* the book is both a bible and a *vade mecum*.

American stations of the first half of the nineteenth century, insofar as they did not imitate European models, had an air of improvisation, of being run up quickly to meet specific conditions. Sometimes inns or dwelling houses were adapted for stations, but one of the earliest building types evolved for the new method of travel was the train barn — again an adaptation of an already-existing model. Arches were cut at either end of the rectangular structure and the trains were run through it, taking on or discharging passengers at platforms on either side. These openings were fitted with doors so that the engines could be locked up at night, like horses in a stable.

This rough shelter was enlarged, as time went on, to include more elaborate station facilities on one or both sides. In America the barn type of station during the early years took the place of the train shed, which was found in England as early as 1830 at George Stephenson's Crown Street Station in Liverpool. It was not until 1869 that the European train shed, as a lofty adjunct to a terminal building, was used at the first Grand Central in New York. After the middle of the century, American depots, as classified by Meeks, usually belonged to one of three categories — the one-sided, with arrival and departure facilities on one side of the line (this has always been the most common American type); the two-sided, with arrivals handled on one flank of the line and departures on the other (uncommon in this country); and the stub type, with the lines ending against the terminal station or head house.

The stations of Pittsburgh are thoroughly representative of the period in general character, nor is there — save in one or two instances — anything especially remarkable about them. There is not here, for instance, nor has there ever been, anything notably grand in the way of termini; the sober tone of the city has, as a rule, eschewed grandeur, and the varied topography of the place contains no plains of sufficient extent which would permit large architectural displays. Our local stations do have, however, a "tone" peculiar to themselves, and it seems fitting, as the Bicentennial of the city approaches, to celebrate them as important factors in Pittsburgh's urban development.

It is obvious that Pittsburgh, due to its geographical position, was destined to be an important channel of commerce, but it was not until the middle of the nineteenth century that a definite attempt was made to connect the city with Philadelphia by rail. The Pennsylvania Railroad Company was incorporated in April, 1846 — not a moment too soon, for the Baltimore and Ohio Railroad Company was trying to secure entry into Pittsburgh. By actually putting part of the line under contract in the summer of 1847, the Pennsylvania was able to force the B. & O. out of the running. A railroad line had already been constructed from Philadelphia to the Susquehanna River, but the Allegheny Mountains constituted a formidable barrier to railroad expansion in the western part of the state. The mountains had been crossed in the 1830s by a series of inclined planes, connected by railroad tracks which pulled canal-boat sections over the ridges, depositing them finally at Johnstown whence they were floated by canal to Pittsburgh. This method of transportation was, however, intricate and cumbersome, and finally superseded by the new railroad, which purchased the Allegheny Portage Railroad (a State-owned concern) in 1857 and dismantled it. The first through train from Philadelphia over the Pennsylvania lines entered Pittsburgh on December 10, 1852, although the new line had to make use of some of the inclined planes until 1854, when the Horseshoe Curve and the Gallitzin Tunnel were completed.

The first passenger station in the Pittsburgh area was built in 1851 at Federal Street in Allegheny by the Ohio and Pennsylvania Railroad. By a process of amalgamation this railroad later became the Pittsburgh, Fort Wayne and Chicago, and later still part of the Pennsylvania system. This, the earliest of the three Federal Street depots, was a two-story brick structure adjoined by a wooden freight shed, and it appears to have been a terminal station until the line was carried across the river into Pittsburgh's Union Station, when it became merely a subsidiary depot. As seen in an old engraving, the structure displays a crude striving for architectural sophistication, an awkward provincial gaucherie not without a certain engaging charm. Typically mid-century and Middle Western, this building has a certain "frontier" elegance. It is a small-town dude tricked out in a store-bought finery.

It seems eminently fitting that Pittsburgh's largest early station should have been devoted to the handling of freight. This huge wooden shed, six hundred sixty-four feet long by one hundred ten feet wide, was known as the Duquesne Depot because it was supposed to have been built on the site of Fort Duquesne, although Neville B. Craig proved conclusively in a newspaper article of 1854, the year in which the station was built, that the structural remnants disclosed during excavation were those of Fort Pitt. The military beginnings of Pittsburgh were by that time rather remote in the popular mind, and the city was so exclusively devoted to commerce that the preemption of its most historic site by a freight station was only to be expected. The land at the confluence of the two rivers is like a palimpsest, a manuscript that has been written over and erased, and the present writing, the Gateway Center, is not, possibly, the most interesting chapter.

Certainly the scene at the Point in the late 'Fifties must have been lively enough. The Pennsylvania had been allowed to lay its tracks down Liberty Avenue to connect with the Monongahela wharves, where goods from the river steamboats were transferred to the railroad for shipment east. The steamers with their tall stacks, the trains and the drays, the clamour and the commerce and the smoke, must have given the scene an animation that it lacks today. The new station needed to be large to accommodate the traffic, and it remained for some years the largest enclosed space in the city.

In November, 1858, the immense hall, decorated with flags and evergreens, resounded to the oratory of the city's first centennial celebration. It is an interesting comment on this sort of building that, in a developing community when a variety of structures for separate functions was lacking, it could and did serve more than one purpose.

As a railroad type, the Duquesne Depot belonged in the train-barn category, although the handling of freight, rather than passengers, was its *raison d'être;* it was built entirely of wood with a curved roof which had a structural ventilator at its apex, running the length of the building. At the ends were round openings with doors which allowed the trains to enter and leave, and to take on or discharge freight at the platforms lining the sides of the interior. Drays could load and unload their burdens from these runways through openings on the longitudinal flanks of the station. The great echoing hall, with its truss roof of a single span, foreshadowed the immense interior spaces of the Pennsylvania's later train sheds.

Stylistically, the Duquesne Depot was a mixture of watered-down "Italian Villa," which was so popular not only for domestic but also for station design in the 'Forties and 'Fifties, and the round-arched style derived from the early Romanesque revival of the last century. The arched doorways might belong in either category, but the brackets were Italian Villa. To add yet a further element to the composition, there is something curiously Baroque about the flattened curve of the roof, an effect which must have added a note of ponderous gaiety to so commercial a quarter.

Even in a freight station of the period, the picking and choosing from the styles of the past is noticeable, for Eclecticism was already well advanced on its course. Fire was, however, the enemy of all these early wooden stations and, owing to the ignition of some oil kegs stored in the cellar, the Duquesne Depot went up in smoke on July 30, 1861. According to contemporary accounts, it burned superbly, providing one of those spectacular conflagrations so appreciated by provincial populations. The station was rebuilt on the same scale but not so stylishly, and the new building survived until 1902, when the new Duquesne freight yard was constructed.

Later Pittsburgh stations, speaking stylistically, fall into three classifications noted by Meeks in his study of the railroad station. The first period in America (c. 1840-70) is Classical, with emphasis on low-lying horizontal masses and detailing derived from the Italian Villa, Italian Renaissance, or Greek Revival styles. Since the Italian Villa in a relatively pure form belongs among the Romantic revivals, the station mass might be given a more varied outline by the addition of verticals in the form of towers. The second period (c. 1870-90) is characterized by an almost unbridled Romanticism of outline and detailing, with much attention to irregular, asymmetrical massing and strong vertical accents. Towers, turrets, and high gables with dormers proliferated in this most complicated and intricate of the three groups, and the styles themselves might be Gothic, Richardsonian Romanesque, or Renaissance. Lastly, another Classical era came into being around 1890, which lasted well into the new century. The Romantic outline sank again into the repose of horizontal masses, and the stylistic detailing might be Roman, neo-Classical, Renaissance, or neo-Baroque. In this last category, domes took the place of towers in providing variety of silhouette. All the stations discussed in this installment of the present series belong roughly in the first classification, and the Pittsburgh station which illustrates it most fully is the second Union Station (1863-65).

The first *passenger* station of the Pennsylvania Central lines in Pittsburgh was located in a warehouse at the corner of Liberty Avenue and Twelfth Street, and this remained in use until the completion of the first Union Station at the southwest corner of Liberty and Grant in 1854. This station, a one-story frame structure, was rendered inadequate by the steadily-increasing passenger traffic, and a new building was begun in 1863, approximately on the site of the present depot. The second Union Station, which was combined with a hotel after the English fashion, was partially opened for use on September 10, 1865 although the hotel portion was not completed until January, 1866. It was, in its day, one of the most elegant stations in the country — certainly the best on the Pennsylvania lines — and its opening was an event of some importance for the city.

The hotel contained in the station building or connected with it developed rather early in Britain, although the type was not completely unknown in America. The British railway station hotel at York (1840-41) was a forerunner of the magnificent and luxurious London caravansaries such as P. C. Hardwick's Great Western Railway Hotel at Paddington (1853) and Sir G. G. Scott's St. Pancras Station hotel (1863-76). In America, there were some depots like the Queen City Station of the B. & O. Railroad at Cumberland, built in the 'Seventies, which accommodated a hotel within the building itself. Some hostelries were built separate from the depot but as near the tracks as possible, such as the Logan House (1855) at Altoona, Pennsylvania. The head-house hotel, as exemplified in the Union Station at Pittsburgh, was probably not emulated to any extent in this country, and it may have been unique, at the time, in bringing to these shores a touch of British architectural magnificence, although it was most un-British in having a series of shed-covered platforms rather than a large train shed.

The building itself covered an area eighty-five by two hundred feet and was constructed of brick with stone trimmings; it consisted of a large block of four stories in the front and another of three in the rear, and both sections had low-pitched slanting roofs. On the first floor were the ticket offices, waiting rooms, and other railroad offices; a dining room and kitchen were the important rooms on the second floor, and the rest of the building was given over to the hotel, which had ninety rooms. Four tracks of the Pennsylvania Central terminated at the building, but the tracks of the Pittsburgh, Fort Wayne and Chicago went out on one side and those of the Pittsburgh and Steubenville on the other, making the structure almost an "island station." The architects were Collins & Autenreith of Philadelphia and the resident architect was J. H. Windrim of the same city.

The general mass of the building was quite Classical in its emphasis on horizontals, and stylistically it was a vernacular exercise in the Italianate "palazzo" manner of Sir Charles Barry mixed, again, with the ubiquitous Italian Villa. The two little pediments, like eyebrows, on either side of the facade may be either Italian Villa, or a last, dying echo of the Greek Revival — for styles that have recently gone out of fashion have a way of lingering on in minor details. Between these gables, perched beneath a flag pole, hovered a great gilded eagle with out-stretched wings that seemed to proclaim American independence from any British influence below. It is interesting to compare the design of the Central High School (Barr & Moser, 1871) on the hillside above; the latter had two symmetrically placed Italian Villa towers. With a superb, breath-taking ignorance,

217

The second Union Station of 1865.

a writer for the *Pittsburgh Commercial* in 1865 described the style of the depot as "Byzantine" and the delicate and charming Renaissance portico which prefaced it as "Arcadian"; one's imagination rather boggles at the wild incongruity of the adjectives, no less than at their ludicrous juxtaposition.

For the term of its existence, the second Union Station, provincial though it was, imparted an air of Romantic Italian elegance to a drab commercial milieu and those hints, those intimations of Florence or Rome, or even Victorian London, contributed poetry to our streets. We are not so fortunate in these days of rigourous modernity, and instead of an "Arcadian" portico, at which we could at least smile, we must be content with colonnades of pipes and avenues of steel which make desolate the soul. Not alone the architecture of the time, but other aspects of the scene have a far-away fascination: through that Italian portico passed gentlemen with tall hats like towers and ladies in crinolines, like blossoms floating, and in and out of the wooden sheds gallantly ran the beautiful small locomotives, the youthful and polished dandies of the shining rails.

This charming backwoods Italian "palazzo" was a victim of the railroad riots of July, 1877, one of those conflicts between Labour and Capital which erupted like bonfires across the social history of the nineteenth century. This particular battle began as a trainmen's strike on July 19, and it was augmented by idle and vicious elements from the urban population. Troops were called in to end the disturbance but they proved ineffective, and for three days a state of anarchy existed in the lower part of the city through which the railroad ran. The freight cars in the yard were pillaged and burned by the mob, and all railroad buildings from the roundhouse at Twenty-eighth Street to the Union Depot went up in flames. All this long area became a lake of fire, a truly infernal spectacle which even the steel mills could not rival. Order was finally restored, but by that time the Union Station was a blackened shell.

Pittsburgh was forced to do architectural penance for the destruction of the station. On the site of the charred ruins, a new brick station was constructed, a barn-like place of a crushing dullness and an overwhelming lack of distinction, save for the station porch which had a vaguely pseudo-Oriental air. There was a train shed, but it was in no way notable.

After the fires of 1877 the first Classical period in Pittsburgh station architecture came to an end, and with the 1880s we find ourselves in another part of the architectural forest, a place full of wayward irregularities and asymmetrical masses, of towers and medieval gables, which attended most delightfully the whistle of locomotives and the movement of trains.

Part II

The state of architectural design in the second half of the nineteenth century might be compared with one of those fountains whose flow is mechanically controlled so that the jets of water rise according to a prearranged pattern. The low play of the water in the fountain is analogous to the first Classical period already noted, but the slow rise of the aqueous jets and columns reminds us of that Romantic ebullience which overtook the art of building in the years 1870-90, and it is that era which is the concern of this section. Behind the rising and the spray of waters appear the towers and the domes, the fairy-tale turrets and the peaked roofs of the court houses, the markets, and the railroad stations which expressed so well the nature and the ideals of that various time. The architects of those days delighted in a multitude of forms and a variety of historical reference, and railroad stations as much as any other building types produced opportunities for displays of stylistic erudition. This wayward carnival of towered fantasy, this make-believe of balcony and bay, may appear dreary and old-fashioned to our Modernists, but we who are now pre-occupied with the elimination of the non-essential, the things which "catch dust," must also consider the gaiety and charm we have lost. The Victorian architect was like a child who has been given too many toys for Christmas, but the Modern designer seems, very often, like the same child who, in glutted desperation, drops the whole bag of tricks and falls to playing with a length or two of iron pipe.

There are certain buildings of the nineteenth century which are of great importance in setting the pace, as it were, for later architects, in establishing pre-eminently a model or type which influenced deci-sively the form of succeeding structures. Such a one was the Houses of Parliament (1835-60) in London by Sir Charles Barry (1789-1850) and A. W. N. Pugin (1812-52) which became the essential prototype for all Romantic buildings until the end of the century. Sir G. G. Scott's reworking of the same theme in his St. Pancras Station (1863-76) in London provided a model for many an ambitious railroad station from Bombay to Philadelphia. The lofty, serrated silhouettes of these railway chateaux, at once passionately medieval and vigourously Victorian, contributed a heavy grandeur, a spiky operatic brio, to the nineteenth-century metropolis. The style of these buildings was often Gothic, but after the advent of Richardson it could just as well be Romanesque — as witness Theodore Link's Union Station at St. Louis (1891-94), which has a generally Romantic outline although the detailing is Romanesque.

Many of these High Victorian buildings, now grimy and neglected, still rise in our increasingly nondescript streets, but they are disappearing fast. Indeed the stations discussed in this article have either been altered considerably or have vanished altogether, and it is a portion of our purpose to define and celebrate their shadows before their memory leaves us forever. It is a sorrow in this day to consider how glamourous they were once. As the nineteenth-century traveler roamed ever-more widely, the ordered Classical station became rather a bore. Variety and picturesque fantasy became essen-tial to the public that rode the rails, and the railroads gave those who traveled what they wanted. In an age of great competition, the com-panies tended, thereby, to rival each other in arch and tower, as well as to see which of them could build the biggest train shed. Halls of Wagnerian grandeur vaunted themselves under aspiring gables, and castellated roofs were attended by flights of histrionic turrets and declamatory chimneys. And the trains ran from castle to cathedral, from French Renaissance chateau to Dutch town hall, traversing the gamut of the styles.

It is with a little section of that world, two points on the railroad map, the cities of Pittsburgh and Philadelphia, that we wish to deal. Three stations by Frank Furness illustrate admirably the architectural ideas of the time, and Pittsburgh's Federal Street Station, very late and rather out of period, sums up the case for the Romantic railroad structure.

Despite the fact that Pittsburgh was rather eminently the focus of much of Richardson's final architectural activity, no Richardsonian Romanesque station was ever built in the city. However, the old Baltimore and Ohio Station (1888-90) was so described, albeit erroneously, in the *Railway Review* of August, 1888. The B. & O. had finally secured entry into Pittsburgh in 1871, but it was not until the late 'Eighties that a large terminal was erected on a magnificent site beside the Monongahela River near the Smithfield Street Bridge. Placed on heavy stone foundations at the very edge of the wide, brown river whose surface is always shadowed by the looming ridge of Mount Washington on the opposite bank, the compact, irregular bulk of the station, looking like a nineteenth-century commercial edition of Chenonceaux, composed rather well with the iron-latticed walls of the train shed and the graceful Pauli trusses of the bridge (constructed by the engineer Gustav Lindenthal, 1881-83). The bridge still stands, but the depot and shed were recently demolished to make way for the Penn-Lincoln Parkway. Although there were no "cloud-capped towers" or wonderful chimneys here, the group did form an ensemble extremely characteristic of the late nineteenth century.

The architect of the station, Frank Furness (1839-1912), who also designed the B. & O. Station at Philadelphia in 1886, was a Romantic — but a Romantic with a difference. A "rugged individualist" according to surviving descriptions of him, he probably would have scorned the imputation of Romance. One of those figures whose importance in our architectural history has only recently been recognized, he has been considered merely one of the "pioneers of the Modern movement," a forerunner of the present Children of Light. However we are now able to see him as a man of his own time, an "original" designer who had a notable sense of constructional frankness and a vigourous and forthright way of handling the forms and the styles of his day. His manner may have lacked refinement, but it never lacked strength.

Furness, it is probably safe to say, was the dominant personality in the firm of Furness & Evans. His chief partner was Allen Evans, and sometimes there were others, but it is doubtful if any of them had any decisive influence on Furness' work.

Furness' early work is his most interesting, inasmuch as he became more conservative in his later years — a tendency apparent in the design of the Pittsburgh station. Much of his *oeuvre* shows the influence of the French theorist Eugene Viollet-le-Duc (1814-79) with whose drawings he was undoubtedly familiar (as William Campbell has demonstrated in a recent article on Furness), but in spirit he was near to that English "original" William Butterfield, who also liked to compose his masses vigourously and who delighted in harsh clashes of form. A close comparison of Furness' manner with that of other English contemporaries — William Burges for instance, whose name has been suggested by N. Pevsner — might yield more evidence of parallel trends. Furness' buildings fail ultimately to satisfy us as works of art. We are often shocked into a kind of startled admiration, but we are also too conscious of his harshness and lack of repose, the absence of refinement of form. His whole performance, although vastly interesting, just does not quite "come off." One is reminded of his American contemporary — William Halsey Wood (1855-97), an architect of less talent and vigour who belongs essentially in the same category. Why these American architects of the late nineteenth century never made the grade would make an interesting study, but we have no space for it here.

Inasmuch as Furness' B. & O. Station at Philadelphia (also a riverside depot) set the tone for the Pittsburgh structure, it would seem proper to consider it first. Located at Twenty-fourth and Chestnut Streets, beside the dreary channel of the Schuylkill, it is still extant,[1] but it was remodeled in 1943 and it must be understood that the description given here refers to the building as it was designed by Furness — and this is also the case with the Pittsburgh depot, which was much changed even before its demolition. The Philadelphia design was boldly conceived, consisting of loosely-disposed low masses dominated by a tower of almost excessively Romantic aspect, in contrast to the more compact, compressed bulk of its western follower. Since the Philadelphia station faced the approach to the Chestnut Street Bridge and the tracks were below street level, Furness made the most of the disparity in designing floor plans which were as contrived as the exterior mass. The detailing of the exterior shows particularly the influence of Viollet-le-Duc, or to be more specific, the influence of his draughtsmanship, since the French architect sketched more than he built. In this, as in other examples of Furness' work, one senses the knife-like plasticity of mass, particularly of the smaller volumes, and the crisp, nervous line of the illustrations to the *Dictionnaire Raisonneé de l'Architecture Française* and the *Entretiens*. These are not the only historical references, however, for the treatment of the roofs has a vaguely Scandinavian air, and one is reminded of the medieval stave churches of Norway. The tower on the Chestnut Street front is typically Furness — here our old friend the Italian Villa tower has gone Second Empire with a mansard roof (this sort of thing was legion in the High Victorian period) — but Furness has placed on top of the mansard, like a plum pudding piled on a cake, a rather Germanic low steeple with four dormers. Coarse and harsh as it is, the whole building has a sharp, tense angularity that is most effective, and its aggressive vigour has a certain fierce attractiveness.

The B. & O. Station in Pittsburgh lacks the dispersed rambling silhouette of its eastern counterpart, and the style shows rather pervasively the influence of the early medievalist manner and the Queen Anne of Norman Shaw (1831-1912), bringing it more nearly in consonance with much of the American brick and "shingle" vernacular architecture of the 1880s. The chimneys with flared caps, the triplets of windows with their multi-paned transoms, and the general feel-

The Baltimore & Ohio Station.

ing of the surface texture are derived from Norman Shaw, but the heavy stone voussoirs of the first floor are perhaps an echo of Richardson's Pittsburgh Jail (1884-86). It is the corner tower, with its low dormered steeple, which continues the Viollet-le-Duc motif and which shows unmistakably the hand of Furness in its vigourous composition and the clash of forms represented by the harsh verticals of the central bay and the arcs of the wrought-iron porches. The railroad age, it announces, has unequivocally arrived, and the tower has the air of a huge freight locomotive advancing from the train shed, thrusting itself forward into the city.

The train shed of this station, although much smaller than the giants that the Pennsylvania was beginning to build, is interesting because of its site — like a bridge, it was built on columns over the wharf at the edge of the river — an unusual feature noted by Berg in his book on railroad buildings published in 1893. It was three hundred eighty-five feet long and had a clear span of eighty-four feet — wide enough to accommodate four tracks and platform space. It was not, however, designed by Furness, since it was, like most train sheds, an engineering job. Although these structures had, very often, a magnificence all their own, they were considered purely utilitarian and divorced from the art of architecture. Sometimes the station architect would work with the engineer, as did Sir Matthew Digby Wyatt and I. K. Brunel at Paddington in London (1852-54), and sometimes, as in the case of several Continental stations, the two parts of the building were very well integrated. In America, however, the two usually had to get along together as best they could. It was always a marriage of convenience but only occasionally of compatibility.

The most splendid of Furness' stations, possibly the most notable of all Romantic stations in America, was Broad Street in Philadelphia. Wilson Brothers & Company, the Philadelphia firm of architects and engineers who executed so much work for the Pennsylvania, were responsible for the first station, built in 1881-82 on the model of St. Pancras in the Ruskinian Italianate Gothic style. The "stylist" of this building was Arthur Truscott. Furness & Evans won the competition for the much larger addition toward Market Street, which was erected 1892-94. Furness used here a tough, hard Gothic manner which had been fashionable in England during the 'Sixties and 'Seventies, but which had become by the 'Nineties rather out-moded, particularly when one compares Broad Street with F. H. Kimball's Reading Station (1891-93) nearby, which is in the new Classical manner. Both the mass and detailing are handled with Furness' early vigour, but the general tone is much tamer. Here again is the tower, now incorporated into an office building, with the low steeple and the four huge dormers (which remind one of early Gothic canopied tombs) surrounded by thickets of Furnessian crockets and finials. Masses of terra-cotta sculpture (executed by Carl Bitter) blossomed expansively at strategic spots on the walls of both station and shed, and all of it was rather Classical in feeling — indeed the group which surrounded the clock on the corner was almost Baroque. The fierce competition of the age may be noted again in the juxtaposition of this Gothic structure and the Renaissance City Hall across the way; Broad Street faced up to its rival belligerently and quite held its own. With its coarse confectionery grandeur, its huge honey-combed bulk, it seemed like a giant's birthday cake, complete with candles — all alight, and triumphant.

The interior plan of the station was remarkably "open" and functional, with its great wide rooms and spaces that proceeded easily into one another. Between the lower level and the waiting room rose broad stair cases notable for their almost Baroque pomp and ease of movement.

The train shed was a *tour-de-force,* the giant of all the steel pavilions that engineers were constructing in that time of unlimited rivalry to market and define the power of the railroads then at its zenith. This was the largest shed of a single span ever constructed (three hundred feet) and vied with such exhibition halls as the *Galerie des Machines* (three hundred sixty feet) at the Paris Exposition of 1889. It was as if the engineers wanted to see what they could do with the new materials, and the results were truly wonderful. These tissues of steel and glass, which seemed to float remotely over the platforms and the tracks, these vast almost undefined spaces filled with smoke and the sound of bells, the breathing of iron dragons, and the echo of hundreds of footsteps, were among the most splendid and dramatic structures ever devised by any builder. Alas, the pride of our engineers was one with the vanity of Babylon, and the halls of their triumph have fled away like visions of the night. For all their poetry, they were dirty, grimy, and difficult to maintain. The end of the Broad Street shed was as spectacular as its existence — it burned in a dramatic fire in 1923 and was never replaced. An end so Wagnerian was overwhelmingly appropriate for such a structure, and it foreshadowed the demolition of the station in 1953.

From these grandeurs and from Philadelphia we must retire nearer to our theme and to a smaller scene, the surburban hinterland of the way station. We shall desert the tumbling and aspiring jets of water, and beyond the turbulence and the spray we may discern

225

some minor displays which have a charm all their own. The suburban station's function was considerably more limited than that of the big terminal — waiting rooms must be provided (but for a smaller group of travelers); there had to be a ticket window and general office, and possibly a freight and baggage room. As Meeks has remarked, they all have one feature in common — a bow window of some sort in front of the structure so that the movement of the trains might be observed by the station personnel. The stations that Richardson designed for the Boston and Albany Railroad are well known as examples of what this type of building could be at its best, and their grounds, landscaped by Frederick L. Olmsted, provided models for other depots.

Two very agreeable examples of the small Romantic railroad station near Pittsburgh are Homewood, built in 1883 and Shadyside (1887), both by Wilson Brothers & Company, who for a time seem to have been architects in ordinary to the Pennsylvania. Of brick and shingle, picturesquely massed, these charming structures, whose scale is essentially domestic, are, again in the 'Eightyish American vernacular Norman Shaw style which we have already noted. The verandahs of these stations, so like those of the houses of the time, extend the mass of the structure pleasantly into the surrounding landscape. Both of these stations, which are now well within the city limits, have survived, but they are not used for their original purpose — the one is now a track supervisor's office, and the other the headquarters for the Pittsburgh Model Railroad Club.[2]

Long after the fountain has subsided again to a low, even flow, there may still be a stray jet or two which rises here and there to remind us of its past activity. After 1900, the Romantic efflorescence of the building mass sank for the most part into the relative quiet of the new Classical mode, but an occasional building will display all of the stylistic qualities of the displaced fashion. Such a one was the third Federal Street Station, built in 1905-06 on Pittsburgh's North Side, which was designed by the Philadelphia architects Price & McLanahan, who were also responsible for the Hotel Traymore (1906) at Atlantic City. Federal Street was a brick, stone, and terracotta building whose elaborate style was inspired by late sixteenth- and early seventeenth-century Netherlandish work, particularly such structures as the Weigh House at Alkmaar (1582-89) and the Butcher's Hall at Haarlem (1602-03). Although these buildings were the essential prototypes, the direct stylistic sources of our station were probably the Anglo-Dutch manner of Norman Shaw, as exemplified in his New Scotland Yard, London (1887), as well as more archaeological imitations like the Van Houten Chocolate Refectory

Federal Street Station.

at the Chicago World's Fair of 1893. Montgomery Schuyler has noted the similarity of Federal Street to the former Post Office at Paterson, New Jersey, by Wentworth & Vreeland (1899) which may also have inspired Price & McLanahan.

This station provides rather eminently a specific instance of the influence of nineteenth-century exposition architecture on contemporary building. The Van Houten Refectory was one of those picturesque oddments so characteristic of the great fairs of the time, and must certainly have attracted the architectural as well as the popular eye. After the Chicago Fair closed the building was sold and re-erected, with some changes, as a residence at Brookline, Massachusetts, where it had a strangely exotic look among its staid neighbours. Both as a refreshment pavilion and a house, it was illustrated in the *American Architect* and the *Inland Architect,* and it is not too fanciful to assume that, due to so much publicity, it eventually metamorphosed into Pittsburgh's Federal Street Station. So did this phantom from the provincial Dutch past, this architectural "Flying Dutchman," appear beguilingly in various forms in the alien streets of our American cities.

With its copper-cupolaed tower, its steep green-tiled roof, its dormers and its chimneys, Federal Street Station was certainly as

Romantic as anything that had gone before. The station was placed at right angles to the tracks, which were above street level so that the plan, like that of Furness' B. & O. Depot at Philadelphia, exhibited a certain ingenuity, although it was not as successful as that of the earlier structure. The architects of the day seemed to be losing interest in the multi-formed variety, the contrived intricacy of the Romantic silhouette and plan, and Federal Street appears, as it were, to be softening, settling toward the new Classical mass. The bescrolled gables with their obelisks and aedicula, and the stair turret with its peaked cap were already just a trifle old-fashioned alongside the Beaux-Arts suavity of the waiting-room windows and the canted walls of the tower. Architecture had never been more various, more "traveled," but the vogue for fairy-tale palaces was waning.[3]

Thus the last high jets subsided and we are prepared for the lower play of the fountain. With the Classical silhouette, the round arch, the colonnade, and the dome became the approved motifs. Stations of the post-Romantic period were to set a new standard of gigantism, and the grandeurs of Rome and the pomp of the Parisian neo-Baroque were to be the familiar stage scenery of the traveler.

[1]It was demolished in 1963.

[2]The Homewood Station was demolished in 1963, and the Shadyside in 1980.

[3]This station was demolished in 1955.

Part III

You are not the same people who left that station
Or who will arrive at any terminus,
While the narrowing rails slide together behind you.

These lines from T. S. Eliot's *The Dry Salvages* are among the last vestiges of the Railroad Age in our literature, just as the great Classical stations must be classified with the ultimate railway architectural relics of that era. The future of the railroads, like that of humanity, is uncertain — the narrowing rails are not only sliding together behind us, they are also vanishing — leaving uncertain the question of whether there soon will be any stations for travelers to leave, any termini at which they may arrive . . .

At the beginning of our century, however, the hopeful, expansive tone of the times augured quite otherwise, and the railroads, then at the apogee of their power and filled with the glory of their pride, adorned themselves with imperial vestments. Stations became not only Classical in style but gigantic in extent, and termini colossal in scale were conceived on monumental lines. The traveler of that magnificent day was to be left in no doubt as to his point of departure, or the terminus that was to receive him.

Pittsburgh, which had become by the end of the nineteenth century one of the great industrial cities of the Western World and one of the wealthiest, had its portion in this great spectacle of imperial display. Its three large stations of the Edwardian period, two of which are still extant, have very eminently the tone of the time, although they are not so enormous as those of New York or Washington.

Towering with Baroque insistence above the undistinguished length of Liberty Avenue looms the Beaux-Arts ornateness of the Pennsylvania Railroad's fourth Union Station — a much-needed replacement for the barn-like structure which had done duty as a depot since 1877. Truncated as it is without its great train shed, it still proclaims the lavish ebullience and brio of America's Age of the Moguls and exemplifies the grandeur and display, the extravagance and pomp, that were the order of that gilded day. Gateways were then much thought of. The year 1900, when the depot was building, was the Gateway to the New Century, and the vehicular rotunda in front of the station was a very conspicuous, one might say seductive, entry to the city.

The sharp and aspiring Romanticism of the second stylistic period in railroad architecture had subsided into the new Classicism, which made use both of the imperial forms of ancient Rome and the dramatic composition and ordered movement of the Baroque. Other stylistic influences, chiefly Renaissance, were much in evidence — the Italian fifteenth century, the Georgian and the French eighteenth century — the last named being one of the components of the neo-Baroque style of the Ecole des Beaux-Arts. Towers, so important in the design of older depots, were disappearing, but the body of the newer structures seemed to be elongating and expanding into the office-building form which was becoming increasingly the commercial archetype of the modern metropolis. Had it not been for the rotunda and the train shed, the Union Station might have been mistaken for just another office building.

The station was commissioned in 1898 from the office of D. H. Burnham & Company of Chicago — one of the chief purveyors of the new monumental Classicism and the Beaux-Arts neo-Baroque (which C. L. V. Meeks has dubbed the Burnham Baroque). Burnham's first important commission in Pittsburgh, it was the prelude to many other jobs in the city, most of them office buildings. The first studies for the project were published in the *Inland Architect* (March, 1899), showing the structure as a relatively small four-story office building with a rather dull entrance pavilion — a heavier version of the "Arcadian" portico of the second Union Station. But in the final plans, dated June 8, 1900, the head house has "lengthened" into the present twelve-story office tower and the square entry has wonderfully changed into the rotunda. The detailing of both the head house and the cab stand is noteworthy; the standard Beaux-Arts devices were used with restraint and taste (Burnham's office was particularly good at this sort of thing), and the brown brick and terra-cotta envelope of the building has a smooth, even texture, a decorative suavity, that is especially commendable. Both the head house and the cab stand were finished in 1902, but the train shed (a creation of the Pennsylvania's engineers) was not finished until 1903.

It is the domed rotunda, above all, with its magnificent four-centred arches and its elegant turrets, which distinguishes the station and gives the whole ensemble a special glamour and *élan.* Very nearly related to the exposition architecture of the time, it has at once a bright, festal gaiety and, in the interior, a mysterious cave-like air; it is a pavilion of enchantment and light, and a grotto of contrived curvilinear shadows, endlessly fascinating. One of the finest things in Pittsburgh from an architectural standpoint, it is certainly one of the most fantastic and delightful railroad structures ever erected.

The rotunda of the Pennsylvania Union Station.

The huge train shed, which was demolished in 1947, was not only the last of the great single-span sheds to be erected by the Pennsylvania but also the last structure of the kind to be built in America. According to the surviving construction drawings, it was huge — two hundred fifty-eight feet wide, five hundred fifty-six feet long, and one hundred ten feet high. To the casual beholder, there seemed to be a subtle wizardry, some incalculable magic, in this great web of steel and glass upheld by what appeared to be the slightest of supports — the pins at the base of the walls. This shed was interesting in that its supports were fixed at only one side — the lattice ribs of the great steel arches had fixed shoes with built-in anchor bolts at one end and roller shoes, rollers, and bed plates at the other. Among the shed drawings are some studies for the ribs which, with their mathematical diagrams, illustrate perfectly the unconscious poetry of the engineers; they resemble certain sketches by Paul Klee whose dream-world hieroglyphs and delicate trellises have a strange crepitant life of their own. The life of the actual lattice ribs — those aspiring and splendid arches which seemed to be trying to enclose as much space as possible — was relatively brief, and with them departed much of the drama and glory of the station. In 1953, work on the modern low sheds (part of a great terminal improvement project initiated by the Pennsylvania) was begun and is still to be completed.

The new sheds are clean and quiet, and the trains glide in and out with a minimum of noise. One is very conscious of the streamlined atmosphere. One is even more aware of the omnipotence of modern machinery in the new ticket sales and service bureau which has become the heart of the station. Located at one end of the main waiting room, it seems, with its huge canopy, to be a cave of light carved out of the former stately and shadowy reaches of the great hall. Above, the skylight is blacked out, the Beaux-Arts cartouches decay, and under the new pool of mechanical light, a diminished group of travelers wait.[1]

The most fascinating of our three neo-Baroque stations, from the human interest viewpoint, was the Wabash, George Gould's Folly, which has vanished utterly except for two forlorn bridge piers on the Monongahela River banks. This fugitive palace, this monumental and inspired foolishness, deserves here some small memorial.

A certain wayward magnificence inheres in great human folly. The individual who courts ruin or invites disaster in pursuit of some whim or ideal or ambition will, if only his ardour be sufficiently excessive, compel our attention and command, perhaps unwillingly, our respect. Such a one was George Jay Gould (1864-1923), son of the financer Jay Gould, whose dream of a great American railroad empire came to an ignominious end. His activities in connection with the Wabash-Pittsburgh Terminal Railroad (now the Pittsburgh and West Virginia Railroad) were perhaps the most potent, if not the sole, instruments of his downfall. The terminus of this line — the great million-dollar Wabash "Palace" depot — was abundantly the symbol of his overweening pride, and ultimately the sepulchre of his ambitions.

Had Gould been a really forceful man, it is just possible that he might have succeeded in his enterprise, but as it was his plans were foredoomed to failure. Ambitious, daring, and capable of conceiving grandiose schemes, he was also arrogant, constitutionally unable to give full attention to his business, and possessed of an indecisiveness of character which rendered inconclusive those projects initiated during his intermittent and frantic bursts of energy. Burton J. Hendricks called him the Hamlet of the railroad world.

His empire in that world consisted of some nineteen thousand miles of track, one of the largest systems ever to be held by one railroad power. Its enormous extent — through great areas of the West and Midwest from Detroit to Ogden, Utah — was matched only by defects in its management and maintenance. When, in 1900, Gould determined to extend his rail empire from coast to coast, the great battle began.

To connect his existing system with the West Coast, Gould began construction of a road called the Western Pacific from Salt Lake City to San Francisco. At the same time, in the East, the real test of his mettle lay, and it was here that, like Hamlet, he took arms against a sea of troubles. Pittsburgh then became the scene of one of the most formidable and dramatic financial wars of the twentieth century. For when Gould determined to enter Pittsburgh, he clashed head-on with a redoubtable antagonist — the Pennsylvania Railroad — an emperor old in power and almost impregnably seated in the Steel City. The city was then one of the important freight centers of the country and was necessary to him as one of the chief links in his chain of empire. He had already purchased the Western Maryland (Baltimore to Cumberland) and also the Wheeling & Lake Erie which gave him a line from Toledo (the terminus of his Wabash road) to Jewett, Ohio, only sixty miles from Pittsburgh.

Andrew Carnegie, wishing to break the Pennsylvania's freight monopoly, had offered Gould his patronage if the latter could provide easy means of transport. The prospect of such golden rewards acted as a further spur to Gould's ambition, and he elected — against full and active opposition of the Pennsylvania — to thrust his line like a sword into the very heart of the city.

The attempt seemed foolish in the last degree, since the Pennsylvania commanded all the easier approaches to the city which, with its surrounding hills, was almost a fort. Nevertheless, across the rugged terrain south of Pittsburgh, Gould ordered his engineers to construct the Wabash-Pittsburgh Terminal Railroad — one of the engineering marvels of its day. Beginning at Jewett, the sixty miles of bridges, tunnels, and fills culminated in a great cantilever bridge (at that time, after the Forth Bridge, the largest in the world) which crossed the Monongahela River at high level and carried the line into downtown Pittsburgh.[2] Everything seemed to be against Gould; the Pennsylvania attempted to block him at every turn, construction accidents on the line abounded, and he was hard put to find the necessary millions, but he persisted against all difficulties. The Wabash terminus, opened finally in June, 1904, was, like the triumphal arches of Roman heroes, erected extravagantly as a symbol of Gould's victory.

The Wabash Station was only another variation on the imperial neo-Baroque theme. A little more ornate than most of the Beaux-Arts depots, its very abundance and profusion of garlands and columns, its air of being so victoriously *en fête,* disarmed criticism. Here again was the office building head house of nine stories, placed rather dramatically on a triangular site at the corner of Liberty Avenue and Ferry Street. The first floor (entered through a circular vestibule at the apex of the triangle) was given over to a huge room which contained ticket offices. The second floor was the main waiting room, elaborately decorated and connected (by means of a hall called the Midway) with the train shed and the platforms, which were some thirty-five feet above street level. The shed was by no means a giant like that of the Pennsylvania since it was only ninety feet wide and accommodated six tracks, but it was interesting because the two stories beneath it housed a freight station which possessed a driveway running down the middle of the lower level. Both freight station and shed were destroyed by fire in 1946.

The passenger station was designed by Theodore C. Link of St. Louis, famous for his great Romanesque Union Station in that city. There is a set of plans dated April, 1903, in the files of the Pittsburgh and West Virginia Railroad (the receivership firm), but the building as executed exhibits several changes in exterior detail — mostly for the better.[3] Nothing is missing, on the exterior at least, of the Beaux-Arts ornamental vocabulary, and everything was used to produce a

The Wabash Terminal.

declamatory, dramatic effect — a triumphant proclamation of the battle won. Even the small, charming neo-Baroque dome with its banded columns, which looked impudently up Liberty Avenue toward the Pennsylvania's festive cab stand, seemed almost like a laurel wreath on the victor's brow.

Gould's victory was a Pyrrhic one, however, and the opening of the new station heralded disaster. It was estimated that the cost of the Wabash-Pittsburgh Terminal Railroad was not less than $45,000,000, and of this sum the station alone had consumed $1,000,000. The freight business Gould counted on never materialized, since his facilities for handling it were inadequate — with only a single line of track crossing the great cantilever bridge to serve the huge station! Passenger traffic was from the very beginning meagre. The great gates of the Station lifted up their Classical heads, but nothing glorious went in. The freight rooms were capacious, but the important commerce of the city avoided them — only a few rural travelers and some straggling crates of chickens and wilting lettuces occupied this glorious palace. George Gould, finally, was unable to beg or borrow any more money with which to maintain a line that was not paying its own way. In 1908, the Wabash-Pittsburgh Terminal Railroad went into receivership; most of his other lines, which had been mulcted to finance his new construction, were in financial straits, and the break-up of the Gould empire was imminent.

Gould's Folly survived, however, somewhat anti-climactically for many years, its urns and garlands becoming dingier as time passed while the steel trusses of the cantilever bridge and the train shed lingered like a gigantic stage setting for a play on which the curtain had never risen. Gradually the great structure began to disappear — the dome first, then the train shed, and the bridge followed in 1948. In 1955, the station was finally demolished and, at the end, the broken fragments of its colossal columns and aedicula constituted, briefly, a small poetic epitaph on the ambitions of George Gould.

From the *sturm und drang* of the Wabash drama and from the vanished blatant splendour of the Gould depot, it is pleasant to turn to the quiet history of the Pittsburgh & Lake Erie Railroad and to the third of our Beaux-Arts stations. The railroad itself was first chartered in 1873, but no actual construction resulted until 1877, when a line from Pittsburgh to Youngstown was begun. In the same year agreements were made with two railroads, the New York Central and the Erie, by which connections could be made with Cleveland and Ashtabula — an arrangement beneficial to all three roads over the years. In 1877, also, William H. Vanderbilt subscribed to part of the road's stock, and since 1882, as a result of additional purchases, the Vanderbilt interests and later the New York Central directly have held a majority stock interest in the firm. The P. & L. E. has always been closely and amicably associated with the New York Central, but it has its own corporate structure.[4]

Not as large as the other two stations already discussed, the P. & L. E. is still a sizeable building having some eighty thousand square feet of floor space. The standard theme of the office building head house appears again, and this example has a basement, a ground floor which is below street level with six stories above. Inasmuch as part of the railroad line passed to one side of it, the depot was, like the Union Station (with which it is exactly contemporary), only partially of the stub type. Designed in 1898 by William George Burns, it was completed in 1901. Its large single-span train shed, one hundred fifteen feet wide and five hundred feet long, was extended by two hundred feet in 1911, only to be dismantled in 1935.

The compact, but hollow, cube of the station, located at the opposite end of the Smithfield Street Bridge from the old B. & O. Station, formed, with the older structure, an interesting contrast in changing architectural fashions — the asymmetrical Romantic mass of Furness' station looked old-fashioned beside the severely Classical, rigidly ordered horizontals of the P. & L. E. across the river. This again is "no-nonsense" architecture, quite in keeping with the rugged and severe Pittsburgh tone. Burns has sparsely adorned the muscular brick and stone flesh of his building with very subdued Beaux-Arts detailing, and there is a minimum use of carved garland, fret, and cartouche. The one lively note on the exterior is a large relief of a moving locomotive — Number 135 — in the square pediment at the centre of the ornamental roof balustrade. It advances proudly, emitting clouds of stylized smoke, serving admirably to announce on the facade the purpose of the building.

The interior of the building is undoubtedly the finest of the three Pittsburgh neo-Baroque stations. The main waiting room, two stories high exclusive of its great coffered tunnel vault, occupies the bottom of the court at the centre and rear of the building. At the level of Smithfield Street is the main station entrance, which leads to a vestibule of two stories. The elaborate Renaissance arcades of this entry have an intricate, contrived effect which subtly prepares one for the great staircase which plunges down into the waiting room like a waterfall. From the top of the stair the whole length of the great hall is visible — a *coup d'oeil* of Baroque magnificence which is too little known and appreciated by Pittsburghers. The tunnel vault of the waiting room not only symbolized the train shed but prepared the way for it, and it now exists as a memorial of the vanished shed. At the platform end of the room, the half-circle window, like a great open fan, announces the same theme and is an echo of those incorporated into the facades of Cubitt's King's Cross Station (1851-52) in London and Duquesney's Gare de l'Est (1847-52) at Paris.

Both the vestibule and the waiting room are marked by great richness and profusion of decorative detail — some of it a little heavy in scale and awkward in conception and execution. Marble, gilt, mosaic, and "art glass" abound, and the place has a sort of ice-cream grandeur, a glittering confectionery charm, which delights the eye.[5] One can overlook the gauche minor details of the decorative scheme, however, when one considers the really masterly and dramatic treatment of interior space, the sheer Baroque extravagance of vista which

The Pittsburgh & Lake Erie terminal waiting room, 1900s.

is so rare in Pittsburgh. After the Music Hall Foyer at Carnegie Institute, the P. & L. E. waiting room is the finest Edwardian interior in the city.[6]

The P. & L. E. Station is still well maintained, but the same cannot be said of the Pennsylvania's East Liberty Station, a large, forlorn, and decaying structure which illustrates forcibly the twilight of the railroad station as a type. A good example of the big subsidiary urban station, but preserving many characteristics of the suburban depot, it belongs to the one-sided type — the arrival and departure platforms are approached by tunnels under the raised tracks. On the "main line" of the Pennsylvania, it was built to serve the prosperous eastern quarter of Pittsburgh, and at one time was surpassed in importance only by the Union Station. Erected in 1906, at the very height of Edwardian prosperity, after the designs of Wilson Brothers & Company of Philadelphia,[7] it reflected in the upper portions of its two waiting rooms a provincial shadow of the Baths of Caracalla, which McKim, Mead & White were then resurrecting on a grand scale for the same railroad's great station in New York. The Venetian hooded chimneys and the quasi-Gothic detailing of the butterfly sheds at track level are echoes of the Romantic period, but here again the accent is on horizontality.

Set in its own small park of smooth lawns and flower beds, the building, with its elegant suburban verandahs, was approached by broad curving drives, whose very lampposts in summer were festooned with ivy and petunias. The lawns are weedy now and the driveways rutted; where once the locomotives and cars roared in and out of the station, day and night, the diminished procession of trains glides into the platforms in ghostly silence. There are few passengers nowadays. The luxury and the life of the station have departed, and the roses and geraniums have withered away. The autumnal solitude of this station, to one who knew it well in its prime, seems a desolation beyond the elegiac word. In this day of frenzied air and diesel travel, it is a wise traveler who knows his exact whereabouts, but once there was, at this suburban depot, a giant flower bed like a cushion which spelled out "East Liberty" in artfully planted blossoms.

The floral sign has long since disappeared, and one day, possibly soon, the station will also vanish.[8] Today's uncertain traveler has gone elsewhere.

Everywhere stations and termini, the great and little railroad palaces, are falling — all across the land they lie like the bones of pre-historic animals which have had their day. The great halls and the platforms are deserted, and the poets must find new metaphors. It seems improbable that this cycle of decay and death can be arrested, but it would be fitting if some of these stations could be preserved as memorials of a past era.

Who shall breathe upon these slain that they may live?

[1]Presently, the station is deserted save for a marginal Amtrak operation, and no one knows what its future will be.

[2]The Firth of Forth is an inlet of the sea on the east coast of Scotland, crossed by a cantilever railroad bridge 5,350 feet long, completed in 1890.

[3]The present whereabouts of the plans are now unknown to the writer.—JVT

[4]And is now, again, independent.

[5]The marble, in fact, is simulated.

[6]The P. & L. E. station building is now The Landmarks Building; the waiting room and adjacent rooms are now the Grand Concourse Restaurant. The terminal complex as a whole is now Station Square.

[7]This has since proven not to be true; the designers were Furness & Evans.

[8]It did, in 1963.

The Charette, December, 1957 and January and February, 1958.

East Liberty, East Liberty!

I have always said that, as a Pittsburgher, I am decidely provincial, but I am more than that in possessing a certain refinement — some might say a diminution — of that local commitment. I am also what might be called parochial, inasmuch as I am devoted to one neighbourhood or parish. I am, I say proudly, an East Ender, a native of East Liberty.

Anything that has to do with the eastern quarter of our city still interests me, but, as so often happens with old inhabitants, I am something less than happy with many changes that have occurred, over the years, in my native place.

Eastward in Pittsburgh, I count the ravages of time and misplaced governmental zeal, but if I must deplore the often-sorry state of the present landscape, I have at least the consolation of my memories of earlier and brighter days.

Among this great crowd of witnesses from the past, perhaps the most salient is the East Liberty Station of the Pennsylvania Railroad. From the date of its construction in 1905-06 it was certainly one of the most important buildings of the city. After the mid 1950s, it began to fall into decay and disuse as the passenger traffic of the railroad disappeared. The merger of the Pennsylvania and the New York Central in 1968 to form the Penn Central did not restore the health of either line, and the final bankruptcy of the new corporation in 1970 was disastrous. East Liberty Station, which had once been one of the most elegant on the Pennsylvania line, had already been demolished, in 1963.

It was the Pennsylvania Railroad, chartered in 1846, that changed East Liberty from a small village on the eastern marches of Pittsburgh into an important section of the city. The first through train from Philadelphia stopped at East Liberty in 1852, and it was near this spot that the first station was built: a frame building of undeniably Victorian vintage that became much too small for the increasing passenger traffic by the end of the nineteenth century. As a child, I remember old-timers telling me of great crowds of people waiting in the rain around the old station at Station Street, simply because there was not sufficient shelter for them.

As the East End became an increasingly busy and fashionable residential district, it became apparent that the railroad would be forced to construct a new facility. After the turn of the century, the railroad began to acquire land around the old station until the company finally owned a tract of seven acres. It also commissioned the Philadelphia architectural firm of Furness & Evans to design a handsome, red brick and terra-cotta station on the southern side of the line, which at that point consisted of two platforms and four tracks. The lines going out of Pittsburgh were on the south side and those going in on the north; they were all connected by a wide passenger tunnel underneath the line. The waiting rooms, baggage room, ticket office, etc. were in the main station building, which was surrounded on three sides by wide driveways and landscaped lawns. In its heyday, East Liberty, although always quasi-suburban, was a metropolitan station of the first order, always full of movement, elegant and visually fascinating. In 1913, more trains ran through it than entered Broad Street Station in Philadelphia.

Although it has been necessary to give a factual introduction to my reminiscences, I wish to speak here only of my memories of the station between 1915 and 1920, when my family and I used East Liberty a great deal. We were moving back and forth between Pittsburgh and Philadelphia, New York, and the Jersey shore during that time. It was in one of those old maroon and sage-green Pullman cars that I first heard the conductor's cry as we approached the station: "East Liberty, East Liberty!" and there was, suddenly, in the deep, gliding syllables, the subtle thrill of being home again. One would go to the front of the car to be ceremoniously "brushed off" with a whisk broom by a black porter.

Then the door would be opened, and I would rush down the steps to greet my grandfather or my aunt, who would be standing on the concrete platform under the upthrust wings of the sheltering "butterfly sheds." When my mother had more decorously descended from the car, we would make our way among the other passengers and the great baggage trucks to one of the stairways that led down into the passenger tunnel, with its steel roof. While we were all trying to talk at once, another train might come in on another track, and in an instant the low, echoing space would be filled with a tremendous roaring sound.

Laughing, we would move on into the station, with its white marble floors. On either side of the central corridor were waiting rooms two stories high. We usually waited in the women's waiting room while Jim the chauffeur went to collect our luggage from the baggage room. I was always fascinated by a large planter of white marble in the centre of the room, with its dense population of palms and other tropical plants. The room had a sort of large Roman quietude, a spacious calm quite at variance with the roaring bustle of the building around it. On the white brick walls were large framed photographs of "sights" along the Pennsylvania line, like the Horseshoe Curve.

When Jim had retrieved our luggage, he would escort us to my grandfather's car, which was parked alongside one of the entrance porches. Since it was a large 1914 touring car, we climbed up into it and drove along one of the driveways toward my grandfather's house, past the wide green, closely-clipped lawns on one of which, facing the station, was a large raised flower bed, rather like a cushion, on which was spelled out in artfully-placed, small coloured plants: EAST LIBERTY. I always looked for it when our train approached the station, and I got a chance to see it closer when we drove past. It was a real masterpiece of the gardener's art, and I was very fond of it. In back of it were large tropical plants that had been brought out for the summer from the railroad greenhouse, whose glass roofs were visible behind a screen of shrubbery and trees. The greenhouses disappeared along with the flower bed some time in the 1920s, and the station was never the same without them. Labour was no longer cheap, and good gardeners were hard to come by.

Leaving the station on a journey out of Pittsburgh was even more exciting. Jim, for some reason, liked to use for departures the other entrance driveway from Penn Avenue. If we left the station by night, the great buildings blazed with light, and the driveways were all lit by Classical standards, each having a circular glass globe on top; each globe seemed to be a separate moon in the darkness. Below the globes were circular boxes filled with petunias, and the whole area on a summer night was filled with their haunting scent, which seemed to be stronger than the pervasive smell of coal smoke. On this drive was another large lawn, with a huge flower bed in the shape of a star.

On one night of our long-ago departures, there were three trains in the station, all of them steaming and puffing as our car descended the long sloping drive. When we stopped before one of the porches, the whole process of arrival was reversed, and we walked toward the waiting room while Jim took care of the luggage. We stopped at the news vendor's shop in the main hall to pick up some magazines. This was a fascinating place, jammed, to my childish eye, as full as Aladdin's cave with wonders including some marvelous glass toys in the form of locomotives or signal lanterns filled with candy. That night I managed to get a glass locomotive.

The night being fine, we decided to wait on the open departure platform, but as we made our way to the tunnel, a strange, solemn figure passed us, the train caller, who for many years was one of the fixtures of the old station. He was a small, pompous, vain man with a hatchet-like face and dyed hair. He always wore an immaculate dark blue uniform, and he had a voice with the volume of a pipe organ. That such a diminutive man should have such a huge, sonorous voice filled me with wonder. His job was to call the trains, and I knew that he would shortly be announcing ours: "Manhattan Limited — train for Greensburg, Latrobe, Johnstown . . ." He was the great high priest of traindom, a notable functionary of travel. Like all the rest of East Liberty, he vanished long ago.

We had scarcely reached the platform when his long incantatory call came from below and a subdued roar from underneath the Penn Avenue bridge announced the arrival of our train. With much smoke, steam, and noise the locomotive slid past like a great fire-breathing dragon, then the baggage and mail cars, the day coaches, and then the sleeping cars. We found our sleeper without much trouble, and amid the hurrying passengers Jim managed to get us aboard the train.

The porter having gone to make up another berth, I sat with my small suitcase in my section looking out at the last flurry on the platform. Then the locomotive bell began to ring, from near and far — " 'Board!" — followed by the slamming of doors. The engine began to huff, and the train began to jerk forward. We were off for New York!

The train gathered momentum as I sat watching the lighted platform signs move past, East Liberty, East Liberty; finally there were no more, and the platform ended. So it went that night in 1916, and now the whole station is utterly gone, like a dream.

"Jamie's Journal," *The Pittsburgher*, September, 1978.

The Skyscraper as Monument
A Field of Commemorative Buildings in Pittsburgh

In Lucian's *Dialogues of the Dead*, Mausolus speaks to Diogenes of his earthly glories which should be held in remembrance: "Because I have been a king . . . and have ruled over a large country, not to make mention of my beauty, nor my valour. Moreover, I have a tomb in Halicarnassus adorned with marble figures. . . ." The desire for monuments is perennial in the human heart, and that tomb which became one of the Seven Wonders of the Ancients has variously haunted the imagination of the Western World. All history, echoing the boasting of the Asian king, is nothing but a memorial field in which monuments are the visible exclamation points.

"I have a tomb in Halicarnassus" was echoed rather insistently in the architecture of the late nineteenth and early twentieth centuries, and the Mausoleum's conjectural physical form, like a recurring motif in a Wagnerian opera, appears again and again in the small field of monumental buildings under consideration.

The great business men of the nineteenth century, the financiers, stock brokers, and industrialists, were — if not the beautiful — at least the valourous and mighty of their day. They had no armies, but their wealth and power were enormous. Pittsburgh especially is a city of monuments to its great industrialists, who left behind them not only steel mills, factories, and banks, but also a number of huge buildings which perpetuate their names. Frick, Carnegie, Oliver, and Phipps resound in the city's architectural as well as its financial annals. Like the princes of the Renaissance, the masters of these great fortunes loved to build. In steel, marble, and granite is memorialized much of the history of the Pittsburgh Age of the Moguls.

In their way, these men were as colourful and forceful as the conquerers of the past, and their achievements were vital to the commercial development not only of Pittsburgh but the nation as well. They had consolidated their triumphs in the business world, and building was the best way of memorializing their conquests. Statuary, even for deceased tycoons, was not exactly appropriate. A mill owner in a frock coat or an engineer in a business suit quite lacked the glamour of generals and princes in armour. The funerary monuments

243

of business leaders in suburban cemeteries, although costly in material, were usually discreet in form, style, and size. For monuments commensurate with their importance, the financial great ones had to look elsewhere. The skyscraper seemed to be the answer.

Towers, in this case, could easily have another dimension beyond that of commemoration; the monuments of Pittsburgh coal and steel barons had to be good investments in real estate as well.

The downtown section of Pittsburgh, known as the Golden Triangle, was therefore selected as the chief field of both commemoration and exploitation. The new steel-framed skyscraper was being developed in the late 1880s and 1890s, just at the time when the local industrial aristocracy was reaching the height of its power. The tall building was a natural for the business man looking for both a monument and an investment. An outsize obelisk with the maximum of rentable floor space became the order of the day.

A really big man in Pittsburgh industry might build more than one of these rentable towers, and a tycoon's importance could be estimated not only by the height and extent but also by the number of his buildings. Within the Triangle, these structures tended to develop in colonies. Each industrialist carved out a tract of his own — H. C. Frick in the area near Richardson's Court House, Henry W. Oliver along Oliver Avenue, and Henry Phipps beside the Allegheny River.

Their great buildings, all of which date after 1900, were preceded by some trial runs. George Westinghouse (1846-1914), one of the great inventors of the nineteenth century whose headquarters were in Pittsburgh, dealt extensively in real estate. At Penn Avenue and Ninth Street he built the first of these monumental buildings in 1888-89. Of nine stories, it was raised to twelve around the turn of the century; this augmentation also graphically illustrated the change in tall building style from the Romantic, turreted mass of the 1880s to the simple Classical rectangularity of the 1900 type. This structure did not have a steel frame, but it did have elevators. Most notably, it proudly bore George Westinghouse's name, and it was the visible symbol in the city of the great manufacturing empire his genius had founded.

Another forerunner was the Vandergrift Building on Fourth Avenue, designed by Longfellow, Alden & Harlow in 1890; it commemorated the business acumen of Jacob Vandergrift (1827-99), a former river steamboat captain. This structure of only seven stories was in reality little more than a glorified loft building, dignified by some fashionable Richardsonian Romanesque detailing.

At this point the physical form of Mausolus' tomb enters the Pittsburgh picture with George B. Post's 1896 Bank of Pittsburgh. The great Halicarnassian sepulchre had quite fallen into ruin, but its remains were excavated by Sir Charles Newton in 1856. From the resurrected stones and carvings, nineteenth-century architects attempted, with the help of Classical literary descriptions, to make paper restorations; from there it was only a step to adapt the restored form to contemporary uses. Post's study for the Bank suggests the influence of the Mausoleum.

The steel-frame building was a little late in arriving on the scene in the steel centre of the nation. It did not appear until 1893-95, when the Carnegie Building (also by Longfellow, Alden & Harlow) was constructed on Fifth Avenue as a memorial to Thomas M. Carnegie (brother of Andrew and a prominent industrialist in his own right) by his widow, Lucy C. Carnegie. It was taller than the earlier buildings, but not of mammoth size.

All these early tall buildings have been demolished within recent years, because early-model skyscrapers are nowadays held in little regard. More ways must be found to make use of our public buildings of this sort, because their demolition is not only difficult but costly.

Still extant of this early group is the Park Building at Sixth and Smithfield, built in 1896 by D. E. and W. G. Park, Pittsburgh steel men. Exuberantly designed by George B. Post, it features a frieze of terra-cotta telamons.

The first real giant among these monuments is the twenty-one-story H. C. Frick Building on Grant Street, designed by D. H. Burnham and erected in 1901. With its steel frame enclosed in a severe neo-Classical masonry envelope, it marks the emergence of the great slab skyscraper in Pittsburgh. Massive and powerful in both form and detail, eminently suited to the spirit of the city and the time, there seems to be little doubt that H. C. Frick, (1849-1919), one of Pittsburgh's great industrial princes, intended it as a monument to his financial might. The marmoreal severity of the lobbies reinforces this impression.

With a later addition, the former Frick Annex, also designed by Burnham and erected in 1906, it towered over and partly surrounded the older and smaller Carnegie Building. The two Frick structures might be considered an architectural *riposte* in the great Frick-Carnegie battle of the turn of the century.

Across Fifth Avenue, Frick also built in 1916 the Union Arcade, now the Union Trust Building, designed by the Pittsburgh architect

The Frick (left) and Carnegie Buildings on Fifth Avenue.

F. J. Osterling in an elaborate late Flemish Gothic style, emulating the Woolworth Building that had just been completed in New York. Frick was also interested in the William Penn Hotel (now the Penn Sheraton) in the next block, built in 1915-16.[1] Janssen & Abbott were the architects, and Janssen & Cocken designed the additions of 1929.

Across Mellon Square from the Italianate facade of the Penn Sheraton the Oliver domain begins.

The largest of these monumental Pittsburgh buildings is undoubtedly that named for Henry W. Oliver, another of the great steel princes. It is located at Sixth and Smithfield. Oliver died in 1904, but in 1908-10 his estate built the twenty-five-story slab-type skyscraper as a monument to him: an expanded version of the Frick Building, it was designed by the same architect in the same coldly Classical style, but the outer severity of the immense slab is softened by some Renaissance ameliorations of style. The main entrance and the elevator lobby, however, manifest the same sepulchral serenity as those of the Frick Building.

Some smaller Oliver buildings, also designed by Burnham, lie along Oliver Avenue on the road to the Phipps colony.[2] Henry Phipps (1839-1930), a partner of Andrew Carnegie, was a conservative business man, and it seems proper that his towers should occupy a peripheral position in the Triangle. None of his several buildings bore his name. The two best known (and still extant) of these are the Bessemer Building (1904-05) and the Fulton Building (1906), both designed by Grosvenor Atterbury.[3] Together they form a kind of Phipps triumphal arch at the entrance of Sixth Street, although neither now belongs to the Phipps estate.

Sharing honours in elaboration of detail with the Park and the Union Trust structures is the Keenan Building[4] at Liberty and

The Fulton (left) and Bessemer Buildings, with the third Sixth Street Bridge in the foreground.

Seventh Avenues, built in 1907 by T. J. Keenan, at one time one of the largest landowners in the Triangle. Featuring a circular concrete dome, it was designed by the local architect Thomas Hannah, probably in emulation of the Reid Brothers' Spreckels-Call Building in San Francisco.

"I have a tomb in Halicarnassus" are words that are echoed even more strongly in two Pittsburgh structures outside the skyscraper colony, but which are just as commemorative in their horizontal fashion. Andrew Carnegie's greatest Pittsburgh monument is undoubtedly the Carnegie Institute in Oakland, the city's cultural centre. Two of the main elements of the Mausoleum, the pyramidal roof and the exterior Ionic colonnade, are to be found in this great building, which was erected in 1904-07 after the design of Alden & Harlow. Here the massive central dome exhibits the Halicarnassian structure flattened and turned outside-in, with the colonnade on the interior.

A very ebullient, Beaux-Arts version of the Mausoleum theme (although here the architect played it straight) is to be found in Henry Hornbostel's Soldiers' and Sailors' Memorial Hall of 1907, also in Oakland. Here the central mass accommodates an auditorium.

These structures constitute in Pittsburgh the fullness of Halicarnassian memory, but Mausolus' boastful words have a thin but definite echo in the terminal roof of the Gulf Building, erected in 1932 at Grant Street and Seventh Avenue downtown. Here the architects Trowbridge & Livingston have used a stripped, modernized version of the Mausoleum theme perched atop their Banker's Trust Company Building of 1913 in Manhattan. The Pittsburgh pyramid is also used as an atmospheric beacon, and flashes in red or blue neon according to the weather in the streets.[5] Doubtless Mausolus would approve.

With the Gulf Building, which emphasizes the corporate structure, the skyscraper in Pittsburgh has ceased to be a personal monument. Mausolus' words are heard no more and we must look elsewhere for monuments to the great and powerful of our own day.

[1]The hotel is once more known as the William Penn.

[2]Most of them are also now demolished.—JVT

[3]The Bessemer Building was demolished in or around 1964; the Fulton Building remains.

[4]Now called Midtown Tower.

[5]Presently, colored light appears only in the uppermost feature, a lantern.

The Charette, April, 1963; presented as a paper at the 1963 national meeting of the Society of Architectural Historians.

An Early Tycoon Palace
The Isaac Meason House at Mount Braddock

The Meason house and dependencies in recent times.

The Meason house is perhaps the grandest image of the domestic architecture of the eighteenth century remaining in Western Pennsylvania. Magnificently sited among the long, rolling hills at the foot of one of the brooding ridges of the Alleghenies, it was liberally conceived by its English designer, Adam Wilson, in the formal manner of the European Baroque mansion, but it was informed also with the youthful vigour of the American frontier. Its date, 1802, just over the turn of the century, insures the continuity of the Georgian tradition, but a certain high-shouldered quality in the main body of the house prefigures the emergence of the American Greek Revival. Solid, forthright, firmly and judiciously established, it both inherits and demonstrates the felicity of the Renaissance tradition, as it celebrates the openness and rugged grandeur of the country in which it was built. It is situated about four-and-one-half miles south of Connellsville on State Route 119 in Fayette County.

The grand Georgian style of the place would probably reflect the personal preference of its builder, Isaac Meason (1743-1818), who was one of the great iron-masters of Pennsylvania's Iron Age — an era which culminated in the careers of Andrew Carnegie and Henry Frick in the late nineteenth century. Meason, like many early settlers of Southwestern Pennsylvania, came from Virginia, but other than that not much is known about his origins. He seems to have had a passion for secrecy — as witness his mysterious marriage in 1772 to a neighbour, Catherine Harrison — a union which was, in 1777, proven legally. Meason came to the Mount Braddock region about 1770. It is not sure whether or not he served in the Revolutionary War, but as his business dealings became more important and fruitful he began to buy land extensively. He built several iron furnaces and forges, and for the first time in America he proved that rolled bar iron could be manufactured successfully. It was he who sponsored the first iron suspension bridge in the world, at Jacob's Creek.[1] Later he took his seat in the State Assembly and later in the Supreme Executive Council of Pennsylvania. It is difficult to overestimate his importance as a really great industrialist; he was the early iron and coal Titan of the Western World.

All great industrialists usually have great houses, and Mount Braddock by no means diminished the splendour of the industrial domestic image. When the young George Washington reconnoitered the adjacent territory, Mount Braddock was known as Gist's Place. Christopher Gist, the wilderness scout and Washington's guide, had chosen this area between the last mountain ridge and the headwaters of the Ohio as the site of his trading post. In 1788, Meason bought the property from the Gist heirs. Mount Braddock is named after the unfortunate British officer who commanded the disastrous expedition against Fort Duquesne [in 1755] and who is buried just east of the property. When Isaac Meason built his great house in 1802, it was intended as a grandiloquent statement of his dignity, power, and affluence.

The land on which the Mount Braddock house stands was in the late eighteenth century claimed by Virginia, and did not definitely become part of Pennsylvania until 1786. Under these circumstances, there were in Southwestern Pennsylvania many architectural influences from Virginia — as witness the Presley Neville house "Woodville" of 1785 near Pittsburgh (which reflects, however, an entirely different type of Virginia country house from the Meason mansion). Certainly the symmetrical lay-out of the latter, with its balanced

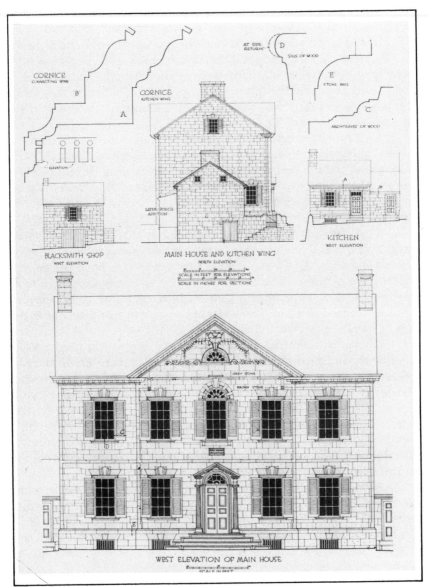

CORNICE
CONNECTING WING

B'

A

ELEVATION

BLACKSMITH SHOP
WEST ELEVATION

CORNICE
KITCHEN WING

MAIN HOUSE AND KITCHEN WING
NORTH ELEVATION

LATER PORCH
ADDITION

SCALE IN FEET FOR ELEVATIONS
SCALE IN INCHES FOR SECTIONS

AT SIDE
RETURNS

D

SILLS OF WOOD

E

STONE BASE

C

ARCHITRAVES OF WOOD

KITCHEN
WEST ELEVATION

A

B

GREY STONE

BROWN STONE

C

D

E

WEST ELEVATION OF MAIN HOUSE
SCALE IN FEET

Measured drawings of the Meason house.

wings and dependencies, strongly reflects Virginia Georgian practice. Meason as a young man would undoubtedly have been familiar, at least by report, with some of the plantation houses of his native province, such as "Westover" or "Carter's Grove."

There is all the difference in the world between the siting of the Tidewater plantations and the Meason house, although the same principles of Classical planning were applied to both. The mountains in the background of the latter are large in scale, but the house easily holds its own with them and becomes a dominant element in the landscape.

Central to the composition is the two-and-a-half story mansion house itself, whose east and west elevations measure about fifty-one feet across, and the north and south about thirty-nine. (It is to be noted here that these measurements were computed roughly from the scale drawings in C. M. Stotz' book *The Early Architecture of Western Pennsylvania.*)

The long elevations are symmetrically disposed, with central doorways flanked on each side by two windows and five windows on the second floor. There are triangular pediments above the central three bays of these facades. The west or entrance facade is more elaborately treated than the eastern face, having a rich Georgian portal executed in wood. The walls of the mansion and dependencies are of locally-quarried limestone.

Above the central portal, with its Ionic columns, broken pediment, and fanlight, is a rectangular signature stone bearing Meason's name and the date 1802, and in the second story is an arched window with handsome voussoirs and a fanlight that echoes that of the portal below and the lunette in the gable of the pediment. All window openings, with the exception of that mentioned above, have wedge-shaped lintels with central keystones. The windows themselves are double-hung, with six lights over six, the latter with narrow muntins and sash-rails.

A notable feature is the delicate grace of the carved ornament, executed in sandstone on the pediment of the entrance facade, which according to Stotz is unique in Western Pennsylvania. Carved exterior ornamentation in the Late Georgian architecture of that area was usually executed in wood and confined to portals and cornices. The Meason house also has a handsome Classical cornice. The carving generally, in contrast to the robust Georgian mass of the house, partakes of the linear grace so characteristic of the Federal period at the turn of the eighteenth century.

The small one-storied wings, one a kitchen and the other an

office, are connected to the main body of the mansion by low passageways, one of which served as a pantry and the other a hall. In the main block are a living room, music room, study, and dining room, ranged symmetrically on both sides of the wide central hall — which latter has doors at both front and back. The staircase rises at one side of the hall, turning at the back of the house with wide, splayed treads at the angles to reach the second floor, where, generally, the bedroom lay-out matches that of the floor below, although there have been some later alterations. The main stairway also rises from the second floor centre hall to the attic.

Each of the eight principal rooms of the main house has a fireplace, and there is also one in the office. Each of these has five mantels, those of the living room and dining room being the most elaborately treated. These also have panels with mythological scenes in composition ornament — some of which has been lost. The principal rooms' joinery and woodwork, generally — doors, architraves, dadoes, and coving — are notable and exceptional for this region.

In line with the main house and its attached dependencies are two others of the same scale, separated from the central block by driveways that flank the house. The roofs of small buildings, like all the Meason buildings, are gabled.

Not the least remarkable aspect of the former Meason domain is the grand Classical lay-out of the grounds surrounding the house. One approaches the mansion from the public road by a private driveway once lined with trees. Some little distance before the house is reached, the drive divides and sweeps, on either side of the diameter of a great circle, up to the sides of the mansion, which in plan is built into the eastern diameter of the circle. Thus was created a large circular lawn, contained by stone walls and having a gate with gateposts at the point where the driveway divides. There are smaller gates in the walls at the point where they meet the wings of the main house. Appropriate to the abode of a great Western Pennsylvania ironmaster, these gateways were furnished with fine gates of simple but handsome design. There is also a terrace before the house portal.

The grand design of both the house and the grounds is due, for the most part, to Adam Wilson (d. 1824), an expert carpenter and stone mason, whom Meason imported from England to build his mansion. There is little known about Wilson, and most of our knowledge comes from Stotz. His other work, except a house that he built in Connellsville for Isaac Meason, Jr. (a structure now so much altered as to be useless as an example of his work), is unknown. The Meason house must be his monument.

Possibly, more than the Virginia houses, it resembles some of the fine country houses of the Philadelphia region which are now preserved in Fairmount Park; but they, too, are close to the English tradition in which Wilson was trained. There are times when the Meason house seems like a rugged Georgian house on the rolling slopes of the Yorkshire moors.

At the time it was built there was nothing so grand as the Meason house in all the western country; it was a marvel in what was then mostly wilderness. It is tragic that a house which deserves to rank among the first examples of the architecture of its time in America should have been so maltreated by the "developed" wilderness of the industrial age.

This writer is not invariably disposed to houses as museums of past grandeurs, but this building is of such rank that it deserves fully to be a museum in the best sense of the word.

Isaac Meason died in 1818, and his son Isaac, Jr. became possessed of his great fortune, sixteen thousand acres of the best coal and iron land in Western Pennsylvania, and the mansion house at Mount Braddock. The huge Meason family fortune was dissipated as early as 1835, but Isaac, Jr's. wife was able to keep the mansion until 1887 by selling properties in Pittsburgh. The property came into the possession of the Frick Coke Company, which offered it to Fayette County in 1932. The County refused the gift, and the property was sold to Michele Cellurale, whose family lived in the house until 1970 when Maria Cellurale, the widow of Michele, died.

In 1970 the Connellsville Area Historical Society became interested in saving the house, and in 1976 they commissioned Landmarks Planning, Inc. to make a feasibility study under a grant from the National Trust for Historic Preservation. Another study was also made in 1981, but to date efforts to save the house have not been productive.

This great house has endured so much that it should not be allowed to vanish.

What kind fate will breathe upon these ancient stones that they may live once more in something approaching their former state?

---

[1]Actually, the first in America: there was at least one earlier example in Germany from the mid-eighteenth century. The Jacob's Creek bridge was built in 1801 at Uniontown to the design of the amateur engineer James Finley.

Radio script for WQED-FM, 1982.

The Greek Revival Revived

Recently, one of Pittsburgh's prime but little-known architectural monuments — the Croghan-Schenley Ballroom from the large country house called "Picnic" — was very agreeably and deservedly brought back to public notice. The occasion was the re-dedication and the attendant reception at the University of Pittsburgh's Cathedral of Learning that celebrated the current restoration of that magnificent Greek Revival room.

The occasion also revived interest in the most romantic story in all of Pittsburgh's history. "Picnic House" was built in the 1830s by Pittsburgh's richest man, William Croghan, Jr., near the then-rural village of Lawrenceville. It was constructed as an elegant dancing pavilion, although the builders later enlarged it into a country house. Croghan's heir was his sixteen-year-old daughter Mary, who, in the middle 1830s, was enrolled at a "select" boarding school on Staten Island, New York. While she was there, the forty-year-old brother of the head mistress visited the school. He was Captain Schenley, a very glamourous British Army officer who had a way with women; he eloped with the young and very impressionable Pittsburgh heiress, much to the dismay of William Croghan, who had other ideas about the marriage of his daughter.

Even so, there was nothing that he could do about the *fait accompli*. He made "Picnic" into a handsome country house, hoping to lure the glamourous couple to live in Pittsburgh. They did live there briefly before 1850, but soon returned to London.

Mary Schenley bore her husband nine children, and she became an honoured figure in British society, although Queen Victoria refused to receive her. "Picnic House," as a rural dancing place, had always seemed rather anachronistic in industrial Pittsburgh, and as the years moved on, it became even more so. The ballroom was not very felicitously proportioned, being forty feet long and only eighteen feet wide. It seemed to be a rather expensive "folly," erected some years before the attendant country house, which was an altogether more pedestrian structure than the ballroom.

After her father's death, Mary Schenley inherited the house, but she never returned again to visit. A mystery it remained: vacant,

The Croghan-Schenley ballroom as installed in the Cathedral of Learning.

shadowed, and shuttered. A caretaker remained in charge of it, even after Mrs. Schenley's death in 1903. In time, the Stanton Heights Golf course took over the grounds of the former estate, but the house itself was not demolished until the late 1940s.

The ballroom narrowly escaped demolition, but Charles M. Stotz, the Pittsburgh architect and historian, had, in his book *The Early Architecture of Western Pennsylvania* (published in 1936), established its beauty and its importance as unique in our region. Two interested donors presented the room to the University of Pittsburgh, along with the ballroom's elliptical ante-room.

These were installed in the Cathedral and dedicated in 1955 after they had been partially restored by a grant from the A. W. Mellon Educational Trust. In the current restoration, the process has been completed. The magnificent carved decorations in the Greek style, originally executed by Mordecai Van Horne in 1835, now shine in all their original glory as does the great crystal chandelier. The ante-room has yet to be fully restored; it is now an office.

So we have this great Greek Revival room in the midst of a splendid Gothic Revival building — surely a triumph of architectural Eclecticism. The room may be viewed by contacting the Nationality Rooms at the University of Pittsburgh.

Radio script for WQED-FM, 1982.

Medieval Pittsburgh
The Singer House, Wilkinsburg

Old houses are like old people; there are survivors among them, and it does not seem to matter whether they are of high or low degree, or rich or poor. Why do some houses endure longer than others; why do some emerge triumphant, even in their ruin, and why do others crumble and fall? Similarly, why do some senior citizens rise superior to the assaults of the years and others subside into oblivion with scarcely a sigh or moan? Where so much falls, it is heartening to consider what still does stand — whether architectural or human — in the face of time, change, and decay.

On the architectural side, at least, on the score of survival, Wilkinsburg's old Singer mansion is pre-eminent in the Pittsburgh region. It has existed on its hillside for well over a hundred years (which in America, is itself a guarantee of antiquity). It was also *the* great house of Wilkinsburg, which had not many mansions; the town was always simply a middle-class suburb of Pittsburgh. Wilkinsburg always had, in the old days, a special character of its own — sedate, unassuming, and pietistic. The latter adjective so much suited it that it was, because of its disproportionate number of churches, known as the "Holy City." The decay of the town in our own day has rather tarnished its religious image.

It seems appropriate then that the medieval-seeming bulk of the Singer mansion should have been built in the Gothic Revival style of the mid-nineteenth century. This was definitely consonant with the Romantic spirit of the age in which it was built. The real temper of the times was revealed in a rampant materialism which flourished behind the Gothic stage scenery.

And the Wilkinsburg Gothicity was — and is, despite its present ruined state — spectacular, although this kind of domestic medievalism does not make for a durable ruin. But more remarkable than the vision's establishment in the unsympathetic village of Wilkinsburg, and beyond that its survival there, is the fact that it was ever established at all. Who *was* responsible for it?

Certainly no inhabitant of the town could have done it — for Wilkinsburg, it would have been a frivolity beyond comprehension. A Pittsburgher? Pittsburgh was not noted then for wealthy business men who had a taste for large, expensive, and exotic residences, and very probably none that possessed a sophisticated and "advanced" taste for such Gothic caprices. Straight on, I must contradict myself — none *probably* possessed such an interest — save John F. Singer, the builder of the mansion.

John F. Singer (1816-72) was born in Greensburg, one of eight children of George Singer, but he moved to Pittsburgh with his family in 1833. John married Mary Snyder (1823-93), who was later chatelaine of the great manor house. Another Pittsburgher, William K. Nimick, became a partner in the Singer firm, which in 1859 was re-organized as Singer, Nimick & Company. This last organization, which manufactured all types of steel, continued until 1900.

John F. Singer and his business partner William Nimick prospered in the steel business, and in due course they projected to extend their partnership into a neighbourly residential status in Wilkinsburg and the adjoining portion of Pitt Township. In April, 1863, William Singer bought from James Kelly, an early Wilkinsburg landowner, a tract of thirty acres for twelve thousand dollars and on August 21, 1863, another large tract. The Singer holdings extended for nine hundred feet along Wood Street. The smaller Nimick acreage, also bought from James Kelly, adjoined the Singer grounds and lay beyond the village line. For some reason the Nimicks never personally occupied their land or built on it. The boundary between the properties was a lane, now called Nimick Street.

But let us return to the great house itself which, miraculously, is still with us. John Singer, aged forty-seven, and his wife Mary, aged forty, began building operations on their new property at once, in the summer of 1863. The Civil War, then at its height (this was the summer of Gettysburg), seems to have interfered little with construction work on the mansion. The work was completed in 1869, according to a Thomas Russell who worked for John Singer in that year. The great manor house was reputed to have cost seventy-five thousand dollars — a huge sum for those days; in our own over-inflated day [in the early 1980s] it would cost about a million dollars. Even so, its intense, haunting richness could not be duplicated today.

The house is magnificently sited, about halfway up the small ridge that forms the northwest escarpment of the East Liberty valley. Arising majestically, and yet mysteriously, from the intricate hillside verdure, it seems to beckon tantalizingly through its masks of begrimed stone and Gothic traceried wood, saying darkly, "I am the paladin of dreams and the all-powerful lady of a long-gone wonder. Approach, come, and taste my kingdom. You will always be bemused

An old view of the Singer house.

and beckoned; you will enter and look about you, but you will never be satisfied. Even so, will you try to speak of what you have seen and what you have felt? Come!"

I came once on a day, and I have continued to visit it periodically for fifty years. I first encountered the enchanted house in 1926, when I went to art school at Carnegie Institute of Technology. One of my classmates who lived on Singer Place (the street on which the house is located) would ask me out to his house when we had to make tracings for our art history classes. It was then that I first saw the huge house, on its great stone terrace, looming against the darkening sky. I fell in love with its dark medieval-Victorian mystery then, and it has always haunted me since.

It was rather more visible then because the enveloping foliage, so all-apparent now, had not become so oppressive. Under such circumstances the main outlines of the mansion were easily discernible—the grey sandstone masonry, roughly cut and coursed; the Gothic arched windows; the sharp, but ample, gables with their elaborately-carved verge boards; and the Jacobean "stacked" chimneys. All this

259

carved wood and stone is a curious mixture of Victorian Gothic and Second Empire French Renaissance design elements. The architect of this fantasy is not known, although it may have been J. W. Kerr of Pittsburgh, who worked extensively in these styles during the 1860s. One thing is certain: it was certainly not the work of an amateur designer, which rules out John F. Singer.

John F. Singer was, however, an Episcopalian — a denomination which was much preoccupied with neo-Gothic architecture. He had his own detached chapel near the main house; it was, perhaps, the only building of its kind ever erected in Pittsburgh. It was, with its sharply-pointed Gothic bell tower, the most salient building on the grounds, until its destruction by fire about six years ago. Here John Singer would conduct services of matins and vespers, "helped out" on occasion by visiting priests. This unique building should have been preserved.

On the estate were also a large spring-fed lake and boat house, stables (the carriage house was in the basement of the chapel), a gate lodge on Wood Street, and a gardener's cottage. The place was also famous for its gardens and orchards.

The interior of the house was also rich in ornamentation. There were eighteen rooms on three floors and two bathrooms — still in the 'Sixties something of a luxury. The front entrance hall, a *tour-de-force* of the American domestic Gothic of the time, has an inlaid marble floor and a spectacular circular staircase. With the drawing room and dining room, the whole first floor looks like a fabulously rich stage setting for a Victorian opera, say Donizetti's *Lucia di Lammermoor.* These rooms have all been restored and are in good condition.[1]

The house inherited the cloudy fascination of its first owner. John F. Singer remains an intensely Romantic figure — aloof, dreamlike, rather like the hero of a modern "Gothic" novel. Neither he nor his family mixed much with the townspeople, and he appears to have lived his dream of Romantic medievalism in his dream castle. And yet he was a wealthy and successful business man of his time in Pittsburgh. It is possible that he was, as rumoured, devoted to the bottle, but certainly he was passionately devoted to the past. Was he a Romantic poet *manqué?* His enigmatic personality and early death invite Romantic legends.

Alas, he did not live very long to enjoy his cloud castle — he died in 1873 — but his wife and four children continued to live there until 1878, when Mrs. Singer took the entire family on a world tour which lasted a year. On their return, they did not live much in Wilkinsburg. The house was left much to caretakers, and it began to show signs of neglect. The townspeople described Mrs. Singer as pretty and elegant, but she did not seem to care very much for the house and, probably, not much for Wilkinsburg. New York and Europe saw more of her in her widowhood. She died in New York in 1893.

The house and estate were sold to developers. The lake was drained about 1900, and the estate was divided into smaller lots — a not-uncommon American phenomenon. Over the years, most suburban private estates metamorphose into plans of lots.

The half-rural aspect of Wilkinsburg was now completely gone, and the huge, gaunt house (now, after 1905, sheltering a boarding establishment for Westinghouse Corporation students) presided majestically over a collection of smaller Edwardian houses, some of them quite charming. Singer Place, the street "put through" in front of the mansion, has a large group of architecturally-important row houses designed by Pennsylvania's only important proto-Modern architect, Frederick G. Scheibler (1872-1958), who is also the only really original architect that Pittsburgh ever produced. The long terraces of row houses in the 1300 block of Singer Place (1919) are good examples of the designer's middle period — beautifully simple, they seem like strata of brick and glass emerging from the wooded hillside.

The Singer mansion, after 1940, began to show signs of decay as the once handsome Singer Place began to fade into shabbiness and outright ruin — often the fate of Pittsburgh's near suburbs. Some of the best houses on the street are now empty and boarded-up.

In 1960, John Bos, a former student in the Drama Department at Carnegie-Mellon University, bought the house, and he and his wife have remodeled it into apartments. The interior is thus in good condition, but the exterior needs a great deal of work. Now the Boses want to sell the mansion because they no longer live in Pittsburgh and cannot give the place the supervision it should have.

On a day of high summer I recently visited the great grey house again. As long ago, it still *does* cast a spell. It beckons, it invites to mystery and the unfathomable past.

---

[1]The recent architectural survey of Allegheny County (conducted by the Pittsburgh History & Landmarks Foundation) gives the state of the house as a whole "average" — neither outstandingly fresh nor particularly bad.

Radio script for WQED-FM, no date.

The Henry W. Oliver house.

Disseminated Mansion

Victorian mansions, although their number is now much diminished, are still very much with us, and a handsome nineteenth-century millionaire "palace," either in a small or large edition, is nowadays the king of glamourous houses. It is not necessary, however, to have the whole house, eminently desirable as that may be, particularly with all the proper Victorian accoutrements. Very often nowadays the grand effort this requires is much too expensive for the average amateur of the past. And yet, even if the preserver's purse be not fat, he may still be able to afford portions of a real Victorian millionaire house. Even if that portion be only a door or a carved panel, the owner of the artifact may take the part for the whole and thereby be privy to all the vanished grandeur. That which was once part of the wonderful mansion on a luxurious avenue is now, a century later, part of the modern environment. Nowadays the great Victorian house has been widely disseminated.

I am constrained to think in this vein as often as I open the door of my office at the Old Post Office Museum. Even before we opened our museum as a repository for historical artifacts of Allegheny County history, the Pittsburgh History & Landmarks Foundation had been collecting, for several years, portions of demolished houses that we had been unable to save. This particular door, of solid and sombre mahogany, is of no great height or width; its paneling is well proportioned and discreetly severe, its brass fixtures absolutely without ornament (the ovoid door knobs would shame the Moderns in their devotion to Pure Form). Just below the door's midsection is a small panel of graceful Quattrocento carving in low relief. This door is almost redundantly Classical in its restrained calm, its exquisite simplicity. It seems not Victorian, and yet it is. It is my own gateway to the past, although it is part of my daily existence. I never tire of looking at it, ever since I first saw it long ago on the second floor (it was one of the bedroom doors) of the now-vanished Henry W. Oliver house at Number 845 on Ridge Avenue, that rich ambience of the millionaires of old Allegheny.

I have only to look at it to conjure up visions of those suave, gracious rooms, the elegant, fashionable house itself, the wide, shining avenue on the ridge, with its carriages and motor cars, the broad somnolent chateaux (those pedestrian dream castles!), and high above all, rising from the roaring flats below, the smoke that produced this gold-plated quarter of the rich and privileged.

And when I walk through the door, past those delicate panels, that richly reminiscent mahogany, I can see through my office window, as through a proscenium arch, the green trees of West Park that conceal the now-desolate quarter where the mansions used to be.

My portal tells me true! Of all the grand and middling-grand houses of Ridge Avenue, the Oliver house was the grandest. The architecture of the Avenue was like most of Pittsburgh millionaire construction — rather stolid and sober-sided. Among these imperturbable mansions, the Oliver house was rather a Cinderella whose grandeur was not original: rather, as it were, a later addition. Always, in its later, forlorn days, one had the sense that it must *always* have been a little forlorn, out of time and place, a Cinderella dressed for a great ball that never took place.

The beginning of the house was middling; it was a standard Italianate exercise in Pittsburgh architectural probity. It was built by one A. H. English in 1871, and it stood, high and tight, on a commanding site at Ridge and Galveston Avenues. In 1879 it was sold to Henry W. Oliver (1840-1904), who in 1891 commissioned the prestigious Boston architectural firm of Shepley, Rutan & Coolidge, the heirs and assigns of Henry Hobson Richardson who finished the great man's Allegheny County Court House (1884-88).

We, who are now so much concerned with remodeling Victorian houses for modern living, are often prone to forget that the Victorians often altered their own productions as styles changed or more money accrued to the builders. Cinderella? This house presented an intriguing double image because the new grandeur was laid over the shell of a "bracketed" Victorian house of a simpler and earlier day. The particular importance of the mansion lay in the amplitude, the grace, and the sophistication of its rich decoration, which could well bear comparison with anything else produced in America in the same period.

Henry Oliver died in 1904, but the house became the scene of much social activity when his daughter Edith married Henry R. Rea. The Reas, like many other affluent North Siders, eventually moved to Sewickley. In the 1950s the house seemed assured of preservation by the Instruments Publishing Company, but it was acquired by the Allegheny County Community College in the 1960s and demolished by them in 1969 to make way for Tasso Katselas' medieval-modern library, which is, to say the least, no compensation for the lost wonders of the Oliver house.

Although the Pittsburgh History & Landmarks Foundation fought desperately to save the house, we were unsuccessful, but we did manage to save most of the magnificent interior woodwork. In a surprise move, the College had scheduled the demolition of the house for late summer, and we knew that we had little time to rescue the interiors. We managed to get a grant from some members of the Oliver family to pay our expenses; and, since we had only a few days to remove what we wanted, all the male members of the foundation dropped their usual tasks to help our work crew with the removal. We also managed to hire some extra hands to help out.

The College, at least, had allowed us the opportunity to add the best woodwork to our collections, but they had allowed us so little time that we were doubtful of the outcome of our efforts. Late August in Pittsburgh was the last season that I would have chosen for this type of rescue work. It was fearfully hot, and since there was no longer any electricity in the house, we worked from dawn until dusk.

There was, as I have said, a great deal of ornamental woodwork, particularly on the first floor: paneling, balustrades, and elaborate cornices. The two chief interior elements were the great staircase in the main hall and the formal dining room, both massive and intricate masterpieces of the most complicated wood working.

The openwork oak balustrades of the stair were excellent examples of neo-Renaissance carving, while the dining room was sheathed — walls and ceiling — with richly carved and inlaid mahogany. These features were extremely valuable, and, since they were so solidly constructed, were particularly difficult to remove.

Not infrequently — and this when time was of the essence — we had to stop to figure out how certain elements had been installed. It was curiously like a slow-motion movie of certain problems of construction, only everything was in reverse. This was undoing, not doing: demolition and not construction. When the parts of any particular element were finally disassembled, they had to be numbered or coded so that they could, at some future time, be re-assembled. We are still hoping that at some future date they can be.[1] In this case, also, we had to be sure that in transport to our warehouse all the relevant parts be kept together so that we would not have a hopelessly jumbled jig-saw puzzle of unrelated fragments.

The paneling had also, particularly in its unfinished back parts, accumulated decades of Pittsburgh soot. Each day was so hot that we always worked stripped to the waist, and when a section of paneling was pried from one of the walls, a great shower of black dust would descend upon us. This was definitely preservation the hard way, and I have always regarded our Oliver rescue job as a landmark case of what can be done to preserve our architectural heritage when you really have to do it.

Finally the job was completed within the stipulated time, and all the splendid woodwork was safely taken to our warehouse. We had chalked up — in soot — another victory, if only a partial one, for the cause of preservation.

The staircase and the dining room still await resurrection, and they are worthy of stellar treatment in some future restoration. We have used minor elements of the Oliver woodwork in other remodelings. Thus the mansion has been widely disseminated throughout the Pittsburgh region. And so I can say that the door to my office is truly my portal to the past.

[1]Besides the woodwork and other artifacts built into the Old Post Office Museum in 1971, some of the salvaged decorative material has been installed in The Shops at Station Square.

"Jamie's Journal," *The Pittsburgher,* November, 1978.

The Last of "Greenlawn"
My First Demolition in the Chateau Country

I suppose that I have enough experience now to be called a professional preservationist as regards the built environment, but when I was young it never occurred to me that I should become identified with what is now an important field of endeavour. Even as a child, I was interested in architecture, and I was always fascinated by old houses and large gardens, so that I early began to gather and examine what would later become the material of my trade — if something so delightful and absorbing could be called by such a mundane name. Trade or no trade, the contemplation or the exploration of an old building has always seemed to me to be a prelude to high adventure. Was the forlorn structure doomed or could it be saved? If nothing could be done about its salvation, the mere exploration of the ruined structure became a nostalgic foray into a past that one had known only by hearsay. To the Romantic spirit, and mine was always such, my intensive backward glance was searching among scattered artifacts and forlorn vistas for a vision that would remake an old and valid *mise-en-scène,* once so established, so *real,* return in a vision, if only for a moment, before it vanished forever.

The earliest of such adventures that I can remember in sufficient detail to give it a certain validity was one that occurred when I was about fifteen, not far from my home in what is now called North Point Breeze. I always called the area the Chateau Country, at least since the time that my family moved there again in 1922, after we had been living for some years in Philadelphia. I was native to the quarter, so to speak, having been born on Thomas Boulevard not far from the original Point Breeze hill where Fifth and Penn Avenues cross each other.

In 1922, my grandfather had bought a large house on Thomas Boulevard. It was no mansion, but fairly extensive and rather tall, and the first thing I did when I moved in was to climb to the top of the house. As I looked out of the window of the cook's room, I saw, rising on the eastern horizon an amazing collection of tall chimneys and fanciful roofs that looked like a range of high volcanic hills — an amazing agglomeration of varied shapes.

267

"Greenlawn."

This, I knew, was the large mansion known as "Greenlawn," the house of the processed food magnate, the late H. J. Heinz, or the "Pickle King" as he was familiarly known. Scattered over the roofs were a collection of early French Renaissance dormers that reminded me of the chateaux of the Loire, and I knew enough about European architecture then to identify them although I did not know much about the American architect Richard Morris Hunt, who had so richly imitated them on the houses of his millionaire clients. The Heinz dormers, I later learned, were imitations of imitations, being products of the office of F. J. Osterling, a local architect. They were, in their way, highly effective in helping to establish the luxurious architectural ambience of the millionaire colony on Penn Avenue. Doubtless they suggested to me rather abundantly the chateau age — and thus my name for the district.

The general area was, in its period of greatest affluence (and still is), quasi-suburban in aspect, with almost rural overtones, although it was part of the city of Pittsburgh — some of the big estates trailed out into cow pastures and cabbage patches at the back. Earlier in the nineteenth century this rolling floor of the East Liberty valley was decidedly rural in tone. The Greensburg Pike, later Penn Avenue, was then, and still is, the chief artery of the area. Even before 1850 there were some large country estates along the Pike, chief among them being that of William Wilkins, an eminent citizen of early Pittsburgh.

By 1900, however a not-unnumerous colony of wealthy people had built large houses on the stretch of Penn Avenue between Point Breeze and Wilkinsburg. Particularly important were a group of partners in the Carnegie Steel Company whose grandiose houses were concentrated on Penn between Lang and Braddock Avenues. That is, however, a story for another day.

Henry John Heinz (1844-1919) was a wealthy man when he bought the old Italianate Hopkins house on Penn Avenue in 1892. At the time, he had Osterling give the plain brick house a François Premier overcoat of white stone and surround it with Classical verandahs. F. J. Osterling also chateau-ized the house Henry Frick had bought at Penn and Homewood a couple of years before. At the time Heinz bought his property, the frontage of his lot extended the length of Penn Avenue between North Murtland Street and North Lang Avenue. I am speaking now only of what I can remember, because I have never made any real study of the exact extent of the property. Robert Alberts, in his recent biography of Heinz,[1] says that it was one hundred seventy-one by five hundred feet — by no means a small estate for the Penn Avenue of the time. I do not think the domain took in the whole block along Thomas Boulevard, because there were some lots on both North Lang and Thomas that did not belong to Heinz.

Heinz did have a large conservatory with ten greenhouses in the corner of his property at Murtland and Thomas. I had visited this large glass house as a schoolboy in 1915 to see the annual autumn show of chrysanthemums. I particularly remember the large central domed building, once an obligatory adjunct of every millionaire's conservatory. It was full of tropical greenery and had a pool where goldfish swam. I was as a small child charmed with the pool, but I do not remember the chrysanthemums at all.

By 1923, however, the conservatory had quite gone — there was nothing left but the foundation. When Heinz died in May, 1919, he had left his conservatory and an acre of ground to the City of Pittsburgh for the enjoyment of the public, but the gift was refused because the donor had left no money for maintenance. The heirs then offered the entire estate to the City as a public park, but the municipality had just accepted the old George Westinghouse estate, across Thomas Boulevard, as a gift from the Engineers Society of Western Pennsylvania and at the moment it was not interested in taking any more property off the tax rolls.

There was some talk of trying to retain Heinz' Museum (which was housed in a building next to the garage) and the recently completed Oriental Gallery attached to the house, but nothing came of these discussions. None of the heirs wanted to live in the house, and when I saw it on that dreary December day in 1922, it was already doomed — waiting to be demolished. This was not the first demolition to be suffered by the Chateau Country in its relatively brief period of glory. First to go was the great Greek Revival house, Judge Wilkins' "Homewood," which was razed in 1922 — just before I returned to the scene, so I did not witness its fall, as I did not also see the vanishment of the Penn Avenue house of Lucy Coleman Carnegie, Tom Carnegie's widow.[2] Both of these estates were destined to become plans of lots for prospective builders. "Greenlawn" followed suit — it was finally to be divided into thirty-three building lots.

As the actual demolition approached early in 1924, I was not conscious of all this — only in a vague sort of way. I could see, or more accurately feel, that great changes were taking place in the Chateau Country. In this case, the prime chateau documents — the William Morris Hunt dormers — were destined to disappear. The Heinz garage and the old museum were made into apartments, and on the Thomas Boulevard lots where the conservatory had been, developers were already starting to build smaller houses.

As the spring merged into high summer the demolition of the great house began in earnest. Much of the interior woodwork, doors, trim, etc., was removed first, and as people were not so security-conscious in those days, it was not too difficult to get into the house when the demolition crew were not at work. Demolition was done more carefully then, but late Victorian and Edwardian craftsmanship was not greatly admired in the 1920s, and much that now would be salvaged and sold at high prices was simply destroyed. I remember an elaborate frieze in the music room, ornamented with the names of Late Victorian composers, that was broken up when the walls came down. There was also a handsome "landscape" stained-glass window on the landing of the main staircase. I do not imagine that it was executed by Tiffany; it was probably done by the Rudy Brothers of the East End, who were patronized by Heinz. It would be worth a great deal of money nowadays, but then it was treated with no special reverence, as this kind of thing was hopelessly out of fashion, and I do not know what became of it. I suspect the worst.

Many of my young male friends used to like to play softball on the great green lawn in front of the house, now something overgrown and sere, but on a hot Sunday afternoon in August I would steal away to a large Tudor library which had been added to one side of the house about ten years before, when the verandahs were removed to make

270

way for terraces. The library was a marvel of oaken paneling and possessed a handsome stone Tudor fireplace which I coveted. Scattered about on the floor were many art auction catalogues and copies of the *Illustrated London News,* of which I remember a special issue on the funeral of King Edward VII in 1910. How I would sit on the floor and imagine with what style I could have inhabited such a wonderful room. "But out, alack, it was but one hour mine," and its final hour at that.

It disappeared one day, as the demolition overtook it, and, strangely, I later found part of the rain-soaked copy of the *London News* in a weedy corner of the lawn. The last part of the house to go was the large two-story Classical, concrete Oriental Gallery which opened off the library and had not been quite finished at Heinz' death. It was so firmly built that they had to use dynamite on it. I was reading one afternoon on my front porch when I heard a loud boom and I knew that it was gone.

So passed one of the most colourful and various of the Point Breeze chateaux. This was not quite the first demolition in the area, nor was it by any means the last.

---

[1]*The Good Provider: H. J. Heinz and His 57 Varieties.*

[2]The builder of "Homewood" was Judge William Wilkins (1779-1865). The next occupant of "Homewood" was William Coleman, a noted mid-nineteenth-century ironmaster whose daughter Lucy married Thomas Morrison Carnegie (1844-1886), Andrew Carnegie's younger brother. In the 1860s, Andrew Carnegie was also a frequent visitor at "Homewood." These blocks of Penn Avenue were obviously "Carnegie country."—JVT

Radio script for WQED-FM, circa 1980.

The stair hall of "Rowanlea."

Peacock's Pride
An East Liberty Millionaire Mansion
of the Early 1900s

There have been other eras as extravagant, as luxurious, as ornate, as over-blown as the Edwardian period in America and Europe — those gilded and rose-strewn years between 1900 and 1914 — but it would be hard to find one so blatant, so spectacular, so wanton in its shameless disregard of any canons of restraint, in spending the endless, swollen dividends that poured out of the cornucopias of the steel industry in the late nineteenth century.

The younger millionaries of the Carnegie Steel Company, particularly after the Company had been sold to J. P. Morgan in 1901, were often the chief spenders in this near-orgy of extravagance and glittering splendour. Their jobs disappeared with the company, but they did get paid for their stock. They had a great deal of money and more time to spend it in. Some of them were relatively young and the world was their oyster.

Notable in this gilded group was Alexander Rolland Peacock (1861-1928), who was born in Durnfermline, Scotland (the birthplace, also, of Andrew Carnegie). As a young man, he went into the linen business in his hometown, but he decided to come to America in 1879. He continued in the same business and was employed in a New York City department store.

Here his Karma or Fate appeared in its most beneficent aspect, and the Horatio Alger story of the nineteenth century was fully illustrated in Technicolor. He was assigned as a sales-clerk in the laces and linens department, where, one fortunate day in the 1880s, he waited on Mrs. Andrew Carnegie. When he could not provide for her a special type of linen that she wanted, he became so excited that he lapsed into the Scots dialect of his native Durnfermline. Mrs. Carnegie was interested and mentioned the solicitous young man to her husband. The great steel tycoon was always interested in young Scots trying to make their way in America. He interviewed young Peacock and found him to be an exceptionally intelligent and perspicacious aspirant to business honours. Carnegie, with his rare natural judgment as to the abilities of men, decided that here was one who would be able to do him good in the steel business, and in 1889, young Peacock entered the employ of the Carnegie Steel

Company. The story is told that Carnegie, who knew another canny Scot when he saw one, summoned the younger man, after he had performed a spectacular feat of salesmanship, to his office, where he asked him, "Peacock, what would you give to be made a millionaire?" Knowing what would please his boss, Peacock replied, "Two percent discount for cash, sir!" Andrew was pleased, and from then on Peacock never looked back. In 1894, he was elected to the position of assistant general sales agent, and a year later became the general sales agent of the great concern. In 1897, he became first vice president — with a commensurate block of stock in the company. Carnegie had chosen most of his young partners by much the same methods, and thus Alexander Rolland Peacock became one of the two-score millionaires of Carnegie's making.

And so he built his house on North Highland Avenue in Pittsburgh. Like the prince in a fairy tale, he had to have a castle. The castles of all these turn-of-the-century millionaires were almost invariably large and gilded affairs, and often in later years, so ephemeral they were, they seemed like castles in the air.

For a time after his elevation to millionaire status, Peacock and his wife Irene Affeck, whom he had married in Brooklyn in 1887, lived in an old Victorian house at Penn and Lexington Avenues, virtually next to H. C. Frick after he built an elaborate stable which is now part of the Frick estate. After 1900, he bought a large tract of land on North Highland Avenue between Jackson Street and Wellesley Avenue in the East End. When Andrew Carnegie, in 1901, sold the Carnegie Steel Company to J. P. Morgan, who formed the United States Steel Corporation, all Carnegie's partners received very large sums of money for their stock. Peacock was therefore equipped to build a palace. It was also apparent that, in choosing its site in the Highland Park district, he wanted to be independent of the Carnegie-Frick millionaire compound on Penn Avenue in Point Breeze.

Possibly, when all was considered, he wanted to establish a new millionaire compound of which he was king. The Highland district, which a half century before had been farmland, was dominated by his great new mansion. Millionaire domains were proliferating in 1901-02, but Peacock's vied with the best of them — it did occupy a whole block of expensive real estate. It was designed by the most important architectural firm in Pittsburgh, who were particularly the architects in ordinary to Andrew Carnegie — Alden & Harlow. The mansion was the best Alden & Harlow — four-square and solid — constructed of the best materials — red brick of a kind you cannot get nowadays and light-coloured stone carved in a manner that you

The salon of "Rowanlea."

could not manage today. There are estimates as to the number of its rooms — the floor plans still exist, and the rooms could be counted if need be. The house was fireproof (to the degree that houses can be) because it was furnished lavishly with inflammable materials — including gorgeous linens and laces, of which Peacock was a connoisseur.

I can remember Peacock's glorious house as I saw it in my childhood, from the Highland Avenue car in 1915 on my way to the Zoo. My parents had told me about the house and also about Peacock, whom they regarded as a fabulous prince of a golden era. It was a kind of fairy-tale domain that he inhabited, in which every luxury was contained — a resplendent conservatory toward the back of the property, a garage full of elegant motor cars, wrought-iron gates at the entrance, and exotic shrubs in the grounds.

As with an exotic fairy-tale prince, many legends grew up about Peacock. Spending his apparently limitless funds seems to have become an obsession with him. In his great house, called "Rowanlea," more than forty employees were engaged to keep the place in order. It was in those days that the story went the rounds that Peacock rose from bed one morning and, clad still in his pajamas, ordered two seven-thousand-dollar motor cars sent to the house before noon. He hunted out many of his early associates and paid their debts. Another story tells that, being served a cold-storage egg for breakfast, he bought a farm in Allegheny County and spent sixty thousand dollars to insure a supply of fresh eggs and other farm products.

At another time, Peacock's name came into prominence when he took part in a five-hundred-thousand-dollar card game on the liner *Deutschland,* on a trans-Atlantic crossing. In 1902, there was a kidnapping scare in which Peacock's children were threatened unless he turned over several thousand dollars to the letter writers. The Peacocks, guarded by police, fled to New York and remained there until the scare abated.

The Peacocks also had a large summer home at Alexandria Bay in the Thousand Islands area of the St. Lawrence River. Here he maintained in a large boat house — a real marine palace — a large fleet of motor boats, and two steam yachts, the *Irene I* and the *Irene II.* Although his summer home has now vanished, the great boat house is still there.

And then Peacock went into the steel business on his own. It was a costly venture. He tried several other businesses, but he seemed to have lost his magic touch, and it was not long before the Pittsburgh mansion was on the market.

With the remnants of his fortune, he took his five children and his wife to New York (the Carnegie millionaires always had a fondness for the Big Apple) about 1920. He went into the real estate business. He was able to recoup some of his fortune, and he owned loft and office buildings as well as the Hotel Brotzel, in which he lived.

He died on July 13, 1928 in New York. The great mansion in Pittsburgh had already been sold in 1921 with all its contents, including his large collection of paintings. A portrait of Mrs. Irene Peacock, by Raimundo de Madrozo, painted in 1902, is now in the collection of the Pittsburgh History & Landmarks Foundation. A very large painting showing the erstwhile châtelaine of "Rowanlea" enthroned in pink satin, it is an expansive document of Edwardian *luxe.*

The house, the pride of the Peacocks, was sold in 1924 to a developer, and its site is now occupied by several much smaller houses. So it vanished like a golden dream.

Radio script for WQED-FM, 1981.

Lovejoy's Folly
A Vanished Pittsburgh Palace

I first saw it — the great grey ghost palace — riding on the crest of a small hill like an abandoned ocean liner, not far from my house in the East End. Perhaps I found it in the spring of 1925, although it is difficult now to remember. Certainly, whatever the year, the visual impact of this house was tremendous. I had heard about it from some of my adolescent friends who used to play ball in the ruins of the garden. To find it, I had to walk some blocks from my house and then cut off at an angle toward Frick Park.

It looms now in my memory like a dream castle — a fantastic jumble of gables, chimneys, and porches. On that long ago afternoon, I walked up onto one of the porches and looked through the dirty plate-glass windows. Inside, I saw fading vistas of great rooms with rough-plastered walls. The interior had never been finished; no one had ever lived there. It was empty and, I thought, probably haunted.

When I returned home, I asked my parents at the dinner table, to whom the house had belonged. "Francis Lovejoy," they said. "That's Lovejoy's Folly. He was a big man in Carnegie Steel, long ago, and then he lost everything. He never lived in it. It is quite a story." Then they started to talk about something else, and it was only recently that I decided to research it.

Mankind is perennially interested in great wealth and in the works of those who embody their affluence in masonry. A great house is like a fabulous bank statement — it commands respect and awe. Certainly no district in late nineteenth-century Pittsburgh was more affluent and wealthier than that area along Penn Avenue between Point Breeze and the East End. I lived in this enchanted region most of my life and I always called it the Chateau Country, because the great country houses reared their towers and gables to the glory of Mammon all the length of that leafy avenue. Even as a child I contemplated them with pleasure, and even now I regret their passing. They gave you a sense of comfort and repose, just like a fat balance at your banker's.

Among the older country houses dating from the days when much of the area was farmland was that called "Edgehill," on South Braddock Avenue not far from Penn. Built about 1868, simple and unpretentious, it was devoted to other values than those of Mammon; it was the "seat" of Colonel Edward Jay Allen (1830-1916), an eminent citizen of early Pittsburgh but not one noted for his wealth. He was an early explorer in the West, an engineer, a colonel in the Civil War, and a local business man, as well as a poet and writer. He collected a large library which nurtured the talent of his grandson Hervey Allen (1889-1949) the well-known Pittsburgh novelist whose *Anthony Adverse* was a best seller of the 1930s. The Colonel's adopted son, the famous painter John White Alexander (1856-1916), was also brought up at "Edgehill."

In 1899 Colonel Allen sold his house to F. T. F. Lovejoy, one of the younger Carnegie partners who apparently was looking for a prominent perch among his colleagues of the Carnegie Steel Company, many of whom had large houses in North Point Breeze. The lord of the manor here was Henry Clay Frick, whose chateau at Penn and Homewood Avenues dominated the district — and still does, now that the others have gone. Within a block or two lived George Lauder, Lucy Coleman Carnegie, widow of Andrew's brother Tom, and for a time Alexander Peacock.[1] Down the street lived H. J. Heinz and T. M. Armstrong, who were "big men" although they were not connected with Carnegie. By the turn of the century the district was undoubtedly a "choice" residential site. Colonel Allen may have thought that it was time to leave this millionaire pleasance to the big spenders.

Francis Thomas Fletcher Lovejoy was born in Baltimore, Maryland, in 1854. He was educated in Ohio but left home at sixteen to seek his fortune. First he worked for ten years in the Pennsylvania oil fields. He was one of those nineteenth-century young men who were able to do a number of things well, and he tried a number of occupations before he came to Pittsburgh in 1880. A year later he was employed as a clerk and telegrapher in the Carnegie steel companies, of which he became auditor in 1889, so rapid was his rise. In 1892 he was active in the formation of the Carnegie Steel Company and became a member of the firm as well — he was elected secretary and manager. Particularly, he was a protégé of H. C. Frick, who saw to it that he advanced in the company.

At the turn of the century, Andrew Carnegie, the majority stockholder, tried to force Frick out of the Company by offering to buy his stock, but at the book, not the market, value which would have resulted in a considerable loss for Frick. Under the so-called Iron Clad Agreement of the Company, any party to the agreement was bound to sell his stock back to the Company if the partners desired it. The sticking point here was the price, which Frick contended was unjust — which it manifestly was. Carnegie lined up the other partners — his own younger protégés and held fast to *his* price. Henry Phipps and Francis Lovejoy, however, would not stand with the Carnegie faction. Frick brought a suit in equity in the Pittsburgh courts in 1900; it was a battle of the Titans, and not only the local but the national public was all agog.

As the lawsuit would have necessitated opening the books of the Company to public scrutiny, all parties agreed that a compromise settlement out of court was the best solution to the impasse. Henry Phipps acted as mediator, and Lovejoy represented Frick's interest. An agreement was signed by all parties that created a new company with greatly increased capitalization. All partners, including Frick, would retain their interests, but Carnegie insisted that neither Frick nor Lovejoy could ever again hold office in the Company. In the end, it must be said that Lovejoy was the only one of the group that emerged from the imbroglio with his honour intact.

In 1901, the Company was sold to J. P. Morgan, who formed the United States Steel Corporation.

In 1901, as well, Lovejoy had just taken possession of the "Edgehill" property, and he planned to demolish the old Allen house (in which he was then living) and build a larger mansion than any Carnegie partner had yet attempted. Like Frick, who was also no longer involved in the management of the steel company, Lovejoy began to acquire real estate, and the latter's largest commercial development (undertaken with Robert Hall) was the construction in 1902-04 of the Bellefield Dwellings, the first high-rise apartment house in Pittsburgh.

Lovejoy, now free of all his former business ties, was seized by a kind of *folie à bâtir,* a madness for building, another outlet for his dreams of grandeur now that the Company was gone. "Mr. Lovejoy will build a magnificent house," proclaimed the headlines of an article in the *Pittsburgh Leader* on January 29, 1901. The article went on to say that Alden & Harlow, the city's most important architectural firm, had been commissioned to design a great house of some forty or fifty rooms, one hundred sixty-three by one hundred feet in area with a terraced garden in front and a large garage at one side to house Lovejoy's ever-increasing fleet of automobiles — he was one of the city's early devotees of motoring.

The architect's water colour perspective of the projected house was published — Lovejoy was still very much in the public eye — and it does give some idea of what he intended. One might almost call it megalomaniac architecture if only he had not been obviously such

A rendering of "Edgehill."

a "gentleman," but it does serve to illuminate another aspect of his enigmatic character. Essentially, the architect's projected picture shows that the basic mass of the house was symmetrical; it was built on a sloping site, however, and it was so overlaid with bays, projections, porches, gables, and chimneys that it is difficult to form any coherent picture of it: even so, Lovejoy himself.

At the age of fifteen, had I examined the shell of the house, I doubt that I would have known any more than I do now. According to the *Leader,* "it was built of grey brick trimmed with stone, handsomely finished but of the somewhat simple and solid order of architecture now popular." The style might be called "Standard Alden & Harlow Mansion" — a mixture of Tudor, Italian Renaissance, and Colonial Revival elements. The house was said to contain almost a hundred rooms (although this seems a gross exaggeration). There were a little theatre, two drawing rooms, and a great library fifty feet long.

The building on Kensington Avenue housing the automobiles, a stable (never used), and a gymnasium was one of the constructional wonders of the time. This three-story structure occupied an area even larger than the house — one hundred eighty by one hundred feet. On the ground floor was the garage, which housed in almost-princely splendour twelve automobiles of various types (and the cars in those days were very expensive), together with a machine shop where the cars could be repaired. In the basement were dynamos to furnish electricity for the entire estate. Two chauffeurs were always in residence. On the third floor was a large gymnasium where the Lovejoys gave a great reception in June, 1904, when the Annex, as it was called, was finished. Probably no motor cars were ever housed more handsomely.

Having opened the city's largest private garage, Lovejoy seemed to have reached new heights, but all was not well under the bright surface of his prosperity. Lovejoy, as long as he had the backing of the steel company, had prospered enormously, but left to his own devices he began to falter. Restlessly he sought for new financial worlds to conquer, and he needed more funds for the ever-grander state in which he now lived. In 1902 he began to finance a mining venture in Idaho into which he sank most of his not-inconsiderable finances. Unfortunately, although there was gold in "them thar hills," it cost more to extract it than it was worth on the market. Lovejoy's Sunnyside Mining Company met an ignominious end, and its entrepreneur and his family, if not reduced to penury, had to subsist on a much smaller scale.

The new palace, which was to have been occupied in 1905, was never finished, and this great shell of a luxurious dream was eventually sold to an East End real-estate entrepreneur. Lovejoy was essentially a follower and not a leader, and when his venture collapsed, he suffered a complete breakdown. Eventually he recovered and returned to Pittsburgh from the West. In relative obscurity, he lived on well into the twentieth century. He died in 1932 in a small apartment in Shadyside, the then-incumbent of a small position with Gulf Refining Company. *Sic transit . . .*

The great bulk of Lovejoy's Folly was almost an anachronism at the time it was built. No one wanted it; it could not be adapted to any new use. Eventually it was demolished in 1929, and its site is now covered by suburban villas. The Annex-garage lasted longer because it could be adapted to new uses. Artists had a fondness for it as studio space. I remember visiting them there in the 1930s and 1940s. Inevitably the end came, however, in 1966, when the solidly-built structure resisted mightily those who demolished it.

If Lovejoy's palatial vision was the stuff of dreams, at least it was well built, well founded. Perhaps if a dream has been sufficiently well founded it has not been dreamed in vain. If Francis Thomas Fletcher Lovejoy went bust he did it with a very large gesture, and no "boom and bust" figure in Pittsburgh history left, if only for a season, a grander monument.

---

[1]George Lauder (1837-1924) was another canny Scot who married Andrew Carnegie's sister. Andrew often visited them at the large "Queen Anne" house which George Lauder bought on Penn Avenue. T. M. Armstrong was another "big man" if not "Carnegie"; he was a power in the cork business. His Penn Avenue house was another Alden & Harlow "special."—JVT

Focus, Tribune-Review (Greensburg, Pa.), March 22, 1981.

Highland Towers.

Frederick G. Scheibler, Jr.
A Prophet of Modern Architecture in Pittsburgh

Among the green residential streets of the East End of Pittsburgh, in certain avenues and secluded corners, looming gables and asymmetrical chimneys call attention to the buildings beneath them. To the eye that remembers the urban scenery of the earlier part of this century the forms are familiar, the aura of William Morris and the Brothers Grimm unmistakable; but even to the casual glance these structures have a liberal simplicity of distinctive form, a pervasive and enduring originality of design. This is Romantic revivalism with a difference, for the architectural spirit of the present day is to be seen here as well. These walls, these chimneys speak a language which can well be understood today.

Transitional architecture of this sort has a strange fascination, for we seem to be looking at both the past and the present at once, and the work of the architects of the early Modern movement has an interest, a value which deserves to be recorded.

Frederick Scheibler, who died in June, 1958, at the age of eighty-six, was undoubtedly the most important "original" architect that Pittsburgh has produced, as well as a distinguished and unique pioneer of the Modern architectural movement in Pennsylvania. Most local architects are familiar with his apartment houses, and students are always re-discovering him, but his very real and enduring contribution to our regional art history deserves a wider audience, a larger renown. Still fresh and interesting today, his buildings have survived the "poppy of oblivion" and the whirligig of taste, and the best of them should assure him a minor and not unmemorable place in the whole chronicle of American architecture.

Like Frank Lloyd Wright, with whose work and career that of our architect shows certain parallels, Scheibler was an individualist, a dedicated artist who developed his own design theories and refused to be moved by any other standards than those of his art. It must be admitted at once that he practiced mostly in Pittsburgh, and in a particular quarter of the city — the East End — so he was in the narrowest sense, not only a provincial, but a parochial architect. To the old East Ender of Pittsburgh, he must seem a kind of *genius loci,* a tutelary spirit, but he was much more than that.

A modest and self-effacing man, he did not, quite unlike Wright, advertise himself unduly, and his work was not much published during his lifetime. No large buildings attest to his fame, for he worked mostly in the domestic sphere, and even here there are no mansions. Even so, although he was no Wright or Sullivan, his work, both in quality and originality compares favourably with that of less-known men like George Maher of Chicago or Wilson Eyre of Philadelphia, and as an early Modernist he often surpasses them.

His work, in essence, reflects very strongly some facets of the more advanced architectural trends of the late nineteenth and early twentieth centuries, as shown in the English domestic work of such men as C. F. A. Voysey and C. R. Mackintosh, and that of the new men on the Continent, Adolf Loos, Otto Wagner, and Joseph Hoffmann. Voysey's own house at Chorley Wood, Bucks, and Mackintosh's Hill House at Helensburgh are not too far in spirit from Scheibler's work. Again, his manner is similar to that of the Continental group mentioned, but his actual practice was more directly influenced by minor German and Austrian architects of the period, such as those published in *Moderne Bauformen.* Albert Gessner at Charlottenburg and Curjel & Moser of Karlsruhe, particularly the former's apartment houses, would seem to be primary sources of inspiration. In this proto-Modern style, an exploration of vernacular sources as opposed to the grand tradition of the styles, led to a simplification of form and a search for new structural concepts and a contemporary architectural vocabulary in which traditional ornament, and even native or folk stylistic reminiscences, tended to disappear. Of course, some of the new ornament was much influenced by the Art Nouveau, but save in some of his decorative details Scheibler was not influenced by that movement in any great degree.

There was probably something atavistic in this very noticeable bias, for he was of German descent on both sides of his family. Frederick Gustavus Scheibler, Jr., was born in the Oakland district of Pittsburgh in 1872, the son of William Augustus and Eleanor (Seidel) Scheibler. His paternal grandfather, who had emigrated from Düsseldorf in 1825, worked in Pittsburgh as a book binder, and this solid German craft tradition was carried on by his grandson, who had a special feeling for the decorative adjuncts of his own buildings and who specialized in designing tiles.

Scheibler never attended architectural school, but got his training by the old apprentice method, which was still relatively common in his day. At the age of sixteen, in 1888, he left the Central High School, where he was a pupil, to enter the office of Henry Moser, a leading local architect of the time. Here, and in other architectural offices like those of Alden & Harlow and Lou Beatty, he worked and learned, and by observation and experimentation laid the foundations for his later career.

In 1898, about the time of his marriage to Antonia Oehmler, he set up in practice for himself, but there is little in his earliest work to indicate the direction he was later to take. His Joseph Steel house in Greensburg or the hotel built in the Woods Run district of Pittsburgh, both done before the turn of the century, are not too different from the average work of the period, although the latter does display an unusual openness of fenestration. And the cottage he built for himself at the time of his marriage, although a pleasant example of the late nineteenth-century "shingle" type, was not outstanding. As the architect himself said, he went through rather a "half-and-half" period for a time.

The full measure of his talent is manifested in the Old Heidelberg apartments, at Braddock Avenue and Waverly Street, which was constructed in 1905 for a local firm of speculators, Robinson & Bruckman. The building, which still serves very well its original purpose, displays its Teutonic origin in its great gabled mass and its Romantic if simple detailing. But if there are here many reminiscences of the middle-European vernacular — the great arches which house the rear porches, the tall chimneys which seem to cry out for stork's nests, and the corbeled bay windows — there is a kind of vernal freshness, a forthrightness of structural statement, that strikes a new note. Here the old folk tale is retold with a morning accent, a new voice.

To anyone familiar with the period, the sources are obvious. Despite his lack of travel, Scheibler's library was stocked with English and German publications of the period, such as the aforementioned *Moderne Bauformen* and *Der Architekt,* and the books of Muthesius and Walter Shaw Sparrow. These literary sources, however, served Scheibler only as a kind of framework for his own construction.

The main building, constructed of brick covered with two coats of Portland cement and roofed with red tile, is symmetrical both in plan and disposition of mass, but the freely-devised naturalistic ornament (like the mushroom relief on the facade) and the great variety of openings and fenestration (always a favourite Scheibler device) create a feeling of asymmetrical movement in the general composition. The porches, which display a highly original treatment of a standard architectural motif of the period, have exposed I-beams, an uncommon practice for the time, which the architect used also in

The Old Heidelberg apartments.

his later work. In 1908, groups of cottages were added at either side of the earlier building, creating a large complex, which if perhaps overly Romantic in aspect, is still attractive to the modern eye as well as functional in a high degree.

The building attracted considerable attention at the time of its erection, and it was published both here and abroad. The *American Architect* featured it in its issue of January 5, 1907, saying that it "draws its inspiration from the Art Nouveau movement as it is understood in Germany." It was later published in the *Western Architect* of June, 1911 and in *Der Architekt* (Vol. XIV, 1908) in Hans Berger's article "Das Wohnhaus in Amerika."

The central motif of the great gabled mass, as well as the treatment of the porches, is to be found in the roughly-contemporary Linwood apartments at McPherson Boulevard and Linden Avenue, although it is possible that the smaller scale of this structure makes for a more satisfying general composition. Both here and at the Old Heidelberg, the floor plans exhibit subsidiary spaces organized around a central living area, a refreshing formula for the time, but his three-story apartment houses at Braddock and Bennett Streets (1909) show how vigorously he could handle even the standard "railroad" apartment of the period. Another variation on the theme — the urban multiple dwelling with shops underneath — at Walnut and Copeland Streets (1908) displays an original, forceful treatment of the ground floor, with its alternation of wide planes of glass interspersed with bold, sloping, monolithic stone piers. Here again, the traditional shop facade assumes under his hand new and impressive dimensions.

The public hallways of this building are rather more elaborate than those of the Old Heidelberg or the Linwood — marble and mosaic are used, but here, as elsewhere, are his simple oak doors, with their art-glass panels, and the skylight of opaque glass panels embedded in a wooden grid. When one remembers the bleakness of the usual Edwardian apartment hallway, these passages and stairways have a real distinction of design that is still pleasant to contemplate today.

Scheibler continued his rational, if admittedly picturesque, approach to design, and the next outstanding landmark of his career, the Highland Towers apartment house (1913) at 340 South Highland Avenue, is just as striking in concept and design as the Old Heidelberg, if rather different in form and texture.

A four-story brick structure, designed around three sides of an open court, this building has, despite the lavish use of art glass and the free "diaper" treatment of the spandrels (which not unpleasantly recall the period), a very contemporary feeling. The wide areas of banded fenestration, contrasting with the plain wall surfaces, the round cement columns, the long vertical windows, and the turrets of the corner towers all contribute to the Modern effect. The floor plans of the structure, whose apartments have today been subdivided, are elaborations of those of the Old Heidelberg and the Linwood. Of special note are the ingeniously-planned staircases which rise partly against a semi-circular wall of rough brick. This building recalls particularly the work of Frank Lloyd Wright (with which Scheibler was familiar) both in character of ornament and disposition of mass.

The interior of the Highland Towers exhibits as well the pervasive influence of Japan, which is also noticeable in the work of Wright. Scheibler was directly motivated by the Japanese through his association with the Japanese-American artist Kentaro Kato (1889-1926), who sometimes collaborated with him in his decorative schemes. The architect, however, whatever his models, was always interested in the visual aspects of his work; sculpture, colour, flat decoration, and landscaping were integral parts of his buildings.

As an architect he displayed, as well, an intensely practical but inventive attitude toward construction and design. Mill owners, iron workers, brick manufacturers, the proprietors of fixture houses, and others aided him understandingly when he was trying to explore their fields for simpler and better ways of doing things. Scheibler laid claim, as the result of their help, to many innovations in products and equipment — tapestry brick and aluminum casements entered the local scene at his urging.

Scheibler was the first architect in Pittsburgh to be influenced by the "garden city" movement, and in this category, too, he explored the types and forms of his day. England had been the pioneer in the "garden estate" and workers' colony developments before 1900, and the later work of Ebenezer Howard was also influential. London's Bedford Park (1875-   ), Port Sunlight (1888-   ), and the Hampstead Garden Suburb (1907) had influenced German architects, who were also much interested in colonies of workers' houses.

Scheibler designed no large lay-outs of detached or semi-detached houses, but he did some interesting work with the row house by breaking up the larger units and disposing them about a city lot in the interest of variety. All these "court" arrangements or "group cottages" may be spoken of as suburban, since they were all placed in a verdant setting of lawns and trees. Meado'cots (the whimsicality of the title may owe something to the period), built in 1912 in Wilkinsburg, and the Hamilton Cottages (1911-14) on Beacon Street are good examples of this type, since they are complexes of row units re-arranged in a suburban pattern. In both of these appear the motif of the three-sided court as at the Old Heidelberg and the Highland Towers, with semi-detached houses acting as forebuildings to the main row section at Meado'cots and the row units performing the same function at Hamilton Cottages. Neither of these sites is very large, but the judicious placing of the row elements, combined with lawns and greenery, produce an effect of almost rural spaciousness, of romantic seclusion, which even the slum decay which has overtaken Meado'cots cannot negate.

Scheibler's street row houses — Inglenook Place (1907), Vilsack Row (1912) and Singer Place (1919) — have the same openness of site and the same variety of exterior treatment. The rows themselves are usually rectangular and boxlike, consisting of two or more units with small projecting wings at the back. Even his rear or side elevations will often be well-studied, but the street facades display an astonishing versatility of handling — granted the limited means at the architect's disposal. Artfully-disposed projections and recessions of mass, ribbon windows and arches, contrasting flat and sloping roofs, plain oak doors, and simply-designed art glass all combine to make these low-budget, speculative productions usually honest and handsome visual assets to the urban landscape. The continued use of the exposed I-beam, the round concrete columns, the constantly-varied fenestration (particularly the corner windows in the forebuildings at Meado'cots) reinforce his reputation as a Modern forerunner.

As a voice going before, perhaps the peak of his achievement is the Vilsack Row (1912) on Jancey Street, which might well be considered in 1962 as the product of a contemporary architect. Here, the corner entrance pavilions, representative of older volumetric shapes, contrast with the open areas and the slab roofs which suggest the intersection and the interplay of planes enclosing spaces. These simple row houses, now much decayed, must have been almost unique in America in their day, and Scheibler has here transcended his role as prophet.

He continued, like the medieval builder or craftsman, to live and work in his own parish — the East End of Pittsburgh's metropolitan district. He and his first wife were divorced in 1913, and he was remarried in 1923 to Mrs. Blanche Clawson. For the last twelve years of his life he was completely blind, but he had retired from active practice sometime before that. He died in his small suburban home near Pittsburgh in 1958.

His later work, after the Singer Place houses of 1919, became more complicated in massing and heavier both in ornament and texture, developments which were foreshadowed in the Rudolf Hellmund house of 1915 and the Johnston house of 1921. His later manner, which to a degree reflects the lush, vespertine romanticism of the 1920s, is to be seen at its fullest flowering in the Parkstone Dwellings (1922) at 6937-43 Penn Avenue. In this amazing building, which may be taken as his swan song, the long roof lines swoop low over walls of heavy schist stone and banks of heavily-leaded windows. Here the concrete toadstools at the entrance doors, like the reliefs on the Old Heidelberg, attest to his continuing interest in and use of natural forms, as do the swelling mock-thatched roof and phallic chimneys of the Harter house (1923) on Beechwood Boulevard. The note of whimsey, not unapparent in his earlier work, has crystallized at the Parkstone in the amusing tile "rugs" which depend so realistically from the balconies and in the tile overmantels of the interior fireplaces where dinosaurs disport themselves. The interiors generally are more elaborate — if there is no advance in planning beyond those of the Highland Towers. The front gardens of this structure and the Klages house (1923), on Beverly Place, both showing Japanese influence, are rich in pattern and texture, and their sunken lawns display the facades to good advantage.

These late buildings are original and striking, but it is by his earlier work that Scheibler should be remembered; and he is an architect that fully deserves to be held in memory. Although he was no great innovator, he did handle with originality and vigour the more advanced design trends of his time, at least in the domestic sphere, and his best work can compare favourably with any thing of the same sort being produced in America at the time. Scheibler's work is a valuable ornament to the streets of Pittsburgh, but it would also be a credit to any American city.

The exploration of the Scheibler saga has been for the writer a labour of piety and love, a kind of *recherche du temps perdu,* a quest for the life, of the face, of a city neighbourhood long known and held in much affection. It was Scheibler who helped mould that face and gave it an extra clarity, a wider dimension, and for his bounty there are many of us who will especially remember him. City landscapes, at best, do not remain constant; many of his buildings were slightly built, and not a few of them are visibly decaying. The face is changing now, and perhaps, one day, portions of it will disappear; but the younger architects, who are still interested in his work, will mould new faces in other urban quarters, and his dedication, his truth and his example will appear in another form.

Note: More recent research establishes new dates for the following buildings (given with the pages where mentioned): Joseph Steel house (285), c. 1901; hotel in Woods Run (285), 1902; apartment houses, Braddock and Bennett Streets (287), c. 1904; Singer Place (288, 289), c. 1912.

The Charette, October, 1962. An edited version of this article was also printed in the October, 1962 issue of *Carnegie Magazine* under the title, "A Prophet of Modern Architecture in Pittsburgh: Frederick G. Scheibler, Jr."

East Liberty's Liberty Theatre

I was, the other day, looking at a new book on American picture palaces of the 1920s — those fabulous temples of the silver screen — and it set me to thinking of earlier picture houses of the 'Teens of this century. I think particularly of those of East Liberty, where I grew up.

East Liberty was definitely a very expansive part of the city of Pittsburgh, but it always had a certain suburban quality because its ranging hills split up the terrain into ravines called hollows, where a rich diversity of neighbourhood life flourished. The advent of the cinematograph introduced a growing awareness of the great world outside the local boundaries, and the movies were a potent force in introducing these isolated neighbourhoods to that world. As time went on, there was scarcely any collection of houses and shops that did not have its attendant movie house. Movies had become part of the American way of life.

East Liberty, being the business and shopping centre of the East End of Pittsburgh, had a number of the largest and best of these embryo theatres, the earliest of which were just converted shops and business premises in which a cinematograph or projector and a screen were installed. Sometimes a fancy front was added to the original building, and sometimes a kind of loggia with a variation of the old Roman triumphal arch, studded with flashing electric bulbs. It was only a step from there to large electric marquees with the names of the pictures currently playing — or, it would be better to say, showing — as well as the stellar actors and actresses in lights.

After 1910, theatres constructed specifically for the showing of movie pictures became more common as the movie industry expanded and became "big business." One of the largest and architecturally most important of these buildings was the Liberty Theatre, which opened in 1915 on Penn Avenue, not far from the East Liberty Station. It was designed by the architect Henry Hornbostel, who had first come to Pittsburgh in 1904 to supervise the work of his firm, Palmer & Hornbostel, which had designed the first campus of the Carnegie Institute of Technology — now Carnegie-Mellon University. This design of the University, as evidenced by the surviving buildings, was a bravura piece of Beaux-Arts, neo-Baroque planning which has never been equalled in the city. The design of the Liberty Theatre, which coincides with that of the School of Fine Arts at C.M.U., displayed a rather more restrained use of the same Beaux-Arts theme in dealing with a theatre commission.

The moving-picture theatre was demolished about 1963 in a commitment to the Urban Redevelopment Authority regarding the East Liberty area. It was a long, narrow building of considerable height, although it was essentially only one story high; this large, high space constituted the auditorium of the theatre. The screen itself was attached to the back wall of the building, in an ornate false proscenium.

Because of his Beaux-Arts training in Paris, Hornbostel as a designer was extremely devoted to oval or elliptical forms and spaces. His theatre in the Fine Arts Building of C.M.U. (1915) employs an oval plan, and he used the same theme in the lobby in front of the auditorium of the Liberty Theatre.

This lofty space also contained a double staircase with a handsome Renaissance balustrade that led to the entrance of the spacious balcony. The curving walls, which led to a domed ceiling, were plastered and scored to look like masonry. There was rich crimson carpeting on the floor and crimson velvet on the stair railing. It was an elegant room but not overpoweringly so, and a proper dramatic prelude to the darkened auditorium in which the larger-than-life images of stars like Rudolph Valentino and Gloria Swanson were enshrined. In the early days of talking pictures, I remember seeing Greta Garbo in *Romance* there on a winter afternoon. Pittsburgh, then, and the icy streets seemed very far away.

My chief memory of the Liberty, however, is the great rippling American flag in sparkling and flowing light bulbs, a triumph of the electric sign maker's art, which coruscated on the street facade above the marquee. It is long gone, but I can still see it flowing.

Radio script for WQED-FM, 1982.

Denholm's Corner and Fred's Store

Among all the memories of my childhood, Fred's Corner Store in East Liberty occupies a prominent and cherished place; even now it juts forward from the long shadowland of my memory like a benevolent ghost ship laden with fugitive fragments of my far past. Fred's long gone, and the store as well, but the building is still there, despite adjacent and far-flung acres of urban renewal; it looms large, solid, and narrowly triangular at the intersection of two avenues in a once-bustling neighbourhood of the East End. The tall three-story apartment house was built by my maternal grandfather James Denholm in 1910 on the triangular plot of land that he had owned since the 1870s. The intersection really constituted a kind of Five Points. Frankstown was the main avenue from which Lincoln Avenue angled off sharply, but Mayflower and Independence Streets came in laterally. This catalogue of historical names lent the area a certain *élan* which it did not quite live up to, but it was a good solid American neighbourhood of its day. My grandfather added his own name to the mixture — the apex of the apartment building was flattened, and just above the front windows of Fred's Store was a great block of stone inscribed with the Roman letters DENHOLM. Perhaps the utter presidency of that name is the reason that I have forgotten Fred's surname.

I can only recall him vaguely, when, as a child of six, I moved with my family in May, 1914, into my grandfather's new apartment house. I was not allowed to roam very far afield in the new neighbourhood, but the fascinating store at the apex of the triangle was quite within bounds. As I look back on it now, it was the focal point of that neighbourhood. It was in nothing unusual; its like could be found the length and breadth of America — it was a combination newsstand, confectionery shop, tobacconist, stationer, and soda fountain. The form of the shop was, of course, triangular, with the soda fountain at the back and the concomitant twisted wire chairs and tables against the great plate-glass windows of the Frankstown Avenue side. The counters for candy and tobacco were ranged in front of the windows of the Lincoln Avenue side. The magazines and newspapers were at the front. Plate glass was everywhere, and the place was full of light except when the striped awnings offered shade in summer. What I remember most strongly about the place was its smell — a sharp, pleasant odour compounded of ice cream, fruit syrup, chocolate, tobacco, and newsprint. It was an olfactory experience once quite common but now rare, as this type of shop has generally tended to disappear. Sometimes in season there would be lilacs or roses in a cut-glass vase in front of the large soda fountain mirrors.

It was before that mirror that I just remember seeing Fred, when my Uncle Brown took me on my birthday in July, 1914, to get a chocolate soda at the fountain. The usual "soda jerk," a young man with a white apron and cap, was not there, so Fred waited on us himself. He was a tall, dark, rather gaunt man, verging on middle age, with bushy black eye brows and a hawk-like nose. He always seemed to wear grey suits, and his eyes were grey — startling beneath the black brows. His voice was very deep and he was always solemnly affable.

"Well, young man," he intoned smilingly, "what will you have today?" "A chocolate soda," my uncle said in his light blond voice, with its faint teasing tone. It was rumoured that he liked more potent liquids, but I did not know anything about that. I watched Fred while he expertly made the soda with his firm hairy hands. First he pumped the chocolate syrup in the tall glass, added a thin jet of soda from the faucet in the domed marble pillar in the centre of the fountain. From the counter he took a large scoop of vanilla ice cream and dropped it in the glass. Then he drowned it all in a copious flow of soda water, stirring the mixture vigorously with a long spoon, until a collar of foam appeared at the top of the glass. Finally he served it to me ceremoniously with a flourish of straws, while he and my uncle talked about baseball and war. I did not know anything about either of them — and still do not. I was blissfully occupied with the absorption of my first chocolate soda. I have never ceased to be entranced with the sharp, acrid taste of chocolate soda water.

From Fred as stationer, when I started to go to school a month or so later, I bought my tablets, pencils and pens — and even an elaborate, shiny pencil box, a gift from my mother. But for the next couple of years what I most enjoyed was the big show case of penny candy with its curving glass front. All the candies in their multitudinous variety were arranged in sparkling, square glass dishes — licorice straps with drops of coloured sugar on them, little wax barrels filled with vari-coloured liquids, tiny "tootsie rolls," sour balls, gum drops, piles of fudge, rather lurid-looking bon bons, and cheap chocolates (both of these cost a penny each). Ah, it was a treasure house, Ali Baba's glassy sugared cave, where I exchanged my hoarded pennies for these gustatory wonders. "I'll have one of those, and two of those," and Fred would patiently put them in a brown paper bag which I would carry outside on a summer day. I would sit on the ledge underneath Fred's window and watch the long red trolley cars go past either on the Lincoln or Frankstown lines, or the strange, high-shouldered delivery trucks or plodding drays.

Sometimes, if there were no relatives around to buy me a root beer or a lemon phosphate at Fred's fountain, I would lie in wait for the iceman's wagon with its sleepy horse. The iceman was a hulking, good-natured man who wore a piece of soaking burlap over one shoulder where he carried huge cakes of ice up the flights of stairs in the apartment house. While he was scaling the heights, my little friends and I would raid the cold, splintery interior of the wagon, hunting for broken pieces of ice which we would carry off. How wonderful on a hot day were these icy fragments!

Just opposite Fred's Lincoln Avenue door on the Mayflower Street corner was a large granite horse trough which bubbled perpetually in summer. It was fun to plunge my arm into the cool water to feel the mosses that waved in the sparkling depths. Here at noon, along Lincoln Avenue, would gather a long line of drays. When they were "parked" their drivers would dismount and give the horses their nosebags of oats. After lunch, the horses and wagons would advance, one by one, till each horse had had a drink. We boys would creep up to a horse who had his mouth immersed in the water and we would pat the white stars on his bony nose. The horse did not often like it; he would raise his head and toss his mane and his tail. Those heavy plodding creatures were certainly noble and patient animals who worked very hard for little reward. I often wondered if there were a paradise for horses.

Meanwhile in Fred's store, by the tobacco counter, my grand-father's old friend Mr. Edwards was bending over the small gas flame that issued from a brass fixture at one side of the counter, to light his post-prandial cigar. As he puffed out the fragrant smoke, the light gleamed on his refulgent white Victorian whiskers — I often wondered why they did not catch fire during this solemn ceremony. He did look vaguely like Santa Claus, and he behaved toward me with a kind of courtly graciousness redolent of old manners and vanished ways. He told me stories of East Liberty in the 1860s and saved his red-and-gold cigar bands for me, so that I could use them as rings. I loved him very much.

Neither my grandfather nor Mr. Edwards would have anything

to do with the relatively new cigarettes, of which Fred had a plentiful supply. My young Uncle Brown smoked them, though — Lucky Strikes to be exact — but I often wished that he would smoke Murads or Fatimas, because I wanted the very colourful cigarette boxes, and, young as I was, I fancied the smell of Turkish or Egyptian tobacco. My uncle was fashionable, and ordered his suits from London, subscribed to *Vanity Fair* and *The Smart Set,* and sometimes, for his young lady friends, he bought one of Fred's fancy boxes of chocolates with roses painted on their satin lids. I also coveted those painted blooms and hoped that Uncle Brown would give me a box for Christmas. He never did.

Vanity Fair and *The Smart Set* were also to be found on Fred's magazine display racks along with most of the popular magazines. My mother used to stop in to get the *Ladies Home Journal,* and the *Saturday Evening Post* was a great favourite with my grandfather. I liked to look at the comic-satiric magazines like *Life* and *Judge* although I did not always understand the cartoons. I particularly remember some of the sensational dime novels that Fred had on display, with their lurid late-Victorian covers. Were they reprints? The heroines depicted in such perilous situations were certainly not dressed in the costume of the day, for which I had a knowing eye.

During the Easter season, Fred's store was a special treasure house of huge candy eggs and large rabbits made of pink sugar — and at such a time that confectionery smell was almost overpoweringly sweet. At Fourth of July, with the stacked packages of fire crackers piled on his shelves, the acrid odour of gunpowder added yet another dimension to the olfactory medley.

In the summer of 1916, my father and mother moved to Philadelphia, and the halcyon days of almost-daily visits to Fred's were finished. Shortly before we left, my mother took me into Fred's for a farewell visit to the fountain. I remember that my mother was wearing a wonderful wide-brimmed hat of Panama straw crowned with artificial water lilies. As a parting present, Fred made me a banana split — my first. Fred sat down with us as I ate, and I remember a strange warm feeling of affection, which was fortified by the banana split.

It is all gone now, Fred and my mother and the magic hour. Only I now remember. Memory? But perhaps it is something more than that. I remember also Thornton Wilder's final words in *The Bridge of San Luis Rey:* "There's a land of the living, and a land of the dead, and the bridge is love."

"Jamie's Journal," *The Pittsburgher,* July, 1980.

Terrace Life in Pittsburgh IV
Schumann *al Fresco*

In my rather drawn-out series of radio scripts on terrace life in Pittsburgh, there is one terrace incident that I have, curiously, rather avoided bringing to the surface of memory. It would be rather like digging up some long-buried treasure. Would it be as wonderful as one had always thought it to be, would it still be as pristine, as compelling, as I remembered from fifty years ago? Oh, I have pursued the past to folly, I have been prodigal of dreams and transformed my middling store of keepsakes into the patrimony of a prince. We create our own legends as we go. But do our legends, our buried treasures, our magical memories have any currency beyond the confines of our own lost time? Perhaps we should *not* rummage in our dusty cupboards for that superlative memory that shone, but yet shines now, with so refulgent an historical gleam.

This memory, I half say to myself: why now do you think it so transcendent, so wonderful? Why make so much fuss over an evening party at Cousin Lally's house and a song sung on a summer night, and the terrace really was not much of a terrace — only a Late Victorian verandah without a roof — but it did look down on a garden and it was approached from the house by a high French door, the two glass leaves of which constituted the *only* architectural feature of any distinction on the rear elevation of Cousin Lally's rented Queen Anne house.

Well, the evening *was* interesting. I still feel it was — despite everything — engaging, intriguing, for Pittsburgh, but since Pittsburgh has always been my chief interest, anything which has been part of it may be considered worthy of being chronicled. It happened long ago — not long after the end of the First World War — was it 1920, '21 — it does not matter if I get the right year or not. It was Cousin Lally's story, really — not mine — and it is for her memory that I tell it.

I was only about sixteen at the time of her little impromptu evening party, and it still amazes me that the event impressed me so *then*. Lally was rather tenuously related to my family, but I have always felt that it was a relationship of liking rather than duty. I did not see her very often. Her family had been, not rich, but rather

297

"well to do." She did not have to work, she traveled much, and on her infrequent visits to Pittsburgh I saw her fairly often. Just after the First World War, she took a notion to settle in Pittsburgh, and she had rented one half of a large double house not far from my family's house on Madrid Street.[1] At that time Lally was in her early sixties, but she still possessed the remains of a rather wispy beauty. She was well-educated, cultivated, and decorously devoted to the arts. Vaguely sociable, she liked to give small artistic parties. She thought that, young as I was, *I* was artistic and "interesting" — so I was invited to her "evenings."

The party of which I speak must have been given late in June — the weather was hot, and the verdure in Lally's backyard garden almost excessive. There were many roses, and the soft evening air was heavy with their scent. We were also not far from the main line of the Pennsylvania Railroad, and billowing clouds of black smoke from passing locomotives sometimes mingled with the rosey odours.

We were a relatively small party — some older people variously interested in the arts, Lally, me, and a dazzling young mezzo-soprano, very German, pink, and blonde — Elsie Freyer. She lived, I think, in Cincinnati, and she was visiting Lally en route to Europe to study. My mother said that Lally had something to do with the European trip, which implied that our cousin was also a patron of the arts.

We were all sitting on the verandah-terrace, which was elegantly furnished with wicker furniture and bright floral cushions which vied with the vibrant and rampant rambler roses for attention. Beyond the tall elms at the bottom of the garden, one could see the signal lights on the railway line; an express roared past in a cloud of black smoke that drifted toward us slowly. As I remember, I was meditating a poem about roses and the smoke.

I knew that Elsie was expected to sing, but none of us wanted to go inside. Elsie said that the piano was right beyond the French door; she would sing there and we could listen where we were. She also asked Lally if there was anything she particularly wanted to hear. Lally smiled intently up at the young singer, all splendid before her in green-and-gold chiffon. It was, after all, Elsie's farewell song before Europe. Something special, something wonderful, it would have to be. I waited. At her best, Elsie was really good, and best at German lieder. "Oh Elsie," Lally murmured in her crinkled middle-aged voice, "the Schumann — 'Der Nussbaum,'" and she reached out her elegant veined hand to touch Elsie's golden arm. Elsie just looked at her with a long, unfathomable glance and breathed, "Yes." She turned gracefully, went through the door, and sat down at the piano. We could just see her with her hands poised above the keyboard. The roses were almost overpowering, so many of them, so sweet. The railway, *mirabile dictu,* was still. The signal lights changed.

First a brief sprinkle of notes, then the clear, soaring voice:

Es grünet ein Nussbaum vor dem Haus
Duftig,
Luftig,
Breitet er blättrig die Äste aus.

I had never heard the song before. From the first note, I was as one transfixed, held under an enchantment. In the still air, in this rosey June, the song was simply pure beauty. The piano flowed and then the voice, just flowing sound. Sometimes the words came through, sometimes not:

Es flüstern je zwei zu zwei gepaart
Neigend,
Beugend
Zierlich zum Kusse die Häuptchen zart.

My German was then not good, and that language in America, just after the First World War, was not exactly in good odour, but that did not matter. There was only the superlative, flowing sound in the still enchanted air. I was very young and ripe for the beauty and the song:

Sie flüstern von einem Mägdlein, dass
Dächte
Nächte
Und tagelang, wüsste, ach! selber nicht was.

With a long rush and roar another express passed, with flashes of light along the line beyond the shadowy elms. The voice rose again, soft, limpid, unearthly . . . *"Sie flüstern, sie flüstern . . ."* It was only a simple song about a maiden listening to the whispering leaves of the nut tree and dreaming of romance. And yet the evening and the song had enchanted us all — young and old. *"Sie flüstern,"* they whisper.

Just as the spell became almost unbearable (I looked across the terrace to see that Lally was weeping silently) I had the sense that it was about to end:

Das Mägdlein horchet, es rauscht im Baum;
Sehnend,
Wähnend,
Sinkt es lächelnd in Schlaf and Traum.

The last notes trailed away into stillness, but the ghost of the song lingered in the air sinking into dreams. Elsie appeared in the doorway, shining like a goddess in the light from the music room. The spell was still strong upon us; no one, at the moment could say anything.

Elsie looked luminously at Lally. Obviously she understood. Silently she moved across the terrace and bending to Lally's shadowy cheek, she kissed the ancient tears. It was the most simple gesture, but it was supreme and it set the seal upon the evening. Like the song itself it had an irreducible grandeur.

¹Madrid Street was a fanciful name I sometimes used for Thomas Boulevard.—JVT

Radio script for WQED-FM, 1978.

Memories of Highland Park

The parks of childhood memories seem perpetually green, continually open, bright and fair, to the backward glance cast from the dubious preserve of the "golden years." To the dimming eye of age, how sweet, how delectable those far-away pleasances. So I was quite prepared for a reminiscent romp along verdant paths when I was asked to write down some recollections of Highland Park early in the century.

Mine was a family of the East End of Pittsburgh, Point Breeze to be exact, and Highland Park was *our* park, since we did not have the Mellon municipal acres in those days. True, we did drive through Schenley Park in my grandfather's car, but we did not make excursions of pleasure there. We went often to Carnegie Museum, on the edge of Schenley, but rarely ventured beyond it. If we were going on picnics in the city we went only to Highland Park and always in the car, but if we were going to the Zoo we usually went in the Highland Avenue streetcar, as trolley cars were usually called in Pittsburgh. These excursions occurred in the two brief years 1914 to 1916, before we went to live in Philadelphia.

I liked some of the pictures at the Museum, usually the more dramatic ones, and the Diplodocus, whose great bones awed and frightened me, but the Zoo was probably more intriguing because the beasts both great and small were alive and moved so imponderably. Of all of my excursions with my father and mother, I probably most enjoyed the picnics, because it was always summer and it was more fun eating in the open. I particularly liked to eat my deviled eggs and potato salad from a table cloth laid on some grassy space.

My mother, however, liked to be more comfortable, so the preferred picnic spot was a table with benches near one of the shelter houses in the groves opposite Lake Carnegie. The Lake was quite different in those days. It was obviously artificial, but by the time I first knew it, it had had time to settle into the hillside below the great reservoir basins. At one end was a boat house and refreshment stand where you could get livid-coloured pop and boxes of Cracker Jack. Adjacent to this wooden building and along the edges of the lake were wooden walkways built over the water, where a little fleet of canoes and rowboats were moored. These were for hire, and, after we had "staked out" our table in one of the groves, my father would take my mother and me rowing in one of the skiffs. It was fun to glide over the rippling, muddy water, trailing my hand beside the boat and watching the water lilies, not in the lake, but on my mother's hat. I watched the groves filling with other summer picnickers. Distantly, I could smell coffee brewing.

My favourite picnics were the annual Sunday School picnics of my grandfather's church. I knew most of the people, and there was always a much greater variety of food to be had. Such layer cakes, such pies, and ten kinds of potato salad! My young uncle, very smartly dressed in white flannels, would drive us to the picnic in the large open car, along Stanton Avenue, and between the park gates with Moretti's bronze horse tamers. These Classical groups always seemed rather forlorn at this side entrance to the Park, but at least they did herald the green lawns and the picnic grounds.

The rearing horses and their tamers are still there, but Lake Carnegie has changed almost out of recognition. In 1925, the pleasures of boating forgotten, the larger part of it was metamorphosed into a swimming pool. The remnant, where the boat house used to be, became a pool where fishermen practice casting their lines. It has been many a long year since I went to a picnic in the groves. The trees are still there, but I do not know about the picnics.

When we went to the Zoo on a Saturday afternoon in summer, we caught the Highland Avenue car at Penn and Highland in East Liberty. I always hoped that it would be one of the huge double-decker cars that in those halcyon days ran between Highland Park and Schenley Park. These trolley leviathans were utterly fascinating to a young child. When we were fortunate enough to board one, I clambered rapidly up the narrow stairway to the upper "deck," which was enclosed though the windows in summer were always open. My bobbed hair flying in the breeze, I would sit on one of the benches, ecstatically gazing through the tree tops at fabulous mansions, castles in the air, as the car proceeded solemnly along the stately reaches of North Highland Avenue. Years later, flying was never as good as this.

When we reached the Park at the Bunkerhill Car Barn, we set off down the wooded path that led to the Zoo. As I recall there was at the entrance, facing one of the great reservoir basins, another refreshment stand, and nearby a small fountain with a child carved in white marble. Both disappeared years ago. Half-way to the Zoo, the path crossed a mysterious leafy ravine — tropical, it seemed to me

Entering the Zoo, 1900s.

The Highland Avenue entrance to the park, c. 1900.

— where a tiny waterfall fell over mossy rocks. This dreamy place was eventually taken over by the Zoo and it lost all its umbrageous mystery.

At the foot of the hill, we came to the wide flights of stone steps that led up to the long, yellow-brick Zoo building that always seemed to be roaring and mumbling as we approached. At strategic intervals on the stairs and terraces were bronze lamp standards ornamented with griffons. I was told that griffons were mythical, but I was always vaguely disappointed to find no live winged beasts inside. What was inside was always completely captivating. I did not have, as I recall, any favourite animals; possibly I favoured the antics of the monkeys and the sullen majesty of the big cats. Years later, when I was reading Blake and encountered "Tiger, tiger, burning bright," I remembered my first tiger at the Highland Park Zoo.

Of course the Zoo was much smaller then, and it had hardly begun to expand into the surrounding parkland. The selection of "specimens" was much smaller then, but it was sufficient for a child to gain a wide view of the marvels of animate existence. Perhaps it is wise not to be glutted with wonders when one is young.

Again, if I were fortunate, I could ride back to East Liberty on the leviathan trolley, rustling through the leaves and the golden light. The last of my childhood visits to Highland Park took place on a dull, cool day of October, 1916, just before we moved to Philadelphia. My young uncle drove us that day in a car, since we went first for a farewell picnic at Lake Carnegie and then for a visit to the Zoo. It was a sad occasion — all the trees dripped sympathetically; I said farewell to the animals whom I had come to know fairly well.

This last evening my uncle picked us up in the car and took us home, going out by the splendid main entrance onto North Highland Avenue. Looking back I could see the great stone pillars, with their dramatic bronze statues gleaming against a stormy sky. This was the last I saw of the park until the mid-1920s, when it had begun to change.

Radio script for WQED-FM, probably 1981.

304

In a Golden Garden
A Small Suburban Station Garden
of Sixty Years Ago

Gardens, by their very nature, are essentially static; they belong to the places in which they are situated. And yet I was just thinking, the other day, how often I have seen them in connection with buildings associated with some form of transportation. These I have seen most often as adjuncts to railway stations, although they are not often so seen nowadays, inasmuch as there are few stations left. Ah, in the old days the grand stations had expansive lawns and luxuriant flower beds, bright with many brilliant Victorian bedding plants. Then, too, there were the small country stations, some of them little more than wooden sheds, with their multi-coloured tangles of garden flowers.

I remember one small garden at a tiny station in one of the southwest suburbs of Philadelphia. Perhaps I encountered it sixty years ago — or something less — in a Sunday afternoon motor excursion, and it seems to float like a dream on the edges of my consciousness.

It must have been August; it was very hot. I was seated with my grandfather in the tonneau or back seat of his great 1914 Chalmers touring car, en route to a dinner party at the country house of one of his friends. We were to stop at the little station to meet another of the guests and bring him to the party. The train was late, so I had a chance to examine the station master's garden, which was unusual because it was composed only of plants with yellow flowers.

The station itself consisted of a rectangular box, constructed in the best Victorian board-and-batten tradition, painted of course yellow; and there was nothing subdued about that hue — it *was* the purest lemon colour. Above was a sharply-gabled roof, covered in variegated ornamental slate and much ornamented with curlicued cornices and barge boards — these last painted in dark green, so that the very building itself seemed to be part of the floral picture. In the centre of the roof was a narrow yellow-brick chimney ornamented with neo-Elizabethan chimney pots. The station platforms were also paved with yellow brick. From the silvery rails (the line had only a single track) rose a wavering shimmer of heat rays, against a magnificent grove of huge pine trees which acted as a backdrop for the station and the railway line. The late-afternoon light was hot and clear; the air was still. The station master, who seemed half-asleep in his minute ticket office, told us that the train, which was late, *should* be in in another half-hour. He implied, in a tone muffled by his white, but yellowish, moustache, that the rolling stock on this small branch line was not of the best, that occasionally there were mishaps, nothing serious, you know, but when the equipment gets old, things will get out of order, what can you expect? His voice seemed to fade out into the somnolent air and he settled back more deeply onto his high stool.

My grandfather, all immaculate in his striped (were the stripes yellow too?) Palm Beach suit and Panama hat, retired to the car, where he sat dozing in the back seat, waiting for the train and Tom Weatherby, whom we were to meet. Jim, the chauffeur, whom the heat had made more taciturn than ever, sprawled in his shirt sleeves on a bench in the scanty shade of the station platform. A couple of sleepy bees buzzed drowsily above the golden masses of flowers that were clustered in the gardens at either end of the station and along the railway line.

Although I was only eight years old, I missed having the adults to talk to. Because I was used to being around older people, I had, as an extra favour, been asked to the dinner party, which was going to be a rather informal affair anyway. At any rate, it was my first dinner party, and I had started out with grandfather from our cousins' home in West Philadelphia with a sense of high adventure. I was annoyed at this temporary set-back. Now it looked as if everyone were falling asleep. I was getting a little old for fairy tales, but I could not help remembering *la belle au bois dormant* — the enchanted princess in the sleeping castle.

I walked out along the platform, where I was startled anew by the great profusion of yellow flowers. I remembered another old legend — that of the ancient king Midas, whose touch had turned everything around him to gold. I was a fanciful child, and I began to imagine that perhaps I had the golden touch myself and I had turned everybody and everything about me into this splendid gold of sleep. At any rate, the fancy would serve me until the train came in — if it did. I had the feeling that time had somehow stopped at the moment when everything had become golden, and the scene might be arrested here forever and ever.

The heat was so dense as to be almost palpable, and it quite brought me up short as I stood surrounded by all that ineffable yellowness, that golden glow. It was to be presumed that the station master was the man who had created the garden: in fact I seem to remember that our dinner host told us later that it was the station master's only recreation and delight.

The golden garden had no very complex design, merely consisting of stretches of lawn at either end of the station and along the platform opposite the station. The botanical material of its rather large effects was also decidedly *not* exotic. Against the pine trees were long rows of sun-flowers — those coarsest of floral beauties — in an astonishing number of varieties, small and large, interspersed with clumps of brilliant yellow flowers called "golden glow" mingled with profuse stands of black-eyed susans. There were great clumps of yellow marigolds, thickets of golden coreopsis. Had it been earlier in the summer there would have been the common field daisy, but there were in this expansive collection other cultivated varieties. There were zinnias in various shades of the prevailing colour.

In the centre of each lawn were large circular flower beds filled with the livid yellow spikes of cannas. In one corner of the station lawn was a large enclosure devoted to yellow roses. I have never seen such floral yellowness again. It was, in a way, blatant, overblown, and vulgar, but it was also quite splendid in its large, yellow singleness of purpose.

Just as I had almost lost myself in the yellow complexity of that garden, I heard the distant puffing of a locomotive, and it was not long before an ancient engine emerged from the pine trees in great clouds of smoke and, snorting and grinding, drew up beside the station. The station master untangled himself from his dreams long enough to pick up a bundle of newspapers handed down from the car.

For a brief moment the small station was alive with movement. One or two motor cars had also driven up to pick up passengers, but since the small hamlet that the station served was half a mile away, most of them set out to walk home. With a great roaring and intense puffing, the ancient locomotive and its train of cars left the station and disappeared into the pines. The station master disappeared.

Our own party climbed into our car, and in the first rays of sunset light we started off for the dinner party.

As we turned in the driveway, the yellow garden blazed fully in the early-evening light. It seemed to be larger than life and, young as I was, I felt that it possessed the landscape more fully than any of the actors who were leaving the scene.

I never saw the garden again. Years later I heard that the railroad line had been abandoned, and the station demolished. Now I cannot even remember its name, but I like to think that some descendants of that yellow garden still haunt the countryside.

Radio script for WQED-FM, 1978.

Autumn Splendour Remembered
The Indian Summer of 1977

Summer in our local climate usually falls easily into autumn; the progression at times seems so smooth and effortless that it is scarcely noticeable. Indian Summer, that most golden of all seasons, may come in sporadic bursts of warmth and light, or it may abide with us as a fully-rounded entity, a marvelous multi-coloured quietude in which the human spirit exists and expands, content merely to be. At its best, it can be a haven of brightness and felicity which fortifies us for the rigours of winter.

Of this halcyon type was the autumn of 1977, all the more precious and wonderful because it was so unlike that of the previous year, when we were hurried, almost precipitated, much too soon, into a winter that became a nightmare of brutal frigidities and seeming infinities of snow and ice. Before spring came in 1977, the fathomless cold had persisted for so long that we had almost forgotten that there could have been any other kind of weather.

To continue our earlier discomfort, the past summer was extremely hot, breathless, and intense — almost as uncomfortable in its own way as the earlier winter. Possibly, speaking as an older person, these intensities of climate, these wayward excursions of the thermometer, become less tolerable as our capacity for enduring their rigours diminishes. We cannot summon the hey-day of the blood, the noon of the flesh, to meet venturesomely their onslaughts.

Perhaps it is the subtleties, the nuances, the half-tones, the soft airs, the pervasive quiet and muted vistas of both spring and autumn that recommend themselves to the latitudes of age.

Under the first blossoms and the coloured and falling leaves we may, if the day be fair, walk equally still and secure; these seasons accommodate themselves to our lingering pace, our contemplative mood. A few fallen leaves rustle faintly under our feet. If it be spring, these are last year's leaves, still with us in the budding grove, reminding us of that eternal cycle which is life. If it be autumn, one thinks as one walks the autumnal paths that the coloured canopy will soon descend, and passing through death to life will nurture "the darling buds of May." So, meditating on these mysteries, secure in our still awareness, we walk.

In this autumn of 1977 — in this *annus mirabilis* that contained such an Indian Summer — I walked in Oakland, that district in the city which is perhaps my favourite. I favour it because I have known it all my life and mostly because it is now my home — the intimate scene of the autumn of my own life. Certainly, I feel that I may most fittingly celebrate a superior Indian Summer there.

Certainly, in this terminal pocket of the great East Liberty valley, there is an openness of neo-Baroque planned amenity, enclosed widely and ruggedly in the firm but haphazard clasp of the familiar Pittsburgh hills and cut abruptly by the usual Pittsburgh ravines. Above all, for the carnival arrival of autumn there are plenty of trees — trees always so essentially part of the Pittsburgh ambience. Now in Oakland, as ever, are painted leaves and smoke, hints of the last hot passions of summer, and premonitions of the stone breath of winter attend my waking and sleeping hours.

This is eminently September — the heat is still softly in evidence as I walk early on Craig Street to the grocer's to buy bread (alas, one can no longer go to the baker's) and to the "State Store" for wine (alack-a-day, the vintner is even more distant in time!). The bread and the wine are for the Feast of St. Michael and All Angels on September 29, which for me is the beginning of autumn — the harvest festival which heralds the painted wonder of Indian Summer. This day is one of the great turning points in my year, made for a private observance in which a special personal communion is enjoined.

On this day, in this autumn of 1977, the trees in the Cathedral lot at Fifth and Craig were still green, albeit something dim and dusty, with only an occasional premonitory yellow leaf. The sun was bright, and one seemed to walk through a golden haze. That night, after the ritual bread and wine in a wonderful lingering twilight, I went in a Yellow taxi cab, not only into autumn but to dine in a former church in South Oakland (which I hope to speak of again in one of these broadcasts). Once more, with my companion of St. Michael's season, I celebrated the aureate day with yet more golden wine. Later, later, in the glowing September night, we strolled back through the shops and small restaurants of Atwood Street, past the diminutive Victorian houses and festival students. The night fled away like a dream. High autumn would soon be here.

After this splendid beginning, day succeeded day, each seeming to be more warm, more golden than the last. Well into October there were enough cold evenings to ensure the proper development of autumnal foliage. But many nights were as soft, as sensuously calm as that of St. Michael's Day. But the days were really supernal. As

An Art Deco Garden in Pittsburgh
The Perennial Garden of the
Phipps Conservatory, Schenley Park

Pittsburgh has had, and still has, some notable gardens of the grand sort, the large and terraced acres of which, designed by landscape architects, once regally spread their lawns and terraces across our clouded hills. One thinks of the great estate of B. F. Jones, Jr., "Fair Acres" in Sewickley Heights, or of the expansive gardens of Richard Beatty Mellon at 6500 Fifth Avenue in the erstwhile millionaire quarter of East Liberty. The cultivated terrain of the former has now quite vanished, but the latter is still with us in a much-diminished form, inasmuch as the Mellon land became a city park in 1941.

These great green pleasances are no longer part of the American landscape, save as they have been preserved as vestiges of the past. Rarely do modern millionaires care to expand their egos via splendid gardens, and even their houses are not what they were. Even if the desire to create princely gardens existed nowadays, it would still be very difficult and enormously expensive to find personnel for their proper maintenance. The huge private garden exists today chiefly as a tourist attraction, and as such we can walk among them and meditate on past floral glories.

Of course, the great municipalities of the nineteenth and early twentieth centuries tended to develop parks along with their concomitant gardens and conservatories. Some of these gardens tended to rival the best effects of the millionaires — as witness, in Pittsburgh, the elaborate floral displays at the entrance to Highland Park, where complex figured parterres surrounded the central fountain and even adorned the sloping terraces of the public reservoir. As I remember, these great flower beds were well tended until the Great Depression of 1929, which really marked the end of the millionaire houses and the expansive gardens of the nineteenth century.

But not quite. Landscape architects, who now tend to be "site planners," still continued in the 1930s to think and operate in the old ways which had been so long familiar to them. Pittsburgh has a very good example of this type of hold-over from the past in the Perennial Garden of 1935-36, adjacent to the Phipps Conservatory in Schenley Park. Here, a large terraced garden was designed to take the place of a lawn that sloped down to the Schenley Park Bridge from one wing of the Conservatory. Although the essential form of the new garden was based on Renaissance precedent, the architectural elements of the composition — the retaining walls and fountains, although generally rock-face and rustic — are definitely influenced by that part-Classical, part-Modern style known nowadays as Art Deco. As such the garden is a fascinating document of its period.

It was designed by one of Pittsburgh's best-known landscape architects, Ralph E. Griswold who, although he was born in 1894, is still very much extant and who has just published a book on Thomas Jefferson as a landscape architect.[1]

Ralph Griswold had been trained as a landscape architect at Cornell University and the American Academy in Rome. In 1927, at Cleveland, Ohio, he joined forces with a colleague to form the firm of Nicolet & Griswold, and the partners designed gardens for several wealthy clients in Pittsburgh. In 1930, Griswold came to Pittsburgh to practice under his own name, and in 1934 he became director of the Bureau of Parks for the city, a position that he retained until 1945. Probably his chief design projects for the city were the Perennial Garden at Phipps Conservatory and the Beechwood Boulevard entrance to Frick Park.

As I have said, the Perennial Garden was executed in the old aristocratic tradition of landscape architecture, but the patronage and the usage of *this* garden were definitely democratic and municipal; the funds and the workforce were provided by the Works Progress Administration — the well-known W.P.A. — which figured so strongly in many public-works projects of the Great Depression. Construction of the garden was undertaken about the same time as the first complete restoration of the Phipps Conservatory.

These airy constructions of iron and glass are not notable for durability, and the Conservatory is now once more the object of a thorough restoration in which the Pittsburgh History & Landmarks Foundation has been involved. It was our involvement which led me at the beginning of September to visit the garden once more.

Although I had been a not infrequent visitor ever since the garden was installed, I had not been there for about four or five years. The afternoon was one of those brilliant early September days that seem to pulsate with light and brilliant colour. There was not a cloud in the sky, which glowed deeply blue and silent over the green park. As I walked across the Schenley Park Bridge toward the Conservatory all the familiar buildings of Oakland gleamed as if they had been specially scrubbed for the occasion. I particularly noticed the two bright Gothic spires of St. Paul's Cathedral as they appeared between the two great chimney stacks of the Bellefield Boiler Plant, the curious tableau forming a mysterious architectural allegory — a cathedral in the grasp of commerce? But it was no day for allegories; the air was warm, benign — it was a supreme pleasure just to be walking in the sun.

Ahead stretched the lines of spired gingko trees that lined the wide driveway, with its island statue of Director Edward Bigelow in his bronze frock coat. But I turned aside to the terminal feature of the Perennial Garden, a roughly oval fountain basin with parapets of rock-faced masonry, where water flowed downward from embrasures formed of Deco waves. This had always been my favourite water-lily pool, but since 1958 even the grandest water lilies had been dwarfed by Frank Vittor's thunderous granite statue of Columbus.

Once past this domineering presence, the garden terraces loop grandly up the slope to the Conservatory, with, at the top, a flight of stone steps leading to a broad, flat terrace paved with flagstones. This area used to be bordered with flower beds featuring the very tall perennials, but now the beds are small and circular and contained within green lawns. Below this terrace is the rather extensive rose garden whose blooms, near the end of the season, are not as refulgent as they were in June, although they still abound with colour. Stretching down from the rose parterres are beds devoted to the old-fashioned, familiar annuals, zinnias and marigolds of all colours and varieties, dwarf dahlias, cockscomb, scarlet sage, and globe amaranth, to name but a few species of this great floral carpet which glowed grandly on this September day: although there was a faint touch of faded grandeur to the display that portended the end of summer.

At the end of the long upper terrace is another fountain of rustic stone work whose water jets issue from carved Deco iris heads. As I sat on the rim and watched the calm tides of colour gleaming in the sun on the slopes below me, the steady, subdued splash of jets in the basin seemed to emphasize and define the golden silence of the afternoon. So I had sat and watched and listened on silent afternoons long gone and in the still evenings of vanished summers.

The place is not what it was once. It is no longer, save for the roses, a perennial garden, being devoted mostly to annuals. It is not quite so well kept as it was in time past. It is, however, a garden of the old grand dispensation, and even if it is something fallen in estate, we can be thankful that we still have it.

¹Ralph E. Griswold died in 1981; the book, co-authored with Frederick Doveton Nichols, is *Thomas Jefferson, Landscape Architect.*

Radio script for WQED-FM, 1978.

Chronicles of Old Fifth Avenue I
From Pittsburgh's Downtown to Oakland

. . . Before the clearance of the Lower Hill in the 1950s that area still contained a great deal of vernacular, particularly domestic, Greek Revival architecture. I remember that, in the first flush of my interest in that style in the 1930s, I used to take long, exploratory walks in the Hill, and I can remember some very handsome houses which, although somewhat decayed in appearance, still had a certain distinction. Even near the very end of their existence, when the bulldozers were in the field and I warily patrolled some of the old streets in clouds of dust, I made my farewells to some very agreeable houses on Canfield Street, whose cast-iron balconies, however, linger pleasantly in my memory. Of course, I forgot that they had recently been tenements of a quarter of the city abandoned by the respectable classes. *O dolor,* O sorrow — as one gets older oneself, as one's doorstep cracks and the Greek Revival porticoes which once one so held in prideful regard are crumbling, crumbling, one is the prey of an ineluctable sadness. Well, I picked myself up from the vanishment of the Lower Hill. I am stubborn, I still remain in the business of preserving old porticoes and carven facades under the immutable sky, which, however it is ominous or fair, communicates to us only an ambiguous message. "Ah, what a dusty answer gets the soul when hot for certainties in this our mortal life." Even if one does not quite know what one is preserving these fragments of the past *for,* one still wants to preserve these minor monuments.

Radio script for WQED-FM, 1982; an excerpt.

316

Chronicles of Old Fifth Avenue II
Some Old Antique Shops

. . . [The] phenomenon [of outmoded furniture for sale in the East End] was also abundantly evident in the second-hand shops of lower Fifth Avenue during the 1920s and 1930s. About that time some of the large, quaint Greek Revival houses were being finally abandoned on the North Side — the former city of Allegheny — as well as those of the small colonies of mansions of the well-to-do in the Hill District. It was amazing to see the great mahogany ghosts of those now shadowy households crowding the old furniture shops of Fifth Avenue in far-away days before the Second World War. Aside from their massive proportions and overwhelming architectural forms, they were irredeemably sombre, indeed curiously sepulchral. One looked throughout the rather dirty plate-glass windows of the shops as one might have examined the monuments of a nineteenth-century Romantic cemetery. Surely no one had ever lived with these colossal wardrobes and armoires, even when one recalls that built-in clothes cupboards were very rare before 1880. And also on display were the huge bedsteads that resemble antique sarcophagi. One remembers also, from Greek Revival dining rooms, the heavy sideboards and over-whelming dining tables along with solemn rows of Greek chairs ranged around a ghostly feast represented now only by piles of white china plates rimmed in gold.

One fine summer morning about 1932 there was near the door of this shop a monumental Greek Revival wash stand, completely accoutred with an almost-incredible china toilet set adorned with purple and white irises on a green background bordered with great golden scrolls. There it all was — ewer, basin, slop jar, chamber pot, and a great number of smaller vessels. It looked like a stage setting for an imperial levee. It could have attended the ablutions of the ancient gods — it was not Greek Revival, but it was magnificent. . . .

Radio script for WQED-FM, 1982; an excerpt.

317

Light over Pittsburgh—1982

... I can well remember how, before 1960, in the East End or Squirrel Hill the night skies at any season of the year would suddenly be lit with great pulsating flares of red and yellow light as the Bessemers from the mills in the river valley began to blow, when air at twenty to thirty-five pounds-per-square-inch pressure was forced through the charge of molten iron. A complete blow could be accomplished in from eight to twelve minutes. After blowing, the vessel was tilted and the steel was poured into a ladle for turning into ingots. During this latter process the light gradually sank and finally the show was over. It really was a display comparable to that of the Northern Lights or Aurora Borealis, and certainly it was eminently characteristic of Pittsburgh in the great age of steel. We will not see its like again. ...

Radio script for WQED-FM, 1982; an excerpt.

Downtown Restaurants of Yesterday
The Dining Rooms at McCreery's and Kaufmann's

Recently a handsome coloured photograph of the new Equibank Building — that great downtown looking glass — appeared in the Roto section of the *Pittsburgh Press*. The picture had been taken from the Press Club, on the fourteenth floor of the building at 300 Sixth Avenue, which from 1904 to 1938 had been the McCreery Department Store. I had frequently remarked the modern view from the Club, admiring its cool monumental perspectives, but it set me thinking of an earlier view, from approximately the same position but a little lower down — the old dining room of McCreery's as it was in the 1920s when I lunched there frequently.

The coloured photograph, so very handsome, so very modern, so cold, so clean, so austere, struck me as so utterly different from the now-dimmed photograph in my mind's eye of the earlier view — so huddled, so busy, so cluttered, so veiled and begrimed with smoke. The vanished view seemed, as I gazed backward through the years, to be part of McCreery's dining room because, as I recall, one of the chief pleasures of lunching there was to get a table by the window so that one could look out over the densely-packed roofs of the lower buildings, the smoking chimneys, the Edwardian high-rises — and, since this was the time of the great building boom of the 1920s — the steel frames of even larger structures rising near and far. Everything smoked, everything moved, and the view from the windows gave one a sense of downtown-ness so different from the quasi-suburban vistas of the East End. One could, of course, get much grander perspectives in New York, but in those days one did not often get there, and consequently the home views of the commercial city were doubly valued.

It struck me that perhaps a radio discourse or two on some of these downtown restaurants, with or without views, might make interesting nostalgic excursions. Since I started with McCreery's I will continue with it, because it was my favourite among all the "high-up" eating places of Pittsburgh.

I have some old post cards of the place as it was when it first opened, and the views can be dated approximately from the postmarks on the cards — 1906 and 1907. The curious thing about this restaurant was that until the time it closed in 1938, its decor never changed. It occupied the entire ninth floor of the building — it was simply a large rectangular space stretching from the bank of elevators at the Sixth Avenue end to the corresponding elevators on the Oliver Avenue side. No attempt was made to divide the space adroitly, which a modern designer would have done — it was simply a large room for eating, with the tables and chairs ranged along its length with military precision in orderly lines. The chairs were of oak in the most uncompromising Mission style; all woodwork was of dark stained oak, the walls were sage green, and the carpet, wall-to-wall, mostly dark green with a large, but not too insistent, figured pattern. The table linen was of the snowiest white damask, the china heavy but good. It was all tremendously solid, muted, respectable, yet it exuded a sense of luxurious calm, a grand sense of Edwardian establishment.

Getting to the restaurant was half the fun of eating there. Ranges of windows illuminated the elevator shafts, which were entirely open, as the cages themselves were mostly grille-work. One had the sense of moving up or down on a kind of platform in space, a space which also included that outside the building. . . .

Once arrived at the restaurant, one was ushered by a solicitous headwaiter to — if one was lucky — a table by one of the windows, whose large plate-glass sashes would be open if it were summer: this was before the days of air conditioning. On one side, as one sat before the dazzling table cloth like a field of snow, there was the busy bustle of the dining room, and on the other the misty smoke-hung towers of downtown. The dull roar of the city was slightly muted at this height, but always there was the sound of trolley cars and the rat-tat-tat of riveting from the new skyscrapers. Against the view was a tall glass vase of gladiola — those most statuesque of summer flowers. At another table, a woman in a fashionable cloche hat was speaking into a telephone that had been brought to her.

The food was as solid, rich, and abundant as the decor; it was, as well, the edible *luxe* of Edwardian establishment. Heavy soups, roasted meats, and wonderful fresh vegetables soon appeared on the gleaming china above the white napery. Iced tea, one remembers, splendid pies of peaches or cherries, and finally glass finger bowls with, at the side, small paper containers of mints.

What did one say, what did one do? That has all vanished, and one remembers only the fine rich ambience which was already an echo of a time earlier in the century that had passed. Since I did have a strong sense of the past even when young, I appreciated enormously the grand air of establishment, of security mixed with the sheer sensuous "abandon," of lunching in such a setting.

There was another one of these sky-hung department-store restaurants that I frequented when I was not at McCreery's and which I liked almost as well, particularly on Saturdays, when I was not at school and could go off shopping by myself. This restaurant, however, has survived and is still on the eleventh floor of the "Big Store" at Fifth and Smithfield, although it has changed its location and is now nothing like it was. This portion of my discourse is devoted to an attempt to evoke Kaufmann's old dining room.

Kaufmann's was also a dining room of Edwardian vintage with many of the appurtenances pertaining thereto, but, in keeping with the general policy of the store, discreet grace notes of modernity had been added to it. It was a fascinating mixture of new and old.

The dining room was located on the Diamond Street (now Forbes Avenue) side of the store, and along one side was a range of exceptionally broad windows which faced toward the Monongahela River and Mount Washington. There were always green plants in boxes where they would get the best light, and in the corners were potted palms. These windows would also be open in summer, and the view was equally intriguing — the same Pittsburgh smoke scene, but different. Kaufmann's window tables were, like McCreery's, the most desirable in the place.

The furniture was lighter, with touches of Viennese modernity; there were paintings on the walls; the carpet was bright. Best of all, there was an orchestra nestled among the potted palms. Ah, how pleasant it was to sit by the wide windows, above the ubiquitous white table cloths, while the tuxedoed musicians played Boccherini's Minuet or the overture to Auber's *Fra Diavolo*. The air of this restaurant was, essentially, established Edwardian, but one always had the sense of a *presented* Edwardianism, brought up to date. Cloche hats and knee-length frocks did not look out of place in such a setting.

The food also had the air of a modernized Edwardian cuisine, but what I chiefly remember were the desserts that had survived from the earlier time. Ah, those elaborate concoctions of ice creams, fruits, and whipped cream, with their French names: Coupe Delice and Coupe St.-Jacques.

One can still go to Kaufmann's dining room, but all the old glamour is gone, along with the expansive, rich desserts. The windows are now shrouded and opaque. But ah, how wonderful it would be, once more, to eat a Coupe St.-Jacques while one looked out on Mt. Washington.

Radio script for WQED-FM, 1980.

A hat shop, unidentified, c. 1915.

From the Hey-day of the Hat: Miss Rose Chapeaux

On the North Side of Pittsburgh, distantly, on the long stretch of East Ohio Street just west of Chestnut, I have these months past — no, years, I should say — seen a shop which appears, *mirabile dictu,* to sell women's hats. Since feminine head gear is rarely seen nowadays and a hat shop even more rarely, I have been fascinated with this phenomenon, this *rara avis,* ever since I first beheld it. The shop building is tall and ornately Victorian; it impends darkly over the shop itself, which as seen from a passing bus looks both in form and ornament to be rather Deco in style — but it is not very distinguished, it is all commercial Carrara glass and jazzy metal details. The building itself probably dates from the 1860s; the shop, with its angular plate-glass windows, could belong to the 1920s, but more probably the 1930s. The displayed hats are peripherally contemporary, appearing to date from the 1950s when they were last fashionable. Hats, I mean; can it be such a brief span of time since they fell from favour?

I must confess that, even in the days before my accident, when I could have got off the bus to look more fully at its form and contents, I did not do so. For the past few years the arthritic condition of my legs had precluded much walking, and consequently I forebore whenever possible to make the effort. Possibly I had so lost my youthful desire to explore, that I preferred to leave the ancient shop quite alone, frozen in its static calm like a waxwork in a museum.

In this area, which as late as the 1940s had been a bustling shopping district, the hat shop appeared like a wraith, an apparition in an area that had been totally ravaged by its heedless "redevelopment" (ironic and tragic word!) in the 1960s and 1970s. What had once been a viable section of the city was now a ragged remnant of the past, and in that wretched file of buildings, preserved like a fly in amber, is the shop.

I remember reading long ago about a poet who, in wandering about an obscure quarter of London, found an ancient Elizabethan shop which sold old furniture and antiquated pots, and where, at an uncertain hour of the day, he had had a fantastic conversation with an interesting stranger. Unfortunately, in his subsequent rambles through lost London, he could never find it again. Had he dreamed the colloquy, the stranger, and the shop?

But surely my North Side hat shop was no dream unless it has vanished within the last month. Its palpability has been abundantly demonstrated by a myriad random glances as I passed by on the bus. I also have commented on it to a number of my friends as I rode by it in their cars, and I was pleased to point out to them this remaining example of a vanishing shop species. But although I am sure that it is there, I have also asked myself why I have never wanted to stop and look at it, or try its vulgar Deco door to ascertain what might be inside. Possibly I have been fearful that the confronted door might swing wide on an interior that little conformed with my remembered vision of what a hat shop should be. Perhaps it might be best to avoid any chance of interior vulgarity or ruin, and leave simply the exterior to carry the *whole* vision of the past. Or, in stopping, one could see exactly what the non-committal hats looked like, although that might not be much — even the hats of the 1950s tended to lack any real colour or individuality as they ceased to be part of the urban scene. Not that hats do not now and then appear nowadays, but they are usually the vestigial contraptions worn by old ladies in church, and we have to be grateful for those dashing young ladies who on occasion sport molded and flop-brimmed hats out of *Vogue* or *Harper's Bazaar*. But *real* hats are now far to seek.

Yes, I think that I prefer my hat shop to remain an enigmatic element in an urban landscape that has few notes of mystery or grace; some mysteries should not be fully explored, or they lose all viability.

But all this interest in hats and hat shops has led me at the same time to consider those of past years that really were glamourous and fascinating. Once these millinery shops existed the length and breadth of the land. Some were tidy, neat, and humble, some richly and elegantly appointed. Ah, and the great hat shops in the department stores — celestial caves of treasures, gardens of delight! But now, lackaday, I have not even thought to explore the present-day extent of these emporiums. However, I doubt if there is any really important space devoted to the selling of hats in large stores — at least not as in the past.

Before I speak of Miss Rose's shop for *chapeaux,* I suppose that I should say that I have always been fascinated by women's hat shops, ever since I can remember. I was also entranced by old soda fountains, all ancient restaurants with white damask table cloths, church altars with half-burned candles, fountains surrounded by geraniums, and crowded barber shops. It seemed to me, though, that there was also a great deal of sheer fantasy even in the surroundings of hat shops. It was fun getting to them.

The shop that I particularly remember was a small establishment wedged into a kind of cul-de-sac in West Philadelphia. In 1920 my family was living there. The neighbourhood had once been rather more pretentious than it was at that time. The street itself was quite narrow and crooked — an alley, really, which had once housed the garages and stables of the large houses on Walnut Street. It was paved with narrow bricks in a kind of herring-bone pattern, not too well maintained, and rubbish was scattered here and there.

The entrance to the premises of Miss Rose was, however, immaculately kept, and the rubbish always meticulously swept away. The Classical doorway was brightly painted apple green, flanked by two Colonial Revival windows tightly curtained with white muslin. On one pane was a flowing painted inscription: *Miss Rose — Chapeaux.* The door itself was flanked by two small conifers in black tubs. Sometimes a cat or two or a dog would wander about the tiny cul-de-sac, but rarely were there people about, and my mother and I rarely encountered any other customers. The minuscule space was called, rather grandly, Montgomery Place — a grand designation almost as startling as the fancy French word — *Chapeaux* — on the shop itself.

Inside, what one was first aware of was the profound stillness; it was almost as if the place were enchanted. The door was solid, the muslin curtains whitely opaque. There were two vaguely French dressing tables, one on each side of a curtained interior door, each with a small chair in front of it. Curiously, there were no hats visible.

Suddenly, the curtains of the interior doorway were parted and in walked the proprietor, Miss Rose. She was a diminutive figure dressed in discreet black — a good costume for a milliner, where a "muted" background was always preferred (never compete with the hats or the customer!). Her hair was simply coiffed, and her dark eyes welcoming — my mother was a fairly frequent customer, and since I usually came with her, I was welcome too.

My mother was ceremoniously seated before one of the mirrored dressing tables, and Miss Rose politely discussed with her the desired hat. I recall that our visit occurred just before Easter, and since the winter season had passed, the hat must be of straw. Miss Rose said enthusiastically that she had several things that my mother would surely like, and in a moment she had disappeared behind the curtain once more. She made her own hats, and I take it that the workroom and the storage space for the merchandise were elsewhere in the small building, but neither my mother nor I were ever admitted behind the curtain.

I sat and watched the two half-hearted Boston ferns in front of the two windows, and two or three small prints of eighteenth-century ladies wearing elaborate *chapeaux*. Just as suddenly and silently, Miss Rose emerged again from the curtains adroitly carrying several hats. The enormous hats of the early twentieth century were by now unfashionable, and Miss Rose's armful were either small or medium-size and posed no problems of portage. She laid her burden down on the other dressing table and picked up a beflowered creation, seemingly made only of silken rose petals, and placed it artfully on my mother's head, adjusting it subtly to get the best effect. Then my mother gazed intently into the glass before her, and twisting and turning, she viewed the hat from every angle; all the while she was also using the hand mirror.

One by one, the beflowered and beribboned straw hats were tried on, and for me this was always the culmination of my visit. My opinion was always asked on the merits of each hat, and as I always seemed to make the proper responses, I was praised for my good taste: which pleased me.

Finally, *the* Easter hat was chosen — a brimmed straw helmet in pale robin's-egg blue, trimmed with twists of forget-me-nots and some tiny crimson flower. As we bore it away in its blue-and-white hat box, speeded by smiling farewells of Miss Rose, I felt that Easter had been achieved. And now as I write, it has been achieved once more in my memory.

Radio script for WQED-FM, 1980.

On Women, Words, and Pittsburgh

Although Pittsburgh cannot be considered a resoundingly literary city, not a few writers of national stature have called it home. The only native writer of talent who stayed here permanently was Gladys Schmitt (1908-72), and even she lived in New York for three years before her career properly started. Gertrude Stein (1874-1947) was born in Allegheny, now the North Side of Pittsburgh, but when a small child left with her family and never returned, choosing to spend most of her life in Paris. Margaret Deland (1857-1945), another local writer, was born in Manchester, but, as a very young woman moved to Boston. The most considerable literary artist of the group was Willa Cather (1876-1947), who came to Pittsburgh from Nebraska in 1896 and left for New York ten years later. Not the most artistic, but the most popular and prolific Pittsburgh author was Mary Roberts Rinehart (1876-1947), who was also a native. Born in Allegheny, she left the Pittsburgh area in 1923 for Washington, D.C., and later New York.

It will be noted that this brief list of nationally-recognized authors were all women, a fact of more than passing interest in the age of ERA. It is also interesting that none of them save Schmitt remained in Pittsburgh. Despite its infernal beauty and its vibrant drama, the city has seemed to be inimical to literary pursuits. There never was any laureate of the steel mills, and if there had been, it is debatable that Deland's *The Iron Women* (her novel of 1911) would have filled the bill.

The city has been made aware of the Pittsburgh-ness of these feminine writers by a spate of books and articles published recently. The November 1979 issue of *Carnegie Magazine* had Stanley Mayer's article on Deland, and in 1978 appeared *I Could Be Mute: The Life and Work of Gladys Schmitt,* edited by Anita Brostoff and published by Carnegie-Mellon University. This February the University of Pittsburgh Press published *Improbable Fiction: The Life of Mary Roberts Rinehart,* by Jan Cohn. In March, The Historical Society of Western Pennsylvania issued *Chrysalis: Willa Cather in Pittsburgh, 1896-1906,* by Kathleen Byrne and Richard C. Snyder. Branching off the traditional critical biography is the new musical drama, or as they say nowadays docu-drama, by Attilio (Buck) Favorini and Gillette Elvgren, *Hearts and Diamonds,* which is a double dramatic treatment of the disparate lives of Willa Cather, the great novelist devoted to the highest art, and Lillian Russell (1861-1922), the famous music-hall star who spent the last years of her life in the city as the sometimes-writing wife of a Pittsburgh millionaire.

It would seem from all this local activity that Pittsburgh is becoming intensely aware of its literary past. There has been much sifting through dusty archives, much examining of the cityscape to find structures in which the authors had lived or with which they had been associated. If the writers be only sufficiently well known, these relics are cherished fragments of the author's fame for the city dwellers who remember them.

When Cather came to Pittsburgh in 1896, fresh from the University of Nebraska, she edited a women's magazine, *The Home Monthly,* which was published briefly in East Liberty. Until the early 1900s, when she went to Washington for several months, Cather lived in a series of East End boarding houses, all pleasant Late Victorian middle-class structures, substantial and unpretentious. All of them have now vanished, prey to redevelopment, including the house at 304 South Craig Street, which was rather grander than the others. I was fortunate to examine this house before it was demolished a few years ago. The chief interior features were given to the Pittsburgh History & Landmarks Foundation provided the Foundation would remove them.

The chief artifact was a huge pier glass of extraordinary dimensions, which practically covered a wall of one of the front bedrooms on the second floor. I helped our work crew detach the great mirror, with its Second Empire frame, from the wall, but we could not get both glass and frame out the door. Accordingly we tried to separate them, but the silvered glass cracked badly in the process and we had, much to my sorrow, to break it up. The huge looking glass, even on the floor, had a haunting mysterious quality, and when it was broken, light seemed to drain from the room, returning it to dimness and shadow. It lingers in my mind like a persistent ghost. I have often thought that it was the kind of thing — an artifact of grandiose vanity — that Cather would not have approved.

From 1901 to 1906 Cather lived with her friend Isabelle McClung at the house of Isabelle's father Judge Samuel A. McClung, at 1180 Murray Hill Avenue. Perched high on a hill between Shadyside and Squirrel Hill, it was part of a quarter at once fashionable and remote. It still is, and so the house has managed, rather grandly, to survive. In it Cather may be said to have reached the residential heights in Pittsburgh, and it seems to be the symbol of her own lofty idealism. Expansively four-square, Colonial Revival in style, the old McClung home sits sedately on its leafy eminence, prim, elegant, *established,* like an aristocratic, be-pompadoured dowager. It is now the sole surviving memento of Cather's residence in the city. After Cather left Pittsburgh she often visited Isabelle's stately home until her friend's marriage in 1916.

Mary Roberts Rinehart, as a beginning writer, did meet Cather once, around 1906, but there is no further record that the two writers ever met again. Rinehart, a born storyteller (the chief focus of the novel or short story is simply narration), was enormously industrious, indefatigably prolific, and vastly popular. At the height of her career Rinehart was possibly the most popular woman writer in America. Cather was undoubtedly the greater artist, and she too possessed a magical narrative gift, but she was intensely private and eschewed personal publicity. Rinehart did learn from her the art of revision, after the first creative impulse had passed, and her own work improved. Changing literary fashions have caused Rinehart's star to wane. Her name is now not often known to today's young people, while earlier in the century it was a household word. She was especially well known for her mystery novels like *The Circular Staircase* (1908), and they are classics of their kind. I think that these will always be read.

Rinehart represented all that was best in the old American middle class, and, true to the best American success formula, she rose from obscurity to fame and wealth. Hers was no rags-to-riches story: rather more of a paraphrased tale of genteel poverty to affluence.

Born Mary Roberts in Old Allegheny, during America's Centennial year, hers was definitely an unaffluent Victorian childhood. Both her birthplace and the small house on Arch Street in which she spent her formative early years have vanished in the redevelopment that has devoured most of the old central North Side. When she married Dr. Stanley Rinehart in 1896, they lived in two houses on Western Avenue, one of which has survived although much changed. It remains as a three-story double house, where Dr. Rinehart also had his office. In 1907, the Rinehart family, which by then included three sons, moved to a large house at 954 Beech Street, at Allegheny Avenue.

This was Rinehart's last Pittsburgh home (in 1907 Allegheny became legally part of Pittsburgh). In 1911-12, she completed the first part of her own success story by moving her family to a large country house in Sewickley — all successful Alleghenians inevitably went to Sewickley, the oldest and most "select" of Pittsburgh suburbs. From there, she rounded out the fullness of the American success story. She spent much of the new wealth on an old Victorian country house which she remodeled — she was thus an early preservationist. She moved to Washington, D.C. in 1923, then, after her husband's death in 1932, to New York and Bar Harbor, Maine — writing busily and profitably all the while. She died in New York at her Park Avenue apartment in 1958, the much-loved matron of American letters, writing to the end. "She wrote," as her biographer says, "more best selling novels than any other American writer and wrote them over a longer period of time than almost any other American writer."

The house in Sewickley is gone as well, and it was at 954 Beech Street, on a snowy morning in late February, that the University of Pittsburgh Press gave a press party to announce the publication of the new biography. After Rinehart's tenancy the place had sunk to rooming-house depths, but of recent years it has been handsomely renovated. The Rinehart papers and memorabilia have been deposited at the University's Hillman Library, and some of these were on exhibition at the reception.

In this North Side house where she first tasted success, it was not too difficult to recall the handsome and illustrious presence of Pittsburgh's own Mary Roberts Rinehart.

"Jamie's Journal," *The Pittsburgher,* June, 1980.

330

Pittsburgh's Forgotten Toy Theatre: the Kilbuck Playhouse

One morning recently, I was driving down the wide, desolate length of the North Side's Western Avenue on my way to the Ohio River Boulevard. I never pass that way without trying to imagine how the broad avenue, once famous for its opulent Victorian mansions, looked like in its prime, before I first encountered it in the late 1920s. Of all that fabulous panorama of chimneys and gables, once so richly ornamented, there is nothing left now but a couple of scarred and misshapen houses (one of them hideously remodeled) and two stately but crumbling gate posts. The high, brazen sun of last April's excursion to the Boulevard mercilessly revealed the hopeless languor of a decaying commercial quarter, but it did illumine also the high wall of an old factory near Fontella Street. Outlined in faded white paint against the dirty brick was the single word, TOYS.

All down those ruined vistas toward the Boulevard, that almost-obliterated word lingered tantalizingly before my mind's eye, and then it vanished, pushed out before the business of the day. A few weeks later I was talking with an old friend about the history of the "little" theatre in Pittsburgh — particularly its status in the 1930s, when, during the Depression, these organizations proliferated. Suddenly, the painted word, TOYS, flashed through my mind; simultaneously I recalled the Kilbuck Theatre, that most miniature of all "little" playhouses that flourished at 1212 Western Avenue briefly from 1934 to 1937, in an ancient mansion called "Kilbuck," under the beetling walls of the Wolverine Toy Company. TOYS . . . yes.

Long ago, in the early 'Teens of this century, I was first introduced to Kilbuck (although I did not know it at the time) by the way of the Wolverine Toys of stamped metal, which would move by spring mechanisms when you wound them up. So I was introduced to the world of make-believe by clowns and construction machines, all metallic and capable of manipulation. I also wondered why they were called Wolverine. Later I discovered that the toy factory had been established on the North Side in 1903 by a young man called B. F. Bain who came from Michigan, known popularly as the Wolverine State — hence the name of the factory.

Bain's business was well established when, in 1913, he built a new factory in the 1200 block of Western Avenue, which had even then begun to decline from its assured status as a select residential district. Bain and his wife, *née* Dora Elliott (also a Wolverine), disdained the new suburban mentality, and in the old-fashioned bourgeois manner they decided to live close to their work. They bought a large, ancient, and historic mansion next door called "Kilbuck" — it must be remembered here that the large Victorian mansions of Old Allegheny and Pittsburgh often had names as well as street numbers. Sometimes the names were hackneyed and less than inspired, but "Kilbuck" definitely had a real historical connection with the land.

I was never in the house, save in the brief years of the theatre, and even then not in the house proper. I was, in the 1930s, interested in old houses, but not so much so as I became later. The mansion was then, as I could see, much amended, changed over the years, and the general effect was muted, indeterminate. Even so, the great, gaunt mansion did not lack for history or glamour. First of all, it bore the name of a well-known Indian chief, Kilbuck. He was Christianized and friendly with the white settlers in very early Pittsburgh. He died in 1811, at the age of eighty-nine, and was reputedly buried under a white marble slab near a mulberry tree in the back yard of the mansion. Before 1860, there was also a small island named Kilbuck at the confluence of the Allegheny with the Ohio, but it has long since disappeared.

The house itself was built in 1823 by John Henry Hopkins, an Episcopal priest who was rector of Trinity Church, Pittsburgh, and who had a great love for the arts of the Church — music, painting, and architecture. He conducted a private school and seminary in the house, which was then an almost-rural situation. Hopkins, who wrote the first American book on Gothic Revival architecture, painted one of the rooms of his house with pointed arches and vaults to look like a chapel. Appropriate to later developments on the site, this *trompe-l'oeil* (fool-the-eye), this make-believe, was very like a religious stage setting. Under the painted ceilings the bemused seminarians chanted the psalms at matins and vespers.

Hopkins became Episcopal bishop of Vermont in 1832, and the house finally came into the possession of Robert McKnight, a lawyer and politician who married Elizabeth Denny, granddaughter of General James O'Hara. Mrs. McKnight was thus related to two great fortunes of Pittsburgh's early history. As chatelaine of "Kilbuck," she had the house much enlarged and remodeled. She was possibly the chief social hostess of her day. President Grant was entertained at "Kilbuck" because she possessed more china and glass than any other social leader in town. The chanted canticles of Hopkins' Gothic parlor were forgotten; only Kilbuck's marble slab still lay under the mulberry tree in the garden, begrimed now with soot from the forges in the river valleys. There were those who said that they had seen his ghost over misty moonlit nights.

The McKnights' daughter, Kate, who continued her mother's social activities, was instrumental in founding Pittsburgh's Twentieth Century Club, and lived on in the house for a number of years, but after 1900 Western Avenue had begun to fade perceptibly as a prime residential district. When Kate McKnight left the house in 1910, it was vacant for some years. The Bains bought the house in 1913 after having built the factory on an adjoining lot. The factory, a rather pleasant example of "light" industrial architecture, was definitely a portent of the rising commercialism soon to overtake the district. The house itself was converted into flats, whose porches overlooked the sooty lawns and the few remaining mansions across the street. Under the mulberry tree Kilbuck still slept on.

Benjamin Franklin Bain died in 1925, and Dora Bain took over the management of the Wolverine Toy Factory. In 1932, in New York, she married a young actor, Robert Alan Green, and a new era began for the old house called "Kilbuck."

Robert Alan Green was born in Washington, Pennsylvania, in 1889. Much interested in the theatre, he went to New York, where he acted in stock and appeared in early movies with players like Constance Bennett. He was a very handsome young man and also enjoyed a brief stint as an Arrow Collar Man — an advertising symbol for male pulchritude in the early part of this century. He was about to embark with Spencer Tracy for Hollywood when a serious automobile accident ended his acting aspirations. Spencer Tracy, of course, went on to stardom; Robert Green went on to a different fate.

However, now in residence at 1212 Western Avenue, he decided to open, with his wife's help, a miniature playhouse in the basement of "Kilbuck," with himself as manager and director. Opened in the dark aftermath of the Depression, in 1934, it was definitely a Pittsburgh "grace note" of that uneasy decade. I went there myself four or five times. Tickets were only fifty-seven cents in a house that held only forty people. The little playhouse cost about four thousand dollars to install, and it was not a venture undertaken for profit.

When Director Green first put a sign reading "Kilbuck Playhouse" on the mansion's front lawn, the neighbourhood children thought that it was an invitation for them to play in the next-door toy factory. They mobbed the grounds, and he had to put up another sign changing "Playhouse" to "Theatre."

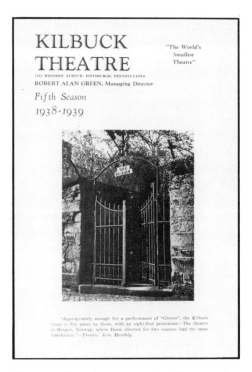

KILBUCK
THEATRE

"The World's
Smallest
Theatre"

1212 WESTERN AVENUE, PITTSBURGH, PENNSYLVANIA
ROBERT ALAN GREEN, *Managing Director*

Fifth Season
1938-1939

"Appropriately enough for a performance of "Ghosts", the Kilbuck
stage is five paces by three, with an eight-foot proscenium—The theatre
in Bergen, Norway, where Ibsen directed for two seasons had the same
dimensions."—*Theatre Arts Monthly.*

It was, as I remember it, an extraordinary place. The director
claimed that it was the smallest legitimate theatre in the world. It
seated forty spectators in rows of ten seats each. The proscenium was
eight feet wide, and the stage, measuring five paces by three paces,
held only five actors at a time. In addition to the stage and air-
conditioned auditorium, the rest of the spacious basement was
honeycombed with shower-equipped dressing rooms, a lobby in silver
and black, a cloak room, rest rooms for men and women, and even
a green room. The latter was four paces around and the dressing
rooms three paces square. Walls throughout the theatre displayed
murals painted by local artists.

The backstage equipment was so complete and well organized
that the most complicated change of scenery took less than ten
minutes. An effect of roominess on the stage was achieved by a clever
use of perspective, involving an arch used to give the illusion of
distance. In such a confined space, the actors had to speak their lines
in low-pitched voices, and conversely, the audience was asked not to
talk while the play was in progress.

The director would re-write and adapt any material used to the
exigencies of the miniature space in which it was performed. He

334

experimented with plays, scenery, and actors until he got just the effect he desired. Since actors usually came to him with little experience he was able, despite all drawbacks, to mould the group into a company that achieved acclaim even beyond Pittsburgh. Dora Green also worked hard to advance the theatre's cause. She was particularly helpful with the business end of the venture, but she could help with the stage settings or even act on occasion.

Bills of one-act plays by local authors were first performed at the theatre, but as the actors became more experienced they attempted full-length dramas. For some reason Henrik Ibsen, the great nineteenth-century Norwegian dramatist, was a particular favourite and I remember seeing both *Ghosts* and the *Doll's House* there. I had seen both plays in larger theatres — *Ghosts* more than once — and it was an intriguing experience to see them very close up and in such a confined space. The action had been so cleverly adapted to the space that, once one got used to the presentation, one was not uneasy with its novelty. I thought it also particularly appropriate that the *Doll's House* should have been given there. As for *Ghosts*, one recalled the apparition of Chief Kilbuck, who was supposed to walk beneath the mulberry boughs in the back garden.

Nora Helmer's *Doll's House,* that earliest and still powerful play on the liberation of women, seemed to have a peculiar cogency as seen in that tiny, silver-walled theatre. I wonder if I could recapture the same impression of stifled captivity that the far-away Nora of that night conveyed at three paces. On consideration, I feel that no other production I have seen could quite equal that miniature of 1936.

But alas, the director's health began to fail again, due to his failing powers. Robert Alan Green closed the little Kilbuck playhouse in 1937 and dismantled it. He died of a heart attack in Miami, Florida, in 1940. *O dolor!* Spencer Tracy endured much longer.

The Kilbuck Theatre enlivened the local dramatic scene only glancingly, it now seems. It appeared suddenly like a dream, stayed a little, and then it was gone again like Kilbuck's ghost. The house called "Kilbuck" has vanished, too, as has also my Sandy Andy, the Wolverine Toy and delight of my childhood ... Ghosts ...

Have I written true or have I dreamt? All that is left now is the time-stained factory wall with the almost-vanished word in mouldering paint — TOYS.

Focus, Tribune-Review (Greensburg, Pa.), June 28, 1981; there it was titled "Kilbuck: Named After an Indian, This Basement Theater was 'World's Smallest.' " Also a radio script for WQED-FM, no date.

Post Office, *oil on canvas, by David Gilmour Blythe, c. 1862-64.*

The World of David Gilmour Blythe
The Spring Exhibition at the Museum of Art, Carnegie Institute[1]

David Blythe (1815-65), America's unique and most mordant genre painter, is back again in the public, and notably the artistic, eye of his native country, for which he ardently hoped much and of which he finally despaired. Possibly the ultimate scholarly chronicle (if one dare say that) of his life and work is contained in the exhibition now showing at Carnegie Institute's Museum of Art.[2]

Genre painting, like the novel in literature, is essentially a bourgeois art, as it was also one of the staple art forms of the nineteenth century. Essentially a depiction of scenes of everyday life, it can be presented realistically without comment from the artist or it can be treated sentimentally, as it often was in the Victorian period, or comically, or satirically. It could be "straight" or carry a message. The message of such genre practitioners as Eastman Johnson or William Sidney Mount was cool and uncomplicated, but the comment of David Blythe on the life around him was generally bitter and sardonic.

He had plenty of material for his disillusion in the expanding, chaotic social condition of Pittsburgh prior to the Civil War; it was here that he did much of his best work. Consequently this exhibition is of particular interest to Pittsburghers. Certainly I have been aware of him for the last fifty years, although genre was not the chief focus of my interest in painting. Gradually, in all my eclectic viewing, I became more and more aware of his tenebrous or palely-coloured cityscapes, inhabited by gaunt and rampant half-crazed animals, slouching half-human louts and vagrants, and especially his inimitable corrupt and abandoned urchins disporting themselves like infernal putti in his lurid industrial vistas.

Gradually, as the years wore on, I became more aware of the full compass of his art. The former Department of Fine Arts (now the Museum of Art), Carnegie Institute collection of Blythe paintings was constantly augmented after 1940. The varied aspects of his genius (and I feel that that is not too strong a word to apply to him) seemed slowly to advance upon me. I remember particularly in the 1950s — possibly also the '60s — the marmoreal corridor between the Hall of Architecture and the Library — a passageway that was always important culturally in the development of the artistic scene in Pittsburgh. There, many paintings (a kind of overflow from the exhibition galleries) were poised against the marble dadoes (possibly because there was not enough room in the formal galleries to contain the lesser paintings). We, who passed daily through the solemn corridor on our appointed rounds, were exposed to paintings that were speaking to the hearts and minds of passers-by. I particularly remember a "prison scene" which seemed to me to be a rather romantic incident in a nineteenth-century melodrama. It is included in the catalogue of the exhibition, and thus seen in the broader context of his other work it seems rather unusual in its subject matter. Perhaps his most famous Pittsburgh canvas, the *Post Office* (c. 1862-64), has been in the Museum for years. The present exhibit is the largest body of his work in a public institution. There are one hundred seventy-one works in all on view, including his painted laminated-wood statue of the Marquis de Lafayette.

This monumental sculpture, eight feet, two inches high, had been commissioned in the winter of 1847-48 to be placed on top of the cupola of the new Fayette County Court House, a handsome example of the Greek Revival style which was demolished in 1890-91 at the time a new Richardsonian Romanesque court house, very close in style to that of Pittsburgh, was erected. At the same time, the statue was taken down from the old cupola and placed in the rotunda of the new building. Originally painted grey, it received a new polychrome coating in 1947, which considerably enhances its appearance. The statue is rather grandly conceived, and not in the least does it resemble a product of the "cigar store Indian" school, although its austere verticality and bold handling have a quasi-primitive directness.

Also in the exhibition is a large, black wooden raven, which apparently was inspired by Edgar Allan Poe's poem. Blythe was also a poet, and some of his pictures were inspired by poetic subjects.

David Blythe was born in East Liverpool, Ohio on May 9, 1815, the son of immigrant Scotch parents. He showed a marked talent for art as a small boy, but he never had any formal training. At sixteen he went to Pittsburgh to study wood carving under Joseph Woodwell, who specialized in designing interior embellishments for the houses of wealthy Pittsburghers. Here he also developed his painting skill further. Eventually, he became a portrait painter, which was the one way an artist of that day could earn a sure living. After serving his apprenticeship with Woodwell, he became a house painter in Pittsburgh. In 1834, the centre of art life was beginning to shift to an art store recently established by a young man hardly older than Blythe, J. J. Gillespie; the artists of the time began to gather there. Blythe was among them, and the friendship started then between Blythe and Gillespie endured until Blythe's death in 1865.

After his first Pittsburgh stay, Blythe traveled restlessly about America, including a stint in the U.S. Navy. He was in his early twenties when he left the Navy; he returned to East Liverpool and lived there for five years. During this time he painted portraits for a living.

Sometime during the winter of 1846-47, Blythe's wanderings took him to Uniontown, about forty miles south of Pittsburgh, where he remained for another five years. There he courted Julia Keffer, who died less than a year after their marriage: a tragedy that may have been one cause of his eccentric, restless style of living and his later painting. Uniontown and the nearby town of Waynesburg inspired most of his poetry, which for all of its irregularities of rhythm and rhyme is an important clue to the understanding of Blythe's character and personality. He tried painting one of the huge panorama pictures so popular at the time, but it was not a success.

He returned to Pittsburgh in 1856. Although Blythe lived and worked in the city only nine years — he died there at fifty on May 15, 1865 — he recorded with amazing insight the men and women of Pittsburgh and the backgrounds of their lives. As Dorothy Miller says in her biography,[3] "He caught in his painting the spirit of the city and its customs and manners."

In a sense, when the exhibition opens on May ninth, the works of the artist will have come home, for this is the city that fired his imagination. . . .

[1]Details of the show and its accompanying events have been omitted.

[2]The show opened on May 9, 1981.

[3]*The Life and Work of David G. Blythe.*

Radio script for WQED-FM, 1981.

Two clowns by Luke Swank.

Luke Swank
A Master Photographer Once More in the Public Eye[1]

Among the notable artistic phenomena of the 1930s in Pittsburgh, the work of the photographer Luke Swank was outstanding. During that decade I was a young man who was always interested in what was going on around town, but I cannot remember now when I first heard his name. I think that it was in connection with the Western Pennsylvania Architectural Survey (1932-35), which was contemporaneous with my own burgeoning interest in local buildings: a preoccupation which has continued to this day. The 'Thirties were a very socially-conscious decade, and it may have been some of my social worker friends who told me of him. In any event, the continuing development of photography, as an art and not just another mechanical process, would have made him an important figure.

Had he lived longer he might be today one of the national "greats" of American photography, but his already-considerable reputation seemed to suffer and eclipse after his untimely death in 1944. The fact that he worked almost entirely in Western Pennsylvania may account, to a degree, for his light being obscured under the regional bushel. Not that his name and his early fame have not "surfaced" occasionally in the decades since his death, but the art of photography is old enough now that its history is being examined closely.

The result has been the resurrection of a once-important but almost forgotten Pittsburgh figure, Luke Swank. Curiously, it was like encountering an old friend after a long absence. I always thought that there was a touch of genius about his photography. Possibly, if he were to hear the word "genius" applied to him, it would have made him uncomfortable. There was never anything fancy or pretentious in his approach to his craft; he never "doctored" his negatives or his prints. He seemed to be instinctively an artist who knew how to get what he wanted with the simplest means, even if he had to try several times to get the desired image. . . .

Swank was not a native Pittsburgher. He was born in 1890 in Johnstown, Pennsylvania, where his father had a hardware store. In 1911, he graduated from Pennsylvania State College School of Agriculture. From 1912 to 1917 he pursued various occupations including truck farmer, police dog trainer and breeder, cattle breeder, clerk in his father's store, and agricultural consultant. In 1917-18 he served in the Army Medical Corps and the U.S. Army Chemical Warfare Services. From 1919 until 1934 he lived in Johnstown and made his living as an auto dealer. Until 1930, he took only occasional weekend snapshots with his Kodak. He sold his first photographs of the local steel mills to his friends at Bethlehem Steel and started entering salons and competitions.

In 1931 he exhibited at the All American Photographic Salon at Los Angeles; First Annual Salon of Photographic Art at Carnegie Institute, Pittsburgh; and the Fifteenth Annual International Salon of Photography in Los Angeles.

Once he had got started on his photographic career there was no stopping him. In 1932, he exhibited at the Brooklyn Museum show of "International Photographers," at the Museum of Modern Art, New York. In 1933, he exhibited in "Photography of the American Scene" at the Julien Levy Gallery, New York. In 1934, he had one-man exhibitions at the Carnegie Institute of Technology art galleries and at the Delphic Studios in New York, the latter showing his circus photographs. During this period Swank met Alfred Stieglitz, who highly praised his work. At the time of the Delphic Studios show, Frank Crowninshield, editor of *Vanity Fair*, a publication that did much to foster the work of the leading photographers of the day, said, "Not only is Luke Swank interested in interpreting American life, but in revealing what is particular to American light and air. Therein, we believe lies his artistry."

About 1934 Swank (according to Charles M. Stotz, author of the *Early Architecture of Western Pennsylvania*) came to Pittsburgh to work with the Architectural Survey of Western Pennsylvania (1932-35) on which the book was based. Stotz acknowledges the debt of the Survey to Swank, not only for providing photographs but also for teaching the Survey members to photograph effectively. He had previously done a large survey of rural architecture in Central Pennsylvania. Swank, in his devotion to Pennsylvania architecture and the local landscape, was a convinced regionalist. Beaumont Newhall, then the chief historian of American photography, wrote about this symbiotic quality between photographer and subject, which is true of all Swank's other work as well. He is the photographic laureate of Pennsylvania.

In 1935, after he had moved to Pittsburgh, Dr. John G. Bowman, chancellor of the University of Pittsburgh, made him official photographer to the University. At this time Swank also initiated the first photojournalism course ever given at an American university. During his stay at Pitt, he was befriended by Edgar Kaufmann, who was a benefactor to many artists. Kaufmann commissioned him to photograph "Falling Water," his famous country house designed by Frank Lloyd Wright, which had been recently completed. Swank also photographed some of the work of the famous Modern architects Walter Gropius and Marcel Breuer. All this time, he was still exhibiting and selling photographs to publications such as *Vogue, House and Garden, Fortune,* and the *New York Times.* He was also listed as a photographer for *Life* magazine, and his photographs of war mothers are part of the *Life* collection.

In addition to his other interests, he still continued his constant social documentation of both urban and rural life. His pictures of Pittsburgh steel mills . . . are superb. Beaumont Newhall, in his 1938 essay on Swank, commends the remarkable restraint of these photographs: "They are the work of a man who has lived among the mills and who has learned to separate the characteristic from the spectacular — he sees with the eyes of a workman." Some of his urban landscapes of the rivers, lined with their smoking mills, and the view down the Pennsylvania Railroad tracks from the Bloomfield Bridge, have a lurid and grimy grandeur that those of us who can remember the old days will recognize immediately.

In 1938, he left Pitt and took a studio on Penn Avenue in the buildings now occupied by the Art Institute of Pittsburgh. At this time another patron, H. J. Heinz II, appeared on the scene. Swank made studio photographs of various Heinz products and compiled an entire portfolio of the Heinz food-processing operations and workers at the North Side Plant. . . . The strange thing about the [presently] exhibited photographs is that they have a curious sense of immediacy. One has the feeling that these images, that were made fifty years ago, could just as well have been made yesterday. Perhaps the sense of the abundant humanity captured on these magic surfaces — a wrinkled face, a stone retaining wall, the clapboard facade of a wooden house, a rutted field of mud — has shown us not the ephemeral but the eternal condition of the world. It is just not possible to pass by these magic images without some emotional commitment to them, some involvement in them as salient aspects of the city.

Many of these photographs are particularly important historically because they show aspects of the local landscape that have quite vanished with urban development, when whole segments of the local landscape disappeared after the passage of the bulldozer. Here are fascinating streets in the old Lower Hill and picturesque corners

343

The Atlantic Refining Company station.

of the old North Side. All of these vistas seem so solid and real, as if we had walked around some mystical corner and here they are, quite as they were once. Also it is wonderful to come across buildings that disappeared a long time ago, like the Atlantic Refining gas station, built about 1915 at Baum Boulevard and Melwood Avenue. Ah, it was so lovely, with its delicate glazed terra-cotta walls and tile roof; there my grandfather's large Chalmers car used to stop on long-ago summer afternoons to have its fuel supply replenished. Again, there is the beautiful Henry W. Oliver house, at 845 Ridge Avenue, where on a much-later summer afternoon I helped to remove magnificent Renaissance Revival artifacts when it was demolished about ten years ago. Then there is the magnificent brickwork of the facade of H. H. Richardson's Emmanuel Church on the North Side, which is still with us, and Richardson's rotunda of the Allegheny County Jail, looking as monumental as one of Piranesi's *Carceri di Invenzione.* The exhibition is like a fascinating tour of the monuments, great and small, of Pittsburgh architecture.

And the people, the faces! What is one to make of the painted head of the circus clown on the cover of the catalogue? That quizzical, yearning face, with its tragic, haunted eyes, seems to be asking a question for which there is no answer.

---

[1]This was written on the occasion of an exhibition of Luke Swank photographs at the Museum of Art, Carnegie Institute, Pittsburgh, in 1980; some material pertaining to the show has been omitted.

Radio script for WQED-FM, 1980.

Memoirs of Old Sewickley
A True Garden Spot of America

There are gardens in this world, even if nowadays they seem less numerous than they used to be. Sewickley, and by implication Edgeworth, is my favourite community of gardens in the Pittsburgh region. The whole area of Sewickley town and the adjacent residential hills might be considered a great garden, depending on how you look at it. Sometimes I am prone to consider the place as medieval theologians conceived of Paradise — *hortus conclusus* — an enclosed garden. Here the industrial roar of Pittsburgh seems remote, almost unimaginable, although it is so near.

Most of the old suburbs of Pittsburgh were industrial rather than residential, particularly those in the river valleys which were served by the railroads. Of the small residential number, Oakmont up the Allegheny and Sewickley down the Ohio were probably the most prominent, but Sewickley has a certain primacy of place. To quote the *History of Allegheny County, Pennsylvania,* published in 1876, "There are few more beautiful places in the whole country than the borough of Sewickley. It is in one of the most favourable situations on the Ohio and has been settled by wealthy families who have united in making it an elegant suburban place of residence. For this purpose they have strenuously opposed all attempts to introduce manufactories in the place, and have even refused to give support to such necessary institutions as hotels. Consequently, although it is a place of between 2,000-3,000 inhabitants, there is not, at present, a single public house within its limits." This was not always so, for there had been in the past taverns on the Beaver Road, and toward the end of the century as the town grew in popularity as a place of resort for Pittsburghers, hotels appeared. It was incorporated as a borough in 1853, as was Edgeworth in 1904.

The original inhabitants of the town had continued to guard the verdant village from industrial or commercial invasion, so that the area seemed ever more residentially desirable as the century wore on. One remembers those sardonic references to some unattractive town as "the garden spot of America." This could never be said of Sewickley because it has always been a garden spot. As Pittsburgh and its neighbouring city of Allegheny became more heavily concerned with heavy industry, the village became more than ever pleasant as a kind of summer resort for Pittsburghers, and one that was not too distant from the city. This coincided with the development of railroad transportation to the point where it was now easy for most male summer visitors to commute easily to their businesses in the city.

More and more, as the 1880s advanced, commerce in the form of summer residents or week-end visitors really began to invade in great numbers the elegant bucolic village which was, by its very nature, prepared to receive them. The new summer people came into the village, so established in its greenery, and sometimes they rented for the summer the fine but not opulent villas on the town's sedate streets. This gave the natives a chance to visit other parts of the country, so everyone was satisfied.

More important, the newly-wealthy industrialists, who had profited enormously by the invention of the Bessemer converter, were looking for convenient places in the near environs of Pittsburgh. For Sewickley the age of steel and great gardens had arrived. Large country estates had become in these affluent years the order of the day all over the northeastern part of the country, and this period inaugurated what historians of landscape design regard as the "country place" era, which extended from about 1880 to 1940, when social conditions changed so radically that it was no longer possible.

Most of these wealthy people had been residents of Allegheny City, but soon it became the fashion to have a summer house in the hills above the village itself. The *Pittsburgh Index* for July 19, 1902, in an article called "Social Life in Sewickley," gives a contemporary account of this change in the village, and I quote verbatim: "The first man to recognize the fact that Allegheny before many years would no longer be a desirable place of residence was Mr. B. Franklin Jones and the beautiful hilltop overlooking Sewickley, the Ohio River and the surrounding country for miles, was purchased by him, and upon it Mr. Jones erected four magnificent country houses, 'Franklin Farm,' occupied by himself, and the others he presented to his three children, Mr. B. Franklin Jones, Jr., Mrs. Elisabeth Horne, and Mrs. William W. Willock."

B. Franklin Jones (1824-1903) — usually referred to as B. F. Jones — was one of the founders of the Jones and Laughlin Steel Corporation as well as one of the important steel-masters of the nineteenth century in Pittsburgh. Many of the turn-of-the-century steel barons had a penchant for buying real estate, and Jones probably purchased the land above the village at a very cheap price. The building

"Fair Acres," the Sewickley home of Mr. and Mrs. B. F. Jones, Jr., c. 1925.

of four houses on his new domain was a very grand gesture, and certainly it made him the *pater patriae*, as one might say, of the new colony atop the hills. Native Sewickleyans, lifting up their eyes unto the hills, called it "Jonesville."

The houses themselves were large, picturesque, and rather lightly constructed, suited for summer habitation only. Such people all had townhouses in the city where they returned in the winter. The continuing development of the motor car and the improvement of country roads were to change profoundly this new colony of the industrial rich, but that is matter for a future discourse.

To continue the chronicle in the *Index* of 1902, "Mr. J. Stewart Brown followed Mr. Jones' lead and his summer home on an adjoining hilltop is plainly seen. Mr. Ralph H. Binns, Mr. Henry W. Oliver and his son-in-law Mr. Henry R. Rea, Mr. James W. Scully, Mr. Harry McFarland, Mr. William P. Snyder, Mrs. William Thaw, Jr., Mr. Charles Scaife, Mr. W. H. Singer, Mr. G. Harton Singer, Mr. Lewelyn Jones, and Mr. Russel Boggs all have beautiful country houses in which they spend a greater part of the summer entertaining house parties in a lavish manner."

Of these summer houses, that of Henry W. Oliver (1840-1904), known as "Farm Hill," became especially notable when his daughter Edith Oliver (1866-1951), wife of Henry R. Rea, inherited the estate in 1904. "Farm Hill" became one of the great formal gardens of the area. The new people on the hill preferred to call their colony Sewickley Heights; in due course, it became a borough.

Again, we quote from the *Index:* "The new Allegheny Country Club and the beautiful golf links added this year are great attractions, and, the informal dinners, dances, music, and golf tournaments contribute much to the gayety of this congenial coterie, not to speak of the many well known bachelors of this set who are domiciled at the club house for the summer. Another year a number of well known people will build picturesque cottages convenient to the club house."

The Allegheny Country Club, an early example of that indispensable element of the contemporary suburb, was founded in the early 1890s as the "country club" of Allegheny City in Bellevue, a contiguous trolley car suburb, but naturally it did not stay there long. Sewickley Heights was calling, and once established there it became truly indispensable. At the time of which we speak, 1902, it was merely working its way up. The young bachelors, like the frieze of young girls at Baalbek in Marcel Proust's *A l'Ombre des Jeunes Filles en Fleur,* were necessary to the action as it stood then — they complemented the supply of marriageable daughters of the country houses.

Picking up the *Index* again, "On what is known as the Mount Sewickley Road, back from Leetsdale, Mr. Hay Walker, Mr. James A. Chambers and Mr. Henry Buhl are building palatial homes which will be ready for occupancy later in the summer. Mr. John Walker of Allegheny has purchased the beautiful old 'Coffin Homestead' on the hill above Leetsdale, Mr. Mansfield Cochran and Mr. Richard R. Quay are erecting country houses out in that direction. A number of people of the social set in the two cities who do not own homes attach themselves to the summer colony by renting desirable places in the valley.

"Every train that stops at the pretty station on Saturday brings gay parties to spend Sunday at the Heights and the smart vehicles, traps, tallyhos, carts, opera busses, road wagons, run-abouts, etc. with the liveried coachmen and fine horses that meet them, give the modest little town an air of elegance of which, in its earlier days, it never dreamed."

This was the Sewickley of long ago at a particularly glamourous turn of its history. . . .

Radio script for WQED-FM, 1981.

348

The Ghost of President Buchanan, and a Town

Spa life has never been quite so important in America as it has in Europe, although possibly this is an overstatement, because therapeutic waters certainly did play a refulgent role in the social history of the United States during the nineteenth and early twentieth centuries. Wherever there was a spring whose waters would seem to have curative or ameliorative properties, a hotel was sure to be built, or even a series of lodging places. Perhaps the most famous American spa of the nineteenth century was Saratoga Springs, in northern New York state — a glittering resort of sin and fashion celebrated in song and story.

Pennsylvania never had anything in the way of spas so fabulous as Saratoga, but there were several in the western part of the state. The Cambridge Springs Riverside Hotel of 1886, in Crawford County, was a quiet, well-run establishment noted for its waters, but it recently has closed. Long one of the most popular health spas was that of Frankfort Mineral Springs, in Beaver County, with a large hotel that burned in 1906. Still extant and flourishing is the Bedford Springs near Bedford, which was established shortly after 1800, when Dr. John Anderson of the town located a lodging house at a magnesia mineral spring. By mid-century additional lodging quarters had been built with a frontage of almost six hundred feet.

Many people prominent in the social, political, and business life of the Eastern Seaboard have been summer guests here, but its most famous visitor was James Buchanan (1791-1868), Pennsylvania's only President (1857-61). During that strange, uneasy, lurid period just before the Civil War, Bedford Springs was Buchanan's Summer White House. In those days there was no Camp David.

I am somewhat familiar with Bedford Springs Hotel — in fact I consider it my favourite American spa of all possible spas — and it seems to me that the long echoing verandahs and solemn Greek Revival halls of the hotel are haunted by the ghost of President Buchanan. In fact, so sure am I of his haunting presence that I have even entertained the idea of some kind of reincarnation. Once, a year or two ago, when I was sitting on one of the verandahs with the high summer sun shining through my expansive white hair and whiskers,

349

a passing summer lady, struck by my mid-nineteenth century appearance, asked me who I was. "The ghost of President Buchanan," I replied solemnly.

But before the advent of the Bedford Springs of President Buchanan there was the town of Bedford itself, and it still abundantly exists as a background to the resort hotel, but has its own existence as the seat of Bedford County. It is one of the most charming towns in the state, having managed to preserve much of its late eighteenth- and early nineteenth-century character. Since it was never much addicted to industrial expansion, the blighting hand of Progress has never lain heavily upon its green calm. Almost fifty pre-1840 houses are still extant in the borough.

Its early nucleus was Fort Bedford, built in 1758 as the chief supply base for General Forbes in his campaign against Fort Duquesne. The fort was named by General Forbes for John Russell, fourth Duke of Bedford. There is now a log museum and park on the site.

The county seat was laid out in 1766 by surveyor General George Lukens on lands belonging to the Penns, and the chief streets were named for members of the Penn family. Dr. John Schoepf, who traveled to Pittsburgh in 1783, observed that Bedford was a little town in a "great wilderness," but commented that the place was "regularly planned, has a courthouse, and is the county seat of the extensive Bedford County . . . and as yet very little peopled." By 1837 the town had been incorporated into a borough and had about twelve hundred inhabitants.

The centre of the town — the Squares — is practically a museum of early nineteenth-century architecture. The County Court House, constructed of brick and timber by Solomon Filler in 1828-29, is now the oldest active courthouse in Pennsylvania. Although stylistically it displays many elements of the emerging Greek Revival, it still has many characteristics of the Late Georgian era. Other buildings in the area, constructed about the same time by the same master builder, include the Bedford Presbyterian Church (1829), the Russell House (1816), and the Lyon House (1833-34). The exceptionally handsome Anderson house on East Pitt Street, built in 1814 by Solomon Filler, now belongs to the borough of Bedford. The stone Espy house of 1770-71, also on East Pitt Street, although it has been altered to commercial premises, is undoubtedly a house where George Washington slept. He spent two nights here in 1794 while inspecting the troops sent to quell the Whiskey Insurrection in Western Pennsylvania.

With all this architectural treasure it is very evident that

Bedford has more landmarks than its resort hotel — I had almost said hotels, because just north of Bedford, near the Turnpike, are the buildings of the former Chalybeate Springs Hotel, whose oldest part was built in 1786-87. In the late nineteenth century this hotel was also very popular, and five Presidents stayed there. It was closed as a hotel in 1913, and the buildings were later made into apartments. At Mann's Choice near Bedford was also the White Sulphur Springs Inn, established in 1884, which is now a club.

From the town Squares one approaches the Bedford Springs Hotel via Route 220, after having passed through the calm residential streets of Victorian and Edwardian Bedford. One skirts a golf course that surrounds another old, high-verandahed hotel now belonging to the Elks (there are rumours that the dilapidated old building is to be demolished). The road enters a narrow gap between two mountains through which flows a small creek. One passes a stone mill of 1797 and, on the other side of the road, a log house of 1798 — both of them in excellent condition. Here, in the green shade cast by the looming mountains, it is not too difficult to imagine what the Bedford countryside must have been like two hundred years ago.

The gap widens again into the beginning of a tree-studded lawn, with the creek murmuring along at the other side of the road. As the valley slowly unfolds and expands, suddenly the hotel unfurls on the right like a long snake of brick and timber. Long lines of verandahs terminate, at the hotel entrance, in a large Classical portico, part of the Greek Revival main building that President Buchanan would have known so well.

The chief dimension of these nineteenth-century resort hotels was almost invariably horizontal; height was eschewed for obvious reasons until elevators began to be introduced toward the end of the century. It is interesting that horizontal construction has come back into fashion with the advent of the motel. But in the old days, if more rooms were needed, another wing was attached to the existing ranges of three- and four-story structures, whose varying styles attest to the dates of their construction. At Bedford Springs verandahs abound, especially on some of the later wooden buildings; the Victorians loved to take the air sedately. I myself prefer a room with a porch. Being elderly and sedentary, I like to sit in the dappled summer light, reading and writing or just contemplating reflectively the past. For those guests who prefer vertical living there is a high-rise tower of the 1920s, attached to the up-valley end of the hotel.

For the younger and more active guests there are all the amenities of the modern resort hotel, save winter sports, because

Bedford Springs is open only from May to November.[1] Up the valley is a great golf course, one of the chief attractions of the hotel. One may ride, like the Victorians in a surrey or on horse-back, walk, hike, or "jog." There are several tennis courts and places for shuffle-board. On the long green lawns in front of the hotel, I have seen ladies and gentlemen playing croquet or practicing archery. Or were these the shades of long-ago visitors? At night, if you want to dance, you may do so at the week-end. If you like to eat and drink, the meals are abundant and good, and they go with the price of your room.

If you want to take the therapeutic waters, they are still there, but they are not so fashionable as they once were. With the development of modern medicine in the last few decades, there has been less and less emphasis on hydrotherapy of the nineteenth-century type. One of the chief springs is located in a small Classical pavilion on the other side of the valley from the main entrance building of the hotel, and it may be reached by an elevated bridge from the Greek Revival verandah.

The architecture of the hotel, in all its variety, is a constant pleasure. The interior of the Greek Revival main building was remodeled in the 1900s with a handsome "grand" staircase and a huge fireplace that always has a blazing fire on cool days or evenings. The main dining room that looks out onto the Classical portico has been delightfully frescoed by the contemporary Irish Romantic painter James Reynolds (1891-1957) who, like me, fell under the spell of Bedford Springs and decorated it handsomely with his paintings. Other examples of his artistry are the painted walls of the Bar on the lower level, and here he was particularly successful in recapturing the wild, untamed wilderness of eighteenth-century Bedford.

Bedford Springs is old, and yet always new. Here you may have both the past and the present, while you enjoy all the comforts of modernity. As I have said, it is my own favourite spa, and my commendation of it is a labour of love.

Best of all, it is only a couple of motoring hours from Pittsburgh via the Pennsylvania Turnpike. And as you walk along the Springs verandahs, you may encounter the ghost of President Buchanan. Or maybe it's me!

[1]The season has since been lengthened.

Radio script for WQED-FM, 1977 or 1978.

Of Christmas Past and Christmas Cards

When I think backward over the entire course of my life, trying to capture the particular character or quality of any Christmas I have known, it is difficult to separate the real holidays from those festivals of which I have perhaps only dreamed or fondly imagined. However, even the Christmases of fact, far off in my own past, may now seem unreal, visions of clouds and tinsel, red and green with glistening holly never grown upon this earth. A rustling of golden feathers, wheaten hair, eyes of glass unknowing and yet all-knowledgeable . . . angels; heads turning, bulbous cheeks and noses, peaked-capped elves turning, turning to the great red-and-white god in the corner, glowing pink face, white hair, curling, crisp — Santa Claus? A department store window? But what image of the god, what angels, elves, what scenery? When? Where? Was it five or sixty years ago? Or was it a vision seen only by the eye of the mind? Something seen and yet not seen, or perhaps seen so many times that it has established itself as a kind of Eternal Now.

The Eternal Now may be that moment at 'quarter past eight in the morning of December second in any recent year you please, when, at the breakfast table, I take my second cup of tea and fall to considering that it is really time to start thinking about Christmas. Even in my warm dining corner, spiced with the odour of hot coffee cake, the air is faintly chilled by the north-west winds outside; a glance from my window reveals the roofs and turrets of St. Paul's Cathedral, over the way, powdered with new snow. The light is clear but subdued; the day will be short, we are nearing the winter solstice. I sit securely in the familiar early December ambience, savouring the dim lustre of the light, the chill warmth of the air, the tea, the spice . . . The calendulas (real ones) in the centre of the table are delightfully anachronistic. They were expensive, but they remind me of California, where, at the moment, I am glad that I am *not* — the long sameness of the California weather is a bore. Early December, the harbinger of Christmas and bright visions, is invigorating — and *different*. All the coloured imitations of autumn are gone, summer is only a memory . . . Christmas is less than a month away — the great feast that divides the year in half, the festival with many faces . . .

But I bring myself up short above my empty tea cup. "It is time to think *practically* about Christmas — there are presents, decorations, holly and juniper, ribbons and pine cones, wreaths and trees — shall I or shall I not have a tree this year? There will be parties to attend. Should I get a new suit?"

What about Christmas cards? You did, I say intently to the unheeding calendulas (even as I admire their passionate colours — the glowing oranges and sensuous yellows — and inhale their curiously acrid summer smell) — you *did* buy some cards in quantity at an after-Christmas sale last year, and what did you do with them? You put them in what you regarded as a place you would surely remember, and *now* you *cannot* remember. Where are they? You will buy some more, and late in January, when you are hunting for that elusive sweater with the Art Deco zig-zags, you will find the cards . . .

Christmas cards — if only you had — if only — my attention shifts from the calendulas to the almost burned-out candles in their silver sticks (on the base of the sticks are repoussé poppies — they were polished yesterday, so they are almost blindingly bright). I polished them, but why? since there is in the cupboard a plethora of unpolished silver. Why? Because I found the silver polish when I was hunting for a cake of soap. I had fifteen uncharted minutes before I left for the office, and the candlesticks were, as old Victorian business letters said, "to hand."

Alas, I said despairingly to the living-room door, this morning you have got an uncharted half-hour before you have to depart for the office, and you *must* decide what you are going to do with *this* Christmas — so many things — and how delightfully the angels turn their heads, the glass eyes which see nothing and yet see everything, gaze outward to the world, the elves turning, turning their bulbous cheeks, their pointed noses and peaked hats at some subtle command from the great red-and-white god in the corner, the huge, fat old man, jolly on a throne made of sacks of toys. He is huge, *great,* and he has been here since the beginning of time — no, wait a moment, since at least the point when he emerged into fable, into the mythology of Christmas which, at this particular point of time, is all that matters — the vision is everything — and I look out at this moment to the roofs and crockets of St. Paul's, powdered so mysteriously and wonderfully with snow. The tea is getting cold in the porcelain cup, but even the temperature of the tea does not matter in pursuit of the vision.

Christmas cards, I said, settling down at the table again with the last cup of tepid tea, Christmas cards — what was that wonderful post card that I got as a child — was I six or seven? — and which

I proudly kept for so many years in my post-card collection until it found its way, probably, into the rubbish bin. What was it? — and now, oblivious of the calendulas, the candlesticks, and the minutes flying away, I pursued it in past time. It was one of those fancy Victorian post cards — out of fashion even when I received it in 1915. I have the vague feeling that it was sent to me by an almost-forgotten great aunt, who knew vaguely that I liked, as she said, "pretty things."

It was made of a kind of heavy paper, repoussé on a backing of lighter paper, and the raised design consisted of a holly wreath coloured almost violently in red and green. In the centre of the wreath was a typically Victorian vignette — a winter scene with a polychrome sunset streaming its lambent colours across a snowy field. In the background was a bare-branched forest and a tall-spired church whose lighted Gothic windows matched the sunset light. In the foreground three carolers walked through the snow toward the church. All this on a post card was, of course, quite miniature, but to my childish eye it seemed quite large and clear; it was invested with a curious importance, a mysterious drama. It was, in some strange way, the very essence of Christmas.

Now in this December, long, long after, I sat at the table, the tea quite forgotten, pursuing in a vision this fragment of the past. It was not *real*, it never happened, and yet it was just as real as anything that ever did. Was I one of the carolers, or did I follow them? I *could* sing — even as a very small child I had sung carols — so I followed after in the snow, which although it seemed fairly deep was remarkably light and powdery. The carolers, two men and a woman, were dressed in what I later learned was Early Victorian costume — they were singing the standard English carols and did not seem essentially much different than members of our church choir, only they were in fancy dress.

We moved through the snow leaving, it seemed, no tracks. The sunset burnt fiercely through the distant network of black branches, the sun itself sent long fingers of flame across the white fields, but there was no heat in them. The air was still and cold. Our warm breath, as we sang, turned into small white clouds before us as we walked.

As we got closer to the tall-spired building, it seemed that it might be a really splendid church, such as I loved to sketch on the leaves of paper tablets that I was forever covering with architectural designs. This could have been also an exhibition hall, like the Machinery Hall of the old Pittsburgh Exposition or even the Phipps

Conservatory, only it was much more elaborate, composed of fantastic Gothic traceries filled with multi-coloured glass that was illumined from within by great bursts of light.

The carolers and I came finally to a great portal, shielded by richly-embossed leather curtains, like that of a medieval cathedral. We parted the curtains, and as we glided inside, the carolers seemed to move into the interior scenery, which resembled nothing so much as a vast circus tent, but there were no performing rings. It was also like the nave of a church or the long exhibition gallery of Machinery Hall at the old Exposition. There were, instead of pillars, long lines of fir trees covered with ornaments and lights, and in between, all the department store window scenes multiplied a hundred times — the angels with the golden feathers and the infinite eyes, the elves with bulbous cheeks and peaked caps, turning, turning toward the great red-and-white god at the end of the fabulous avenue — Santa Claus, Father Christmas, toward whom I walked, wondering.

The clock in the living room struck nine . . . my eyes focused on the calendulas and the candlesticks and the cup of cold tea. I would be late for my appointment at the office. I hurried to get my overcoat and briefcase. Where did I put those Christmas cards from last year? Yes, I might have to get some more . . .

Radio script for WQED-FM, 1977.

356

I Open My Windows to
Summer Stars and Locust Blossoms
in the Night

. . . As I have grown older I have tended, as well, to become more sedentary in my observation and appreciation. Arthritic joints conduce often to a sharpened stationary view, a view lacking when I could move about more freely. It is necessary, therefore, to have a point where one can view as widely as possible, commensurate, also, with what one can afford financially, but even this, if one's view is temperate, need be no problem, no hindrance to the cultivation of really wide horizons. . . .

The sky was cloudless and of an almost indescribable aquamarine colour, shading off toward a dusky sapphire hue in the darkening east. Herron Hill to the west looked like a patinaed Victorian stage "flat" with its lacy trees and shadowy houses. The two transeptal turrets of St. Paul's Cathedral, with their pinnacles and gargoyles, stood out like sentinels at attention, guarding the luminous west. As the dusk deepened into night, I saw a brilliant point of light, small but intense against the cloudless sky, appear to no great distance above the nearest turret. Slightly to the left and beneath the tiny beacon was another star, smaller and, as it were, attendant on its larger companion. My ignorance of scientific astronomy is abysmal. I do not know what the great star was called, and certainly I was equally unenlightened concerning the lesser one. The great star must surely have been one of the first magnitude, perhaps a distant planet, seen at its best only briefly and, perhaps, a star with a glorious name. Was it Venus or Mercury or Saturn? It does not matter — I can react to the stars only poetically. For a long time I watched the two points of light sink lower and lower until they vanished before midnight beneath the Gothic gable of St. Paul's.

Alas, in the city, how little we see of the stars, and all the marvels of the night sky are strange to us. My early summer vision did not send me to reference books in search of the stellar names. Why try to explain the mystery of such beauty? It comforted me the long night, and I fell asleep under the protection of its vanished wonder. Shall I see it again? Perhaps tonight or the next night will be cloudy, but the vision lingers in the heart and sustains the soul.

How glorious that my summer windows were so auspiciously opened on that shining enchantment.

As the night advanced toward the witching hour, the mysterious point of midnight, the circle of lamplight around my chair seemed to become more intense as if it were the centre of the world — as for the moment it was. The magic windows were still open; sounds, much diminished, drifted upward from the wide and traveled streets below, spiraling upward, the cries of the young, the lost, the inebriated, the roar of youthful motors, of insistent motor cycles, late, late — Wordsworth's "still sad music of humanity"? It was not still, nor was it sad — but certainly it was humanity.

When the great stars had disappeared, there existed the muted presentment of the actual world below. And I should not, for anything, have had it otherwise.

Looking out now from the magic circle of lamplight into the luminous dark-grey of the night, I can see a faint glow of light, the aura of the city above the serrated bulk of the Cathedral and Herron Hill. On the hill itself there is a scattering of lights like stars and the solemn red beacon atop the mushroom water tank.

Faintly, faintly, on the soft night wind, warm, I catch the far scent of locust blossoms, which is a pervasive odour that I had smelled often when I passed green hillsides during [a] recent journey. It is a dense, uneasy odour, troubling to the senses, unbearably sweet and yet pungent and almost acrid. It is the smell of life and new summer.

The light on the horizon seems to glow more brightly and circle the whole of my early summer view. Unbidden, to my mind come those haunting lines of Henry Vaughn, the seventeenth-century mystical poet:

> I saw eternity the other night
> Like a great ring of pure and endless light,
> All calm as it was bright.

Radio script for WQED-FM, 1978; excerpts.

358

My Own Birthday Anniversary
— Number 73

This year it happens that Monday, July 20, the day of my weekly
broadcast, also coincides with my seventy-third birthday, so I thought
that it might not come amiss if I celebrate my own personal anniversary on the air. I had not thought about it before Sunday the
fourteenth of July, when I had to speak informally to a small summer
lawn party held by the North Point Breeze Neighbourhood Association in Westinghouse Park. Since I am old enough to have been born
at home, I was born within that district when it was rather different
than it is now. I also lived there, on Thomas Boulevard, from 1922
to 1966. Therefore a large part of my life has been spent there, and
the wide and long green vistas are part of the landscape of my heart.

Similarly, I had to go on business to Greensburg in
Westmoreland County a few days later. After I had finished there,
my driver took me on to the little hamlet of New Alexandria,
where my mother's family had originally settled when they came
over the mountains from the East in the late eighteenth century.

It was a superb day — July at its best. The sky was intensely
blue, with great puffs of white clouds driven like heavenly sheep
across their wide cerulean pastures by a summer wind, warm and
slow. After we turned off Route 22 at Delmont onto Route 66, the
wonderful Westmoreland County farmland began to roll away to the
horizon — green and golden — with now and again a dark patch —
the shadow of a processional cloud. I thought how often I had seen
it before, in summers long ago, under just this superlative light, this
transcendent illumination that seemed to exist beyond any visible
source, and that elegant barn with its attendant silo, just so, tucked
in a fold of one of the recessional hills. Now in this solemn noon, I
felt that it had existed always. Certainly it has been part of me, ever
since I first saw it. Would it be there when I could no longer see it?
When its wheat and corn should have dissolved into snow and winter
darkness, would I remember this summer ecstasy of being. O, I cried
in the fastness of my heart. (The driver was intent on the road — my
private vision made no slightest ripple in the heated air.) I stretched
out my arms to the flooding light, and I swore by the flaming sun
that I would remember forever and ever when the season turned.

And, as for the glorious summer fields, I remembered Thomas Traherne: "The corn was orient and immortal wheat, which never should be reaped nor was ever sown. I thought it had stood from everlasting to everlasting.". . .

We had eaten lunch at a fast-food emporium in the huge Westmoreland Mall — Der Dog Haus, which I found an interesting mish-mash, not only in the amusing nomenclature of the place but also in the culinary fare offered. I do find as I get older that it is more difficult to appreciate these great architectural forms spawned by the fullness of the Motor Age. . . .

At any rate, there we were in Der Dog Haus — a real artifact of this modern shopping eclecticism. I would not partake of any of the proferred international "dogs." Instead I ate a grilled-cheese sandwich. The decor was a kind of jazzed up mid-European Early Renaissance Vernacular, essentially inappropriate to the proffered fodder. One attempted to meet the studied informality of the occasion with a sort of "picnic" mood, but it did not quite work. This careless lunching is the everyday occurrence, the habitude of the modern world. Perhaps as one gets older one prefers something more ceremonial, especially if one is traveling. Perhaps, generally, I could do with more ceremony. (I notice in my present discourse the salient emergence of the impersonal pronoun — one. "One" is vanishing with all the civilities and graces of the Late Victorian period, which had survived so plentifully and — may I say it? — so graciously, into the twentieth century.) Now, at seventy-three, I have not ceased to look forward, but I do it more cautiously, and with a sense of inevitable closure — particularly in the late afternoon of a fine day. Towards evening, we look for shadows.

Mostly, I suppose, I tend to look back. Were the old days with their clustered memories more sweet, more bright, than anything the contemporary day can offer? Probably not, even if in the later latitudes of life we tend to think so.

Toward the middle of our golden afternoon we stopped briefly at Ligonier, which I have known practically all my life; it is a great pool of memories which I can now scarcely fathom. One seemed here, and I have noticed it before, to plunge backward through layers of time with glimpses, now here, now there, of other excursions undertaken, some thirty or forty years ago. I remembered the old hotels — the Fort Ligonier and especially the Breneiser — the latter on the public square, where it was so pleasant to go for Sunday dinners on the long, glass-enclosed porch that abutted on Route 30. The Fort Ligonier had a similar porch, which looked out toward the Loyalhanna, and there was also the bandstand in the centre of the public park, that quasi-Oriental gazebo that represented superlatively Victorian Ligonier and still keeps its memory alive. And then out Route 30 to Laughlintown, with its restored Compass Inn, looking almost too "restored." And, ah, the long narrow ascent of Laurel Ridge on Route 30 which was so difficult for my grandfather's 1914 Chalmers, although it was in its day a powerful car. It was not at all uncommon to get stalled near the summit with an overheated radiator and hunt for water to assist in the process.

Then, in the waning afternoon, back through Ligonier and Latrobe to New Alexandria on the lower reaches of the Loyalhanna. On this present excursion we approached it circuitously, where I was always more used, long ago, to the more direct route from Pittsburgh, through Greensburg. Old Route 22 had once been the main road to Philadelphia, the continuation of the Greensburg Pike, also called the Northern Pike. Just before it entered New Alexandria it crossed the Loyalhanna, there rather somnolent and sluggish, on a covered wooden truss bridge — a strange tunnel of darkness slit with dazzling flashes of light.

On Sundays in summer, in 1916, I would ride with my grandfather in the great Chalmers touring car, seated high in the tonneau at the back while the chauffeur drove us through the fields of ripening wheat to the ancestral town of New Alexandria. Over the undulant seas of grain we rode in the superior galleon, above the tawny wheat, the gold of paradise, propelled by the long, slow winds and the heavenly clouds which moved above us in procession.

Then would appear the sleepy waters of the Loyalhanna to either side of the dark mouth of the bridge. The heavy boards of the bridge deck rumbled and banged in a rhythmic cacophony of sound as the car wheels passed over them. Then out again, up the dusty road to the ancient stone coaching inn at New Alexandria where we were to eat Sunday dinner. The hulking body of the old general store nearby is still there, but the Inn burned sometime during the 1920s and was rebuilt as a private house.[1] The main street of the town when it was part of the main highway was bustling and alive with traffic. Now, since it was bypassed in the 1930s, it is only a somnolent ghost.

But as I get older, I like to think of the Westmoreland wheat fields under the sky and the clouds: "The corn was orient and immortal wheat which never should be reaped nor was ever sown. I thought it had stood from everlasting to everlasting." And now it shall be my standard and my comfort.

[1]This reconstruction has also disappeared.

Radio script for WQED-FM, 1981.

Bibliography

This bibliography of the works of James D. Van Trump from September, 1947 through July, 1983 is based on a list of publications compiled for Pittsburgh History & Landmarks Foundation; on a bibliography compiled by John H. Richman with an introduction by Franklin K. B. Toker which was published in the January, 1980 issue of the *Western Pennsylvania Historical Magazine;* on unpublished manuscripts, principally scripts for WQED-FM radio broadcasts; on periodical articles; on WQED recording tapes; and on discussions with Mr. Van Trump.

Periodicals

The American Cemetery
"A Pittsburgh Pantheon: the Story of Allegheny Cemetery." 31:12 (December, 1959), 16-18.

Antiques
"National Stone: the Cumberland Road and American Architecture." 82:2 (August, 1962), 165-67.

"History in Houses: Hope Lodge, Whitemarsh, Pennsylvania." 89:4 (April, 1966), 542-45.

"Living with Antiques: the Pennsylvania House of Mr. and Mrs. J. Judson Brooks." 95:5 (May, 1968), 656-59.

The Book Collector
"Thomas B. Mosher: Publisher and Pirate." 2:3 (Autumn, 1962), 295-312. With Arthur P. Ziegler, Jr.

Carnegie Alumnus
"Henry Hornbostel and His Campus." 45:3 (December, 1959), 4-7. With Barry B. Hannegan.

"Technology's Temple." 45:5 (April, 1960), 2-7. With Barry B. Hannegan.

Carnegie Magazine
"Gargoyles from Texas." 30:8 (October, 1956), 276-79.

"The Triumphant Stone: a Study of the Foyer of Carnegie Music Hall." 31:5 (May, 1957), 167-75.

"Dramatic Prelude: the Rotunda of the Pennsylvania Station in Pittsburgh." 31:8 (October, 1957), 266-67.

"An American Palace of Culture: the Architecture of the Carnegie Institute Building." 32:1 (January, 1958), 21-30; 32:2 (February, 1958), 51-59, 61.

"The Tomb, the Temple, and the Casts: the Hall of Architecture and Sculpture Court at Carnegie Institute." 32:5 (May, 1958), 167-74.

Bibliography: Periodicals, continued

"Pittsburgh's Buried Bridge." 32:8 (October, 1958), 277-78.

"A Pittsburgh Palazzo: the House of Arthur E. Braun." 33:1 (January, 1959), 23, 27, 29-30.

"A Congress of Muses: the Allegorical Bronze Figures at Carnegie Institute." 33:4 (April, 1959), 135-37, 139.

"The Urn and the Tree: a Commentary on the Early Days of Carnegie Museum." 33:5 (May, 1959), 169-74.

"Art in Greensburg: the Opening of the Westmoreland County Art Museum." 33:6 (June, 1959), 199-201.

"A Pittsburgh Pantheon: Allegheny Cemetery." 33:8 (October, 1959), 271-73.

"Lions in the Streets: a Sculptural Hunting Party in Pittsburgh." 34:2 (February, 1960), 41-44, 52.

"A Garden of Books: the Library of Rachel McMasters Miller Hunt." 34:5 (May, 1960), 167-70, 177.

Review, *The Styles of Ornament* by Alexander Speltz (reprint). 35:7 (September, 1961), 245-46.

"Frederick G. Scheibler, Jr.: a Pittsburgh Prophet of Modern Architecture." 36:8 (October, 1962), 267-70.

"Our First Art Galleries Reappear." 37:1 (January, 1963), 13-15.

"A Wreath for Charles Bulfinch, Architect & Planner." 37:6 (June, 1963), 209-11, 213.

"Christmas and the Past Recast." 37:10 (December, 1963), 343-44.

"The Tenth Muse: Alexander Murals at Carnegie Institute." 39:2 (February, 1965), 63-67.

"A Museum for Pittsburgh History." 42:5 (May, 1968), 173, 175-76. With Arthur P. Ziegler, Jr.

Reprint, "Spanning the Years" (from *The Charette*, 47:7). 42:6 (June, 1968), 203.

"Old-New Home for American Art: National Collection of Fine Arts and National Portrait Gallery in Washington, D.C." 43:2 (February, 1969), 65-67, 69.

"Picking up the Pieces in Dutchtown." 44:6 (June, 1970), 226-28.

"The Crossing in the Valley: Point Breeze." 45:5 (May, 1971), 209-13.

"The New History & Landmarks Museum." 46:2 (February, 1972), 61-65.

"Valley of Memory and Decision: Homewood-Brushton Past and Becoming." 47:6 (June, 1973), 242-47.

"The Gothic Revived in Pittsburgh: a Medievalistic Excursion." 48:2 (February, 1974), 57-69.

"Revived Romanesque in Pittsburgh." 48:3 (March, 1974), 108-13.

"Wilkinsburg: A Personal View." 48:6 (June, 1974), 245-52.

"The Past as Prelude: a Consideration of the Early Building History of the Carnegie Institute Complex." 48:8-9 (October-November, 1974), 346-60.

"The Angelic Eye: Bellefield from the Air." 49:7 (September, 1975), 313-22.

"History at the Point and in the Golden Triangle." 49:10 (December, 1975). Map.

"Henry Phipps and the Phipps Conservatory." 50:1 (January, 1976), 26-35.

"And Always the Play: Historic Theaters of Pittsburgh." 50:2 (February, 1976), 71-79.

"Art Deco." 51:5 (May, 1977), 198-219.

"The Fate of the Anderson Memorial, or What Is the Workman Reading?" 51:8 (October, 1977), 24-33.

"Some Orthodox and Byzantine Rite Churches in Allegheny County." 51:10 (December, 1977), 17-32.

"Mary Roberts Rinehart." (Review, *Improbable Fiction*, by Jan Cohn.) 54:5 (May, 1980), 18-19.

"Memories of the Park." 54:6 (June, 1980), 16-17.

"The Bells of Pittsburgh." 54:10 (December, 1980), 14-27.

"Peter Berndtson, Pittsburgh Architect." 55:9 (November, 1981), 27-29.

"Stations East." 56:6 (November-December, 1982), 20-25.

The Cathedral Age
"The Unsubmerged Cathedral: Trinity, Pittsburgh." 32:3 (Autumn, 1957), 10-13.

The Charette
"Pittsburgh's Church of the Ascension." 36:6 (June, 1956), 14-16, 29.

"The Gothic Revival in Pittsburgh." 37:3 (March, 1957), 23-25, 30-32; 37:4 (April, 1957), 15-17, 32-33; 37:5 (May, 1957), 20-22, 27-30; 37:8 (August, 1957), 14-18.

"Pittsburgh Railroad Stations Past and Present: an Architectural Excursion with Stopovers in Philadelphia." 37:12 (December, 1957), 19-22, 35; 38:1 (January, 1958), 23-26, 33-34; 38:2 (February, 1958), 25-28, 32-33.

"The Church Beyond Fashion: a Discussion of Henry Hobson Richardson's Emmanuel Episcopal Church, Pittsburgh." 38:4 (April, 1958), 26-29.

"The Stones of Carnegie Tech: of Temples and Technology: the Drama of Henry Hornbostel's Buildings at Carnegie Institute of Technology, Pittsburgh." 38:11 (November, 1958), 26-28, 35. Follows an earlier part (September, 1958) by Barry B. Hannegan.

"The Stones of Venice in Pittsburgh: the Pittsburgh Athletic Association Club House." 39:4 (April, 1959), 24-27.

"An Architectural Tour of Pittsburgh." 39:11 (November, 1959), 18-21.

"From Log Cabin to Cathedral: the Pittsburgh Church Building 1787-1940, a Changing Image." 41:9 (September, 1961), 2-8, 11-13.

"Pittsburgh's New Pleasure Dome: the New Civic Auditorium." 41:10 (October, 1961), 8-22.

"Aluminum, Glass, and Books." 41:10 (October, 1961), 24-25.

"The Mansions of Science: Koppers Research Center." 41:10 (October, 1961), 26-27.

Bibliography: Periodicals, continued

"Pilgrimage to the Present: a Commentary on Some Contemporary Philadelphia Buildings." 41:11 (November, 1961), 7-12.

"Images of a Mirror: the 1961 Pittsburgh International." 41:11 (November, 1961), 13-20.

"Space and Art: the New Gallery Installations at Carnegie Institute, Pittsburgh." 41:11 (November, 1961), 26.

"The Christmas City, 1961: a Coronal of Trees." Poem. 41:12 (December, 1961), 5-7.

"Student Design Forum: Model Churches of the Future." 41:12 (December, 1961), 9-11.

"Towers de Luxe: Two New Apartment Houses in Pittsburgh and Philadelphia." 41:12 (December, 1961), 18-20.

"Pilgrimage to the Present: More Contemporary Philadelphia Buildings." 42:1 (January, 1962), 8-13.

"Requiescat in Pace: Modern Style." 42:1 (January, 1962), 19-20.

"Castles in the Urban Air: or The New Mall-to-Mall Magic Carpeting." 42:2 (February, 1962), 12-15, 22.

"Henry Hornbostel (1867-1961): a Retrospect and a Tribute." 42:2 (February, 1962), 16-17.

"Our Academic Suburbs: a Commentary on the Architecture of Non-Urban Elementary and Secondary Schools in Pennsylvania." 42:3 (March, 1962), 12-15.

"The Lamp of Demos: Some Pittsburgh Public School Buildings of the Past." 42:3 (March, 1962), 17-20.

"Burning Bush, a New Window at East Liverpool, Ohio." 42:3 (March, 1962), 26-27, 30.

"The Castle and the Hill: Two Contrasting Examples of the Picturesque in 20th Century School Architecture." 42:3 (March, 1962), 28.

"Pilgrimage to the Present: a Peregrination Among Parks." 42:4 (April, 1962), 8-12.

"The Hill." Poem. 42:4 (April, 1962), 13-16.

"Project H. H. Richardson: the Allegheny County Court House and Jail." 42:5 (May, 1962), 4-5, 20.

"The Sacred Ring: the New National Offices of the American Baptist Churches at Valley Forge." 42:5 (May, 1962), 10-13.

"Pavilion on the Schuylkill: Woodford, Philadelphia." 42:5 (May, 1962), 15-18.

"The Fire City: Steel and a Night Journey." Poem. 42:6 (June, 1962), 15-18.

"Castles Toward Tomorrow: a Brief Commentary on Contemporary Industrial Sites and Parks." 42:6 (June, 1962), 22-25.

"Citizen Grandeur and a Pear Tree: the Powell House, Philadelphia." 42:7 (July, 1962), 12-15.

"Concrete Ship in Shadyside: the Kentucky-Negley Apartments, Pittsburgh." 42:7 (July, 1962), 18-19.

"Faces of City Clubdom: Some Aspects of the Downtown Social Club in Pittsburgh." 42:8 (August, 1962), 14-17.

"The Contemporary Sports Club: a Parade of Modern Clubhouses in Pennsylvania." 42:8 (August, 1962), 19-22.

"Stars in the East: a Galaxy of Philadelphia Churches Old and New." 42:9 (September, 1962), 12-17, 24.

"A Prophet of Modern Architecture in Pittsburgh: Frederick G. Scheibler, Jr." 42:10 (October, 1962), 10-15.

"Circular History: the Visitor Center and Cyclorama at Gettysburg, Pennsylvania." 42:10 (October, 1962), 21-23.

"The Palace, the Loft, and the Tower: Some Notes on the Development of the Urban Hotel in Pittsburgh." 42:11 (November, 1962), 12-17, 20.

"City of God: Symbol and Echo." 42:12 (December, 1962), 6-9.

"Philadelphia and the World of Architecture: a Commentary on the Recent Exhibition at the Commercial Museum." 42:12 (December, 1962), 15-18.

"A Matter of Grace: a Few Words on Architectural Fitness and Some Recent Suburban Houses in Pennsylvania." 43:1 (January, 1963), 6-11.

"Homage to Paul Schweikher: the Man and His Buildings as Seen in a Recent Exhibition in Pittsburgh." 43:1 (January, 1963), 18-20.

"The Groves of Academe: 'Old Main' and the College Campus in Pennsylvania." 43:2 (February, 1963), 5-8.

"Enameled Face: Modern Style (The Erveen Porcelain Enamel Curtain Wall System)." 43:2 (February, 1963), 24-25.

"A Triad of New Towers: the Men's Dormitories at the University of Pittsburgh." 43:2 (February, 1963), 27.

"Castles on the Allegheny: an Architect's Fantastic Demesne near Pittsburgh." 43:3 (March, 1963), 8-10.

"J. Roy Carroll, Jr. the New President of the American Institute of Architects." 43:4 (April, 1963), 6, 22.

"The Skyscraper as Monument: a Field of Commemorative Buildings in Pittsburgh." 43:4 (April, 1963), 10-13, 21.

"The Painted City: Philadelphia as Seen Through the Eyes of Eight Local Artists." 43:5 (May, 1963), 19-22.

"Conference on a Pleasure Coast: a Report on the 95th Convention of the American Institute of Architects at Miami Beach." 43:6 (June, 1963), 16-19.

"Redeveloped Warehouse: 100 Ross Street, Pittsburgh." 43:6 (June, 1963), 24-25, 30.

"An Antiphon of Stones: Some Random Native Notes in Reply to a Visiting Architectural Critic in Pittsburgh." 43:7 (July, 1963), 8-12.

"Design Center Pittsburgh." 43:7 (July, 1963), 24-25, 28.

"The Found City: the Panther Hollow Project of the Oakland Corporation in Pittsburgh." 43:8 (August, 1963), 6-9.

Bibliography: Periodicals, continued

"The Gothic Fane: the Medieval Vision and Some Philadelphia Churches 1860-1900. Part I." 43:9 (September, 1963), 20-27.

Review, *Liturgy and Architecture* by Peter Hammond. 43:9 (September, 1963), 33-34.

Review, *Early American Homes for Today* by Herbert Wheaton Congdon. 43:10 (October, 1963), 10, 12.

Obituary, Hans A. Vetter. 43:10 (October, 1963), 12.

"But Westward Look: an Architectural Tour Beyond the Mississippi." 43:10 (October, 1963), 30-35.

"Suburban Wine: the Paris of Maurice Utrillo." 43:11 (November, 1963), 13-16.

"But Westward Look: the Lake and Ocean Cities." 43:11 (November, 1963), 18-23.

"Architecture and the Nativity: a Christmas Garland from the Philadelphia Museum of Art and Carnegie Institute, Pittsburgh." 43:12 (December, 1963), 4-5.

"The Gothic Fane: the Medieval Vision and Some Philadelphia Churches. Part II." 43:12 (December, 1963), 14-21.

"A Pride of Columns: Classical Philadelphia." 44:1 (January, 1964), 12-16.

"Security in the Round: the Police Headquarters Building in Philadelphia." 44:1 (January, 1964), 27-29.

"Mirror in the West: the Work of Some Philadelphia Architects in Pittsburgh." 44:1 (January, 1964), 34-39.

"A Castellated Metamorphosis: Grey Towers into Beaver College." 44:2 (February, 1964), 17-20.

"Temples of Finance: Philadelphia." 44:3 (March, 1964), 13-16.

"A New Face for an Old Bank: the Provident Tradesmens Bank and Trust Company in Philadelphia." 44:3 (March, 1964), 22-23.

"Banking and Art: the Remodeled Premises of the Fayette Bank and Trust Company in Uniontown." 44:3 (March, 1964), 24-26.

"A House of Leaves: the Poetry of Fallingwater." 44:4 (April, 1964), 13-15.

"Caught in a Hawk's Eye: the House of I. N. Hagan at Kentuck Knob." 44:4 (April, 1964), 20-21.

Review, *New York Landmarks*, Alan Burnham, ed. 44:5 (May, 1964), 3, 47-50.

"Some Prize Winning Works from the 54th Annual Exhibition of the Associated Artists of Pittsburgh." 44:5 (May, 1964), 25-28.

"Temples of Finance: Pittsburgh and a Praise of Pillars." 44:5 (May, 1964), 30-35.

"This Great Hospital: Some Pennsylvania General Hospitals." 44:6 (June, 1964), 20-25.

"Space Age Pavilion: a Plutonium Fuel Development Laboratory in Japan." 44:7 (July, 1964), 10-12.

"This Great Hospital: Some Medical School Hospitals in Philadelphia." 44:10 (October, 1964), 18-24.

"Behold Even I: Two Italian Romanesque Revival Churches in Philadelphia." 45:1 (January, 1965), 14-19.

Review, *The New Churches of Europe* by G. E. Kidder Smith. 45:1 (January, 1965), 28-29.

"Yet Once More O Ye Laurels: Benno Janssen." 45:2 (February, 1965), 8-13.

"The Reconstructed Landscape." Review of *Landscape Architecture: The Shaping of Man's Natural Environment* by John O. Simonds. 45:2 (February, 1965), 25-26.

"The Infinite Flathouse: Some New Pittsburgh and Philadelphia Apartment Buildings." 45:3 (March, 1965), 15-19.

Review, *The Best in Twentieth Century Architecture* (Selective Eye, V), Georges and Rosamond Bernier, eds. 45:3 (March, 1965), 30, 32, 34.

"This Great Hospital: the Porch and the Heart, Four General Hospitals in Pittsburgh." 45:4 (April, 1965), 10-15.

"Primitive Shapes and Shadows." Review of *Architecture Without Architects* by Bernard Rudofsky. 45:4 (April, 1965), 18.

"History in Sculpture: Five Historical Reliefs in the Blue Cross Building, Pittsburgh." 45:5 (May, 1965), 14-15.

"Haarlem at Allentown" (Observations). 45:6 (June, 1965), 10, 23.

"Therefore with Angels: an Architectural Excursion in Los Angeles." 45:6 (June, 1965), 11-16.

Review, *Architecture in New Jersey* by Alan Gowans. 45:7 (July, 1965), 4-5.

Obituary, Frederick Bigger. 45:7 (July, 1965), 18.

Review, *Landscape Architecture as Applied to the Wants of the West* by H. W. S. Cleveland (new edition, ed. Roy Lubove). 45:8 (August, 1965), 2-3.

"Pittsburgh Chapter, A.I.A.: the First Seventy-five Years." 45:8 (August, 1965), 4-5. Reprinted as a pamphlet.

"The Changing Substance of London." Reviews, *Georgian London* by John Summerson and *Town Planning in London, the Eighteenth and Nineteenth Centuries* by Donald J. Olsen. 45:9 (September, 1965), 8.

"The Eagle and the Court: Wanamaker's and the City." 45:9 (September, 1965), 13-16.

Review, *The Spire* by William Golding. 45:10 (October, 1965), 25.

"The House Made with Hands: Recent Houses Designed by Pennsylvania Architects." 45:11 (November, 1965), 10-15.

"Now Rome Return: the Service Tunnel of the Philadelphia Museum of Art." 45:12 (December, 1965), 8-11.

"Medieval Memories in a Victorian Suburb: Two Romanesque Revival Churches in West Philadelphia." 46:1 (January, 1966), 9-13.

Review, *Protestant Worship and Church Architecture* by James F. White. 46:3 (March, 1966), 5-6.

"Elegance on the Mall: the Rohm & Haas Building in Philadelphia." 46:4 (April, 1966), 6-7.

Bibliography: Periodicals, continued

"Henry Hornbostel: the New Brutalism." 46:5 (May, 1966), 8-11.

"The Philadelphia Academy of Music." 46:6 (June, 1966), 10. With Alan Class.

"Shadyside Redivivus: Sutton and Westoration in Pittsburgh's East End." 46:6 (June, 1966), 15.

"A Document of the New Urban Order: the Commercial Area of Allegheny Center, Pittsburgh." 46:8 (August, 1966), 10-14.

"Skyward Conviviality: the New Press Club Quarters in Pittsburgh." 46:9 (September, 1966), 17-18.

"Denver and the Portrait of the Architect." 46:10 (October, 1966), 16-18.

"This Great Hospital: from Baroque to Modern." 46:12 (December, 1966), 6-11.

"The Christian Circle and the Master Plan: the Chapel of the Randolph Macon Woman's College, Lynchburg, Virginia." 47:1 (January, 1967), 7.

Review, *The Architectural Heritage of Western Pennsylvania* by C. M. Stotz. 47:2 (February, 1967), 6-11.

"The Column and the Cross in Philadelphia: Three Victorian Classical Churches by Edwin F. Durang." 47:2 (February, 1967), 9-12.

"The North Side Market House." 47:3 (March-April, 1967), 25-26, 29.

"Mirror of the American Architect." Review of *Images of American Living* by Alan Gowans. 47:4 (May-June, 1967), 7, 8, 41-42.

"Faces of the Past and Present: Four Philadelphia Town Houses." 47:5 (July-August, 1967), 21-23.

"The Chapel on the Hill: the Philadelphia Divinity School." 47:6 (September-October, 1967), 13-16.

"Architecture and the World of Water: the New Aquazoo at Pittsburgh." 47:7 (November-December, 1967), 8-10.

"Spanning the Years." 47:7 (November-December, 1967), 22.

"The Art Gallery and the Fun House: the 1967 Pittsburgh International." 48:1 (January-February, 1968), 8-9.

"Art and Religion on the Campus: the Religion-Fine Arts Center of Roanoke College, Salem, Virginia." 48:3 (May-June, 1968), 16-17.

Review, *The Art and Architecture of Medieval Russia* by Arthur Voyce. 48:3 (May-June, 1968), 29-30.

"The Book and the Land: the Hillman Library of the University of Pittsburgh." 48:4 (July-August, 1968), 6-9.

"Architecture West: the 1968 Convention of the AIA at Portland, Oregon." 48:5 (September-October, 1968), 14-16.

"The Architect as Painter." 48:6 (November-December, 1968), 6.

"Welcome to a Good Guy: Number One, Oliver Plaza, Pittsburgh." 49:1 (January-February, 1969), 12-13.

"Expanding Museum: the New West Wing of the Westmoreland County Museum of Art at Greensburg." 49:2 (March-April, 1969), 8-9.

"Progress and the PNB." 49:4 (July-August, 1969), 13.

Review, *Tasso Katselas, Architect, Planner,* Wile and Ehrman, eds. 50:1 (January-February, 1970), 8.

"The Towers Fall." 51:2 (March-April, 1971), 11. With Arthur P. Ziegler, Jr.

"Quattrocentisteria: the Frick Art Museum, Pittsburgh." 51:4 (July-August, 1971), 5-7.

"Noses and Nostalgia at 800 Feet: Stouffer's Top of the Triangle, Pittsburgh." 51:4 (July-August, 1971), 12.

"A New Publisher for *Charette:* Farewell and Hello." 51:5 (September-October, 1971), 5. With Arthur P. Ziegler, Jr., Charles W. Shane, and A. H. Kiefer.

"Autumn Wine and Preservation: the Heinz Hall and the Old Post Office at Pittsburgh." 51:5 (September-October, 1971), 6-10.

Classical America
"Renaissance at Pittsburgh: the Frick Art Museum and the Pittsburgh History & Landmarks Museum." 1:2 (1972), 41-44.

Ekistics
"Castles Toward Tomorrow." Abridged from *The Charette,* 42:6. 15:90 (May, 1963), 295-96.

"Valley of Memory and Decision." Reprint from *Carnegie Magazine,* 47:6. 15:90 (May, 1963), 295-96.

Focus, Tribune-Review (Greensburg, Pa.)
"Lovejoy's Folly: Intriguing Saga of One Man's Dream to Build the Best." 8:18 (March 22, 1981), 6-7.

"Kilbuck: Named After an Indian, This Basement Theater Was 'World's Smallest.' " 8:32 (June 28, 1981), 2-3.

"Time 'Erasing' Remains of Fayette's Grand Meason House." 8:33 (July 5, 1981), 6-7.

"Singer Mansion: 'Castle' Triumphs over Time." 8:44 (September 20, 1981), 6-7.

"At Johnston House, the Stone Remembers." 9:2 (November 29, 1981), 2-3.

"Yule Memories: the Summer Christmas of 1936." 9:5 (December 20, 1981), 6-7.

"Peacock's Pride: Highland Park Once Boasted Turn-of-the-Century Millionaire's Mansion." 9:18 (March 21, 1982), 4-5.

"St. Philomena's: This Migratory Church Was Dedicated to a Disallowed Saint." 9:23 (April 25, 1982), 4-5.

"Uniontown's Courthouse: Remarkably Similar to That of Pittsburgh." 9:29 (June 6, 1982), 3-4.

"Indiana County's Old Courthouse: Italianate Masterpiece Preserved." 9:35 (July 18, 1982), 4-6.

"Whither, the Wabash?: Traces of a Rail Empire." 9:37 (August 1, 1982), 9-10.

Bibliography: Periodicals, continued

"Linden Hall: Where Sarah Cochran, the Farmer's Daughter, Lived Like a Great Lady." 9:45 (September 26, 1982), 6.

"Victorian Fountain Reborn at Allegheny Cemetery, Pittsburgh's First Park." 10:1 (November 21, 1982), 3.

"Mozart Hall." 10:8 (January 9, 1983), 3.

"From Defense to Domesticity." 10:9 (January 16, 1983), 6.

"Incomparable Chatham Village." 10:14 (February 20, 1983), 6.

"Spanish Villas: a Charming Legacy from the '20s." 10:17 (March 13, 1983), 18.

"A Century of Worker Housing in Natrona." 10:22 (April 17, 1983), 6.

"Dawson's Church by the River." 10:26 (May 15, 1983), 8-9.

"Vandergrift: 'the Worker's Paradise' and the State's Most Famous Example of a Late 19th-century Planned Industrial Community." 10:34 (July 10, 1983), 8-9.

"Tudor Towers in New Kensington." 10:36 (July 24, 1983), 6.

Greater Pittsburgh
"Pittsburgh: a Study in Building Designs." 42:2 (February, 1960), 29-32.

Historic Preservation
"The Beckoning Fair One: or What Is an Historical Structure?" 17:3 (May-June, 1965), 90-92.

Huntia
"The Procession of Flowers in Colorado: a Note on a Picture Album Memorial to Helen Hunt Jackson." I (April 15, 1964), 25-32.

"The Agnes Arber Collection." I (April 15, 1964), 169-71.

The Ivy Leaf
"The Market Square and the Ivy School." April, 1969, 1.

Journal of the Society of Architectural Historians
"St. Peter's, Pittsburgh, by John Notman." 15:2 (May, 1956), 19-23.

"The Romanesque Revival in Pittsburgh." 16:3 (October, 1957), 22-29.

Landscape Architecture
"Flowering Steel: a View of Pittsburgh." Poem. 53:3 (April, 1963), 190-95.

"The Green Thumb and the Early Suburbs." 53:4 (July, 1963), 300.

"Smithsonian Show—Faults are Minor." 54:1 (October, 1963), 44.

"Figures in a Landscape: Simonds and Simonds of Pittsburgh." 54:2 (January, 1964), 127-30.

"Pittsburgh Points to the Great Fountain." 65:1 (January, 1975), 59-63.

Market Square of Pittsburgh
"The Square: How It All Began." 1:13 (March 19, 1971), 1, 4-5, 8.

"The Square: a New Theatre." 1:14 (April 2, 1971), 1, 7, 10.

"The Square: Early Market Scene." 1:15 (April 16, 1971), 1, 6-7.

"The Square: Supplying the Need." 1:16 (April 30, 1971), 1, 8-9.

"The Square: a New Market House." 1:17 (May 14, 1971), 1, 6-7.

"The Square: Our New Tomorrow." 1:18 (May 26, 1971), 1, 8-10.

"Market Square 'Versus' the Diamond." 2:27 (April 7, 1972), 1, 7.

"Local Historian Provides Perspective on the Jenkins Arcade." 2:15 (August 11, 1972), 6, 12.

"Pittsburgh's Forgotten Architectural Monuments." 3 (March 16, 1973), 11.

"Pittsburgh's Forgotten Buildings II: the Americus Club." 3 (June 1, 1973), 9, 14.

"The Arcade: a Downtown Landmark." 6 (August 25, 1976), 7.

New Catholic Encyclopedia (1967)
Articles on eighteenth- and nineteenth-century church architecture. III, 807-14.

Newsletter of the Society of Industrial Archeology
"Station Square." May, 1977.

The Pennsylvania Library Association Bulletin
"The Pittsburgh Bibliophiles." 19:4 (May, 1964), 5-8.

Pennsylvania Professional Engineer
Review, *Tunnels* by Gosta E. Sandstrom. 2:4 (December, 1966), 5-6.

"Cable Roof Conference: Plant Tour, Bethlehem Steel." 2:5 (February, 1967), 12.

PHLF News
"Penn Theater into Symphony Hall." 14 (August, 1969), 4.

"Van Trump Rages Against More Architectural Ravages." 30 (October, 1971), 5.

"The Towers Continue to Fall." 31 (November-December, 1971), 2.

"Preservation in the Banking World." 53 (October, 1974), 3.

"The Grand Concourse." 62 (June, 1976), 3.

"PHLF Assists in the Establishment of the New Courthouse Park." 67 (September, 1977), 2.

Pittsburgh Post-Gazette
"Wightman Manor." November 9, 1974, 18.

The Pittsburgher ("Jamie's Journal")
"Incipit." 1:10 (March, 1978), 47-48.

"Urbane, Cultivated, and Formerly 'Gracious.' " 1:11 (April, 1978), 29-30.

"Of Mann's Hotel and a Bridge." 1:12 (May, 1978), 67-68.

"The Ghost of President Buchanan." 2:1 (June, 1978), 29-30.

Bibliography: Periodicals, continued

"Eccentric Pittsburgh." 2:2 (July, 1978), 69-70.

"Buried Bridges, Lost Ravines." 2:3 (August, 1978), 69.

"East Liberty, East Liberty!" 2:4 (September, 1978), 69-70.

"Disseminated Mansion." 2:6 (November, 1978), 65-66.

"September Christmas." 2:7 (December, 1978), 75-76.

"The Duquesne Gardens." 2:8 (January, 1979), 55-56.

"Baronial Living in Oakland." 3:5 (October, 1979), 23-24.

" 'Alicia' in Oakland." 3:6 (November, 1979), 21-22, 24.

"A 'Palace' Train." 3:7 (December, 1979), 21-22, 24.

"Two Courts, Two Verdicts." 3:9 (February, 1980), 23-24.

"A Palace Up to Date." 3:12 (May, 1980), 25-27.

"On Women, Words and Pittsburgh." 4:1 (June, 1980), 27-29.

"Denholm's Corner and Fred's Store." 4:2 (July, 1980), 23-25.

"Pleasure in the Air." 4:3 (August, 1980), 19-20.

"The Great Unwashed." 4:5 (October, 1980), 19-20.

"Remembering the Bulletin." 4:6 (November, 1980), 19-20.

"Christmas in Polish Hill." 4:7 (December, 1980), 47-48.

"Eastward in Pittsburgh: the Estate of R. B. Mellon." 4:8 (January, 1981), 15-18.

Pittsburgh Quote
"Towers for the Tycoons: Pittsburgh Industrialists and Their Monuments." 5:1 (June, 1960), 18-23.

Preservation News
"Doomed Dome? Pittsburgh's Battle to Save the North Side Post Office." 8:5 (May, 1968), 3.

Réalités
Articles on architectural uses of aluminum, inserted between pp. 4 and 5 of the Alcoa edition in the following numbers: Numéro 169 (December, 1964); Numéro 170 (January, 1965); Numéro 171 (February, 1965); Numéro 172 (March, 1965).

Renaissance
"Pittsburgh's Blossoming Tree: the New Museum of Pittsburgh and Allegheny County History." 1:1 (Summer, 1969), 25-28. With Arthur P. Ziegler, Jr.

Renaissance Pittsburgh
"Art Deco City: in Pittsburgh, the Last Ornamental Style in Architecture Is Still Extant." 4:7 (July-August, 1973), 32-36.

"Remembering the Schenley Hotel." 5:9 (October, 1974), 37-40. With Scott MacLeod and Frankie Gustine.

St. Louis Post Dispatch
"St. Louis Visited." July, 1964.

Sewickley Herald
"Bicentennial Sparks Awareness of Architectural Heritage." Bicentennial edition, July, 1976.

Trinity
"Episcopal Church Architecture in the Pittsburgh Region." 1:2 (Summer, 1976), 2-4.

University Club News
"An Architectural History of the University Club." September, 1966, 11-19.

The Western Pennsylvania Historical Magazine
"King's Folly." 41:1 (Spring, 1958), 11-16. With Barry B. Hannegan.

"The Centennial Celebration of 1858 in Pittsburgh." 41:2 (Summer, 1958), 93-113.

"The Celebration of the Completion of the Laying of the Atlantic Cable." 41:2 (Summer, 1958), 170-71.

" 'Solitude' and the Nether Depths: the Pittsburgh Estate of George Westinghouse and Its Gas Well." 42:2 (March, 1959), 155-72.

"Two Hundred and Fifty Years of Pennsylvania Art at Greensburg." 42:3 (September, 1959), 277-81.

"A Sermon on the Fall of Fort Duquesne." 42:3 (September, 1959), 314-16.

"Of Footbridges and Preservation." 43:2 (June, 1960), 135-46.

Review, *The Antiques Treasury of Furniture and Other Decorative Arts.* 43:3 (September, 1960), 295-97.

"The Mountain and the City: the History of Shadyside Presbyterian Church, Pittsburgh, as Seen Through Its Architecture." 44:1 (March, 1961), 21-34.

"A California Gold Rush Letter from Bernard J. Reid." 44:3 (September, 1961), 217-35. With Alfred D. Reid, Jr.

"Passage Through a Southwest Landscape: a Brief Comment on the Historical Society Tour." 44:3 (September, 1961), 305-07.

"Green Valley and Steel Bridge: the Historical Society Tour of July 14, 1962." 45:3 (September, 1962), 283-86.

Review, *Early American Homes for Today: a Treasury of Decorative Details and Restoration Procedures* by Herbert Wheaton Congdon. 46:4 (October, 1963), 398-401.

Review, *Victorian Antiques* by Thelma Shull. 47:1 (January, 1964), 67-69.

"The Church of the Ascension, Pittsburgh: a Brief Chronicle of Its Seventy-five Years." 48:1 (January, 1965), 1-18. Abstracted from *The Church of the Ascension.*

"Halicarnassus, Pittsburgh and New Alexandria: a Memorial Excursion." 48:3 (July, 1965), 221-34.

Review, *Images of American Living: Four Centuries of Architecture and Furniture as Cultural Expression* by Alan Gowans. 49:2 (April, 1966), 157-59.

"Bellefield's Tower: the Centenary of the Bellefield Presbyterian Church." 49:3 (July, 1966), 213-25.

Review, *The Architectural Heritage of Western Pennsylvania* by Charles Morse Stotz. 50:1 (January, 1967), 68-71.

Review, *Here's to Thornburg* by Alice Crist Christner. 50:4 (October, 1967), 330-33.

"A Heritage of Dreams: Some Aspects of the History of the Architecture and Planning of the University of Pittsburgh, 1787-1969." 52:2 (April, 1969), 105-16.

Review, *A Pencil in Penn* by Edward Brown Lee. 54:1 (January, 1971), 80-82.

"The Sutton-Elkin House, Breezedale, in Indiana, Pennsylvania: a Historical and Stylistic Analysis and a Program for Its Restoration." 56:2 (April, 1973), 107-28.

"An Affair of Honor: Pittsburgh's Last Duel." 57:3 (July, 1974), 307-15. With James Brian Cannon.

"A Trinity of Bridges: the Smithfield Street Bridge over the Monongahela River at Pittsburgh." 58:4 (October, 1975), 439-70.

"The Diary of Samuel W. Ewing—A Forty-Niner" (as editor). 60:1 (January, 1979), 73-88.

Review, *Thomas Jefferson, Landscape Architect* by Nichols and Griswold. 63:2 (April, 1980), 163-65.

Review, *A Pennsylvania Album* by George Miller. 63:3 (July, 1980), 260-62.

Review, *Improbable Fiction* by Jan Cohn. 63:4 (October, 1980), 355-56.

Review, *The Shaping of the Point* by Robert Alberts. 64:3 (July, 1981), 279-99.

Review, *Organic Vision* by Miller and Sheon. 65:1 (January, 1982), 69-70.

The Winged Head

"The Architecture of the Pittsburgh Athletic Association Clubhouse: the Stones of Venice in Pittsburgh." 51:4 (April, 1961), 29-33.

"Athletes and Steel Mills: a Commentary on the Club's Art Collection." 51:4 (April, 1961), 35-39.

The Woman's Home Companion

"When Yesterday Returns." Short story. Vol. 74 (September, 1947), 22-23, 44, 46, 49, 50, 52.

Books, Contributions to Books, Pamphlets, and Catalogues

(PHLF signifies Pittsburgh History & Landmarks Foundation as publisher, with Pittsburgh as place of publication.)

An American Palace of Culture; the Carnegie Institute and Carnegie Library of Pittsburgh. Pittsburgh: Carnegie Institute and PHLF, 1970.

An Architectural Tour of Pittsburgh.. Pittsburgh: Pittsburgh Chapter of the American Institute of Architects, 1960.

An Architectural Tour of Pittsburgh (The Stones of Pittsburgh, No. 1). PHLF, 1965.

The Architecture of Frederick G. Scheibler, Jr., 1872-1958. Pittsburgh: the Department of Fine Arts, Carnegie Institute, 1962. With James H. Cook.

Bellefield's Tower: the Centenary of the Bellefield Presbyterian Church. Pittsburgh: Bellefield Presbyterian Church, 1966. Reprint from *Western Pennsylvania Historical Magazine,* 49:3.

The Bells of Pittsburgh. PHLF, n.d. Reprint from *Carnegie Magazine,* 54:10.

Birmingham, Pittsburgh's South Side: an Area with a Past That Has a Future (The Stones of Pittsburgh, No. 7). PHLF, 1968. With Arthur P. Ziegler, Jr.

By Any Other Name: the Controversial Spelling of "Pittsburgh," or Why the "H"? (The Stones of Pittsburgh, No. 8). PHLF, n.d.

The Centennial of the Episcopal Diocese of Pittsburgh, 1866-1966. Pittsburgh, 1966. With Canon Wilson.

Evergreen Hamlet (The Stones of Pittsburgh, No. 4). PHLF, 1967.

"Glenfield, Past, Present, and Future." In *Glenfield and the Eye of History* (PHLF, 1975), 1-4.

The Gothic Revived in Pittsburgh: a Medievalistic Excursion (The Stones of Pittsburgh, No. 10). PHLF, 1975; reprinted from *Carnegie Magazine,* 48:2.

Grandfather's Attic: the Philadelphia Story of the Pittsburgh Bibliophiles. Pittsburgh: The Pittsburgh Bibliophiles, 1964.

Preface, *Henry Hobson Richardson: Allegheny County Courthouse and Jail,* Part One. Pittsburgh: Courthouse Gallery/Forum, 1977.

Introduction, reprint edition of *Henry Hobson Richardson and His Works* by Marianna Griswold Van Rensselaer. River Forest, Ill.: Prairie School Press, 1969.

A History of the Bridges at the Point of Pittsburgh and the Brady Street Bridge. Washington, D.C.: Historic Conservation and Recreation Service, U.S. Department of the Interior, 1973.

Landmark Architecture of Allegheny County, Pennsylvania (The Stones of Pittsburgh, No. 5). PHLF, 1967. With Arthur P. Ziegler, Jr.

Legend in Modern Gothic: the Union Trust Building, Pittsburgh (The Stones of Pittsburgh, No. 3). PHLF, 1966.

"*Our Eastern Domes, Fantastic, Bright . . . .*": *Some Orthodox and Byzantine-Rite Churches in Allegheny County.* (The Stones of Pittsburgh, No. 12). PHLF, n.d.; reprinted from *Carnegie Magazine,* 51:10.

Pilgrimage to April: the Pittsburgh Bibliophiles' Journey to Washington. Pittsburgh: The Pittsburgh Bibliophiles, 1966.

"Pittsburgh's Court Houses: Two Centuries of Legal Architecture in Pittsburgh." Mimeographed. PHLF, 1975.

Pittsburgh's Court Houses: Two Centuries of Legal Architecture in Pittsburgh. PHLF, forthcoming.

Bibliography: Books, etc., continued

Pittsburgh's Neglected Gateway: the Rotunda of the Pennsylvania Railroad Station (The Stones of Pittsburgh, No. 6). PHLF, 1968.

"Pittsburgh Then: Historical Star of the West." In *Pittsburgh Magazine's Guide to Pittsburgh* (Pittsburgh: Metropolitan Public Broadcasting, Inc., 1976), 7-9.

Porter Garnett and the Laboratory Press. Pittsburgh: The Laboratory Press, 1962.

Railroad Stations of Pennsylvania: an Architectural Excursion: Metropolitan Terminals. Pittsburgh: M. Hugh Wilmoth, 1964. Revised from articles in *The Charette*, 37:12, 38:1, 38:2.

September Solstice 1966: the Virginia Journey of the Pittsburgh Bibliophiles. Pittsburgh: The Pittsburgh Bibliophiles, 1967.

Station Square: a Golden Age Revived (The Stones of Pittsburgh, No. 11). PHLF, 1978.

1300-1335 Liverpool Street, Manchester, Old Allegheny, Pittsburgh (The Stones of Pittsburgh, No. 2). PHLF, 1965. With Arthur P. Ziegler, Jr.

A Trinity of Bridges: the Smithfield Street Bridge over the Monongahela River at Pittsburgh. Washington: Historic Conservation and Recreation Service, U.S. Department of the Interior, 1973. Reprint from *Western Pennsylvania Historical Magazine*, 58:4.

The Walker-Ewing Log House; Built c. 1790. PHLF, 1975.

Papers and Printed Interview

"Architecture Without Armor: the Norse Room of the Fort Pitt Hotel of Pittsburgh." Twenty-first annual meeting of the Society of Architectural Historians. Summarized in *Journal of the Society of Architectural Historians*, 27:3 (October, 1968), 223.

"The Greek Revival in Pittsburgh: an Image of the Nineteenth-century American City." Twenty-third annual meeting of the Society of Architectural Historians. Summarized in *Journal of the Society of Architectural Historians*, 29:3 (October, 1970), 269-70.

"The Pennsylvania Canal in Pittsburgh and Allegheny." Research paper for PHLF I-79 project, in cooperation with Pennsylvania Department of Highways and Federal Bureau of Roads.

"The Skyscraper as Monument." Sixteenth annual meeting of the Society of Architectural Historians. Printed in *The Charette*, 43:4.

"August Interview: James Van Trump," *The Pittsburgher*, 1:3 (August, 1977), 6-9.

Manuscripts Held by the Pittsburgh History & Landmarks Foundation

Where precise dates are given, these are as shown on typescripts. Dates by year have been established from conversations with Mr. Van Trump or from internal evidence. An asterisk indicates that Landmarks has a tape of the work, made for broadcast on WQED-FM.

*"An Aerial View of Oakland in 1924." C. 1978.

"Allegheny Cemetery's Rededicated Fountain." October 8, 1982.

*"Amazing Grace: a New Restaurant at the Freight House in Station Square." 1980.

*"American Photographers and the National Park." August 20, 1982.

"Another Look at Oakland—1982." September, 1982.

*"Another Mountain Inn Closes Its Doors: the White Sulphur Springs Inn." 1977.

*"Architecture and the Pittsburgh Land: the Buildings of Peter Berndtson." December, 1981.

*"Art Deco Exhibited at Pittsburgh: the ASID-PHLF Show at the Old Post Office Museum." 1979.

"An Art Deco Garden in Pittsburgh: the Perennial Garden at the Phipps Conservatory, Schenley Park." 1978.

*"The Associated Artists of Pittsburgh Through Seventy-one Years—1910-1981." 1981.

*"At the University Club: a View of Oakland in Winter." 1978.

*"Autumn Leaves, 1982." November 11, 1982.

"Autumn Splendour Remembered: the Indian Summer of 1977." C. 1978.

*"Brandy's: a New-Old Restaurant in the Strip District." C. 1979.

"The *Bulletin Index:* an Important Chapter in Pittsburgh Journalism." January, 1982.

*"The Cameraphone: a Youthful Memory." December 15, 1982.

*"The Carnegie Institute Christmas Trees—1982." February 3, 1983.

*"*Carnival In Flanders:* a Further Excursion into Re-seeing the Movies of One's Youth." 1978.

*"A Celebration of Feathers: the Feather Arts Exhibition at the Museum of Natural History, Carnegie Institute." 1980.

*"Charles Rosen—The Pennsylvania Years." February 16, 1983.

*"The Charm of Old Post Cards: George Miller's *A Pennsylvania Album: Picture Post Cards 1900-1930.*" 1980.

"Christmas and the Colonial Revival: a Holiday Party in September." 1978.

*"Christmas Before Christmas—1980: an Excursion to a Holiday Church Bazaar." 1980.

*"A Christmas Party at Hartwood: a Holiday Excursion." 1979.

*"Chronicles of Old Fifth Avenue I: From Pittsburgh's Downtown to Oakland." August 20, 1982.|

*"Chronicles of Old Fifth Avenue II: Some Old Antique Shops." August 20, 1982.

*"Chronicles of the Pennsylvania Railroad: a Terminal Station That Never Got Built." July, 1982.|

*"The Cinderella Ball, 1982." February 3, 1983.

"C.M.U.'s Tower Logo Again." November 1, 1982.

*"Commodore Joshua Barney Remembered." April 13, 1982.

Bibliography: Manuscripts, continued

*"Constructivism and the Geometric Traditions: the New Exhibition at the Museum of Art, Carnegie Institute." 1980.

*"*Crime Without Passion:* a Nostalgic Essay on Re-seeing the Movies of One's Youth." 1978.

"The Disseminated Mansion: Mementoes of the Henry W. Oliver House." 1978.

*"A Document of Early Modern Architecture." February 16. 1983.

*"A Doll House from California and Some Paintings." 1980.

*"Downtown Pittsburgh Today." April, 1982.

*"Downtown Restaurants of Yesterday: the Dining Rooms of McCreery's and Kaufmann's." 1980.

*"The Drama Department at Carnegie-Mellon University." September, 1982.

"Duquesne Gardens: Victorian Adaptive Re-use in the Twentieth Century." 1978.

*"Early Railroad Architecture on the Main Line of the Pennsylvania—Water Stations." August 20, 1982.

"An Early Tycoon Palace—the Isaac Meason House at Mount Braddock." 1982.

*"Easter and the Opening of the Floral Season." April, 1982.

*"East Liberty's Liberty Theatre." December 7, 1982.

"Eastward in Pittsburgh: the Estate of R. B. Mellon at 6500 Fifth Avenue." 1980.

"Eccentric Pittsburgh—Some Figures from the Past." 1978.

*"Ecclesiastical Architecture de Luxe: the Interior of Calvary Methodist Church in the North Side." 1981.

"1890." December, 1981.

"1895: the Port of Pittsburgh in 1895, Looking Up the Valley of the Monongahela River Which Flows Down (Not Up) from West Virginia." December, 1981.

*"English Romanesque Cathedrals and the Buildings of Western Pennsylvania." August, 1982.

*"Epiphany at Aaron's Rock: a Modern Holiday Fantasy."

*"Epiphany at Ascalon Cottage." June, 1983.

*"The Ethnic Church, Old and New, Near and Far: Pittsburgh and Gracanica."

*"An Excursion in May: a Late Spring Trip to Natrona and Some Houses." 1981.

"A Fairy Tale Christmas at the Hall of Architecture: the Annual Holiday Trees of '81." January, 1982.

"Fantasy on the Roof, or Architecture Overhead." 1978.

*"The Fascinations of August and Old Magazines." August 23, 1982.

"The First Journey of the New Year—1982: a Trip to Indiana, Pa." February, 1982.

*"Flowers of India: an Exhibition of 'A Selection of Late Eighteenth- and Early Nineteenth-century Indian Botanical Paintings.' " 1980.

*"The Fountain on Gunn's Hill: a Pittsburgh Vignette." 1981.

*"Fox Hall: the Decorator's Show House 1978." 1978.

*"Fred's Place: the Corner Store at the All-American Corner."

*"From Bowling Alley to Art Gallery: the New Pittsburgh Plan for Art Building." 1980.

*"From Realism to Fantasy: the Malcolm Parcell Exhibition at CMU." March, 1982.

"From the Hey-day of the Hat: Miss Rose Chapeaux." 1980.

*"A Further Chronicle of the William Penn Terrace Room." June, 1983.

"The Ghost of President Buchanan and a Town." C. 1978.

*"A Glimpse of Romantic East Liberty in the 1850s." August 20, 1982.

"Glimpses of East Liberty II." October 26, 1982.

*"*Gone With The Wind:* a Varied Disquisition on Its Past." 1978.

"*El Grande de Coca Cola.*" October 27, 1982.

*"Great Shakespeare Exhibition and the Three Rivers Shakespeare Festival." 1980.

*"The Greek Revival Revived." February, 1982.

*"Happy New Year for Pittsburgh's Penn Station: Long Live the Rotunda." January, 1982.

*"The Haunted House: a Hallowe'en Meditation." 1979.

*"*Die Heimkehr aus dem Fremde:* a Return to the Home Place." 1979.

*"The History of the Present Wilkinsburg Station on the Pennsylvania Line." August 20, 1982.

*"The Hotel by the River and the Railroad: the New Sheraton Motor Hotel at Station Square." December, 1981.

*"*Impressions du Voyage:* a Visit to San Antonio, Texas."

*"In a Golden Garden: a Small Suburban Station Garden of Sixty Years Ago." 1978.

"Incomparable Chatham Village: a Pittsburgh Landmark." February 15, 1983.

*"In Praise of Kennywood: a New Book on an Old Theme." August 20, 1982.

*"In Search of Harmony: a Brief Overview of Some American Communitarian Societies in the 19th Century and Their Architecture" (two parts). February, 1982.

*"I Open My Windows to Summer Stars and Locust Blossoms in the Night." 1978.

*"Islamic Renaissance at Carnegie Institute." June, 1983.

*"Journey to the Centre of the Earth: the New Hillman Hall of Minerals at Carnegie Institute." 1980.

*"Kate Greenaway and the World of the Child: a New Art Collection at the Hunt Institute of Botanical Documentation." December, 1981.

"The Ladies of the Post Office." August 5, 1966.

*"The Last of Greenlawn: My First Demolition in the Chateau Country." C. 1980.

*"The Last of Summer and Early Autumn in Pittsburgh: a Few Mixed Cultural Notices." October, 1981.

*"The Last of Webster Hall: the Passing of a Famous Oakland Hotel." 1977.

*"Light over Pittsburgh—1982." December 7, 1982.

*"A Long Lost Botanical Treasure Trove on Exhibit at the Hunt Institute of Botanical Documentation." December, 1982.

"Louis Comfort Tiffany and His Stained Glass Windows at Calvary Methodist Church." 1981.

*"Lovejoy's Folly: a Vanished Pittsburgh Palace." 1981.

*"Luke Swank: a Master Photographer Once More in the Public Eye." 1980.

"Medieval Pittsburgh: the Singer House, Wilkinsburg."

*"Memoirs of Old Sewickley: a True Garden Spot of America." 1981.

"Memories of Highland Park." 1981.

*"Memories of Whitby Hall: a Grand 18th-century Country House of Philadelphia."

*"More Memories of East Liberty Station and a Praise of Petunias." July 8, 1982.

*"The Most Recent Mutation of Sharpsburg: Il Geranio and the River." 1979.

*"My Own Birthday Anniversary—Number 73." 1981.

"The New Building for the Pittsburgh Centre for the Arts."

"A New Exhibition at the Westmoreland County Museum of Art." November 1, 1982.

*"A New Gallery for the Westmoreland County Museum of Art." September, 1982.

*"A New Guide to Pittsburgh's Public Sculpture." June, 1983.

*"A New Ornament for an Old Neighbourhood: the Cafe Stephen B's in the East End." 1979.

*"The New Realism: Two Pittsburgh Art Exhibitions Now on View." 1981.

*"New Year's at Montalto: a Green Hill from the Past." 1981.

*"New Year's Eve, 1915: a Pittsburgh Festal Vignette." 1977.

*"Of Castles: a Medley of Dream Towers in Miniature." C. 1977.

*"Of Christmas Past and Christmas Cards." 1977.

*"Of Clubs and Cornices: from Pittsburgh to Cleveland."

*"Of Gateways: Some Pittsburgh Entrances." 1980.

*"The Old City Hall of Pittsburgh: a Glimpse of Our Victorian Past." C. 1980.

*"On the Terrace: Vignettes of Life *al Fresco* in Pittsburgh." C. 1978.

*"On the Terrace II: the Roof of the University Club in Pittsburgh." C. 1978.

*"The Opening of the Commerce Court Building." December 7, 1982.

*"The Opening of the East Busway." June, 1983.

"A Palace Up to Date: the Recent Renovation of the William Penn Hotel." 1980.

*"Palladio Again and Another Lecture." April, 1982.

*"Pavane for an Oakland Spring." C. 1978.

"Peacock's Pride: an East Liberty Millionaire Mansion of the Early 1900s." January, 1982.

*"The Penn Central Station at Pittsburgh: Some Recent Preservation Notes." 1978.

"*A Pennsylvania Album: Picture Post Cards 1900-1930.* By George Miller." 1980.

"The Pennsylvania Canal in Pittsburgh and Allegheny." 1969.

*"The Philosophy of the Interior: Mario Praz and the Miniature Room." C. 1979.

*"A Pittsburgh Bridge That Was Never Constructed." April, 1982.

*"A Pittsburgh Migratory Landmark: St. Philomena's Roman Catholic Church in Squirrel Hill." December 3, 1981.

"Pittsburgh's Buried Bridges and Lost Ravines." 1978.

*"Pittsburgh's Forgotten Buildings II: the Former Americus Republican Club." 1973.

*"Pittsburgh's Forgotten Toy Theatre: the Kilbuck Playhouse." 1981.

*"Pittsburgh's Grand Gateway: the Pennsylvania Station." C. 1981.

*"Pittsburgh's Great Walls: a Selection of Revetments." 1980.

*"Pittsburgh's Newest Marvel: the Opening of the Freight House at Station Square." 1979.

*"Polar Preview." June, 1983.

*"Reflections on the Carnegie International of 1982." November 1, 1982.

"The Remembering Stone: the Alexander Johnston House at Kingston."

"Renaissance at Pittsburgh: the Frick Art Museum and the Pittsburgh History & Landmarks Museum." 1971.

"Renaissance in Pittsburgh: the New History & Landmarks Museum." 1972.

*"Restoration of the College of Fine Arts, C.M.U." June, 1983.

"Restoration of a New Old Fountain." September, 1982.

*"Return of the Human Image: a Review of the Associated Artists Show of 1978." 1978.

"The Saga of Sarah Cochrane of Linden Hall." August 9, 1982.

*"Some Stray Thoughts About Pittsburgh Fountains." April, 1982.

*"Southwestern Pennsylvania Painters 1800-1945: an Exhibition at Greensburg." February, 1982.

"Spanish Villas near Greensburg." December 7, 1982.

*"Station Square: a Great New Project in Urban Preservation." 1977.

"Station Square: Pittsburgh's Newest Pleasure Place." 1978.

"The Summer Christmas of 1936." January, 1982.

*"The Summer of 1980 in Pittsburgh: Our Own Shakespeare Festival." 1980.

*"Tea for Two at the William Penn." February 16, 1983.

*"Terrace Life in Pittsburgh III: the Cathedral of Learning from the University Club Roof." 1978.

*"Terrace Life in Pittsburgh IV: Schumann *al Fresco.*" 1978.

*"Texas—Gargoyles and Preservation: Calvary Methodist Church on Pittsburgh's North Side." 1980.

*"Thomas Jefferson as Landscape Architect: a Review of a Recent Book." 1980.

*"A Three Rivers Evening Party: an October Cruise on the *Gateway Party Liner.*"

*"The Tradition of Fine Bookbinding in the Twentieth Century: an Exhibition at the Hunt Institute of Botanical Documentation." 1979.

"Two Recent Art Exhibitions in Pittsburgh." 1981.

"Uniontown's Romanesque Courthouse." April, 1982.

*"Uphill and Downdale in Pittsburgh: a Night Journey at the New Year." 1978.

*"Vanished Pittsburgh Watercourses: the Four Mile Run Drainage Basin." 1980.

*"The Venetian Glass House: a Vitreous Excursion into the Past." 1978.

"A Victorian Gem at Latrobe." December 15, 1982.

*"Vision of the Heart: the Pittsburgh Paintings of Peter Contis."

"The Wabash-Pittsburgh Terminal Railroad: High Drama in Early 20th-century Pittsburgh." June 9, 1982.

*"A Wooden Hotel by the Sea: Ocean City in 1916." C. 1981.

*"Works on Paper from the Museum of Art." June, 1983.

*"The World of David Gilmour Blythe: the Spring Exhibition at the Museum of Art, Carnegie Institute." 1981.

WQED-FM Recording Tapes

These tapes have been donated to the Pittsburgh History & Landmarks Foundation; each tape box is identified by the number given by the station, where such a number exists. An asterisk means that the script is in the manuscript collection of the Foundation.

S-Jv01-SP
> Chronicles of Grant's Hill, Pittsburgh, No. 1: the Hill as It Was in the Early Days of the City
> Chronicles of Grant's Hill, Pittsburgh, No. 2: More Notes on the Hill and the Early City of Long Ago
> (same, No. 4, title not announced)
> (same, No. 5, title not announced)

S-Jv02-SP
> Chronicles of Market Square, Pittsburgh, No. 1
> Market Square or Diamond: What's in a Name?
> Chronicles of Market Square, Pittsburgh, No. 3
> Treasure Trove at the Courthouse: the Current Exhibition of the Competition Drawings of 1883 for the County Buildings
> Grant's Hill and the New Courthouse Courtyard

S-Jv03-SP

Dramatic Prelude: the Rotunda of the Pennsylvania Station at Pittsburgh

The Phantom Railway Station: the East Liberty Station of the Pennsylvania Railroad

*Station Square: a Great New Project in Urban Preservation

*In a Golden Garden: a Small Suburban Station Garden of Sixty Years Ago

*The Penn Central Station at Pittsburgh: Some Recent Preservation Notes

S-Jv04-SP

Victorian Christmas at Pittsburgh: a Fantasy on the 1890s Exhibit at the Old Post Office Museum

*Of Christmas Past and Christmas Cards

*New Year's Eve, 1915: a Pittsburgh Festal Vignette

The Decorator's Show House, 1977

Hill and Dale: the 1976 Decorator's Show House

*Fox Hall: the Decorator's Show House, 1978

S-Jv05-SP

*On the Terrace, No. 1: Vignettes of Life al Fresco in Pittsburgh

*On the Terrace, No. 2: the Roof of the University Club in Pittsburgh

*Terrace Life in Pittsburgh, No. 3: the Cathedral of Learning from the University Club Roof

*Terrace Life in Pittsburgh, No. 4: Schumann al Fresco

Fantasy on the Roof, or Architecture Overhead

S-Jv06-SP

Chronicles of Oakland, No. 2: East Oakland and the Civic Center

*Pavane for an Oakland Spring

*I Open My Windows to Summer Stars and Locust Blossoms in the Night

*An Aerial View of Oakland in 1924

*The Last of Webster Hall: the Passing of a Famous Oakland Hotel

Schenley Farms: the Green Garden of Oakland

S-Jv07-SP

Pittsburgh's Unknown Streets, No. 1: Melwood Avenue

Pittsburgh's North Side: the East Street-Dutchtown Area—the District, Its People, and Its Business

Pittsburgh's North Side: East Street-Dutchtown as an Architectural Entity

(title not announced—concerns Shadyside West)

Pittsburgh's Lawrenceville

The Territory of the North Negley Neighborhood Alliance: a September Walking Tour

S-Jv08-SP

By Any Other Name: the Controversial Spelling of Pittsburgh

History of the Point and the Golden Triangle

George Washington in Western Pennsylvania: a Holiday Review and a Brief Modern Go-around Again

Pittsburgh in New York: the Smithsonian Institution's National Museum of Design

The Rededication of Trinity Cathedral Burying Ground on 21 April 1976

S-Jv09-SP

Rockfaced Pittsburgh: the Mirror of the Richardsonian Revived Romanesque in This City

Bibliography: WQED-FM, continued

Three Rivers and Bridge Technology: the Nineteenth- and Twentieth-century Metal River Bridges of Pittsburgh

Bank Building as Art Gallery: the New Albright Gallery on Fourth Avenue

An Architectural Excursion in Pittsburgh's Financial District: the People's Savings Bank Building

*Pittsburgh's Forgotten Buildings, No. 1: the Former Americus Republican Club

The Art Deco City: Modern Architecture and Decoration in Pittsburgh from 1920 to 1940

S-Jv10-SP

A Pittsburgh Pantheon: Allegheny Cemetery

A Room with a View: Looking at the Allegheny River from the Pittsburgh Press Club

A Room with a View, No. 2: Trinity Cathedral and the First Presbyterian Church, Pittsburgh, as Seen from the Press Club Bar

Death of a Chateau: the Demolition of 928 Ridge Avenue, the John Moorhead, Jr. House

Pittsburgh's William Penn Hotel

*At the University Club: a View of Oakland in Winter

S-Jv11-SP

Renaissance at Pittsburgh: the Frick Art Museum (portion of an article, "Renaissance at Pittsburgh")

*From Bowling Alley to Art Gallery: the New Pittsburgh Plan for Art Building

*Of Gateways: Some Pittsburgh Entrances

An Art Deco Garden in Pittsburgh: the Perennial Garden of the Phipps Conservatory in Schenley Park

*Vanished Pittsburgh Watercourses: the Four-mile Run Drainage Basin

*Pittsburgh's Great Walls: a Selection of Revetments

S-Jv12-SP

Of Time and a Horse: an Excursion in a Hansom Cab

Herron Hill and the Seasons: a View from My Window

Dans le Vieux Parc (In the Old Park): an Excursion Through Time at Idlewild Park

*Of Castles: a Medley of Dream Towers in Miniature

*Autumn Splendour Remembered: the Indian Summer of 1977

*Uphill and Downdale in Pittsburgh: a Night Journey at the New Year

S-Jv13-SP

*Crime Without Passion: a Nostalgic Essay on Re-seeing the Movies of One's Youth

*Carnival In Flanders: A Further Excursion into Re-seeing the Movies of One's Youth

*Gone With The Wind: a Varied Disquisition on Its Past

*Another Mountain Inn Closes Its Doors: the White Sulphur Springs Inn

*Downtown Restaurants of Yesterday: the Dining Rooms of McCreery's and Kaufmann's

*Fred's Place: the Corner Store at the All-American Corner

S-Jv14-SP

*A Wooden Hotel by the Sea: Ocean City in 1916

387

Bibliography: WQED-FM, continued

Two Late Nineteenth-century Courthouses in Pennsylvania: Warren at Warren and Sullivan County at La Porte
*My Own Birthday Anniversary—Number 73
Lions in the Streets: a Sculptural Hunting Party in Pittsburgh

(no tape boxes marked S-Jv31-SP to S-Jv35-SP)

S-Jv36-SP
*Memories of Whitby Hall: a Grand Eighteenth-century Country House of Philadelphia
*Ecclesiastical Architecture de Luxe: the Interior of Calvary Methodist Church in the North Side
*Memories of Old Sewickley: a True Garden Spot of America
Two Classical Courthouses in Eastern Pennsylvania: Northumberland County at Easton and Bradford County at Towanda
Two Pennsylvania Courthouses: Doylestown in Bucks County and Smethport in McKean

S-Jv37-SP
*The World of David Gilmour Blythe: the Spring Exhibition at the Museum of Art, Carnegie Institute
*Pittsburgh's Grand Gateway: the Pennsylvania Station
*An Excursion in May: a Late Spring Trip to Natrona and Some Houses
*Terrace Life in Pittsburgh, No. 4: Schumann *al Fresco*
Two Modern County Courthouses in Pennsylvania: Lebanon and Beaver
Two Italianate Courthouses in Central Pennsylvania: Adams County at Gettysburg and Juniata County at Mifflintown

S-Jv38-SP
*Happy New Year for Pittsburgh's Pennsylvania Station: Long Live the Rotunda
*Pittsburgh's Forgotten Toy Theatre: the Kilbuck Playhouse
*The First Journey of the New Year—1982: a Trip to Indiana, Pennsylvania
*Lovejoy's Folly
The *Bulletin Index:* an Important Chapter in Pittsburgh Journalism
A Neglected Sculptural Ornament in Pittsburgh
*The Greek Revival Revived
From Realism to Fantasy: the Malcolm Parcell Exhibition at Carnegie-Mellon University
*Palladio Again and Another Lecture

S-Jv39-SP
*In Search of Harmony: a Brief Overview of Some American Communitarian Societies and Their Architecture in the Nineteenth Century
*In Search of Harmony: a Brief Overview of Some American Communitarian Societies and Their Architecture in the Nineteenth Century, Part 2
(no title announced: WQED fund-raising speech)
*A Fairy-Tale Christmas in the Hall of Architecture: the Annual Holiday Trees of 1981

S-Jv40-SP
*The History of the Present Wilkinsburg Station on the Pennsylvania Line
*More Memories of the East Liberty Station and a Praise of Petunias
*Chronicles of the Pennsylvania Railroad: a Terminal Station That Never Got Built

*English Romanesque Cathedrals and the Buildings of Western Pennsylvania
*In Praise of Kennywood: a New Book on an Old Theme
*American Photographers and the National Park
*(title not announced; MS. title is "The Drama Department at Carnegie-Mellon University")
*The Fascinations of August and Old Magazines
*(title not announced; MS. title is "A New Gallery for the Westmoreland County Museum of Art")

S-Jv40-m
*Downtown Pittsburgh Today
Carnegie Tech Reconsidered
*A Pittsburgh Bridge That Was Never Constructed
*Some Stray Thoughts About Pittsburgh Fountains
*Commodore Joshua Barney Remembered
*Easter and the Opening of the Floral Season
Symbols of a Lost Past in Pittsburgh's Market Square
*Chronicles of Old Fifth Avenue, No.1: From Pittsburgh's Downtown to Oakland
*Chronicles of Old Fifth Avenue, No. 2: Some Old Antique Shops
*A Glimpse of Romantic East Liberty in the 1850s
*Early Railroad Architecture on the Main Line of the Pennsylvania: Water Stations
The Pennsylvania Railroad Station at Greensburg

Unnumbered A
*Reflections on the Carnegie International of 1982
*Autumn Leaves, 1982
*East Liberty's Liberty Theatre
*Light over Pittsburgh, 1982
*The Opening of the Commerce Court Building at Station Square
*The Cameraphone: a Youthful Memory
*The Carnegie Institute Christmas Trees, 1982
*The Cinderella Ball, 1982

Unnumbered B
*Epiphany at Ascalon Cottage
*Charles Rosen: the Pennsylvania Years
Two Recent Pittsburgh Exhibits at Carnegie Institute
*Tea for Two at the William Penn
*A Document of Early Modern Architecture
*Works on Paper from the Museum of Art
*A New Guide to Pittsburgh's Public Sculpture

Unnumbered C
*The Opening of the East Busway
*Islamic Renaissance at Carnegie Institute
*Polar Preview
*Restoration at the College of Fine Arts, Carnegie-Mellon University
*A Further Chronicle of the William Penn Terrace Room

Unnumbered D (copied from other tapes)
Two Courthouses in Indiana County: One Vanished and One Renewed
*Flowers of India: an Exhibition of a Selection of Late Eighteenth- and Early Nineteenth-century Indian Botanical Paintings

391

Bibliography: *WQED-FM, continued*

Two Neo-Georgian Courthouses in Western Pennsylvania: Meadville and Indiana

*The Ethnic Church, Old and New, Near and Far: Pittsburgh and Gracanica

*A Great Shakespeare Exhibition and the Three Rivers Shakespeare Festival

Two Italianate Courthouses in Pennsylvania

Unnumbered E (copied from other tapes)

*The Old City Hall of Pittsburgh: a Glimpse into Our Victorian Past

*The Last of Greenlawn: My First Demolition in the Chateau Country

A Richardsonian Courthouse in Southeastern Pennsylvania: Pottsville in Schuylkill County

*The Associated Artists of Pittsburgh Through 71 Years: 1910 to 1981

*Memories of Whitby Hall: a Grand Eighteenth-century Country House of Philadelphia

*Ecclesiastical Architecture de Luxe: the Interior of Calvary Methodist Church in the North Side

Unnumbered F (copied from other tapes)

*(title not announced; MS. title is "Journey to the Centre of the Earth: The New Hillman Hall of Minerals at Carnegie Institute.")

(title not announced; concerns courthouses of Butler and Monroe counties, Pennsylvania)

Two Classical Courthouses in Western Pennsylvania: Mercer and Kittanning

*Constructivism and the Geometric Traditions: the New Exhibition at the Museum of Art, Carnegie Institute

The Gigantic City Hall and Courthouse: Municipal and Legal Grandeur in Philadelphia

(title not announced; concerns courthouse of York County, Pennsylvania)

Unnumbered G (copied from other tapes)

Two Greek Revival Courthouses in Northern Pennsylvania: Erie and Bellefonte

*A Doll House from California and Some Paintings

Two Greek Revival Courthouses in Pennsylvania: Wellsboro and Carlisle

Three Quasi-Georgian Courthouses in Pennsylvania: Clearfield, Coudersport, and Middleburg

Two Modern Pennsylvania Courthouses and Their Predecessors: Williamsport and Allentown

Index

This is primarily an index of architects, collaborating artists, and others discussed in connection with buildings in the Pittsburgh area; of buildings and interiors; and of geographical areas. Passing references with little informational content in the text have not been included.

Life and Architecture in Pittsburgh was typeset by Cold Comp in Century Schoolbook with Goudy chapter headings, and was printed on 60 lb. Warren Olde Style by Broudy Printing, Inc., Pittsburgh. Cover and book design by Thomas S. Stevenson, Jr., with the assistance of Jacqueline Snyder, Laura A. McDonald, John O'Connell, and Brenda A. Harford.